HOSTILE TAKEOVER

Also by Matt Kibbe

Give Us Liberty (with Dick Armey)

HOSTILE TAKEOVER

RESISTING CENTRALIZED GOVERNMENT'S STRANGLEHOLD ON AMERICA

Matt Kibbe

wm
WILLIAM MORROW
An Imprint of HarperCollins*Publishers*

HOSTILE TAKEOVER. Copyright © 2012 by Matt Kibbe. All rights reserved. Printed in the United States of America. No part of this book may be used or reproduced in any manner whatsoever without written permission except in the case of brief quotations embodied in critical articles and reviews. For information address HarperCollins Publishers, 10 East 53rd Street, New York, NY 10022.

HarperCollins books may be purchased for educational, business, or sales promotional use. For information please write: Special Markets Department, HarperCollins Publishers, 10 East 53rd Street, New York, NY 10022.

FIRST EDITION

Library of Congress Cataloging-in-Publication Data has been applied for.

ISBN 978-0-06-219601-9

12   13   14   15   16   DIX/RRD   10   9   8   7   6   5   4   3   2   1

For Terry. You saw more in me than was readily apparent. You are everything.

"Their motto is Don't Tread on Me"
—*Uncle John's Band* by Jerry Garcia and Robert Hunter

CONTENTS

PROLOGUE: THE HOSTILE TAKEOVER

IMAGINE A ONCE SUCCESSFUL ENTERPRISE, LONG AGO BUILT ON THE principles of hard work, growth, and innovation, that has grown arrogant, fat, and happy from earlier successes. Achievement, once sought out, strived for, rewarded, is now assumed as given. But there are telltale signs of trouble: Expenditures are skyrocketing even in the face of declining revenues. Debt servicing now dominates the company's balance sheet. Leadership has been replaced with a stultifying bureaucracy, and hard work has given way to cynicism and complacency among the rank and file. Customers no longer want to buy what senior management is selling.

There was a time when things were good. "The customer is always right," was the mantra that drove the corporate culture, and the CEO and senior managers vigilantly guarded against unnecessary spending, any hint of waste, or any deviation from the core mission of the enterprise. But now continued success is treated as a birthright, and innovation has been replaced with an aggressive sales pitch for tired ideas and bad products that customers don't want.

It is a story that plays out time and again in the life cycle of a business. Over time, innovators are replaced by bureaucrats, and future managers lose sight of the values and principles that made the venture strong in the first place. As Apple founder Steve Jobs describes it in one of his last interviews, companies often lose their purpose and fail because producers who had a keen sense for innovation, and the drive to constantly create value for customers, are eventually replaced by salesmen simply intent on moving product and collecting new revenue. "I have my own theory about why decline happens at companies like IBM or Microsoft," Jobs tells Walter Isaacson. "The company does a great job, innovates and becomes a monopoly or close to it in some field, and then the quality of the product becomes less important. The company starts valuing the great salesmen, because they're the ones who can move the needle on revenues, not the product engineers and designers." "So," says Jobs, "the salespeople end up running the company."

> John Akers at IBM was a smart, eloquent, fantastic salesperson, but he didn't know anything about product. The same thing happened at Xerox. When the sales guys run the company, the product guys don't matter so much, and a lot of them just turn off. It happened at Apple when [John] Sculley came in, which was my fault, and it happened when [Steve] Ballmer took over at Microsoft.[1]

Sounds familiar, doesn't it? In America, our political management has failed us, attempting to replace founding principles with a slick sales pitch for tired, bad ideas. The American enterprise grew exceptional based on the bedrock foundations of individual freedom, decentralized knowledge, and accountable, constitutionally limited government. But our "leaders" in Washington, D.C. have systematically replaced the dispersed genius of America with top down dictates and expensive schemes designed to expand the power of insiders and protect the privileged positions of politicians and bureaucrats.

Senior management has failed us, and it's time to clean house.

The American people know that it's time to shake up senior management, and as shareholders we are acting swiftly to protect our interests and those of our children. But entrenched management—everywhere inside the Beltway, but particularly in the U.S. Senate and the West Wing of the White House—is circling the wagons. They don't want change. Solutions are being ignored, and outsiders rebuffed.

We know where our problems begin, and they begin in Washington, with a political elite that has neither the will nor the inclination to do what must be done. But we do. And so America needs to *take over* Washington. Blithely ignoring our entreaties, the powers that be in Washington say: "no thanks, we got this." Our shareholder proposal has been roundly rejected by the CEO and the Board of Directors, the microphone has been shut off, name placards removed, conference tables broken down, and naysayers herded out the front doors. In effect, America has been thrown out of its own shareholders meeting.

Things are getting, in the parlance of corporate governance, "hostile."

On August 17, 2010, just a few months before the November 2, 2010, mid-term elections, Dick Armey and I called for a "hostile takeover" of the Republican Party in the *Wall Street Journal*.[2] The logic was simple: we had to beat the Republicans before we could beat the Democrats. We needed standing within the operations of government, a minority position in the company that would at least allow us entry into the room, a seat at the table. We got more than a few angry calls from the leaders of the Grand Old Party, but we meant it precisely, in the exact use of the phrase. Takeovers replace failed business practices and failed managers. *Hostile* takeovers do the same, but are decidedly unwelcomed by the existing management regime.

If you think of Congress as America's Board of Directors and the federal budget as the annual operating budget for our country, it is immediately clear that something is fundamentally wrong with our company's management team. In the private sector, showing no cash-on-hand and an operating debt equal to or exceeding total output, the heads of the entire finance team would roll. Shareholders would act swiftly to protect their interests. When a failing company burdened with entrenched, visionless executives is challenged by insurgent entrepreneurial leadership from outside the corporation, expect those in privileged positions to do whatever it takes to cling to power regardless of what is best for the company and its customers. Often CEOs pad their boards of directors with friends and other CEOs that manage related firms in a similar fashion. In this case, change is difficult, and any friendly takeover is rebuffed immediately.

It's only "hostile" because the interests in Washington—the political class, the rent-seekers, the power-hoarders, the government-employees-for-life, the moochers and looters—like things just the way they are. The mere presence of citizens with better ideas and the will to implement them is viewed as a hostile act.

The only way we will ever reduce the debt, balance the budget, and restore constitutionally limited government is if America first beats Washington.

In the private sector, a "hostile takeover" seeks a controlling interest in a publicly traded company against the wishes of the current management. When you think about it this way, it seems like a perfect description of what needs to be done to take back control of our government. In our democratic republic, the people need to get involved again. As stakeholders in the American dream, as Sons and Daughters of Liberty inspired by our Founding Entrepreneurs, we need to take it over. We need to take it back from the Washington establishment, and from the crony capitalists that lobby through their "man in Washington" in lieu of producing better goods and services at lower prices. We need to pry it from the hands of well-heeled progressives that would block the unwashed *nouveau* from getting *riche*, through higher tax rates and government-imposed barriers to success. From the professional tax consumers—the public employees unions—who feed off the fruits your hard labor. And from a growing class of well-paid bottom-feeders who expect—no, are self-entitled to—a handout, a subsidy, a loan or a payment they did not earn and do not deserve, from each according to his ability and to each according to the loudest demands.

Know that "We the People" will not consent to this fiscal misman-agement by our government leaders, just like the citizen activists who did not consent to Crown-protected monopoly tea, choosing, instead, to spill it into Boston Harbor. We will not subjugate our voices to the whims of a king or a czar or a senate committee chairman, or even a president. We will not be silenced.

The shareholders need to take America back. We need to break up the privileged collusion of Washington insiders and return power from self-appointed "experts," back to the people. This book tells you how we are going to do it, from the bottom up.

HOSTILE TAKEOVER

CHAPTER 1

THE CENTRAL PROBLEM

"THE CHAIRMAN TELLS US THIS EVENT HAS TO BE MOVED."

So decreed the chief clerk of the Senate Rules Committee, Lynden Armstrong, as he and his colleagues proceeded to expel about 250 citizen activists from the Russell Senate Office Building's Kennedy Caucus Room. It was November 17, 2011, and the room was already packed with regular folks who had traveled from across the country at the invitation of Republican senator Mike Lee of Utah. Months earlier Lee had offered to host a meeting of a grassroots group, the "Tea Party Debt Commission," in the Russell Building and had gotten Senate Ethics Committee approval to do so. Together, we wanted to offer a budget-balancing alternative to the Joint Select Committee on Deficit Reduction (aka the "supercommittee"), and provide a hearing where the people would speak and members of Congress could listen.

The grandiose, century-old room (officially known as SR-325) with its thirty-five-foot ceilings was filling not only with senators and congressmen to listen, but also reporters and TV cameras from

C-SPAN, Fox News, and other network outlets. The room seemed like an oddly discordant place for We the People to congregate, and a far cry from the street-corner protests Tea Partiers had started organizing in February 2009. As the U.S. Senate website describes it:

> The interior decoration of the room is classically grand yet refined, much in the tradition of Versailles. Twelve Corinthian columns along the longitudinal walls flank three French windows and support an architrave and frieze. Above the frieze are classically derived motifs of dentils, egg and dart molding, and brackets. A Greek key forms a ribbon at the top of the Corinthian pilasters. . . . A large keystone crowns each window arch, and over the main doorway is a triangular pediment as found in ancient Greek temples.[1]

Most who were gathered in the Kennedy Caucus Room that Thursday in November had made extraordinary sacrifices—traveling many miles away from job commitments and families—to petition their elected representatives with the commonsense proposition that our government cannot keep spending money it does not have. We were not in town to protest. Despite a certain let-them-eat-cake air about the Rules Committee staff, this was no modern-day Women's March on Versailles. We had come peacefully and respectfully to the seat of federal power to offer budget solutions.

The Tea Party Debt Commission (TPDC) plan stood in perfect contrast to the way Washington typically conducts business. The process was completely open and transparent. Everyone was welcome to participate. A series of field hearings across the country asked local residents to take the microphone to offer to the TPDC commissioners—twelve community leaders who volunteered their time to oversee the process—their ideas to balance the budget. The TPDC crowd-sourced (i.e., surveyed) one million answers to budget priorities online, receiving input from more than 50,000 citizens.

This is hardly the way things work in Washington. The very idea of the supercommittee was founded on the proposition that an elite group of insiders knows better than the public what the people want and need. Of course, when you get twelve members of Congress together in one room—each beholden to interests other than the interests of the people, each of the opinion that his or her "expertise" trumps the will of the people—then you end up with what the country got: nothing. (Some would argue this was the goal all along.)

Contrast the Washington way with the people's way: our work would quickly balance the budget using the Congressional Budget Office's own scoring.

No matter: "The chairman tells us this event has to be moved." Our ideas were unwelcome. So were we, apparently.

As remarkable as it seemed, we were getting kicked out. Who could possibly be so threatened by a mob of citizens armed with . . . notebooks, spreadsheet printouts, and a budget plan? Who would go to such extraordinary lengths to shut down a conversation (a particularly risky public relations move, given the reporters and cameras, and the way and speed with which information spreads these days)?

"Who told you to do it?" Senator Lee asked the chief clerk as Senate staffers collected our name placards and attempted to break down our conference tables. Who was kicking us out of a building financed by our tax dollars?

"Uh, Schumer," the Senate staffer responded condescendingly, referring to his boss, Senator Charles Schumer, the hyperpartisan Democrat from New York and chairman of the Senate Rules Committee.

"Does the First Amendment have no application here?" asked an incredulous Lee.

"SIMULATING A HEARING"

IT IS OFTEN SAID THAT HUMAN HISTORY IS WRITTEN BY THE VICTORS. But that was before YouTube. That was before the democratization of information and knowledge online.

Julie Borowski, a young economist from FreedomWorks, had the foresight to capture the terse exchange between Senator Lee and the Rules Committee enforcers on her handheld camera just as they were evicting us, and she quickly posted the video on YouTube. This turned out to be the essential record of what actually happened, because as soon as we had left the hearing room the Rules staffers went into full spin mode to cover up what had just gone down.[2]

Sony Bloggie HD Pocket Camcorder with 4GB memory and 360-degree lens: $79.97. The truth: Priceless.

Initially the Schumer staffers argued that Lee was violating Senate rules by "simulating a hearing," despite the fact that senators make a regular practice of holding mock hearings on Senate property. "Funny thing is," blogger Michelle Malkin later reported, "members of Congress have been able to convene politicized 'hearings' in government buildings for years. On the House side, Democrat Rep. John Conyers' 'basement hearings' on everything from impeachment to illegal immigration are legend. On the Senate side, such non-official, non-hearing 'hearings' are plentiful."[3] One such pretend hearing Malkin identified was in 2009 on climate change, presided over by then-senator Robert Bennett, Republican from Utah, and Senator Lamar Alexander, Republican from Tennessee. Another involved none other than Senator Schumer: the 2005 show trial on the Valerie Plame affair, which was referred to as a "forum on national security implications of disclosing the identity of a covert intelligence officer—committee hearing."[4]

So which was it? A "forum" or a "committee hearing"? Any rule of conduct ought to be applied consistently across the board; otherwise it can't possibly maintain legitimacy. This seems so obvious and simple that even a senator can get it. Remarkably, one of Senator Schumer's staffers, having been inundated by angry phone calls from disenfranchised Tea Partiers, actually argued that Senate rules don't apply to Senate Rules Committee members. Surely that frazzled staffer misspoke. Surely Senate rules apply equally to all senators, even those writing the rules. Yet one can't help but wonder what type of office culture would enable a young phone attendant to so casually channel

Hugo Chávez or Vladimir Putin. Maybe this is where the problem starts?

And then there was also the odd coincidence that Shaun Parkin, the other "non-partisan" Rules staffer caught on video evicting the group, had long worked for the aforementioned Senator Robert Bennett, whom Lee, the Utah Tea Party, and FreedomWorks PAC had ousted in the 2010 elections. He now works as deputy staff director for the aforementioned Senator Lamar Alexander, the ranking minority member (i.e., Republican) on the Rules Committee. Presumably, the minority staff is present to protect the legitimate rights of minority members from arbitrary dictates from the majority, right? Is it possible that freshman Republicans, particularly members of the Tea Party class like Lee, were effectively treated like second-class legislators within the Republican caucus's pecking order?

Even odder was the ex post facto decision by the U.S. Capitol Police (USCP) to demand, and receive, a correction to a *New York Times* online report that had originally described the ousting pretty much as it had happened.[5] In e-mails to reporters who covered the story, the chief information officer for the Capitol police wrote the following:

Re: the story you wrote here that you said you sourced from Freedom Works, here's what really happened. . . . The USCP responded to room SR-326 in the Russell Senate Office Building for the report of a suspicious package. As a security and life safety measure, the USCP evacuated the immediate area until we could determine that nothing hazardous was found in SR-326. Obviously, SR-325 [the Kennedy Caucus Room] which is adjacent was affected by this suspicious package. I'll look for the update soon & thanks in advance for making the correction.[6]

Now it was "security" concerns and a mysterious package down the hall that forced the evacuation of all of us from the Kennedy Caucus Room that afternoon. There's just one problem with this account. It's not true. In addition to Borowski's video, Ben Howe at *RedState* quickly posted a meticulous accounting of the facts, times, and e-mails of what actually happened. E-mails from Schumer's staff belie the USCP's claim that "a suspicious package" made them do it. An hour before the event was scheduled to begin, the aforementioned Rules staffer Lynden Armstrong sent an e-mail to a Lee staffer, time-stamped 1:03 p.m.: "Please call me ASAP or meet down at SR-325 about the Tea Party Budget Hearing that is scheduled at 2:00pm. There are two problems with this and that is they are simulating a hearing which isn't allowed and the Rules Committee has determined events of this nature are political and not allowed."[7]

Two minutes later, the Lee staffer responded by e-mail: "This was an event to get input from some Utahns and others about the Debt."[8] Five minutes after that, Lee's staff replies, "Lynden I will be there in 10 minutes."[9] Armstrong doesn't wait, but instead responds, "Ok. At this point, we have to pull the plug on the event."[10]

During the next twenty minutes, Senator Lee confronts the two Rules Committee staffers in the corridor outside the Kennedy Caucus room (as shown in the Borowski video). Then, in an e-mail time-stamped at 1:31 p.m., the Capitol police broadcast the following message to all Senate staff:

> The U.S. Capitol Police are responding to a suspicious package in Room 326 of the Russell Senate Office Building. All staff and other personnel are directed to avoid this area until further notice.[11]

At this point, frustrated, but graciously concerned about his hundreds of guests, Senator Lee decided to relocate the meeting rather than make a stink. His staff began searching for an off-campus meeting place. At 2:08 p.m. a follow-up e-mail from the Capitol police declared that the "investigation of the suspicious package in Room 326" has concluded and that "all tests are negative and the area is now open."[12]

Was the "suspicious package" just a bizarre coincidence? Perhaps. But the USCP account is clearly not accurate. The e-mail evidence alone makes clear when the decision to "pull the plug" on the Tea Party meeting was made and why. We weren't evacuated for safety reasons by the Capitol police; we were evicted for political reasons by the thought police. Why, then, did the Capitol police feel a need to make sure an inaccurate version of events got into the *New York Times*? What motivated them to "correct" the story soon after it had appeared online? At whose behest? Such palace intrigue raises serious questions. Is it the regular practice of congressional staffers and other government employees to manipulate media stories and misrepresent the facts?

One thing is for certain. If Julie Borowski had not captured the bouncers from the Senate Rules Committee red-handed in the act of evicting Senator Lee and his guests, the "history" of what happened that day would have been rewritten forever. If Michelle Malkin and Ben Howe had not reported on events in real time, digging up the facts and doing the type of investigative journalism that gets all the sources out in the open—reported—the version of the "truth" that came out would have conveniently protected Senator Schumer and his staff from the light of day. As it turns out, we are no longer dependent on one authoritative source for news. We are wholly independent of the old information monopolies, in fact.

WHOSE RULES?

IS IT PARANOIA IF THEY REALLY ARE OUT TO GET YOU? IT WAS CLEAR TO those present that the powers-that-be conspired to block outside voices from disrupting business as usual inside the marble walls of the Russell Senate Office Building. But our experience that Thursday was no watershed. They didn't stop us. We simply relocated down the street, beyond the purview of Senate authority, at Hillsdale College's Kirby Center—a move that Senator Lee, in a nice turn of phrase, dubbed the "walk of freedom." But the experience is emblematic of the extent to which those in power will go to protect their station. It seems obvious that the Beltway establishment views any citizen seeking fiscal responsibility and an adult approach to making unlimited budgetary demands fit within scarce means as a hostile threat to be ignored, derided, demonized, and, when necessary, expelled from the building.

This is a pattern that can be documented over and over again since the emergence of the Tea Party and its massive grassroots uprising against our fiscally lascivious government. On September 12, 2009, more than one million people showed up for the Taxpayer March on Washington in Washington, D.C., gathering in Freedom Plaza and marching all the way to the U.S. Capitol's steps. It was—by orders of magnitude—the largest gathering of limited-government activists in our nation's history, the size of which caught FreedomWorks and the U.S. Capitol Police, the District of Columbia Police, and the National Park Service all by surprise. It was logistical chaos, as you might imagine.

Despite being in possession of an agreed-upon plan and the proper permits, FreedomWorks' Brendan Steinhauser was directed by the National Park Service to start the march itself several hours earlier than planned because the sheer size of the crowd had shut down the streets surrounding Freedom Plaza. "It's time. You have to go now," ordered National Park Police Sergeant Stephanie Clarke. She probably made the right call, and Steinhauser started directing people to move east down Pennsylvania Avenue. The crowd was so large, the *New York Times* reported that the "magnitude of the rally took the authorities by surprise." All seven lanes of the 1.2 miles of Pennsylvania Avenue from the White House to the Capitol were filled with a constant stream of marchers for more than three hours. The article went on to note that the "sea of protesters" were not an angry mob, but "expressed their views without a hint of rage." [13] Many marchers were frustrated that they had missed the scheduled beginning, but it was the right thing to do, so we all just rolled with it. Fortunately the march was captured by a rooftop security camera. That video was an instant hit on YouTube, providing objective evidence of the size of the crowd, to counter many of the reports filed that day by the mainstream media.

At the other end of Pennsylvania Avenue, the gathering crowd was so overwhelming that security and safety personnel could not pass on the streets that surrounded the east front of the Capitol. The whole Capitol expanse was shut down with a happy mass of freedom-loving humanity. And yet the Capitol police refused to let the crowd set foot on the National Mall from Third to Sixth streets, Northwest—open, unused space that could have eased the congestion and allowed for a safer experience for everyone involved.

Why would they do that? To what end if not to prevent a better picture—a more iconic image of an iconic day—from being taken of the size of the crowd. If you look at the panoramic photo taken by activist Michael Beck from the top of the Capitol steps that day, you can see that the crowds were packed all the way from Independence Avenue to Constitution Avenue, while the open space on the Mall went empty and unused. A few days later, an informed source told me that then-Speaker Nancy Pelosi had issued the order: Not a single Tea Partier would be permitted to set foot on that section of the National Mall. Really? Did the Speaker herself—arguably the single most powerful Member of Congress and second only to the vice president in the presidential line of succession—really take time out of her busy day to impede this peaceful gathering of her fellow citizens? We will probably never know for sure. Regardless of who gave the illogical command, hundreds of thousands of Americans, while standing on what is widely referred to as "the People's space," were denied their right to peacefully petition their government for a redress of grievances. It seems that the political establishment's adherence to the First Amendment of the U.S. Constitution is up for circumstantial interpretation depending on who's doing the talking.

One can't help but wonder about the blatant double standard of those who blocked the marchers that day. Though it has grown into something much more than a protest movement, the Tea Party first arose in early 2009 as just that: a cry of protest from an alarmed citizenry. It wasn't easy. From day one, Tea Partiers struggled to get the permission, the approvals, and the permits to allow them to protest against big government. Many government officials went so far as to insist on a demonstration of proper insurance to cover the cost of any property damage. For example, a planned Tea Party in the Park to be held in Cape Coral, Florida, on April 1, 2009, was blocked by city bureaucrats who insisted that, because the event was likely to attract more than 500 people, no permit would be granted unless volunteers obtained liability insurance for the event. "WINK News spoke to the director of parks for Cape Coral. He says that even now if [Lynn Rosko, the initial organizer] is willing to get insurance for the event he'll likely re-authorize it." [14] Because of the onerous requirement, the protest was temporarily canceled. Rosko understandably felt she could not bear that financial risk alone. The event went on as planned after Mary Rakovich, with help from a FreedomWorks-provided insurance policy, picked up the ball and charged past the city's bureaucratic roadblocks. Obviously the city knew that a disparate group of citizens could not possibly purchase an insurance policy just to exercise their First Amendment rights.

Despite such onerous requirements, we all did what was required. Every local Tea Party group raised and spent the dollars required to comply with the rules. For the 9/12 march in 2009, I was tasked with raising a total of $500,000 to fund the portable toilets, health services, security fencing, and other infrastructure required to keep the permits. Much of that money was raised online, one portable toilet at a time. Lefty bloggers had great fun mocking our efforts to provide proper sanitation, with the far-left blog the Democratic underground posting the funding request from FreedomWorks, emphasizing in bold letters: "There are fundamental things we need to have like more portable restrooms to accommodate a crowd like we are expecting and they cost $185 a piece." "You will know them by their trail of port-o-potties," sneered one commenter.

Only later, with the emergence of Occupy Wall Street, would we discover that this mocking attitude toward tending to proper sanitation was a structural deficit with the progressive mind-set. I'm not suggesting that anyone liked the unhealthy squalor that Occupy encampments became; it was simply someone else's problem to tend to. For the contemporary Left, many of the things that we need to function, including bathrooms, are taken as given; it's someone else's responsibility. Bathrooms, like good jobs, wealth, food, and prosperity, are simply assumed to exist, there to be redistributed by smart, compassionate planners, or General Assemblies.

Two years after the 9/12 march, when Occupy Wall Street appeared, there were no such logistical roadblocks to their protests. Without ever acquiring permits, they proceeded to occupy both public and private spaces. The cost to taxpayers—for extra police and crowd control, for sanitation, for the substantial damage to both public and private property—has been staggering. In November 2011, a survey by *Associated Press* estimated that the cost to taxpayers of the Occupy encampments totaled $13 million, according to figures from government agencies in eighteen of the hardest-hit cities across the country. The AP survey was not intended to be comprehensive and did not estimate damage to private property, including smashed windows. The biggest tab was racked up by taxpayers in New York City, at $7 million so far. "In Oakland," the AP reports, "where protesters temporarily forced the shutdown of a major port, the city has spent more than $2.4 million responding to the protests. The cash-strapped city, which had to close a $58 million budget gap this year, was already facing an uphill battle when Occupy Oakland began Oct. 10." [15]

In Virginia, members of the Richmond Tea Party watched as Occupy protesters were allowed, gratis, to protest in the same park that they had been required by the city to pay to gather in, to the tune of $8,500. Frustrated by the blatant double standard applied by Mayor Dwight Jones, a left-wing Democrat, the Tea Partiers sued the city for reimbursement. Instead of cash back, they were immediately hit with a tax audit from the city.[16] According to Patrik Jonsson of the *Christian Science Monitor*:

> Tea party activists have noted instances of public solidarity with the Occupy protests that suggest different free-speech standards based on political affiliation. Such solidarity has been expressed by mayors like [Antonio] Villaraigosa in Los Angeles and Dwight Jones in Richmond. Tea party activists say they've paid their way and followed the law. . . . By some estimates, Richmond taxpayers paid $7,000 to supply the Occupy protesters with portable toilets and other services during the two weeks they camped at Kanawha Plaza.[17]

Justice, according to Adam Smith, the Founding Fathers, and every Tea Partier I have ever met, means treating everyone exactly like everyone else under the laws of the land. Colleen Owens, a local Tea Party activist, told the *Christian Science Monitor* that everyone should be treated the same. So imagine her frustration: "We challenged the mayor's unequal treatment between groups, and he responds with even more unequal treatment."

DON'T WALK ON THE GRASS

EVEN MORE OUTRAGEOUS IS THE DOUBLE STANDARD IMPOSED BY THE United States Park Police in Freedom Plaza and McPherson Square in downtown Washington, D.C., two public spaces that have become permanent Occupy encampments. The Park Police were so accommodating, in fact, that many protesters migrated south to D.C. from Zuccotti Park in the heart of Wall Street, New York City. "As officials shut down Occupy encampments across the country," reports the *Washington Post*, "protesters streamed into the District, eager to join the movement in the nation's capital, which has so far enjoyed protection from supportive local and national police." [18]

Congressman Darrell Issa, chairman of the House Oversight Committee, suspects a politically motivated double standard is at play. In a letter to Interior Secretary Ken Salazar, dated December 12, 2011, Issa argues that "this situation raises questions about why those decisions were made, who participated in making them, and whether political judgments played a role in not enforcing the law." [19]

At issue is the fact that the park police, blatantly it seems, ignored the law, which prohibits overnight camping in the parks. "But the National Park Service, which is in charge of McPherson Square, has applied the most liberal interpretation of rules against overnight camping, and officials instead consider the makeshift tent city a '24-hour vigil,'" reports CNN. "A handwritten bulletin board maintained by the protesters Monday noted it is 'Day 93' of the demonstration there." [20]

So the Interior Department of the Obama administration now defines ninety-three days of camping as "a 24-hour vigil." And we wonder why they can't balance the budget.

Speaking of the budget, the real agenda here may be to stimulate the economy by destroying the newly restored McPherson Square, which was resodded and refurbished, at a cost to taxpayers of over $400,000, as part of the Obama administration's failed economic stimulus bill. As I will discuss in the next chapter, the logic of Keynesian economics upon which that $768 billion legislation is built argues that any expenditure by government during times of economic downturn is good because it will stimulate new "aggregate demand." How the money is spent is not particularly important to the theory.

So, how many jobs will Occupy Wall Street "create or save" simply by destroying the sod in public and private spaces? Only Obamanomics can answer this question. Back here on terra firma, regular grassroots Americans know that trampled turf is a net loss to taxpayers totaling that same $400,000, and that restimulating the economy will cost us another $400,000. That's jobs and wealth destroyed, never to be reimbursed by the Occupiers.

FILTHY-RICH ONE-PERCENTERS

NANCY PELOSI, WHO LOST HER JOB AS SPEAKER IN THE 2010 TEA Party wave election, once actually referred to Tea Partiers as "un-American" and "astroturf." [21,22] But she has celebrated Occupy Wall Street with unrestrained zeal and fully embraced its particular brand of civil disobedience. "God bless them for their spontaneity," said Pelosi on October 6, 2011. "It's independent people coming (together), it's young, it's spontaneous, it's focused, and it's going to be effective." [23]

The irony, as they say, is thick. Pelosi and her husband, Paul, are superwealthy—card-carrying members of the Occupy-reviled "one percent." "House Minority Leader Nancy Pelosi (D-Ca) saw her net worth rise 62 percent last year, cementing her status as one of the wealthiest members of Congress," according to *The Hill* newspaper. "Pelosi was worth at least $35.2 million in the 2010 calendar year, according to a financial disclosure report released Wednesday. She reported a minimum of $43.4 million in assets and about $8.2 million in liabilities. For 2009, Pelosi reported a minimum net worth of $21.7 million." [24] This massive wealth comes from her husband's investment firm, Financial Leasing Services. "The bulk of the Pelosis' money comes from investments in stocks and real estate," according to the *San Francisco Chronicle*. Their holdings include "Microsoft, AT&T, Cisco Systems, Disney, Johnson & Johnson and a variety of tech stocks." [25]

Why would the former Speaker, a filthy-rich One-Percenter, celebrate Occupy Wall Street? Surely, the Tea Party can be equally characterized as "independent people coming together." They too are focused and effective. What's up with that? It may seem hypocritical for Pelosi to stand with Occupy Wall Street. (It is.) It may seem like a blatant double standard to revile Tea Partiers and then embrace OWS. (It is.) But it is predictably consistent, too. There is a pattern to the madness. If you want to increase accountability, reduce costs, and rein in the power of Washington, the political elites will attempt to block you at every turn. Your efforts will be greeted with abject hostility. You will be scorned, kicked out of the halls of power. You may even get audited. But if you want to grow the confiscatory power of government, the political establishment will applaud you, defend your First Amendment rights as sacrosanct, and bend over backward to accommodate even your worst behavior.

It's all a means to an end.

NOT TOLERABLE

THIS IS NOT A NEW PHENOMENON. IT GOES ALL THE WAY BACK TO THE beginnings of the Republic. Like the folks in the movement today, the original "Tea Partiers" were a community of patriots who had self-organized in defense of their threatened liberties. On December 16, 1773, a band of Bostonians styling themselves "Sons of Liberty" and led by Samuel Adams gathered in Boston to petition His Majesty King George III and the British Parliament for redress of grievances. They did so, of course, in that wonderfully memorable—and nonviolent—way of holding a "tea party" in Boston Harbor. The following year, Parliament responded—with abject hostility—to the Boston Tea Party, closing the city harbor and passing a series of repressive edicts that history remembers as the "Intolerable Acts." These laws systematically stripped colonial Americans of their individual rights. One of those dictates, the Massachusetts Government Act, included a provision that prohibited citizens from assembling in town meetings more than once a year, subject to the discretion of the Crown-appointed governor. This was the British government's attempt to force American citizens to subjugate themselves to Parliament's unquestioned authority over the freedoms and prerogatives of colonials.

But the Intolerable Acts backfired: American moderates who already sympathized with the grievances of the radicals flooded to the cause of revolution. As Parliament continued to erode the liberties of the colonies, the oppressed colonists responded by organizing among themselves. The theory of American unity was not a novel idea—Benjamin Franklin had proposed a loose confederation among the colonies as far back as 1754—but the practicalities of such an arrangement proved too difficult to overcome. The colonies after all thought of themselves as independent from each other, subject only to the British Crown. Although the Intolerable Acts didn't apply to all the colonies equally—the Massachusetts Government Act applied only to Massachusetts, obviously—the colonists feared the precedent. If Parliament could eradicate freedom of assembly in one colony, what would stop it from doing so in others?

The colonists responded to this real fear in a variety of ways, the most effective of which was the creation of the Committees of Correspondence. By 1774, eleven colonies had set up their own Committees, which functioned as a de facto "American" government, acting in secret from British authorities. It was the individual Committees that, in September 1774, established the First Continental Congress in direct response to the Intolerable Acts.

Today, the revolution that followed is too easily summarized as a reaction against "taxation without representation." While that was certainly part of Parliament's offenses, the colonists didn't revolt only because of taxes. They revolted because, by steps large and small, Parliament had gradually eroded their historical rights as British citizens. Beginning with the Magna Carta in the thirteenth century and through subsequent eras, with the establishment of common law and the principle of representative government, the Englishman in the 1700s enjoyed a level of freedom unmatched in the rest of Europe, never mind the world. More to the point, wherever Britain planted its flag, there British common law—and the rights of Englishmen—would follow.

Except that by 1774, the British colonists in America were beginning to realize that this ancient balance between citizen and government no longer applied to them. Their revolt was an attempt to retrieve a level of freedom that had been gradually destroyed after, in Jefferson's immortal phrase, "a long train of abuses and usurpations." That—and not simply "taxes"—was the principal cause and justification of the American Revolution.

Similarly, the Left and the mainstream media like to dismiss the Tea Party as a group of people disgruntled over paying taxes. They're half right. Taxes are too high, and when our taxes go toward wasteful government spending, we justifiably become disgruntled. But the grievances of the Tea Party go deeper than that, just as the grievances of the colonists went deeper than taxation without representation. Out-of-control spending and high taxes are just the symptoms of a government system that is eroding the individual rights of American citizens. As the example of the American Revolution shows, attempts to redress this erosion are met by subtle and not so subtle forms of government repression of our individual voices. The arbitrary differences in treatment between two groups of Americans—the Tea Party and Occupy Wall Street—both attempting to exercise their First Amendment rights is just one small example.

But the Second American Revolution will not involve violence, throwing tea into Boston Harbor, overthrowing the government, or the destruction of anyone's property, private or public. The Tea Party revolution is about education and the decentralizing forces of cheaper, quicker information. This revolution does not require a better leader or "another Ronald Reagan." The next revolution in America involves individuals, in voluntary cooperation, holding government accountable. This was our original mandate from the Founders: to protect, as eternally vigilant individuals, that "sacred fire of liberty" George Washington spoke of so eloquently.

UNDERWATER, DROWNING IN DEBT

IN THE NINETEENTH CENTURY, BRITISH STATESMAN WILLIAM GLADstone coined a set of "golden rules" for economy in government:

"Limit spending, tax lightly, borrow the minimum, maintain a surplus, pay off debt."[26] These days, it seems the only people in our society who don't have to abide by these rules are politicians and children. Children, at least, have an excuse. Our politicians, meanwhile, have turned every one of these maxims on its head. And the result is a nation drowning in debt.

Fiscal profligacy is as inimical to individual liberty as any overt oppression. In some ways, it's even more dangerous, because it tends to creep up on an unsuspecting populace. How bad has Uncle Sam's fiscal problem become? Let's start by putting it in "kitchen-table" perspective. Imagine Uncle Sam really is our uncle—a living, breathing individual. If you take the existing federal budget figures and simply erase the last eight zeroes from each, you can immediately see how serious his problem is.

OUR UNCLE SAM'S
PERSONAL BUDGET, 2011*

	Amount	% of income	% of spending
Outstanding credit card balance	$154,762	672	430
Income received	$21,700	—	64
Amount spent	$36,011	156	—
New debt added to credit card	$12,986	56	36
Total spending cuts this year	$385	2	1

*Actual U.S. government budget figures, in tens of billions of dollars

Uncle Sam owed $154,762 last year. But because he spent 56 percent more than he took in, he added nearly $13,000 to his outstanding debt. He borrowed 36 cents for every dollar he spent. And the trouble is, he's been living this way for years. Now he's asking us for another $13,000 loan for next year. Should we give it to him? Or should we do what any sensible family would do and take away his credit card and ask him to revise his consumption pattern?

By the way, I could have included in this table a line showing the House Republican pledge to cut $1,000 from Uncle Sam's 2011 budget (that is, $100 billion). Instead, they only managed to produce the $385 you see listed ($38.5 billion). That puny 1 percent savings came about only after much gnashing of teeth and threats of partial government shutdowns. Imagine what it will take to produce real change.

From 1790 to 1930, federal spending averaged just 3 percent of national output. From the end of World War II through 2008, it averaged about 19.3 percent. In 2009, it shot up to 25 percent, and the average for the past four years has been 24 percent.[27] Uncle Sam is consuming nearly one out of every four dollars in value generated in the United States every year. In 1960, the government spent approximately $97 billion, or about $500 per person. This year, 2012, federal spending is expected to surpass $3.7 trillion or nearly $12,000 per person.[28] Federal spending has increased thirty-eight-fold over the past half century; twenty-four-fold on a per person basis.

As our government has grown, so has its chronic habit of borrowing. From 1790 to 1930, our federal deficit, the amount of money our government spends annually that it does not have, averaged one-third of 1 percent (0.3 percent) of national output. From 1947 through 2008, deficits averaged 1.5 percent of output. Since the end of 2008, they've averaged 8.6 percent.[29] The deficit hit $1.4 trillion in 2009, the highest yearly shortfall since 1945.[30] In fact, the three largest deficits of postwar history have all occurred in the past three years: 2009 (10 percent), 2010 (8.9 percent), and 2011 (8.6 percent). The fourth biggest postwar deficit is expected to occur this year, 2012 (7 percent).

The result of all this borrowing? A truly staggering debt. Two years ago, Admiral Mike Mullen, chairman of the Joint Chiefs of Staff, shocked the Washington establishment by declaring that "the single-biggest threat to our national security is our debt."[31] He was right. As of December 7, 2011, the gross debt of the United States Government stood at exactly $15,046,397,725,405.16 (i.e., more than

$15 trillion[32]), and the most debt in our nation's history, in dollar terms, and the second most as a share of the economy. The all-time peak was in 1946,[33] when it was equal to 126 percent of the nation's output. Three years ago, the debt equaled 75 percent of output; today, it's 103 percent and rising. This generation of Americans has managed to pile up almost as much debt as did the generation that waged World War II, and more debt than the generation that waged the Civil War (on both sides!).[34]

To put this in perspective, during the past four years, the debt has been growing by an average of $1.7 trillion a year, $139 billion a month, $32 billion a week, $5 billion a day, $190 million an hour, $3.2 million a minute, $53,000 a second. In the time it will take you to read this sentence, Washington, D.C., will have added roughly a quarter of a million dollars to the national debt. In the time it has taken you to read this paragraph, the debt will have grown by nearly $2.5 million.[35]

Divide the national debt by our current population of about 310 million people, and each American's personal share of the debt—your share and mine—is about $46,400. This amount is currently growing at the rate of $5,400 a year, $450 a month, $100 a week, $15 a day, 60 cents an hour, one cent a minute, every minute, without cease.

Using accounting practices that would make even Bernie Madoff blush, our staggering national debt does *not* account for an additional $100 trillion in unfunded liabilities that will come due as the baby boomers retire and our Medicare and Social Security programs attempt to fulfill their obligations to retirees. Add that $100 trillion to the $15 trillion that *is* on the books, and every single one of us owes roughly $370,000.

SPENDING LIKE PIGS?

When we compare our situation with that of other countries, things look even worse. Europe has been trying for the past few years to stave off a domino effect of national debt crises among its member states. At the time its debt crisis began, Greece's debt load was roughly 137 percent of its national output; for Portugal, the comparable figure was 82 percent. Together with Spain and Italy, these countries are members of the notorious PIGS group of European nations teetering on the brink of financial default. With a gross debt load equal to 103 percent of GDP, we are second only to Greece. And we definitely exceed her, if we count those unfunded liabilities.[36]

Greece's debt has already been downgraded by her global creditors, creating a domestic budget crisis, political unrest, and rioting. The only thing keeping Greece from defaulting on her massive debt is the generosity of European taxpayers, especially the Germans, who have agreed to massive bailouts. A lot of experts think these bailouts won't work, and ultimately American taxpayers will be asked to bail out the bailouts, as it were. If that fails, who will bail *us* out?

You say, *But we're America, the world's economic superpower. What happened in Greece can't happen here.* Global bond markets say otherwise. The first serious sign of impending crisis came last year, in the wake of the Great Debt Ceiling Debate in Washington. Seeing our leaders utterly unable to agree on even modest changes to stanch the massive flow of red ink, Standard & Poor's downgraded U.S. government-issued debt from the highest possible level, AAA, to the next highest, AA+. This was a gentle warning shot across the bow. Next time, they won't be so kind. All three of the top global credit rating agencies—Fitch, Moody's, and S&P—have warned that they intend to downgrade us in 2013, absent serious deficit reduction.[37]

Merely to stabilize the debt as a share of the economy, we would have to reduce annual deficits to no more than 3 percent of national output. Recall that deficits are currently in the 8 percent range. What happens if we don't stop the debt? Downgrades will force us to pay higher interest rates when we borrow, which will make our fiscal challenge even worse. Federal interest payments today equal about 1.2 percent of national output, but on our current course they will quadruple to about 4 percent by 2020.[38] Many economists define the "point of no return"—the point at which some form of debt default becomes unavoidable—as having been reached when interest payments exceed 10 percent of revenue. Because of our unique position in the global economy, Moody's grants the U.S. leeway on this metric, generously defining our "point of no return" as occurring when our interest payments exceed 14 percent of our revenue.[39] Either way, we're in trouble. Interest payments currently equal 10.5 percent of revenue, and are expected to exceed 14 percent in the next two or three years.[40]

The root problem underlying every fact and figure I've recited is centralization of power and information in big institutions that lack accountability. The biggest culprit is the tendency of the federal government to centralize authority from the top down. Governments naturally collect responsibilities, grow budgets, and expand their reach. The Founders were keenly aware of this trend, having lived under the arbitrary tyranny of a parliament and of a king who decided from across an ocean—effectively a different world, then—for the people he supposedly governed.

Today, the Constitution seems to have diminished in its relevance to the actions of the legislative and executive branches of government. There are no practical limits on government action. For every problem—real or imagined—there is someone inside or outside demanding a government solution.

FAILED MANAGEMENT

Despite the ominous statistics, Senate Majority Leader Harry Reid, Democrat of Nevada, has refused to pass a budget resolution—the blueprint that sets the agenda for annual appropriations and program authorizations for the fiscal year—for three years running. The Budget Act requires that Congress pass a budget resolution by April 15 of each year,[41] the same day Americans are required to pay their taxes: "On or before April 15 of each year, the Congress *shall* complete action on a concurrent resolution on the budget for the fiscal year beginning on October 1 of such year." [42]

This is an abdication of Congress's first responsibility. Why doesn't Senator Reid obey the law? Someone should be fired, you say. If the U.S. government were a private company, surely the CEO would fire the entire finance department for failing to come up with an annual budget plan. Of course, the federal government's chief executive, Barack Obama, is in no position to enforce regular order when it comes to congressional budgeting and deficit spending. The Obama administration's last budget blueprint actually proposed an additional $2.3 trillion in new spending on top of current red ink. [43] There is no hope of adult supervision coming from the current resident at 1600 Pennsylvania Avenue when it comes to questions of fiscal discipline.

Adding insult to injury, the forced removal of We the People from the Russell Building that Thursday in November coincided with the inglorious collapse of the extraconstitutional "supercommittee," a secretive, extremely powerful conclave of six Democrats and six Republicans that was created to come up with modest spending reductions. This was the legislative solution to public opposition to increasing the government's authority to borrow still more, to "raise the debt ceiling," in lieu of actually reducing the amount of deficit spending actually spent. This was the *second* debt-cutting commission created during the Obama administration in the hope of solving a problem that Congress and the White House have been unwilling to solve for years. Given the size of the problem, their agreed goal of $1.2 trillion in savings—or, to put it in terms of our "Uncle Sam's personal budget," their goal of a mere $120 a year, for ten years—was just a small haircut in projected new spending.

In the commonsense methodology you and I use to think about our family budgets, this sort of trim isn't a "cut" at all, but rather a decrease from a hoped-for rate of increase well beyond our means. This practice of calling anything below a rising baseline a "cut," known as "current services" or "baseline" budgeting, is a fiction that makes it very difficult for taxpayers to even understand the budgeting that comes out of Washington. To put it less delicately, it's a lie.

Lie or not, the supercommittee failed anyway. It could not even agree to noncut cuts. It could not even agree to reduce the rate of increase in expenditures of taxpayer monies that we do not have. Their inability to come up with even a nominal $1.2 trillion "cut" from an artificially bloated ten-year baseline was a new low, and the likelihood of any movement toward a balanced budget was put off yet again. That Monday, November 21, 2011, just four days after 250 American taxpayers were kicked out of the Russell Senate Office Building for committing serial acts of good citizenship and fiscal responsibility, the supercommittee members released this helpful statement:

> After months of hard work and intense deliberations, we have come to the conclusion today that it will not be possible to make any bipartisan agreement available to the public before the committee's deadline. Despite our inability to bridge the committee's significant differences, we end this process united in our belief that the nation's fiscal crisis must be addressed and that we cannot leave it for the next generation to solve. . . .
>
> *Most importantly, we want to thank the American people for sharing thoughts and ideas and for providing support and good will as we worked to accomplish this difficult task.*[44]

Say what?

TAKE IT OVER

WELCOME TO BUSINESS AS USUAL IN OUR NATION'S CAPITAL: BEREFT of new ideas, poorly managed, failing to perform its most basic functions, and utterly contemptuous of anyone from outside the Beltway establishment who is armed with facts, better ideas, and a belief that

America can and must do better. Every time Washington fails, wagons are circled and almost everyone colludes around the pretense that nothing's really wrong: *Everything is fine if we just let the process work its will—and by all means, we welcome your input.*

So it was on November 17, 2011, when the twelve commissioners of the Tea Party Debt Commission were literally thrown out of Congress for having the audacity to bring specific ideas to balance the budget to a "boardroom" in desperate need of new ideas. This is the classic behavior of entrenched management circling the wagons against any entreaty that might undermine the status quo.

The Hostile Takeover of the U.S. Senate by the American people was now in full tilt.

CHAPTER 2

WHAT CZARS DON'T KNOW

*I don't sit around just talking to experts because this is a
college seminar. We talk to these folks because they potentially
have the best answer so I know whose ass to kick.*
—Barack Obama

HOW IS IT POSSIBLE THAT MILLIONS AND MILLIONS OF PEOPLE LO-
cated in disparate places—each individual in possession of a unique
perspective, particular goals, wants, and needs, and a personal knowledge of their community and circumstances—can come together in
voluntary cooperation to create something far greater and more valued than any one individual could have achieved alone?

It's a great question. It is a particularly humbling question for a
so-called public policy expert to ask, because just by asking it I have to
admit that I don't know a lot of what is happening in the world at any
moment in time. The question itself *acknowledges* that at any moment
in time there are many things in an infinite sea of facts, data points,
and bits of knowledge that you and I can't possibly know.

This humility—knowing that there is much you don't know—is

one of the foundational principles of a political philosophy based on individual freedom. It's the bottom-up approach. But for a simple, timeless set of rules that protect life, liberty, and property, we should all be left alone to pursue our own interests as we define them, because we know best what is good for ourselves and our families. That's very personal knowledge, not known by anyone else. Only freedom lets us use, in voluntary cooperation with others, what we alone know. Freedom works to best meet everyone's goals in a world of uncertainty, trade-offs, and scarcity. Adam Smith wrote of this dynamic in 1776 in *The Wealth of Nations*, describing how it is that freely acting people can lead to an unintended coordination of individual interests:

> Every individual is continually exerting himself to find out the most advantageous employment for whatever capital he can command. It is his own advantage, indeed, and not that of the society which he has in view. But the study of his own advantage naturally, or rather necessarily, leads him to prefer that employment which is most advantageous to society. . . . [H]e intends only his own gain, and he is in this, as in many other cases, led by an invisible hand to promote an end which was not part of his intention.[1]

The freedom-based, bottom-up approach does not depend on centralized direction, or the good intentions of a central director.

The opposite political philosophy, the top-down approach, requires that someone be "in charge." Without adult supervision, things may not progress, and may even collapse into chaos. Someone needs to direct things. *Someone needs to dictate.* The top-down approach implicitly assumes, but seldom says explicitly, that certain people—those smarter than you and me—know certainly, and can act to improve things based on a better set of data, a more comprehensive set of facts, and a superior wisdom to do better than free individuals could do for themselves. Those special people just need the authoritative power of government behind them to succeed.

There is a certain arrogance to this top-down approach that presumes to know better. This presumption is what Nobel laureate economist Friedrich Hayek called "the pretense of knowledge."

Economist Ludwig von Mises and his protégé Hayek developed their critique of top-down government planning based on their understanding of market interaction as a process between people choosing in real time. They understood the world to be driven by purposeful humans—folks who in the very act of living and working set out to accomplish things with every waking moment. But all this purpose yields results that are never predetermined, not by a design. This is not a world of perfect knowledge but of knowledge gained as life actually happens in the real world. Everyday life is a world of uncertainty, where the outcome of future decisions cannot be known for sure; instead they are guided by past experiences, traditions, informed risk-taking, and the knowledge that emerges from this push and pull, conveyed by institutions such as money and prices.

How is the coordination of individual plans even possible in such a complex world? The feedback mechanism is success or failure and profit or loss based on the choices made. This process, this feedback loop of new information, corrects itself untold times a day. This is how real people in their everyday acts of living, planning, failing, regrouping, pursuing, and dreaming solve the ubiquitous "knowledge problem." We don't know what we don't know, but the process of figuring things out—the market process—coordinates our efforts with those of others. "The evolution of markets has delivered us into a world too complex for any individual intelligence to comprehend in detail," wrote Don Lavoie in his important critique of top-down economics, *Rivalry and Central Planning*. Understanding this necessitates "our reliance on the greater social intelligence embodied in market processes."[2]

Can you know what the best outcome is without undergoing the process that reveals individual preferences, corrects mistakes, rewards risk, and punishes bad behavior? This is perhaps the most important question economists and policymakers can ask, and too many experts in Washington, D.C., fail to ask it before they act.

Whenever faced with a public policy proposal, a potential "fix" to a very real problem facing our society that involves more government—more spending with money we don't have or more government control over the decisions you and I make—I always ask myself two simple questions. First, do those elected officials and government employees involved in developing and implementing proposed new laws face the proper incentives to get the job done? In other words, do they have your best interests at heart, or their own? Second, even if they do have your best interests in mind, do they have the knowledge to outsmart the market? Do they know better what to do? Virtually every policy architect who has ever proposed a grandiose macroeconomic scheme involving a new and better government redesign of some or all of the private economy has simply ignored the question. From Karl Marx to John Maynard Keynes to Paul Krugman to Ben Bernanke, it's the same. They feel no need to answer the question, because they assume they know.

Any bureaucrat or committee chairman who wants to adjust economic outcomes to correct real or perceived market failures has to first come to terms with the very real possibility that a disruption of the market's corrective processes—millions and millions of individuals learning and acting on new information—might lead to an unintended, more catastrophic government failure.

THE KNOWLEDGE PROBLEM

WHAT DO WOULD-BE PLANNERS KNOW? HOW DO THEY KNOW IT? These questions defined the work of Mises, whose research into the nature of economic coordination was no doubt spurred by the rising popularity of central planning in Europe after World War I. Until 1934, he had been a well-respected scholar in Vienna, Austria. The so-called Austrian School of economics is named after the geographical origins of its best thinkers: Carl Menger, Eugen von Böhm-Bawerk, Ludwig von Mises, and Friedrich Hayek.

Mises moved to Switzerland with the rise of the National Socialist Party in Germany. After the Anschluss, the occupation of Austria by Adolf Hitler, Mises joined many other Jews and fled Europe for the United States. There he took up a position at New York University. Perhaps because of his own personal knowledge and experiences with practical outcomes of the theoretical constructs of socialism, Mises's initial work was on the nature of money, and its necessary role in facilitating economic calculation in a market economy. This led directly to a fundamental critique of socialism, one that is now acknowledged even by his fiercest critics to have been irreparably devastating to Karl Marx's original vision. Mises predicted that even the best-intended policies under government ownership of the means of production would lead to economic calamity because there would be no rational basis for sorting things out, for the allocating of scarce resources. He recognized that the relevant information was not already "given" to government planners and that no one mind or group of minds could possibly possess all the knowledge necessary to plan a complex economic system. Instead, monetary calculation and prices are the indispensable "guide amid the bewildering throng of economic possibilities."[3]

Mises understood socialism in terms of its original Marxian aspiration: complete elimination of the monetary economy. Marx wished to replace *production for exchange*, which was directed by the blind forces of the market, with consciously directed *production for direct use*. It simply does not work. Mises argued,

No single man can ever master all the possibilities of production, innumerable as they are, as to be in a position to make straightaway evident judgments of value without the aid of some system of computation. The distribution among a number of individuals of administrative control over economic goods in a community of men who take part in the labor of producing them, and who are economically interested in them, entails a kind of intellectual division of labor, which would not be possible without some system of calculating production and without economy.[4]

Central planners cannot know which production projects are economically possible and which are not precisely because such knowledge is not merely data to be gathered and crunched.

Mises's critics at the time failed to appreciate the fundamental nature of the Austrian's critique, not just of Marx's wholesale vision, but for piecemeal government planning. Most economists incline toward more government planning, intervention, and fine-tuning, because they view prices and knowledge as objective data points that exist independent of the process of the market, understanding the whole problem of economic organization as merely a technical one. With the right inputs and outputs, they believe, an economy can still be rationally directed toward a preferred state of equilibrium.

POLITICAL PRETENSE

SOUNDS FAMILIAR, DOESN'T IT? YOU LIKELY HEAR THIS PRETENSE OF knowing better whenever a politician opens his or her mouth and starts fixing problems. No politician in my lifetime better personifies the hubris of knowing better than Barack Obama. His administration, in all its various attempts to "fix" the economy, has sought to replace the corrective forces of the market process with a better plan, or a new direction that better masters "all the possibilities of production, innumerable as they are."[5] Consider Obama's confidence in his administration's "green jobs" agenda, circa May 2010:

The true engine of economic growth will always be companies like Solyndra, will always be America's businesses. But that doesn't mean the government can just sit on the sidelines. Government still has the responsibility to help create the conditions in which students can gain an education so they can work at Solyndra, and entrepreneurs can get financing so they can start a company, and new industries can take hold. . . . Around the world, from China to Germany, our competitors are waging a historic effort to lead in developing new energy technologies. There are factories like this being built in China, factories like this being built in Germany. Nobody is playing for second place. These countries recognize that the nation that leads the clean energy economy is likely to lead the global economy. And if we fail to recognize that same imperative, we risk falling behind. Fifteen years ago, the United States produced 40 percent of the world's solar panels—40 percent. That was just 15 years ago. By 2008, our share had fallen to just over 5 percent. I don't know about you, but I'm not prepared to cede American leadership in this industry, because I'm not prepared to cede America's leadership in the global economy. So that's why we've placed a big emphasis on clean energy. It's the right thing to do for our environment, it's the right thing to do for our national security, but it's also the right thing to do for our economy. And we can see the positive impacts right here at Solyndra. Less than a year ago, we were standing on what was an empty lot. But through the Recovery Act, this company received a loan to expand its operations. This new factory is the result of those loans.[6]

This particular solar panel manufacturer filed for bankruptcy just a few months after Obama spoke at the newly constructed, government-financed facility. The dubious entanglements between the Obama administration, Obama's political patrons, and the financial investors in the project rightly generated a public outcry over who exactly helped procure a $535 million government outlay of taxpayer dollars in the new president's very first legislative initiative, the 2009 stimulus package. The scandalous facts in this instance make Solyndra an easy target for critics of the Obama administration. But the more fundamental point is the underlying audacity of a president who is so confident that he knows better—certain of "the right thing to do"—than the entirety of all the actors playing in global markets. He's second-guessing billions of people, innumerable competing firms, every type of energy production that is a viable substitute for solar power, and other command and control governments. That's an awful lot for a politician and a few bureaucrats to know about. This is more than pretense. The arrogance of big government is, as Hayek put it, a "fatal conceit."

According to Jonathan Rothwell, a senior research analyst at the Brookings Institution, at the time that the administration was making its initial investments in green energy, *"there just wasn't much known* about the size of the green economy. It was hard to come up with precise numbers."[7]

At the U.S. Department of Energy, the epicenter of informed strategic thinking on green energy within the Obama administration, "there just wasn't that much known." True enough, the very nature of capital investment and risk-taking in an inherently uncertain future always involves the potential of failure and loss. But in the private economy, the risks are borne by the same individuals and interests that will foot the tab for failure. Do you see a possible incentive problem with politicians and bureaucrats risking your money for their potential benefit? Does anyone believe that someone else will be more cautious with your money than you would be? Planners like Obama do, apparently.

President Obama is an unusually easy target when searching for politicians who think they know better than you do, even in Washington, D.C., where virtually every politician is likely to believe that they have been especially blessed with a vision to lead. Whenever Obama goes off script, his "vision thing" gets more transparent, easier for the rest of us to see. "We're not trying to push financial reform because we begrudge success that's fairly earned," he told an audience in Quincy, Illinois, in April 2010. "I do think at a certain point you've made enough money, but you know, part of the American way is, you know, you can just keep on making it if you're providing a good product or you're providing a good service." [8] There's that word again—at a "certain" point he knows certainly that enough is enough. Which successes are "fairly earned"? How much money is "enough"? President Obama has never publicly revealed his economic calculations on these points, but all this was said without the benefit of a teleprompter, so presumably with great personal conviction.

Democratic congressman Barney Frank, former chairman of the House Financial Services Committee, is also a regular culprit when it comes to political expressions of certainty. "It is also clear," Frank said, "that left entirely untouched by public policy, the capitalist system will produce more inequality than is socially healthy or than is necessary for maximum efficiency." [9] How much touching by public policy do you suppose gets the market process to "maximum efficiency"? You may not know the answer to that complex question; I sure don't. But Congressman Frank thinks he does.

Frank was also infamously certain about the financial soundness of Fannie Mae and Freddie Mac, the massive government-sponsored enterprises so culpable for putting buyers into homes they could not afford. He argued for "rolling the dice" in 2003: "I do think I do not want the same kind of focus on safety and soundness that we have in OCC [Office of the Comptroller of the Currency] and OTS [Office of Thrift Supervision]. I want to roll the dice a little bit more in this situation toward subsidized housing." [10] In July 2008, just weeks before the whole subsidized-housing house of cards collapsed, Frank knew that "Fannie and Freddie are fundamentally sound, that they are not in danger of going under. They're not the best investments these days from the long-term standpoint going back [but] I think they are in good shape going forward." [11] He was certain it was so, because he was the chairman of the House committee of jurisdiction.

Think about how the housing bubble and the 2008 stock market crash was driven by the collapse in value of mortgage-backed securities. Now think about the culpability of the Federal Reserve, and the role of Fannie Mae and Freddie Mac. Didn't they enable the bad actors and deceive the rest of us into making calculations based on corrupted price signals? To make matters worse, instead of acknowledging their mistakes and allowing the needed corrections to take place, the instigators of the first crisis now presume to know how to fix what they caused. Their "fixes" to the perceived failures of markets are making things worse. The presumption of knowledge and multiple efforts to improve on market outcomes by the government has resulted in systemic damage to the economy and real pain for countless individuals caught up in the boom and bust of government intervention. The unintended consequences of government decisions from on high seem only to encourage more intervention, but little accountability. There is no built-in correction mechanism in the top-down approach.

Before you leap to the conclusion that this "pretense of knowledge" is a disease that afflicts only Democrats, think again. Republican President George W. Bush proposed in 2004 "that mortgages that have FHA-backed insurance pay no down payment. . . . What we're trying to do is make it easier for somebody to own a home, and there are practical ways the government can help." [12] As it turns out, making it easier for people to buy homes at the near peak of a government-induced bubble was exactly the wrong thing to do. Those mortgage contracts became a government-induced form of financial servitude for folks struggling to make their monthly payments on a home that was now underwater. But how could the Bush administration have known?

Former Massachusetts governor Mitt Romney, a Republican who made his fortune as a management consultant, is widely viewed as a technocrat, and he does little to dissuade people from the characterization. Governor Romney, as everyone knows, aspires to be our next president; and he touts as his chief qualification his experience at taking over and fixing failing companies. A particularly revealing interview by Joseph Rago and Paul A. Gigot in the *Wall Street Journal* showed the planner inherent in Romney's thinking. On the one hand, "Mr. Romney describes the core failure of Mr. Obama's economic agenda as faith in 'a wise group of governmental bureaucrats' rather than political and economic freedom." Romney called it "a refrain that we have seen throughout history where smart people are convinced that smart people ought to be able to guide an economy better than hordes of individuals pursuing their self-interest, the helter-skelter of free people choosing their course in life." [13]

But in a 2007 *Journal* interview, that same Mitt Romney revealed a very different outlook: "In that meeting the candidate began by declaring 'I love data' and kept on extolling data, even 'wallowing in data,' as a way to reform both business and government. He said he'd bring in management consultants to turn around the government, mentioning McKinsey, Bain and the Boston Consulting Group. Mr. Romney seemed to elevate the power of positive technocratic thinking to a governing philosophy." [14]

Has he had a conversion? Like Congresswoman Michele Bachmann, who once confessed she reads Ludwig von Mises at the beach, did Mitt Romney sneak-read a copy of Hayek's *Constitution of Liberty*? Not so fast, you hopeless optimist. When asked by the *Journal*, again in December 2011, about his views on how to fundamentally reform the monstrous labyrinth that is the U.S. tax code, he dodged the question, saying, "I simply don't have the team . . . to be able to model out what will happen to all the different income groups in the country, what will happen to the different sectors of our economy based on dramatic changes." [15] The whole point of tax simplification is to eliminate the political biases and social engineering in the tax code that requires a team of experts to model, and an army of professional tax preparers to comply with. Wanting to redistribute income in a better way than the current tax code does make Romney almost sound like a wise "governmental bureaucrat," doesn't it?

Democrats and Republicans alike think that they know better, or at least can hire the experts who know better, than millions and millions of people acting on their own behalf. Sometimes their knowing is piecemeal, tinkering around the edges of the market process. Romney, for instance, seems more inclined to pick up a tuning fork than a hammer. But for some, like Obama, you really get the sense that his vision is, like the progressive planners before him, a wholesale re-booting of our economic system. Indeed, his whole mind-set—collect the dispassionate analysis of the smartest guys in the room, armed with the best data, and you've solved the problem—is an inherently progressive approach to public policy. William Schambra argues that Obama's approach to public policy is textbook progressive, preferring "an approach to public policy that would make greater use of objective evidence, scientific facts, and expert counsel." [16] Obama, writing in *The Audacity of Hope*, argues for "having a nonpartisan group like the National Academy of Science's Institute of Medicine determine what a basic, high-quality health-care plan should look like and how much it should cost." [17]

AGGREGATING KEYNES

EITHER WAY, WHEN INTERVENTIONS ARE TRIED, PIECEMEAL OR wholesale, they fail to produce the desired effect. Interventions can lead to destructive, unintended consequences that cause real suffering for real people, many of them deceived by government-distorted signals. And of course, each intervention is followed up by still more interventions to fix the problems caused by the presumption of knowledge from the top down.

Part of the problem with planners wanting to plan is the aiding and abetting they get from the economics profession and its flawed assumptions. "It is vitally important to always remember," says Peter Boettke, one of the brightest of a new generation of Austrian economists, "that in the field of economics bad economic ideas lead to bad public policies which in turn result in bad economic outcomes." [18] He is referring specifically to major government-induced economic dislocations attributable to the intellectual legacy of John Maynard Keynes. According to Boettke, Keynes got it wrong by throwing basic economics out the window. He misrepresented markets as inherently unstable, and his arbitrary use of aggregation had no economic meaning, but allowed for simplistic, politically attractive policy prescriptions of aggregate demand management through more government spending.

Keynes was the first "macroeconomist," and the author of *The General Theory of Employment, Interest and Money*, published in 1936. Around that time, a famous series of "debates" broke out between Keynes, who was at the University of Cambridge, and Hayek, who had just arrived at the London School of Economics. In many ways it was a debate between the classical traditions of fiscal responsibility and balanced budgets that had been, pre-Keynes, the accepted wisdom of public finance, and a wholly new way of thinking, from the top down, introduced by Keynes. The two academics' arguments are brilliantly captured in the popular rap videos—"Fear the Boom and Bust" and "Fight of the Century"—of John Papola and Russ Roberts. The "fight" video depicts Hayek winning the intellectual argument but Keynes winning among the political and academic elites in the court of public opinion. And that's exactly how it played out.

Not surprisingly, Hayek's ideas about the decentralized power of freedom fare much better in the decentralized world of online media than they ever did in the cloistered monopoly of elite university academia. Freedom sells better in a world where people are free to choose what information they will consume. With total views of the two videos exceeding 4.5 million, Hayek is more relevant today than he ever was in his own lifetime.

There is, in fact, a boom in the market for Hayek's ideas. "Fear the Boom and the Bust" was uploaded to YouTube on January 23, 2010. Glenn Beck featured a discussion of Hayek's *Road to Serfdom* on June 8, 2010. "Aren't you just a little curious," Beck asked his audience, "if this is the first time you've ever heard of *The Road to Serfdom*, why that is? Gosh, it seems like a pretty important book. Why don't we teach this everywhere?"

"Decide for yourself," Beck advised. "Go online now and order it—*The Road to Serfdom*."[19]

The endorsement, like a proverbial injection of artificial credit by the Federal Reserve Bank, created an immediate boom in sales. "The University of Chicago Press found itself in an unprecedented position: number one in Amazon and Barnes & Noble's sales rankings with F. A. Hayek's anti-big government book *The Road to Serfdom,*" according to a June 10, 2010, report from *Publishers Weekly.* "The 66 year-old book bested Stieg Larsson and Stephenie Meyer—at least for a day. . . . Press director Garrett Kiely told *PW* that the book has been a consistent seller since the election of Barack Obama in November 2008, selling about 27,000 copies annually. Although he declined to quote exact numbers, Kiely said that with Beck's endorsement, the book has sold about half its annual number in a 24-hour span." [20]

Even Steve Rattner, who served as Obama's "car czar," acknowledges the importance of Hayek's ideas in the coming election. Writing in the *Financial Times,* he claims that the "2012 rivals can be named: Hayek vs. Keynes. . . . Providing intellectual underpinnings to each side—while lurking mostly out of sight—is the work of long-dead economists. The White House continues to lean heavily on the playbook of economist John Maynard Keynes—without uttering his name. As huge deficits have failed to lift the economy, 'Keynes' has almost become a vulgarity in US discourse, in part because a very Keynesian Obama initiative—the 2009 $825bn stimulus (another banished word)—has been widely derided as ineffective." Rattner went on to observe that "Republicans have been less coy about their favourite school: Ludwig von Mises and Friedrich Hayek. The quasi-libertarian, anti-statist sensibilities of these philosophers appeal to a public that has soured on government." [21]

ALIEN CONCEPTS

KEYNES REPLACED CLASSIC MICROECONOMIC TERMS LIKE *DEMAND* (how much you want to consume at a particular price) with a new, imaginary construct of *aggregate demand*. He argued that government needed to step in to spend more money and boost aggregate demand to stimulate the economy because of chronic underconsumption by consumers. Hayek argued that government policies had, in fact, caused an artificial boom by distorting price signals with easy money. The bust comes when the false signals are discovered. More government distortions would prevent economic recovery, prolonging the economic pain.

Keynesianism legitimized the idea that governments can stimulate economic activity and lift the economy out of recession through deficit spending and public works projects. Whether or not such spending projects are "shovel-ready" investments in infrastructure projects that make sense is beside the point. "If the Treasury were to fill old bottles with banknotes, bury them at suitable depths in disused coal mines which are then filled up to the surface with town rubbish, and leave it to private enterprise on well tried principles of laissez-faire to dig the notes up again," Keynes wrote in *The General Theory of Employment, Interest and Money,* "there need be no more unemployment and, with the help of the repercussions, the real income of the community, and its capital wealth also, would probably become a good deal greater than it actually is. . . . It would, indeed, be more sensible to build houses and the like; but if there are political and practical difficulties in the way of this, the above would be better than nothing." [22]

If you worry that I am taking Keynes's argument out of context, consider this August 15, 2011, exchange on CNN between Fareed Zakaria and Nobel laureate economist Paul Krugman, a preeminent advocate of Keynesian fiscal stimulus who has repeatedly argued that the failure of the Obama administration's economic policies is a failure to spend far more money on far more stimulus. "Wouldn't John Maynard Keynes say that if you employ people to dig a ditch and then fill it up again, that's fine?" Zakaria asked. "They're being productively employed. They're paying taxes." Krugman responds by wishing for "a program of government spending plus an expansionary policy by the Fed."

What kind of spending?

If we discovered that, you know, space aliens were planning to attack and we needed a massive buildup to counter the space alien threat and, really, inflation and budget deficits took secondary place to that, this slump would be over in 18 months. And then if we discovered, oops, we made a mistake, there aren't any aliens, we'd be better. . . . There was a Twilight Zone episode like this, in which scientists fake an alien threat in order to achieve world peace. Well, this time we don't need it [to achieve world peace]; we need it in order to get some fiscal stimulus.[23]

I am not making this up, but Hayek anticipated such absurd outcomes from the "logic" of the Keynesian method à la Krugman, noting that "some of the most orthodox disciples of Keynes appear consistently to have thrown overboard all the traditional theory of price determination and of distribution, all that used to be the backbone of economic theory, and in consequence, in my opinion, to have ceased to understand any economics."[24]

Be that as it may, by all accounts Hayek lost the "Fight of the Century" among economists and politicians looking for an intellectual defense for bad behavior. It really came down to the incentives of planners to plan and the incentives of advisers who wanted to advise the planners. But the greater misunderstanding was with the Austrian view of markets as a discovery process, not a mathematical problem of inputs and outputs that could be tweaked and micromanaged. It was this misunderstanding that led Hayek to write his seminal paper on "The Use of Knowledge in Society," published in *The American Economic Review* in 1945. Hayek posited that each individual, because of his unique situation within society, possesses a great deal of knowledge that is known to him alone—the knowledge of the particular circumstances of time and place. The individual may not even be able to articulate what he knows in explicit, rational terms. Institutions such as the price system emerge and continually adjust in an ongoing expression of these particular "bits of knowledge" that are dispersed throughout the market. Such market prices serve as a dynamic "system of telecommunications," or better, as "guideposts to action."

For Keynesians, times of downturn call for stimulating new demand. Any demand for anything will do because it's the aggregate that matters. Government spending is, by definition, a component of Gross Domestic Product, the official government measure of economic output. We could literally spend our way to prosperity, if we just had the courage of Paul Krugman's convictions. Can you imagine why Keynes's ideas have such lasting appeal to congressional committee chairmen and presidents? As the great public choice scholar P. J. O'Rourke so precisely explained it, "giving money and power to government is like giving whiskey and car keys to teenage boys."[25] Think of Keynesianism as the car, and your tax dollars are the whiskey. It's actually a Mack truck, and it has no brakes.

KEYNESIAN CONCEIT

HERE'S THE CONCEIT. ACCORDING TO HAYEK, KEYNES "WAS GUIDED by one central idea—which in conversation he once described to me as an 'axiom which only half-wits could question'—namely, that general employment was always positively correlated with the aggregate demand for consumer goods."[26] Get it? Macroeconomists are really smart, much smarter than the "half-wits" who still think governments shouldn't spend money they don't have, particularly on public projects that are never going to be "shovel ready."

Conceited government, it turns out, comes from conceited economists.

The problem with the Keynesian view is that it ignores the fact that public expenditures must come from somewhere. Each dollar spent on burying old bottles filled with banknotes or spent on building solar panels at three times the cost of what you can sell them for means that someone else will not spend that dollar. That someone else, by the way, is you, the person who earned it. That someone else would otherwise have been able to use that same dollar in ways that are informed by a real understanding of their personal needs. That someone else was highly likely to make a better decision that made better economic sense. This is what old-fashioned microeconomists call "opportunity cost." If you do this, you can't do that. There is a real opportunity cost, something better is always forgone, when the government raises taxes, raises the debt ceiling, or expands the supply of money and credit. That forgone opportunity might have been food on your family's table, an investment in a new idea by a struggling entrepreneur, or a new hire by a small businesswoman trying to figure out how to keep the doors open and still comply with the new health care mandate under Obamacare. You might consider this common sense, but the experts, like Keynes himself, think you're a "half-wit."

The absurd policy conclusions that can come from aggregate-demand thinking are caused by using the wrong method to understand how the world works. The bottom-up view of economic organization is unique in that it does not focus on the imaginary equilibrium states typically employed by macroeconomists, where all relevant information is already assumed to exist. Everything is known, given by definition. Too often, macroeconomists think about the economy as if it were a chessboard, where all potential moves are potentially knowable, dependent on the intelligence and strategic acumen of the player moving the pieces. This standard equilibrium view begs the key question of economic organization. "*If* we possess all the relevant information, *if* we can start out from a given system of preferences, and *if* we command complete knowledge of the available means, the problem which remains is purely one of logic," Hayek argued. "That is, the answer to the question of what is the best use of the available means is implicit in our assumptions." [27]

Planners can justify anything they want, even malinvestments in green jobs, by starting with the "right" assumptions. One great example of this was the estimated number of jobs "created or saved" crunched by Obama's economic advisers that were used to sell nearly a trillion dollars in deficit stimulus spending to a skeptical public in early 2009. Those numbers were contrived, and ultimately proven absurdly off the mark, but they were presented with an air of scientific certainty.

THE SEEN AND THE UNSEEN

IN THE REAL WORLD OF MARKET PROCESSES, INDIVIDUALS DEPEND ON the reliability of relative prices as guideposts to action. They depend on money as a stable standard of value that facilitates economic calculation. Investors use these market signals to determine where to invest and where to allocate resources. Do I build more housing? What is the expected value of a new home should an individual borrower default on their mortgage? Do I buy more house for my family than I need, or can really afford, because the annual double-digit increase in its value over the past three years makes it a sure bet? What are competing returns on capital if I pull out of mortgage-backed securities and seek less-risky financial instruments with a lower yield?

Every government action creates unforeseen consequences that must distort relative prices. There is a difference between what is seen, or intended, and what is not seen—the unintended consequences. The nineteenth-century economist Frédéric Bastiat described this, the seen and the unseen, particularly well: "In the economic sphere an act, a habit, an institution, a law produces not only one effect, but a series of effects. Of these effects, the first alone is immediate; it appears simultaneously with its cause; *it is seen.* The other effects emerge only subsequently; *they are not seen;* we are fortunate if we *foresee* them." [28]

In terms of their methods and their policy prescriptions, this was the unbridgeable gulf separating Hayek from Keynes. Hayek wanted to "pierce the veil of aggregates and look at the distortive effects on relative prices and relative output produced by boom-time credit expansions," says economist Mario Rizzo. Hayek's view says: "Let us look at the distortive effects that booms leave us as we work our way through a recession. Let us concentrate on sustainable lines of expenditure both during the boom and during the road out from the bust." [29]

As clever as Keynes was, he presumed too much. He didn't know what he could not know, but he was too arrogant to admit it.

HAIL, CAESAR!

AND THAT'S THE PROBLEM WITH CZARS.

They presume the knowledge necessary to outguess the millions of people who reveal their preferences in the marketplace, in a kaleidoscope of decisions, actions, and reactions to the decisions of others. And they have the power to act whether you agree with their dictates or not.

By the way, when exactly did it become acceptable in the United States of America to confer the title of "czar"? Particularly to describe the politicians and bureaucrats who supposedly work for We the People? America does not do the "czar" thing.

Americans, whose founding was a revolt against the tyranny of King George III, should revolt against the very suggestion that anyone holding public office hires a "czar" to oversee anything. It's offensive. A czar is a dictator by another name. Former senator Russ Feingold, a progressive Democrat, said it well at a Senate Judiciary Committee hearing in 2009:

> I should note that while the term czar has taken on a somewhat negative connotation in the media in the past few months, several presidents, including President Obama, have used the term themselves to describe the people they have appointed. I assume they have done so to show the seriousness of their effort to address a problem and their expectations of those they have asked to solve it. But historically, a czar is an autocrat, and it's not surprising that some Americans feel uncomfortable

about supposedly all-powerful officials taking over areas of the government.[30]

As Jonah Goldberg, author of *Liberal Fascism*, has pointed out, *czar* derives from *Caesar* and *Kaiser*, words not typically associated with constitutional governments. Yet the word *dictator* was used to describe various potentates in FDR's administration. "We had a 'dictator for steel' and a 'dictator' over at the NRA and elsewhere," wrote Goldberg. But "you can see the appeal as pretty much no one has a living memory of life under the Czars. Americans wouldn't tolerate a 'car king' or 'car dictator' or even a 'car Caesar.' But 'car czar' sounds both ironic and quaint."[31] The Russian people probably had a different view of life under real czars.

This is one of the more disturbing rhetorical turns in modern American political discourse—the casual comfort with which the press and government officials seem to use the term *czar*, more and more often to describe politically appointed Schedule C bureaucrats assigned to various government policy portfolios. Intended or not, the term seems to cede more power, greater expected responsibility onto government officials to "take charge," to "do something." A "green jobs czar" infers that we need to create green jobs as a national imperative, regardless of the opportunity cost. A "car czar" suggests that America is no longer capable of making cars without the financing, control, and top-down direction of the federal government. A "health care czar" seemingly implies that decisions of patients and doctors are to be superseded by the decrees of experts who will better manage the cost and quality of the care you and your children can receive.

The very nature of our constitutional democracy prohibits such concentrated power with any individual, including the President of the United States. But it particularly prohibits such power seated with an unelected, not-accountable-to-anyone bureaucrat.

It's a careless, sloppy misuse of language.

Or is it? The growth in use of the term seems to coincide with the expanding power of the executive branch of government over the prerogatives of the legislative branch. By some accounts, President Obama has somewhere between thirty-three and thirty-eight individual public policy "czars" working for him, the most of any U.S. president. There is no fully objective, agreed-upon use of the term, as it is used to refer to high-ranking policy officials working in the executive branch, but it usually denotes White House–appointed bureaucrats who can operate without congressional oversight and can avoid the bright spotlight of Senate confirmation hearings. Simply by appointing policy czars with direct access to the West Wing, the Obama administration has been able to avoid a great deal of congressional scrutiny that certainly would have occurred otherwise.

In April 2011, for instance, House Republicans attempted to defund four of Obama's most prominent and controversial czars, notably his "health care" and "climate change" czars, by including language that defunded the positions in budget legislation that was signed by the president. Obama responded with "a relatively rare 'signing statement' after he inked the budget deal in which he argued that the legislative effort to eliminate those positions was an unconstitutional infringement on the executive branch," according to the *Huffington Post*. That statement read, in part:

> The President has well-established authority to supervise and oversee the executive branch, and to obtain advice in furtherance of this supervisory authority. The President also has the prerogative to obtain advice that will assist him in carrying out his constitutional responsibilities, and do so not only from executive branch officials and employees outside the White House, but also from advisers within it. Legislative efforts that significantly impede the President's ability to exercise his supervisory and coordinating authorities or to obtain the views of the appropriate senior advisers violate the separation of powers. Therefore, the executive branch will construe [the law as to] not to abrogate these Presidential prerogatives.[32]

Translated, for us non-legal-scholar types, this says: "Screw you, Congress. We're doing it."

The late senator Robert Byrd (D-W.V.), who was highly critical of the George W. Bush administration for its accumulation of executive power, expressed alarm over Obama's czar power grab early in his administration. "As presidential assistants and advisers, these White House staffers are not accountable for their actions to the Congress, to cabinet officials, and to virtually anyone but the president," Byrd wrote in a letter to the president. "They rarely testify before congressional committees, and often shield the information and decision-making process behind the assertion of executive privilege. In too many instances, White House staff have been allowed to inhibit openness and transparency, and reduce accountability." [33]

PROGRESSIVELY WORSE

IN FAIRNESS, OBAMA IS CERTAINLY NOT THE FIRST PRESIDENT TO USE czars as an end run around Congress. The practice appears to have begun in earnest with the administration of Franklin Delano Roosevelt. And the idea of centralizing power to "experts" in Washington who can sagaciously determine how best to improve social welfare goes back to the Progressive movement of the late nineteenth and early twentieth centuries. The Progressive aim was to concentrate more and more power in the executive branch, where enlightened experts— today we call them czars—would govern the country.

In effect, the Progressives were turning the Founders' vision upside-down. Individual liberty was not viewed as the standard by which to judge policy. Rather, Progressives sought to improve society as a whole, which meant a far greater degree of intervention into the affairs of its citizens. Hayek's attack on "scientism"—the belief that well-educated public servants have the knowledge and skills to better run society with a certainty sought in the physical sciences—applies in spades to the Progressives and their reform agenda, which included two constitutional amendments that were perhaps the most direct attacks on individual freedom—the Sixteenth Amendment, authorizing an income tax, and the Eighteenth, prohibiting the manufacture and sale of alcoholic beverages. The Progressives also ushered in the Federal Reserve, seeking a central authority to control the money supply.

And much like today's ever-expanding government, the Progressive movement expanded in the 1870s by seducing both Republicans and Democrats with the lure of federal power. As historian Arthur Ekirch noted, elements of both political parties were drawn to "the idea of reform from the top under the leadership of the patrician or aristocratic classes of the community. . . . The reformers particularly emphasized the necessity of a civil service merit system. Better men in public positions, they hoped, would result in improved government."[34]

Perhaps the first major victory of the Progressives was the accession of Theodore Roosevelt to the presidency in 1901. Roosevelt clearly identified with the Progressives and sought to stretch the Constitution to its limits. Viewing himself as a "steward of the people," he aggressively expanded the role of government at home and abroad. "I did not usurp power," he famously declared, "but I did greatly broaden the executive power."[35]

Others did not view this expansion so kindly. Writing on Roosevelt, the legendary journalist H. L. Mencken (using the term *liberal* in the classic sense, before Progressives hijacked it to hide their true motives) wrote:

He didn't believe in democracy; he believed simply in government. His remedy for all the great pangs and longings of existence was not a dispersion of authority, but a hard concentration of authority. He was not in favor of unlimited experiment; he was in favor of a rigid control from above, a despotism of inspired prophets and policemen. He was not for democracy as his followers understood democracy, and as it actually is and must be; he was for a paternalism of the true

Bismarckian pattern, almost of the Napoleonic or Ludendorf-fian pattern—a paternalism concerning itself with all things, from the regulations of coal-mining and meat-packing to the regulation of spelling and marital rights. His instincts were always those of the property owning Tory, not those of the romantic Liberal. All the fundamental objects of Liberalism—free speech, unhampered enterprise, the least possible governmental interference—were abhorrent to him.[36]

Franklin Delano Roosevelt's New Deal piled on to the Progressive movement's push for more government, expanding government far beyond its constitutional mandate, and creating the culture of dependency through Social Security and other welfare programs that have categorically changed the relationship between citizens and the state. Likewise, President Johnson's Great Society expanded the entitlement state's future promises far beyond our ability to finance them.

Even Charles Beard, one of the most popular Progressive intellectuals, became disillusioned with the FDR's New Deal and the federal spending it entailed: "The principal weakness of the whole program is its heavy dependence upon government spending and lending policies. . . . Only one thing seems to be certain. When all the merits and accomplishments are duly appreciated, it remains a fact that this dispensation has been made possible only by enormous increases in the national debt."[37] The only way the new welfare state could survive is by commanding more and more of the nation's resources.

In addition to the direct expansion of government, the New Deal also ushered in the era of the rent-seeking society.[38] If you fill the trough, feeding will commence. As the reach of government grew, more and more decisions that were once left to the market were now routed through Washington. This centralization of economic power tended to favor the crony capitalists and corporate interests with the resources required to influence the federal government. Economist Mancur Olson explained the issue very precisely in *The Logic of Collective Action,* first published in 1965. Specifically, he examined how interest groups operated, highlighting the benefits that accrue to small groups.

Creating an interest group is not cheap; there are resources required to maintain a presence in Washington. Further, the more members of the group, the more difficult it becomes to reach a consensus opinion for the group. Consequently, Olson reasoned, small groups will form first. In addition, the only motive to participate in a group is if it provides benefits to the individual members, and the fewer members, the greater benefits per member. For Olson, this meant concentrated benefits provided the rationale for creating special interest groups. At the same time, the costs of their demands—higher tariffs, tax complexity, barriers to entry—will be spread across the entire taxpaying population.

This iron trap of concentrated benefits and dispersed costs provides incentives for groups to come to Washington, and feeds the progressives' push to centralize and expand the role of government, creating a symbiotic relationship between the moochers and the looters. The rest of us pick up the tab. It's a downward spiral that is driven by the concentration of money and power in Washington.

Unfortunately, it will be the larger, well-heeled interests that come to Washington, such as GE and other corporate giants, because they have the resources to hire an army of lobbyists. Smaller businesses struggle to make payroll and their voices are not heard, just as consumers are often left out of the top-down approach to economic policy, because they have no time or resources to devote to politics and federal regulations. The larger government grows, the more inequitable things become.

This should come as no surprise to proponents of big government. After all, such concerns were raised during the Progressive era. Charles B. Spahr raised these concerns about the centralization of power in 1896: "The smaller the area, the stronger the pressure of public opinion. As a rule, the middle class can control the legislation enacted under their eyes by those whom they know, but only the wealthier classes can act unitedly and effectively upon legislation at the national capital." [39]

The great push to centralize economic decision making from the top down was a fundamental departure from the laissez-faire principles that our nation was founded on, contrary to the *republican* ethos of Jefferson and Madison and the decentralized gaggle of pamphleteers and citizen activists that drove the Spirit of '76. Those at the top have failed to solve the knowledge problem. Economic decision makers in Washington can never grasp the particular knowledge of time and place that Hayek so eloquently described in his study of prices and information—essential knowledge that is generated from the bottom up, not from the top down.

The Progressive goal of centralizing decisions, power, and authority in the presidency seems utterly contrary to the trends everywhere else in life. We live in a world that is more decentralized than ever before. Individuals have more power and control. We are more mobile, get our news and information from a multitude of sources, communicate via Twitter, and connect on Facebook. We are typically free to choose our own destiny, thanks in large part to the liberating forces of the Internet.

And yet we see this trend toward centralization in government and the proliferation of czars wanting to tell us what we can and can't do with our lives and our hard-earned pay. At the top, the president is gathering executive power, wanting to redesign things in a way that no human possibly could.

Something's got to give, one way or another.

But think about the power of decentralization, how it is possible for millions and millions of people located in disparate places—each individual in possession of a unique perspective, particular goals, wants, and needs, and a personal knowledge of their community and circumstances—to come together in voluntary cooperation and to create something far greater and more valued than any one individual could have done alone. Is it possible that freedom, from the bottom up, can beat entrenched management, from the top down?

The answer, I think, is yes.

CHAPTER 3

THE TRUTH CARTEL

Information is not knowledge.
Knowledge is not wisdom. Wisdom is not truth.
—Frank Zappa

HOW DO WE GET TO THE TRUTH OF THE MATTER? IS WHAT WE BE-lieve to be true more legitimate if it's vetted and dispensed by the experts, from the top down?

There once was a time in the United States when we relied on Walter Cronkite to tell us what to think. He was "the most trusted man in America." We had no choice but to trust him, along with some nameless producer behind the scenes at *CBS Evening News,* two other television networks, and a handful of national newspapers, all part of an insular cartel that sorted through the infinite bits of information of the day and determined, for us, the Truth. In this top-down system, Truth came in a one-size-fits-all package, and was allocated to the public twice daily, with delivery of the morning paper and the start of the six o'clock news.

"And that's the way it is," Cronkite would say, concluding the half-hour right on cue, effectively ending any debate on the subject. There would be no argument, no alternative opinions. There was no easy mechanism by which viewers could push back. An individual's only recourse if he wanted a different set of data filtered through a different conventional wisdom was to switch channels to the strikingly similar versions of the truth offered by ABC and NBC.

Not surprisingly, Cronkite was a big believer in the positive power of centralization. He believed that the smartest people could get together in one room to solve the world's greatest problems, even the most elusive of challenges to social order and the human condition itself. Consider the quixotic quest for world peace, as an example. "It seems to many of us," he pronounced in an October 1999 speech before UN delegates, "that if we are to avoid the eventual catastrophic world conflict we must strengthen the United Nations as a first step toward a world government patterned after our own government with a legislature, executive and judiciary, and police to enforce its international laws and keep the peace. To do that, of course, we Americans will have to yield up some of our sovereignty," he continued. "That would be a bitter pill. It would take a lot of courage, a lot of faith in the new order."[1]

According to America's most trusted man, you and I need to stop clinging to our outdated notions like individual sovereignty and find more "faith in the new order." The experts have it all figured out. And that's the way it is.

Frank Zappa, the contrarian musician and guitarist, had zero faith in the journalistic profession, or in any journalistic pronouncements from the top down. Circa 1979, the halcyon days of Walter Cronkite's power over what average Americans could see and hear, Zappa was particularly peeved with the complete centralization of journalism in highly controlled, exclusive enclaves. Someone else's conventional wisdom, based on someone else's information, determined the rules of the game and the perceived truth of things. Reporters "walk in the door seeking a method by which they can reinforce conclusions they've already arrived at," Zappa said.[2]

This was true in Los Angeles for entertainment news, what the late Andrew Breitbart dubbed "Big Hollywood." It was equally true in New York and Washington for political news. As the only markets in the country with a national reach, these three cities enjoyed significant control over the flow of information, framed by someone else's values, filtered by preconceived notions of what the story was, and organized for us, creating an unchecked echo chamber—a one-size-fits-all message of the day.

Even as ideas based on economic freedom and individualism gained a foothold in politics, it seemed the flow of information would always be handicapped in favor of predetermined big government agendas. The Cronkite-Chancellor-Reasoner Cartel in the 1970s gave way to the Rather-Brokaw-Jennings Cartel of the 1980s. New names, same bent. It had become, for all intents and purposes, a single manufacturing facility for the political establishment to craft and distribute its messages, keeping the voters in the dark about many things, by omission, with the help of their friends at the networks and big newspapers.

This centralization of control and power in journalism was bad news for the American people, who rightly view the free and unfettered dissemination of information as foundational to the working of a free society. Because of the centralized media, they didn't have access to relevant information about what the government was up to with their money and their personal liberties.

One-size-fits-all press was not just a concern from right-of-center. As the iconic leftist press critic A. J. Liebling wrote in *The New Yorker* in 1960, "Freedom of the press is guaranteed only to those who own one." Liebling had a detailed critique of the problems with centralized journalism even in the 1960s. "What you have in a one-paper town is a privately owned public utility that is Constitutionally exempt from public regulation, which would be a violation of freedom of the press," he wrote. "As to the freedom of the individual journalist in such a town, it corresponds exactly with what the publisher will allow him. He can't go over to the opposition, because there isn't any." [3]

The problem Liebling saw wasn't just for journalists who lacked diverse job opportunities. "In any American city that I know of," he wrote, "to pick up a paper published elsewhere means that you have to go to an out-of-town newsstand, unless you are in a small city that is directly within the circulation zone of a larger one. . . . Even in New York, the out-of-town newsstands are few and hard to find. The papers are, naturally, late; they cost more; and most people would use up a sizeable part of every day just traveling to get one."

Who controlled the distribution of information, knowledge, wisdom, and truth was a question that got to the very functioning of our democratic republic. It was the very life blood of the bottom-up system established by the Founders. In January 1789, while in Paris, Thomas Jefferson wrote to British minister Richard Price about the adoption of the Constitution and his hope for a government of and by the people in spite of consolidation:

> I did not at first believe that 11 states of 13 would have consented to a plan consolidating them as much into one. A change in their dispositions, which had taken place since I left them, had rendered this consolidation necessary, that is to say, had called for a federal government which could walk upon it's [sic] own legs, without leaning for support on the state legislatures. A sense of this necessity, & a submission to it, is to me a new and consolatory proof that wherever the people are well informed they can be trusted with their own government; that whenever things get so far wrong as to attract their notice, they may be relied on to set them to rights.[4]

Jefferson, the most radically democratic of the Founding Fathers, was deeply distrustful of consolidated government power. He had great faith in the ability of the people to self-govern, to constantly question the prerogatives of centralized authority, and to limit, through grassroots vigilance, the power of government. But he understood the clout of information. He knew that a "well informed" public was required as a check on the necessary evil of the accumulation and centralization of control in the new federal government. And, he noted, it was within an informed public's rights to change the government if things "get so far wrong as to attract their notice."

THE FCC WON'T LET ME BE

ONE OF THE MAIN CONTENTIONS OF THIS BOOK IS THAT THE CONSOLIdation of power in so-called "private" enterprise is often the result of an unholy alliance between big business and big government. The two often collude to fix prices, limit supplies, and prevent choice and competition. It is a symbiotic arrangement in a politically defined marketplace—you scratch my back and I'll scratch yours—which is mutually beneficial to the colluders but harmful to the rest of us. Monopoly market power typically has to be enforced by the power monopolists, that is the politicians and bureaucrats, the "dictators" and "czars" of the government. Thus, the special relationship between the Truth Cartel in top-down media and the string-pullers inside the political establishment. Committee chairmen and information czars are protected by their effective control of the media's message, and those granted a special position in media markets grow fat on a privileged market stake. Host or parasite, puppet or master, both feed off you and me.

The first customer served by the crony capitalists in Big Media is "their man in Washington, D.C."

Not surprisingly, the heavy hand of government played a key role in propping up the cartel that created Walter Cronkite. From the earliest years of radio, federal regulators seized control over the airwaves and established rules to allocate the airwaves according to the "public interest," a nebulous term akin to "social justice," open-ended and conveniently defined by the bureaucrats. Not only did the Federal Communications Commission control the allocation of the airwaves, it also controlled the radio and television markets. The FCC viewed anyone granted a license to broadcast as a "public trustee," which meant there were strings attached. Pulled just right, the strings will make the puppet dance.

In fact, this is where the Fairness Doctrine emerged, the necessary result of puzzling bureaucratic logic. Because broadcasters were federally created monopolists, regulators required stations to ensure that both sides of the debate were heard, all in the name of fairness. Equal time for the opposition, as it were. Additional restrictions on media ownership and reach were also imposed. For example, no broadcaster could own stations that reached more than 35 percent of the population. In other words, media was the perfect example of a top-down, centrally controlled market with a rule for everything. Did it ever occur to the bureaucrats that removing barriers to entry might be an easier way to ensure all sides of the story are heard? Probably not, because the lucky station owners benefited, along with their political allies, who had an interest in how the news was told.

As economist Thomas Hazlett notes, "The licensing bargain struck between broadcasters and regulators was a political accommodation that drove the 1927 Radio Act and has determined essential aspects of spectrum allocation ever since. The bargain relied on spectrum regulation to create gains for both parties. Allocation and 'technical' rules protected broadcasters from competition as well as from fees or competitive bidding (for licenses), and gave political incumbents (both in Congress and the executive branch) the opportunity to leverage 'public interest' discretion for some measure of control over content. Given the ban on regulation of free speech in the U.S. Constitution, this was a formidable regulatory achievement."[5]

The establishment's stranglehold on information flow was so bad that, in 1987, a group of conservative news junkies started the Media Research Center to act as a watchdog against the liberal press. They couldn't break into the carefully guarded ivory towers of New York newsrooms, so they decided to at least document what the media were up to. As it happened, 1987 was also the year that the Reagan administration repealed the Fairness Doctrine and laid the groundwork for conservative talk radio. A year later, Rush Limbaugh would begin his wildly successful radio show.

It was only the push of technology that offered any relief to the stifling regulations. For decades most Americans had, at best, access to only a handful of stations: the Big Three—ABC, CBS, and NBC—along with a PBS channel and perhaps a few fuzzy UHF channels on a clear day. But technological innovation has pushed us into the information economy, fueled by rapidly decreasing computing costs and increasing bandwidth through both wireline innovations such as fiber optics as well as the booming new market for wireless communications and products.

Technology has transformed the way we live, touching almost every aspect of our lives, from how we talk to others, to how and what we listen to, to what we watch and where we watch it. Smartphones, tablets, and other computing advances are at the forefront of a technological revolution that is providing dramatic consumer benefits. Indeed, the entire technology sector is in the midst of a paradigm shift. And these changes occurred because market forces chipped away at the government's information cartel. The Fairness Doctrine fell in 1987, ownership rules began to ease after the Telecommunications Reform Act of 1996, and soon auctions were created as an alternative approach for allocating spectrum. As the market was allowed to evolve, consumers went from set-top rabbit ears to high-definition television. We don't have to worry about getting two sides to a story; with a few simple keystrokes we can find hundreds of perspectives competing with one another.

As long as technology keeps one step ahead of the regulators, the benefits to consumers are astounding. Today, instead of four channels, we can access hundreds of channels provided by cable and satellite, 255 million websites, and 152 million blogs that provide information virtually in real time.[6] While most of us are awestruck by the new world of technology, bureaucrats at the FCC see an open-ended world of communications that makes no sense to a planner. *Who's in charge?* Today's dynamic marketplace is striking evidence that the FCC has outlived any purported purpose. Indeed, its continued meddling in markets only undermines the public interest. As media titans of the past lose their grip on political power, a new group of tech giants are fast rising to the top, none faster than Google. As if to justify its existence, the FCC is shifting gears to control the Internet, pushing new regulations that will benefit the new industry leaders. This is nowhere clearer than in the debate over "net neutrality," a debate couched in terms of Internet freedom, but very much a power play that provides immense benefits to corporations with a large Internet presence like Google. Despite the fact that prices for Internet services are falling and consumer choice is booming, the FCC asserts the need to intervene in this actively functioning marketplace.

Like the other czars pushing to expand the regulatory state throughout the Obama administration, FCC Chairman Julius Genachowski—Harvard Law classmate and longtime political ally of President Obama—has ignored both the courts and the Congress in order to impose net neutrality regulations. Using a very loose interpretation of the FCC's authority, the agency proposed new rules to put the FCC in charge of the Internet, the emerging center of power in the world of information. This led to a sharp rebuke by the courts, which slapped down the regulations, stating the FCC clearly did not have the authority to regulate the Internet; only Congress, not unelected bureaucrats, can write the laws to provide such authority and they have not done so. Undaunted, the FCC took a second run at the regulations, issuing final regulations in December 2010 that provide the agency with control of the Internet. Those rules took effect November 20, 2011.[7] This is yet another example of the growing muscle flexed by the executive branch, expanding government power against the intentions of Congress. For the sake of innovation, the courts should remind these information czars just who, under the Constitution, writes the laws of the land.

FEWER EYEBALLS

IN THE LAST TWO DECADES, THE INFORMATION CARTEL HAS CRUM-bled. In 1980, more than 52 million people tuned into the networks' evening news shows. In 2006, 26 million did.[8] Recently, *CBS Evening News*, which once commanded the attention of upwards of 20 million viewers, couldn't muster even 5 million.[9] Most of the people who still watch probably do so only out of routine. By late 2011, roughly 75 percent of nighttime network news broadcasts were outside—that is, older than—the important 25- to 54-year-old target demographic.[10]

Newspaper circulation has been on the decline too, dropping by 8 million subscriptions between 1990 and 2004. Over the same period, the number of U.S. households grew from 93.3 million to 112 million.[11] The number of daily newspapers in the U.S. has been steadily declining since 1940, dropping by more than 400 through 2005.[12] While the trend had been occurring for years, recent data is no more reassuring for the establishment journalism's cheerleaders. Twenty-four of the twenty-five biggest newspapers saw a decline in weekday readership between 2009 and 2010. The *New York Times* dropped 8.5 percent. Only the *Wall Street Journal* saw a small increase of 0.5 percent.[13]

Why this erosion in audience and readership? Simple. The people finally had a choice. The web offered a new way to share information that was increasingly accessible to average people. A modem was all one needed to connect to vast, if still highly unorganized, quantities of information. Indeed, the first industries to recognize the potential of the Internet were media outlets without a national distribution. The Internet negated the need for expensive printing presses, distribution overhead, and the nineteenth-century model of delivering paper copy.

Even more revolutionary was that citizen pamphleteers and home-grown investigative reporters suddenly had a ready avenue to the connected world. True, the promise was still much grander than the reality at that time, but the opportunity was before everyone: plug in, connect, inform.

Slowly but surely, the American people started to realize they no longer had to rely on the Big Three networks, the *New York Times,* or the *Washington Post* for their news. The old model that Liebling wrote of began to crumble: American news consumers didn't have to spend a day tracking down an out-of-town newsstand to get the rest of the story or hear a dissenting voice. All they had to do was surf to a different website.

Of course, reading different outlets, critiquing old media, and disseminating your own views constituted just the first wave of the "New Media," which saw the explosion of self-funded blogs around the time of the 2000 election. Indeed, many of the most popular blogs today—like Instapundit, Hugh Hewitt, and Michelle Malkin, to name just a few—all began during this first phase. In time, everyone had his own blog. But this was only the beginning.

DEFENDING THE CARTEL

THE ABILITY TO CONTROL THE FLOW OF INFORMATION IS VITAL FOR centralized politics. Just look at the communist states of the twentieth century, each of which repressed free speech and operated their own media outlets. The new attempts to control the media in the United States are defended through a progressive lens: information must be sorted through by experts, and knowledge vetted by the most knowledgeable among us. Leave it to experts so that nothing is left to chance. This is the "public interest" rationale used by FCC bureaucrats to justify their various Internet power grabs. This, ostensibly, is also the rationale of Democrats who pushed for the reestablishment of the Fairness Doctrine. But in both instances, one suspects another, less noble motive. One of those Democrats demanding radio "fairness," as it happens, was none other than Senator Charles Schumer of New York. In 2008, the day after the election with Democrats approaching monopoly control of the executive and legislative branches of government, Schumer told Fox News that he supported government controlling the content on talk radio, saying, "The very same people who don't want the Fairness Doctrine want the FCC to limit pornography on the air. I am for that. . . . But you can't say government hands off in one area to a commercial enterprise but you are allowed to intervene in another. That's not consistent." [14]

That's right, the same Senator Schumer who would later anoint himself the sole arbiter of speech content inside the walls of the Russell Senate Office Building wanted to control speech on the radio in 2008. The same Schumer, now chairman of the Senate Rules Committee, who told Senator Mike Lee, through Rules Committee staff, "that the event has to be moved." He seems eager to try any means at his disposal to control what you can say, hear, or, presumably, think. Schumer saw then, through reimplementation of the Fairness Doctrine, a window to reassert his control over your speech.

I'm not certain of the legal definition of tyranny, but I know it when I see it.

For good reasons, this attempt to control talk radio never gained traction. But in March 2009, with a number of major news corporations on the brink of default, Democratic senator Benjamin Cardin proposed what the *Hill* described as a "newspaper bailout bill," the coyly named "Newspaper Revitalization Act." [15] The proposed legislation "would allow newspapers to operate as non-profits, if they choose, under 501(c)(3) status for educational purposes, similar to public broadcasting. Under this arrangement, newspapers would not be allowed to make political endorsements, but would be allowed to freely report on all issues, including political campaigns." [16] Free to report, that is, what is deemed to be "in the public interest," as determined by the government officials fortified with the monopoly power to make your business go away.

"I haven't seen detailed proposals yet," Obama said of Cardin's proposal, "but I'll be happy to look at them." Why? "I am concerned that if the direction of the news is all blogosphere, all opinions, with no serious fact-checking, no serious attempts to put stories in context, that what you will end up getting is people shouting at each other across the void but not a lot of mutual understanding." [17] There it is again, our top government official slipping easily into a presumption of which news is "serious" and which is mere "opinion." Do you trust Barack Obama and Charles Schumer, or a free community of bloggers scrambling and digging to get the story first, and to get the story right? It's the difference between central planning and robust competition that exploits the personal knowledge of dispersed individuals.

The Truth Cartel is pushing back, trying to protect its cozy relationship with the old institutions of the media that limited our direct access to things. But how could any single person actually have access to all the particular facts, as innumerable as they are, and always be able to know better, with certainty, what is legitimate, serious news, and what is just "people shouting at each other"?

(ONLINE) VIDEO KILLED THE RADIO STAR

THE DISAGGREGATION OF INFORMATION ONLINE COMPLETELY changes the way we discover, learn, share, and organize. The new paradigm is a rowdy, decentralized model of exchange in which news consumers bypass the gatekeepers to share facts and opinions directly with each other on a grassroots level. This democratization of information and knowledge formation online is, in effect, radically Jeffersonian, enabling We the People to find out for ourselves what is actually going on inside the government fortress.

Today the New Media, made up of independent newspapers, online news outlets, blogs, radio shows, podcasts, and more, are breaking news and driving the conversation. In an age in which a "citizen journalist" can capture images or video of a news event on her handheld camera and immediately upload it to the Internet, it's impossible to calculate the reach and impact of the New Media. American ingenuity drives us to continue to find new ways to use the tools we have— whether Facebook, Twitter, or smartphones—and the old methods of tracking influence are no longer applicable. The Old Media's ability to control the content and flow of information is dead and gone. The nature of the decentralized structure simply won't allow it.

The American people still turn to traditional media for news, but it's clear they prefer options less encumbered with bureaucracy and tradition. CNN's website, which leads other "mainstream" news outlets on the web, averages roughly 8.5 million unique visitors a day,[18] compared to 800 million active users on Facebook, more than 400 million of whom log in on a given day.[19]

Impact is now measured by outcome, rather than with ratings and hit numbers—the way the Old Media calculates their importance even in the new paradigm. Stories the centralized news media and their friends in Washington, D.C., used to be able to ignore are now seeing the light of day, and the grassroots, bottom-up model for dissemination of information is proving to be even more potent than the old guard feared.

Drudge Report was the pioneer of this model. It began in 1996 as—and largely still is—a one-man operation, little more than a clearinghouse of the most interesting stories of the day, from anywhere in the world. In fact, according to a 2011 report from Outbrain, a content recommendation engine whose clients include the *New York Times, The Atlantic,* and the *New York Post*, Matt Drudge drives more traffic to news sites than Facebook or Twitter combined, even though these sites dwarf *Drudge* in unique daily page views.[20] This is not to discount the impact of Facebook or Twitter. Rather, it reveals that the "one guy with a modem" power of the Internet still exists even today.

In June 2011, Glenn Beck left his successful program at Fox News (where he helped create a boom in sales of F. A. Hayek's *The Road to Serfdom*) to start GBTV, an Internet-based live streaming video network. The move represents one of the latest, and potentially the most radical, departures from the one-size-fits-all mentality of mainstream media. It is a logical step in the market-driven evolution of news media, away from the top-down to a decentralized system where the customer is always right. Speaking at a *Business Insider* conference on the state of the media industry, Beck described the high speed with which the world of media is disaggregating as the "most dangerous and the most exciting era of our lifetime." We used to "go to the Sears Catalogue and get it," Beck argues, referring to the old centralized model of doing business, necessitated by the pace of snail mail.[21] With the Internet, customers now find the products and entrepreneurs they want online, cutting out the middleman, eliminating a need for a Sears catalogue. Our entire society is individualized, publishing, in effect, our own private, virtual Sears catalog every time we choose. We go to print in real time, based on what we do, view, reject, buy, and consume.

"This is the struggle," Beck told his media-industry peers. "This is the answer for business. This is the answer for the [TV] networks. This is the answer for politics. The individual is the answer. You have the opportunity for the first time in all of human history to connect with the individual. Stop trying to be all things to all people. It won't work. It worked in 1950; it won't work in 2050."[22]

When GBTV launched, on September 12, 2011, Richard Greenfield, a media industry analyst from BTIG, predicted "a watershed day for the media/television industry, with Glenn Beck set to launch a direct-to-consumer video network utilizing IP-enabled devices called GBTV. Despite the significance of GBTV, top media executives are not terribly focused on what Glenn Beck is doing, let alone concerned by it. Yet," Greenfield predicted, "we believe they should be very afraid of the disintermediation underlying the launch of GBTV."[23] The new Internet-based network began with 230,000 subscribers, compared to an average of 156,000 watching OWN, Oprah Winfrey's new yet traditional cable network.[24]

It's as if Glenn Beck's business team, in addition to his Fox viewers, were encouraged to read up on their Hayek as well.

NOT AFRAID OF AUGUST

THE LIBERATING POWER OF SOCIAL MEDIA AND A DECENTRALIZED, open-ended online discovery process is integral to the story about the emergence of the Tea Party movement. There once was a time when there stood a virtually impenetrable wall—an inaccessibility of good information—between those inside the legislative process and the rest of us. On occasion, the political elite would cast their gaze down at the rest of us on the other side, but their focus was always inward-looking, focused toward their agenda, not ours. They wrote the laws and we would typically discover, after the fact, who did what to us. We might eventually discover the real story—if we were lucky, that is. In that world, the insiders had special knowledge that went hand in hand with being there, on the inside. Those committee chairmen writing the laws, their legislative staff, and the special interests who presided over the process by lending opinions and expertise were the primary inputs into the legislative process.

The rest of us were "rationally ignorant," because the cost of finding out what was actually going on, and then doing something to stop it, was prohibitive. Good, timely information was too expensive. This was a competitive advantage for the looters and moochers inside the process. They had better access to information because they were willing and able to pay the price of admission. That made them hard to beat. This is the "concentrated benefits" and "dispersed costs" of political decisions. If you want something from government, a provision that would benefit you at the expense of everyone else, you have an extraordinary incentive to show up. The rest of us take it on the chin.

One indication that this dismal decision paradigm was shifting—that the constant ratcheting upwards in the size and scope of government driven by this political insider trading might slow—was the defeat, albeit temporarily, of the Troubled Asset Relief Program (TARP) in 2008. The falling cost of real-time information was leveling the playing field between the insiders and the rest of us, and that had big implications for the future ability of participatory democracy to break into the closed system known as Washington, D.C. There were new rules.

House Speaker Nancy Pelosi, for one, had completely missed the broader implications of her own failure to collect enough votes in support of the first TARP bill, which failed on the House floor on September 29, 2008. After all, she and her Senate coconspirator, Harry Reid, had just larded the legislation up with more spending and passed it on the second round.

Surely she could just pull this stunt again on a health care takeover, right? She certainly seemed to think so. When asked by a reporter if she needed to pass the bill in July 2009, before legislators went home to face their constituents at town hall meetings back home, Pelosi said "I'm not afraid of August—it's a month." [25] If you think that sounds arrogant and out of touch, you are missing the point. It was *her House.* Speaker Pelosi was in charge.

Or so she thought.

Under the old system, politicians would have voted on a bill they'd never read and that, thanks to the centralized media, Americans knew little if anything about. Members of Congress were shocked when they attended town hall meetings with their constituents in August 2009 and discovered that the voters knew more about the contents of the bill than they the lawmakers did. We didn't need national reporters to track down a hard copy of the bill, study it, gather "expert" insight, and neatly package a message-managed story that reinforced foregone conclusions.

One of the defining moments in the debate over Obamacare was the speed with which tens of thousands of individuals learned about the actual contents of the bill. Untold numbers of online "eyeballs" read, parsed, analyzed, and then shared their own personal breakdown of the House legislation introduced by Democrats and made available online on July 14, 2009.

For all the fevered conspiracy theories promulgated by leftist advocates of Obamacare, there is only one reason why so many angry constituents showed up for the August recess town hall meetings. Unlike the members of Congress who were about to pass it, We the People had actually read the bill. The process had a striking similarity to the process of knowledge conveyance through voluntary exchange and shifting price signals typical of market processes. A "social intelligence" emerged as people debated, studied, reconsidered, and compiled a virtual community's understanding—more informed, more aware of the implications of the proposed legislation than that of any one of the congressmen and senators standing there, haplessly, in front of angry constituents.

The media chose not to celebrate the democratization of the process but instead demonized the demonstrators, calling them "ugly," "unruly," "nasty mobs."[26] Try finding such unsavory pejoratives in the mainstream media's coverage of Occupy Wall Street. Even the actual rats that occupied Occupy D.C.'s encampment at Freedom Plaza received less-hyperbolic coverage.[27]

But no one, not even in our democratic republic, loses power politely—especially not a centralized media regime that has reigned unchallenged for so long. What Democrats and the media discovered in the summer of 2009 was perhaps more frightening than the decades-long decline of the power of the Old Media cartel. It was the rise of the information-powered electorate.

TURNING UP THE HEAT

THE MEDIA RESEARCH CENTER HAS FOUND A CONSISTENT PATTERN of New Media beating Old Media to the story and the scoop time and again. It almost seems willful. From Van Jones to ACORN to Climategate, major news stories surface in spite of the mainstream cartel's attempts to ignore, bury, or otherwise control the story. For example, networks and major newspapers "were stubborn in their avoidance" of Van Jones's involvement in a nutty "Truther" petition supporting the idea that 9/11 was a carefully orchestrated government conspiracy. Most didn't cover the story until it was clear Jones would resign his post as Obama's "green jobs czar."[28] The Old Media was well behind the curve, which wouldn't have been a story at all if they had still been in charge.

The Climategate scandal of 2009 featured classic information management tactics from the Old Media. The *New York Times* and the *Washington Post* both reported hacked e-mails from climate scientists. The story, according to MSM, was that they trash-talked skeptics of global warming. Only one outlet—*CBS Evening News*—reported the real story: that scientists had discussed how to hide a decline in global temperatures from one popular chart. The mainstream media—longtime global warming alarmists—had a vested interest in managing the narrative of this story.

Fortunately, the American people could read the e-mails for themselves, and had access to a wide range of analysis and opinions on the scandal thanks to bloggers, Fox News, talk radio, and online outlets. Had the scandal occurred in the 1970s, when the media were warning about global cooling and the coming ice age, we would never have heard the story.[29] But thanks to the decentralization of news and information, we had access to the whole story, which is not a trivial event in this case. Without access to this kind of information, the global-warming alarmists, led by guru Al Gore, might have already steamrolled Congress to fix a supposedly dire problem based on cooked science. Indeed, what was once considered a fait accompli by the bipartisan duopoly in Washington, D.C.—that "impartial" science justifies the legislative rationing of energy in America—has suffered mightily under the decentralized accountability of activists, energized citizen reporters, bloggers, and just-plain citizens armed with e-mail or Facebook.

The media establishment has resisted change for so long they have missed the opportunity to change their behavior and adapt to the new world, while bloggers ensconced in their basements get the facts and uncover the real story. Welcome to Joseph Schumpeter's "creative destruction" writ large. In 1942, this maverick economist described a "process of industrial mutation—if I may use that biological term—that incessantly revolutionizes the economic structure from within, incessantly destroying the old one, incessantly creating a new one." This process "is the essential fact about capitalism."[30]

The establishment's news organizations are stuck playing catch-up to the thousands of newsletters, social networks, blogs, and other information outlets that redefine themselves on an hourly basis. It's a harsh world when you are on the receiving end of market accountability.

CENTRAL SCRUTINIZERS

RATHER THAN ADAPT AND COMPETE WITH THE NEW ROUGH-AND-tumble style of journalism, the old guard is on the attack, fueling skepticism of New Media standards, questioning motives, and writing off results. It's a remarkably *progressive* approach to things.

Journalist Tom Price summed up the establishment's feelings about the New Media in a 2010 essay in *CQ Researcher*, an industry publication that analyzes issues facing the news business and claims to offer, in their words, an "in-depth, unbiased coverage." Referring to A. J. Liebling's observation on freedom of the press, Price wrote:

A half-century later, everyone with an Internet connection owns a virtual press. And many of them scorn the journalism standards that have guided America's mainstream media since before Liebling penned his famous aphorism. Among those standards: accuracy above all else, plus fairness, balance, thoroughness, independence, civility, decency, compassion and responsibility—along with a clear separation of news from opinion. Now, operators of some news-like websites unabashedly repeat rumors and throw accuracy to the wind. Vile, anonymous reader comments on mainstream media websites mock civility. Add the pressures of Internet speed and shrinking news staffs, and serious journalists wonder what kind of standards—if any—will prevail during the next 50 years.[31]

What people like Tom Price fail (or refuse) to understand is that the decentralization of information has increased transparency and accountability. To Old Media apologists, the infallibility of "serious journalists" is assumed, as is the cynical belief that bloggers are little more than hacks. The fact of the matter is that pajama-clad reporters are just as serious as Price's deified newsmen, and reading news into a camera doesn't mean you're not a hack. The Internet gives news consumers an invaluable tool to keep all the hacks in check—whether they're in a newsroom in New York or a basement in Des Moines.

Centralized control of information is predicated on the notion that one person, organization, or industry can decide what is best for society. The Old Media still believe this, and they see themselves as the rightful disseminators of information and the sole purveyors of intellectualism and insight. In short, they think they're smarter than the rest of us, and they view it as their duty to educate the unwashed masses about how things really work in Washington.

Again, this mentality is hardly exclusive to the Left. In a 2010 discussion about Old Media versus New Media, *New York Times* resident "conservative" David Brooks explained that the old model of journalism is better because the serious work of governing, and reporting on the process of governing, "isn't a debating society. Usually there are 30 pressure groups pushing on each decision, and the outcome depends on a complex web of personalities and relationships. You can't understand the flux of the forces unless you are inside the conversation."[32]

Brooks admitted that the old model for journalism results in favors. "It is true that when you interview people you do develop relationships, and there is some pressure not to burn the people you admire and rely on. Nonetheless, I think the deal is worth it for the reader. In the first place, you learn what's not true. Pundits who don't do interviews often speculate on what is happening, but they usually don't know what they are talking about. I'll read some theory by a pundit about why something is happening, and I know it's complete hokum because I just spoke with the people who are doing it."[33]

This of, course, naively assumes that those "who are doing it" inside the halls of government are always pure in their motives, would never "spin" a story to put a political agenda in the best public light, would never be biased themselves, and would never, ever put their personal interests before the "public interest." These are odd assumptions for an investigative reporter, to say the least. Maybe the challenge from outside the process, from pundits and citizen journalists, is vitally important to getting the story right?

Another bizarrely top-down attitude comes from "liberaltarian" policy analyst Brink Lindsey, whom Jonah Goldberg and I once debated at a Reason Foundation forum. Lindsey misses the days of the centralized media cartel, "a critical constraint" on who was allowed to speak for conservatism.

> To be visible at all in the nation's public debate, conservatism was forced to rely on intellectual champions whose sheer brilliance and sophistication caused the liberal gatekeepers in mass media to deem them suitable for polite company. People such as [William F.] Buckley, George Will, and Milton Friedman thus became the public face of conservative ideology, while the rabble-rousers and conspiracy theorists were consigned to the shadow world of mimeographs, pamphlets, and paperbacks that nobody ever reviewed. The handicap of elite hostility thereby conferred an unintended benefit: It gave conservatism a high-quality intellectual leadership that, to some extent at least, was able to curb the movement's baser instincts.[34]

I can't imagine a less libertarian attitude toward the process of truth-seeking and opinion-making than this. I also can't imagine a Declaration of Independence without "rabble-rousers" like Samuel Adams and pamphleteers like Thomas Paine. Neither was deemed "suitable for polite company," then. But it is hard to imagine our great nation, conceived in liberty, without them.

In defending the centralized model, both Lindsey and Brooks demonstrate the very essence of the problem. Our political culture is built around an insiders-only philosophy. It's not a good deal for readers to only have access to what David Brooks's insider friends are thinking. We don't want or need someone to tell us, as the final word on the matter, what they think is true based on their inside-the-Beltway friendships. We don't need journalists who reinforce the status quo and perpetuate the insiders-only mentality by working within the broken system. We need access to information and the freedom to decide for ourselves how best to change the system and reshape it.

If Walter Cronkite said the wrong thing on the *CBS Evening News,* it became "the truth." There was no one to fact-check him, other than internal ombudsmen and colleagues at other outlets who were all part of the same centralized information machine. There was practically nowhere else to turn. In contrast, if a blogger says the wrong thing on his website, ten of his friends—and more of his opponents—will correct him within minutes, often in the most unsubtle of terms. Talk about creative destruction. Entire websites exist to debunk Internet rumors and urban legends. (It took the *New York Times* fifteen years to notice Snopes.com, one of the most popular rumor-debunking sites on the Web.[35]) The nature of the Internet is such that even the fact-checkers are fact-checked again and again.

If the successful blogger Ace of Spades—the man in the black pajamas, a worthy adversary—gets the story wrong, Ed Morrissey at *HotAir* gleefully flames him with a furrowed brow, better information, and another link. When the *New York Times* gets it wrong, Julie Borowski, with her Sony Bloggie camera, captures the story and posts it on YouTube, where it is immediately picked up by Michelle Malkin and by *RedState.* If this seems like chaos, it's the beautiful chaos of Jeffersonian democracy setting "them to rights."

Freedom, and the discovery process driven by millions of free people, is the best way to get to the truth of things. It is the "greater social intelligence" that results from our natural tendency to act, to discover, make mistakes, adjust, refine, and move forward. This is what fundamentally differentiates my argument from the standard conservative complaint against the liberal media. It's not that the left-leaning mainstream media are always wrong and that Fox News and Glenn Beck are always right. My contention is that freedom works better, and an open-ended system of aggressive competition will produce a fuller understanding of what is actually going on in the world. As Beck says: "It's about the individual." It's not us versus them. It's about them serving us.

DRINK YOUR TEA

As THOMAS JEFFERSON FORESHADOWED IN HIS LETTER TO RICHARD Price in 1789, a well-informed public is likely to notice when the government is getting it wrong, and has a right to do something about it. One CNBC commentator's cable tirade about mortgage bailouts, "The Rant Heard 'Round the World," helped brand and galvanize an entire movement.

"How many people want to pay for your neighbor's mortgages that have an extra bathroom and can't pay their bills?" Rick Santelli asked from the floor of the Chicago Mercantile Exchange during a regular appearance on *Squawk Box* on February 19, 2009. "Raise your hand! President Obama, are you listening? . . . You know Cuba used to have mansions and a relatively decent economy. They moved from the individual to the collective. Now they're driving '54 Chevys. . . . We're thinking of having a Chicago Tea Party in July, all you capitalists that want to show up to Lake Michigan, I'm going to start organizing." [36]

There are roughly 180 "Rick Santelli Rant" videos on YouTube, with well over 2 million combined views, and countless other versions of the video posted on other sites. (CNBC doesn't publish its online view counts.) A Google search for "Rick Santelli Rant" returns 119,000 results. While elements of what became known as the Tea Party were operating well before February 2009, Santelli is widely credited with issuing the call to action that inspired so many people to make it the movement it is today. Unintentionally, Santelli linked an already burgeoning movement to its own revolutionary heritage, a set of tried-and-true values based on freedom, and a Whig intellectual tradition that put the individual first in the pecking order. The Tea Party, in the words of Van Jones, became our "meta-brand."

Without the Internet to fan the flames of Santelli's rant, spreading it across the country in mere hours, few people beyond the 185,000 who were watching *Squawk Box* in early 2009 would have ever seen it.[37]

This phenomenon, by the way, isn't restricted to the political Right. Occupy Wall Street was another movement that masterfully utilized Internet tools to organize its protests and spreads it messages. Indeed, the Left realized the tremendous potential of the Internet long before the modern Tea Party existed. In 2003, during the Democratic presidential primary, Howard Dean galvanized an entire movement into action through unprecedented use of the Internet—and scared the daylights out of establishment Democrats. Though Dean flamed out with one spectacular scream, the movement he spawned did not, and it could be argued that the people-powered grassroots that donated millions to a first-term senator from Illinois, and which eventually coalesced around the OWS movement, began with Dean in 2003.

Nor is it playing out only in America. The Arab Spring of 2011 and other protest movements were fueled by the free exchange of information on social media sites like Twitter. The sites not only empowered protesters to organize; they also kept supporters around the world updated on the news coming out of countries notorious for controlling the messaging of official press outlets.

Just as we no longer have a need for a centralized clearinghouse of information in the form of a news cartel, the power of political parties has diminished. Before the information revolution, we needed centralized parties to find candidates, raise money, buy ads, craft messaging, and organize supporters. Now we can do all that for ourselves. The people can connect directly with one another, whether through general social media tools like Facebook and Twitter, or through more niche social networks like my organization's FreedomConnector.

Remember, information is not knowledge. There are simply too many bits of information out there for any single mind to know; even if you are the editorial page editor at the *New York Times* or the information czar at the head of the Federal Communications Commission. Even a properly progressive president "talking to experts" who "potentially have the best answer" doesn't have the best information at his disposal. Knowledge is "personal," in the words of philosopher Michael Polanyi, and only through interaction, cooperation, and competition can we ever get from here to there.[38]

Remember also that knowledge is not wisdom. Our personal knowledge of time and place—what is happening in our lives and with our family in our local community—is part of what we use to figure things out as everything changes around us. We also depend on things that don't change very often, institutions and rules that guide our actions in an uncertain world. Laws such as "don't hurt others" are a product of human action but not of human design, and they represent common wisdom that has made sense for a long time. We need both knowledge and a little wisdom for freedom to work.

Walter Cronkite, or "news-like websites"? "Serious journalists," or the Ace of Spades? Top-down or bottom-up? Keep your top-down solutions, Walter. I'm clinging to my individual sovereignty and my RSS feed.

CHAPTER 4

DON'T HURT OTHERS AND
DON'T TAKE THEIR STUFF

VAN JONES IS BAFFLED. STANDING AT THE PODIUM, HE IS THE MAIN event, speaking to a full house at Netroots Nation 2011. The audience is clearly on his side. Jones is one of the most important community organizers in the progressive movement, and he is trying to wrap his mind around the notion of freedom-loving individualists working together toward a common end, "collectively." "Here's the hypocrisy, the irony," Jones says. "They talk rugged individualism—that's their whole schtick, right? This is the Tea Party. 'If you had a problem, don't look to the government. Just be more rugged, and more individual and your problem will be solved.' That's their schtick, rugged individualism." [1]

If you have heard of Van Jones, it is likely because of his short stint as the "green jobs czar" in the Obama administration. In the bizarre world we live in today, apparently "green jobs"—like those illusory jobs "created" at Solyndra with Obama stimulus dollars—require their own special czar, someone who can really take charge and fix things. Jones describes himself as a "globally recognized, award-winning pioneer in human rights and the clean energy economy."[2] Jones's support for radical socialism and his dabbling in 9/11 Trutherism resulted in his swift excision from the administration. He now markets himself as a "leading champion of smart solutions for America's middle class" and a "successful, innovative and award-winning social entrepreneur." That sounds a lot safer than his earlier days of progressive radicalism. These days, however, he mostly spends his time trying to replicate the decentralized grassroots power of the Tea Party and teach his fellow progressives to be more like us.

THE PARTY LABEL

VAN JONES USED TO BE A SOCIALIST, BUT "SOCIALIST" IS NO LONGER the preferred nomenclature of the far Left in American politics; indeed, they get quite testy about the label. In the early twentieth century, the American Progressive movement closely identified with socialism, and the politics of the Bull Moose Party and Teddy Roosevelt always involved more government power and control over individuals and the private means of production. Eventually, Americans figured out what the progressive agenda was really all about, so in the FDR era progressives co-opted the word *liberal,* which was audacious, since *liberal* then still meant something akin to "the federal government should mind its constitutional limits and its own damn business." Later, "liberal" became associated with the Left's own big government failures, so unpopular that the Left had to give up that label as well. So today, Democrats and the broad array of left-wing interests that make up their coalition are no longer "liberals"; they are once again "progressives."

The new progressives passionately disavow the "socialist" lineage of their failed ideology. The president himself, piqued by the question, went out of his way to tell the *New York Times* that he was "not a socialist."[3] Of course, a rose by any other name is still a rose, and "socialism" refers to a system of economic organization where government owns the means of production. Like car companies, or the provision of health insurance, or seats on the governing board of investment banks. In fairness, maybe their real goal is government *control*, rather than ownership, of the means of production. But that system of economic organization effectively functions in the very same way, and has its own history of catastrophic failure. Just ask the Italians.

But whatever you do, do *not* call them "socialist." It's not polite.

Progressives pursue government ownership/control of the means of production because their philosophy is based on the belief that government can know better and plan better than free individuals could ever do on their own. Progressives have a plan for everything, and they want to reorganize things and redistribute your hard-earned money to their ends. It's all a means toward their definition of "social justice." The American definition of "justice," from the Founders and the traditions of classical liberalism back to the Scottish Enlightenment and beyond, has always meant treating each individual just like every other individual under the laws of the land, "with liberty and justice for all." "Social justice," as far as anyone can tell, always requires someone presumed to be smarter than you—a government czar—telling you what you can or cannot do with yourself or your property. These are not new ideas. Imposing a better plan and second-guessing everyone else have been the fools' errands of all would-be central planners for centuries.

So, when Van Jones and the Netroots Nation label Tea Partiers as "rugged individualists," you can be quite certain they are not paying a compliment. People like Jones don't understand how people who value individualism can act collectively. As far as they're concerned, only collectivists can act collectively, because only they care about their fellow man. The other guys, the rugged individualists, at best care about no one other than themselves. But the progressives suspect far worse of us: that individualists are willing to do just about anything to get ahead, regardless of who gets hurt. President Obama, an ardent aficionado of debating imaginary straw men, simply loves to set up this parody of individualism, and then knock it right down.

Coincidentally, he invoked the ominous specter of "rugged individualism" just a few months after Van Jones spoke at Netroots Nation. On December 6, 2011, Obama spoke to a campaign rally in Osawatomie, Kansas:

> Now, just as there was in Teddy Roosevelt's time, there is a certain crowd in Washington who, for the last few decades, have said, let's respond to this economic challenge with the same old tune. "The market will take care of everything," they tell us. If we just cut more regulations and cut more taxes—especially for the wealthy—our economy will grow stronger. Sure, they say, there will be winners and losers. But if the winners do really well, then jobs and prosperity will eventually trickle down to everybody else. And, they argue, even if prosperity doesn't trickle down, well, that's the price of liberty.
>
> Now, it's a simple theory. And we have to admit, it's one that speaks to our rugged individualism and our healthy skepticism of too much government. That's in America's DNA. And that theory fits well on a bumper sticker. But here's the problem: It doesn't work. It has never worked. It didn't work when it was tried in the decade before the Great Depression. It's not what led to the incredible postwar booms of the '50s and '60s. And it didn't work when we tried it during the last decade.[4]

Freedom "doesn't work," says Obama. A lot of this is just textbook Chicago politics—literally. Saul Alinsky, Obama's mentor and the founding father of leftist community organizers, wrote about how to effectively demonize your opponent regardless of the facts. Alinsky's Thirteenth "Rule for Radicals" states: "Pick the target, freeze it, personalize it, and polarize it."[5] Dutifully, the president has set up a straw man to polarize. Rugged individualism: bad.

On one level, you have to assume that Van Jones's and others' bewilderment about the Tea Party is disingenuous, for as progressives they are not terribly interested in understanding how freedom works.

They ask, à la Alinsky, how do I demonize freedom effectively so that the public turns to my agenda of more government and the redistribution of wealth?

But on a more fundamental level, Van Jones really is baffled. *How did those rugged individualists pull it off?* It's not just that he doesn't understand *how* we could work together, but *why* we would work together for the seemingly individualistic goals we have set. This is part and parcel of the hubris, arrogance, and lack of humility that are ingrained in the ethos of big government. Do they really believe that free people won't care about others unless compelled, from the top down? Do they really believe that people won't cooperate unless guided by a master plan?

So, true to instincts, Jones needs a plan to counter this thing called the Tea Party, even if he's not sure what it actually is. What might community organizers do to counter the obvious effectiveness of the Tea Party movement, particularly when it comes to its measurable impact on driving public opinion and getting out the vote?

If you are a planner, you believe that you can fix it, no matter what the "it" is. "Just give me your power and your cash; I'm the man for the job." A program, an earmark, a green jobs czar—each of these is presumed to be a better alternative to letting market forces punish bad behavior and reward the good.

This attitude requires action, even if it's destructive. In political discourse, it is a given that those in power, or those seeking power, will make promises and propose new programs funded with your money. Will the programs work? Likely not, but it really does not matter, because more funding for education, as an example, even if it is putting good money after bad, is a proposal to do *something*. The response is not always so simple, because an alternative to the *educratic* status quo, based on empowering parents with individual choice, is often a prospective expectation of what would happen if we let freedom work. It requires a bit of vision, and for elected officials, the courage of your convictions (if you brought such things with you to Washington, D.C., in the first place).

This is the flip side of Bastiat's *seen and unseen* in public policy.[6] We can see, clearly, a $535 million earmark to fund green jobs at Solyndra, at least for a while, until our attentions are drawn elsewhere and the company goes belly-up. We can't see, by definition, the opportunity cost, the path not taken, if government had not misappropriated those resources.

So what's the plan, Van?

It seems to be Occupy Wall Street, at least as an opening bid. One essential characteristic of the progressive mind-set is a willingness to just toss an idea against the wall, hoping it sticks like spaghetti. Though Jones did not create Occupy Wall Street, he certainly has stuck to it. "They've got moral clarity," Jones says of OWS. "They're as clear as a bell, and that's what's been missing. You should not ask folks who have been hurting, sitting on a white hot stove for three years . . . to holler properly."[7]

Attached at the hip, now Jones himself faces the same dilemma— the seen and the unseen of progressive principles—in the increasingly unpopular behavior of his values put into practice. This is why the emergence of Occupy Wall Street, a cause to be celebrated among progressives and their leaders, proved such a vivid and useful experiment in their values applied, and the practical results of top-down collectivism. The OWS movement was lionized by the mainstream media and liberal politicians from the get-go. It was celebrated by Hollywood stars, bona fide one-percenters like Michael Moore, Alec Baldwin, and Kanye West.

Occupy Wall Street was also a living, breathing manifestation of the values of redistribution and class envy put to practice. Or should I say petri dish?

THE GREAT DIVIDE

At first blush, I wanted to like Occupy Wall Street. Having suffered the isolation of being one of the very few opposing the 2008

Wall Street bailout—TARP—from inside the Beltway, I felt their pain. I shared their outrage. I wished they had been there on the streets when we were fighting—against both Republicans and Democrats— the bailouts of irresponsible fat-cat investment bankers and dishonest home-flippers. We needed help then, as everyone, including Senator Barack Obama, lined up like panicked lemmings and wrote an unconstitutional blank check to an unelected Treasury bureaucrat (who happened to be the former chairman of Goldman Sachs) to "fix it."

I wanted to understand Occupy Wall Street, particularly for students and young graduates already underwater with college tuition debt and with few prospects of employment. Chronic unemployment rates over 8 percent are particularly punishing to new job entrants, and the double whammy of debt and joblessness creates a dark outlook for the Millennial Generation, who had been so optimistic about the promises of "hope" and "change" they were fed during the Obama campaign.

I wanted to connect, somehow, with Occupy Wall Street. Indeed, friends who attended the first rallies saw signs lifted straight from any one of the Tea Parties that I had personally attended. "End the Fed." "Stop Crony Capitalism." Was there a potential populist meeting of the minds? Had some on the Left finally reached the same conclusion that we had, that the unholy collusion between big business and big government undermines growth and opportunity for everyone unlucky enough not to have some special relationship with a Senate committee chairman or the U.S. Treasury secretary? Could we together take on the bottom-feeding politicians who wallow in the economic bog created by government-granted privilege?

Would they join in a hostile takeover bid of Big Government, Incorporated?

At the time of the initial protests in October 2011, I happened to be in Sestri Levante, Italy, giving a talk on the decentralized nature of the Tea Party to European graduate students participating in the Istituto Bruno Leoni's annual Ludwig von Mises Seminar. The students wanted to know my take on OWS, and I was eagerly talking to friends on the ground back in the States. Was it possible that many of the same troops organizing for Obama were now rejecting his cozy relationship with corporate rent-seekers?

The answer, it turns out, was no. But why not? What was the disconnect between freedom-loving Tea Partiers and Wall Street–hating Occupiers?

The answer came from economist and Nobel laureate Vernon Smith, who was delivering the keynote lecture at the same Mises seminar, on Adam Smith's *The Theory of Moral Sentiments*. His address focused on the question "How do social norms emerge spontaneously?" As I listened to a brilliant talk, I was answering a very different question in my mind: What is the difference between OWS and the Tea Party?

Both Smiths, Adam and Vernon, argue that individual freedoms and individual property rights are the foundations of moral behavior—the values that bind a community. Individuals, with full ownership of their life, liberty, and property, judge themselves and care about the positive judgments of others. This accountability is the moral basis that binds a community, allows for cooperation, and enables human prosperity.

Adam Smith said it this way: "The most sacred laws of justice, therefore, those whose violation seems to call loudest for vengeance and punishment, are the laws which guard the life and person of our neighbour; the next are those which guard his property and possessions; and last of all come those which guard what . . . is due to him from the promises of others."[8] Most Tea Partiers have not likely read all 546 pages of *The Theory of Moral Sentiments,* but have nonetheless inherited this foundational insight genetically from America's Founding Fathers, who themselves cribbed it from Scottish Enlightenment thinkers like Adam Smith.

We can boil it down to this: Don't hurt other people and don't take their stuff.

From this "sacred law" comes grassroots activists' righteous indignation toward bailouts of the irresponsible, and deficit spending on special-interest earmarks. Both reward bad behavior and are paid for with other people's stuff. We oppose other government intrusions in our lives, such as the Obamacare mandate that every American must buy health insurance that will decide, without our input, which treatments we may or may not be allowed. We oppose government forcing the responsible to subsidize the irresponsible, because these policies hurt other people and take their stuff.

DOMESTIC TERRORISTS

WHEN MORE THAN 1 MILLION CITIZENS PETITIONED THEIR GOVERNMENT for a redress of grievances at the September 12, 2009, Taxpayer March on Washington, our critics hoped that the overwhelming mass of humanity would devolve into chaos. Based on historical experiences with radical leftists, it should have. People still recall the violent "Battle in Seattle" in 1999, the infamous protest against the World Trade Organization that resulted in much violence and damage to both the city and private property. Grassroots protesting before the emergence of the Tea Party—dominated by leftist nihilists, socialists, progressives, and the like—usually devolved into incivility or worse, so if you were not really paying attention to what was happening, you could reasonably have expected more of the same.

Professional leftists, acolytes of Alinsky, eagerly attacked our community early on, trying to define us as angry and violent, a fringe element that was dangerous to America. My favorite smear came from David Axelrod, now chief campaign adviser to President Obama's 2012 reelection campaign. In an April 2009 interview, right after an estimated 800-plus Tax Day Tea Parties demonstrated the growing power of this fledgling movement for fiscal responsibility, Axelrod was interviewed about the phenomenon by Bob Schieffer on *Face the Nation*. Speaking then as a senior White House adviser, he suggested that "there is always an element of disaffection that can mutate into something that's unhealthy." Was the Tea Party protesting "unhealthy"? Schieffer asked. "This is a country where we value our liberties and our ability to express ourselves," Axelrod responded, "and so far these are expressions." [9] This shockingly conditional endorsement of our civil liberties and the right to free speech was particularly disturbing coming straight from a White House official. Was Axelrod hedging his bets on the future wisdom of the Bill of Rights, taking a wait-and-see attitude?

Outside the West Wing of the White House, the accusations from Team Obama were even more unhinged. Organizing for America, which was once the grassroots arm of the 2008 Obama presidential campaign, then called Organizing for Obama, put out this beauty on the eve of the September 12, 2009, March on Washington: a national call to action to its members to "fight back against our own Right-Wing Domestic Terrorists who are subverting the American Democratic Process." [10] The "domestic terrorist" motif, quickly pulled down from the OFA website, had a second life when top Democratic legislators and Vice President Joe Biden used it again to describe Tea Party opposition to increasing the national debt ceiling in the summer of 2011.

As *Politico* reported:

Vice President Joe Biden joined House Democrats in lashing Tea Party Republicans Monday, accusing them of having "acted like terrorists" in the fight over raising the nation's debt limit, according to several sources in the room.

Biden was agreeing with a line of argument made by Rep. Mike Doyle (D-Pa.) at a two-hour, closed-door Democratic Caucus meeting.

"We have negotiated with terrorists," an angry Doyle said, according to sources in the room. "This small group of terrorists have made it impossible to spend any money."

Biden, driven by his Democratic allies' misgivings about the debt-limit deal, responded: "They have acted like terrorists." [11]

How disappointed they all must have been that September morning in 2009, as the largest gathering of limited-government activists in history converged on the Capitol steps. It should have been chaos. As primary organizers who had supplied the stage, security fencing, and other safety and crowd control measures required by the permits, all of us at FreedomWorks were caught totally off guard. So were the National Park Service and Capitol police, who clearly had not anticipated such a massive crowd. And yet, despite it all, there was no pushing, no shoving. There were no fights. No one got arrested. We said "excuse me" as we waded through shoulder-to-shoulder crowds. We said "thank you" when someone we had never met and would likely never see again helped us reach the stage in time to speak. We waited in hopelessly long lines for too few portable toilets. We picked up our trash and we left both public spaces and private property exactly as we found them. If it was chaotic, it was the most beautiful chaos I have ever seen in my life.

Needless to say, there were no videos of public pooping, on police cars or otherwise, as we later had the misfortune of seeing at OWS. We didn't realize this as a great community accomplishment at the time.

Individualism, personal responsibility, and respect for property form the operating philosophy that allows for peaceful order to emerge where violence and chaos might otherwise explode. No one told us to do these things; we just believe that you shouldn't hurt other people and you shouldn't take their stuff.

THIS UNCHECKED AGGRESSION WILL NOT STAND

OCCUPY WALL STREET ACTIVISTS, IN SPITE OF THE FACT THAT THEIR ranks were a small fraction of the size of the Tea Party community, struggled to maintain basic civility, let alone peaceful cooperation in their tent cities. My early hopes quickly evaporated as I watched the initial protests quickly devolve into ugliness. The term *occupy* itself seems to imply a zero-sum gain, an act of taking, by conquest, someone else's property. *It's unchecked aggression.* Like when Saddam Hussein *occupied* Kuwait.

The attitude was illustrated even at OWS's home base in and around Zuccotti Park in lower Manhattan, which is private property in the heart of New York City's financial district. From the very beginning, there were reports of stealing, property damage both in the park and at small businesses surrounding it, and arrests, often of protesters who had provoked conflict with the police.

Local Panini & Co. owner Stacey Tzortzatos said that she "had a lot of damage from the protesters. . . . I've had to put a $200 lock on my bathroom because they come in here and try to bathe. The sink fell down to the ground, cracked open, pulled the plumbing out of the wall and caused a flood. It's a no-win situation." Another nearby businessman has had similar problems: "They want to use the toilet, the phones, we give them free water and free ice," says the frustrated restaurateur. "They sit here and don't buy anything, but they recharge their phone batteries with our plugs, and I tell them, 'Hey, if you guys are going to come, I need to do some business here. We are suffering, too!' And then they start with their own words, going against you." [12]

Another small group of Washington, D.C., OWS activists inexplicably tried to force their way into the National Air and Space Museum. According to the *Washington Post*: "The demonstrators carried large signs and other items not allowed inside the museum. . . . When a security guard told them they could not enter, demonstrators pushed the guard outside and up against a wall." [13] Pepper spray came out, the police were called, and one person was arrested.

The problems have only escalated since the beginning. According to a list compiled by blogger John Nolte, more than 400 Occupiers had been arrested by the end of December 2011. [14] An *Associated Press* report added up the damage and found that the first two months of OWS resulted in $13 million in damages. [15]

Things have gone far worse at OWS events across Europe. In Rome, for instance, one OWS protest quickly devolved into a full-on riot, with protesters smashing shop and bank windows and torching cars. "Clad in black with their faces covered," the Associated Press reported, "protesters threw rocks, bottles and incendiary devices at banks and Rome police in riot gear. Some protesters had clubs, others had hammers. They destroyed bank ATMs, set trash bins on fire and assaulted at least two news crews from Sky Italia." [16]

Can you imagine a Tea Partier ever behaving in such a way? The 9/12 Taxpayer March on Washington had at least ten times as many attendees as anticipated, and yet all day I saw activists shaking hands with various law enforcement staff and thanking them for their help in a logistically confused gathering.

A woman named Latoya, who was working at a local Chicago TV studio where I was doing an interview about the differences between the Tea Party and OWS, described it this way: "The difference between the Tea Party and Occupy Wall Street is the difference between Martin Luther King and Malcolm X. Malcolm X said: 'By any means necessary.'" [17]

She's right. In fact, the 9/12 March consciously channeled the iconic 1963 march, inspired by MLK's purposefully nonviolent model for social change. The Boston Tea Party, once lionized by radical leftists as the historical model for "direct action," was always more MLK than Malcolm X. The original Tea Party protest was a carefully orchestrated event designed to galvanize colonial opinion in favor of American independence. Sam Adams trained protesters to ensure that no one was hurt, and that only East India Company tea, protected by the British government's monopoly status, was destroyed. As far as I can determine, no dodgy Bank of America mortgage-backed securities, protected by the U.S. Treasury Department with your hard-earned tax dollars, were burned in effigy at Zuccotti Park. But windows have been smashed in Oakland, California, by out-of-control Occupiers.

Tactical nonviolence is smart strategy, as everyone from Dr. King to Mahatma Gandhi has demonstrated in practice. But for modern

Tea Partiers, it is really just a practical outgrowth of the values that define our community's ethos. No one could possibly have trained more than a million marchers in the tactics of nonviolence, as was done by civil rights activists before the Greensboro, North Carolina, Woolworth's sit-in. The spontaneous community of Tea Partiers that emerged in Washington, D.C., on 9/12/09 simply believed, to a person, that you don't hurt other people and you don't take their stuff.

And that's where the Occupiers ultimately fell short. Stuff was taken. People were hurt.

SPENDING MONEY YOU DON'T HAVE

PART OF THE PROBLEM SEEMS TO HAVE BEEN THE OCCUPIERS' INABILITY to identify a unifying sense of purpose in their uprising. When you look for a coherent set of policy goals in the Occupy Wall Street crowd, you discover a very disparate set of demands coming from various factions of the "social justice" coalition, all competing with one another for a bigger share of the pie and a larger take of somebody else's stuff. To be sure, some of the original protesters were real people with righteous anger at the crony capitalism and high unemployment that have defined the first three years of the Obama administration. Likewise, many of the young people protesting in the euro zone can't find jobs despite their costly college degrees, and face a perfect storm of no-growth economies, crushing sovereign debt fueled by cradle-to-grave entitlement spending, and public unions that serve as ironclad barriers to entering the job market.

Young people *should* be pissed off. Someone *should* be fired. But the focus of Occupy Wall Street seems fundamentally off target. The problem is concentrated political power, not wealth per se. The problem is the unholy collusion between well-heeled interests and government's monopoly on power. Shouldn't Bank of America have to sink or swim on the merits of its business model, just like the mom and pop store around the corner? But if we rightly hold Bank of America to that standard, don't each of us as individuals have to live by it as well? Justice is equal treatment under the laws of the land. Instead, more typical targets of OWS protesters are capitalism, capitalists, "the top one percent," wealth possession, and wealth creation in general. They want to redistribute the pie, not grow it.

Why aren't they angry at the politicians and the interests and corporations that feed off government failure, who create government barriers to their success?

This cognitive dissonance is on full display in the person of Sarah Mason, an Occupy Los Angeles protestor made famous in a composite image on the cover of *Time*'s 2011 "Person of the Year" issue, dedicated to "the Protestor." The day before the magazine was published, *360 Magazine* posted a full profile of Mason and her motives for joining the movement. "I think the Occupy Wall Street Movement has shown that a lot of attention has been going to the fact that students have made an investment in their educations," Mason said, "then they come to the real world and they realize that that investment is essentially worthless."[18] Fair enough. The inflated cost of higher education and the government-generated student loan bubble is a real problem that needs to be addressed.

But Mason's bigger gripe seems to be with Bank of America, who offered her a credit card, a card she accepted and ran up. "I still have debt and I'm not paying it back because I feel like at this point, I have an obligation to try and disrupt and upset the financial industry, the credit industry. This industry is built off of the belief that it is okay to exploit poor people in order to make a profit," said the *Time* magazine icon. But is her financial situation really someone else's fault?

Each paycheck that I would get, I would overspend. I got a credit card because I had no money and I needed a credit card to buy things that were essential to my life during this time. I had already spent all this money on clothes, make-up, accessories, and I got the credit card because I needed to [pay] my electric bill. Bank of American [*sic*] offered it to me, so I was like, "Yeah, of course—I'll pay my electric bill with it." . . . I think that some of it—most of it was feeling inadequate and insecure and feeling pressure to look a certain way. What I also think it was that you're just surrounded by these messages telling you to buy, buy, buy, consume, consume, consume. . . . I frequently find myself walking around stores in the mall, ready to make big purchases, and buy impulsively just because I feel insecure.[19]

What would Adam Smith do? The laws of justice, according to Smith, "guard what is due . . . from the promises of others."

Not so for Sarah Mason, who feels no compunction to honor a contract that she voluntarily entered into, of her own free will. "They make money off this bad shit, so why am I going to walk around and feel like this moral obligation to pay them back?"[20]

There you have it. Government failure is certainly culpable for the financial dilemma of many Americans caught between a rock and a hard place. But individual freedom comes with a responsibility. With profit comes the potential for loss. With contracts come "what is due from the promises of others." That should be true if you are Bank of America, too: in a free society, you don't get a bailout when you take on too much risk, even if you have the best lobbyists in Washington, D.C. You go out of business, ingloriously scooped up at pennies on the dollar by a more financially conservative, properly managed bank.

One of the most corrosive effects of top-down government, where winners and losers are chosen by someone else, is the destruction of the values that allow for peaceful cooperation among individuals. Individual responsibility is replaced with a sense that someone else owes you something. "If Bank of America gets a bailout, where's mine?"

Where is the sense of responsibility in Occupy Wall Street? What do they stand for? The closest thing to a central organizing principle is an overarching sense of entitlement. But who is entitled to what, and who has the authority to decide? The real questions in the OWS's world of social justice are: By what standard are decisions made? Whose claims are legitimate, and how might you reallocate the wealth of some to the benefit of those deemed more deserving?

THE DRUMBEAT OF CHANGE

IN ZUCCOTTI PARK, REAL LIFE ILLUSTRATED THE TROUBLESOME TASK of doling out resources in a centralized regime. The group gathered there quickly created a "General Assembly," à la the United Nations' General Assembly, to come up with a set of demands and to allocate resources among competing protestor factions. The purpose is the pretense of true participatory democracy, but that's not how things really work. These assembly gatherings quickly devolved into arguments over who gets what, and whose opinions matter most.

According to a report by the *Huffington Post*:

> There's no shortage of talking, and you never know who will take hold of the People's Mic. Persuasive speakers on all sides can give General Assembly meetings a roller-coaster feel. Someone always seems to oppose a budget proposal, or have a strong dissenting opinion on something that seems on its way to sure passage. Just one voice joining the debate at the last minute has the power to sway the entire discussion.
>
> With every proposal, there are questions and there are concerns, and the process continues and continues. The facilitators say numerous times the group has strayed off process. Questions are sometimes ignored for being "off-topic" even when they aren't, time constraints are cited and frustrations boil over. Occupiers curse, speak out of turn and sometimes they just keep on talking, despite "Mic Check" calls over them. Those on all sides alienate each other.[21]

One seemingly inconsequential fight was reminiscent of the saga of the Twentieth Century Motor Company in Ayn Rand's novel *Atlas Shrugged*, where ability and hard work were replaced with a compensation system based on needs. The *Huffington Post* reported:

> On Thursday, the matter at hand was a proposal from Pulse—the group of drummers—for $8,000 for new musical instruments. They say they hoped to secure the funding after a $5,000 handmade drum was sabotaged and destroyed during a rain storm. They say that because they've been there since Day 1, they deserve the funding more than anyone.
>
> "We have worked for you! Appreciate us!" the leader of the proposal shouted angrily to the GA [General Assembly] in response to voices of dissent.
>
> After a long debate, the proposal was tabled. No funding for the drummers. After the meeting, one drummer cursed and yelled at GA members for their decision. He confronted another occupier and the two shouted obscenities back and forth; a physical fight nearly erupted but a peacemaker came between them.[22]

Mediating the squabbling over who is entitled to what is apparently an essential part of managing any coalition of progressive interests. Van Jones himself lamented the dynamic in his Netroots Nation speech. Along the garden path to peace and love and social justice for all, there has apparently arisen a fundamental conflict between utopian rhetoric and the actual process of wealth redistribution in a centralized system.

"We talk, 'kumbaya,'" Jones said. "We talk, 'Solidarity Forever!' We talk, 'Can't we all get along?!' But we have enacted the most individualistic approach to politics. 'Why she'd get that grant!?'"[23]

Why indeed. Was she more deserving than you? Only one thing is for certain in a world where someone else is doing the deciding: You don't get to decide for yourself.

In the fictional *Atlas Shrugged*, and in the all-too-real catastrophic experiments in socialism put into practice across the world, this is what happens. Where the edict "to each according to their contribution" is replaced with "to each according to their need," the disastrous results leave most of society—the 99 percent—jobless, angry, hungry, and destitute.

APPLES AND ORANGES

DESPITE VIOLENCE, PROPERTY DAMAGE, AND LACK OF A COHERENT "set of demands," Occupy Wall Street has been celebrated by the media as a legitimate counter to the Tea Party movement. Indeed, the *Time* "Person of the Year" write-up that accompanies the image of Sarah Mason favorably compares the cause of Occupiers with that of the young street vendor in Tunisia, Mohamed Bouazizi, whose death triggered a grassroots revolution against an oppressive, autocratic government regime. According to international development economist Hernando de Soto, Bouazizi "was a repressed entrepreneur" who struggled against arbitrary government rules and corrupt law enforcement—all insurmountable obstacles that prevented him from earning a living for his family:

> For years, Bouazizi had endured harassment at the hands of deeply corrupt petty officials—most notably, the municipal police officers and inspectors who lived off street vendors and other small-scale extralegal business-people. The police officers helped themselves to the vendors' fruit whenever they felt like it or arbitrarily fined them for running their carts without a permit. Bouazizi complained about the greed of local officers for years. He hated paying bribes.
>
> But on Dec. 17, 2010, this otherwise uneventful life took its place in history. That morning, Bouazizi got into a tussle

with town inspectors who accused him of failing to pay a fine for some arbitrary infraction. They seized two crates of pears, one crate of bananas, three crates of apples, and his electronic scale—worth some $225, the entire capital of his business. A municipal police officer, a woman named Fedia Hamdi, slapped Bouazizi across the face in front of the crowd that had gathered at the scene. With his uncle's help, Bouazizi appealed to the authorities for the return of his property. But he got nowhere—a common outcome in a society where small-scale business-people were treated with contempt by local official-dom. One hour after the confrontation with Hamdi, at 11:30 a.m., he doused himself with paint thinner and immolated himself in front of the governorate building in Sidi Bouzid.[24]

Mohamed Bouazizi set himself on fire because someone else, a government agent, took his stuff, the means of his livelihood. There was no path to justice, no rule of law that existed, no legal recourse available to Bouazizi to get his private property back. The false equiv-alency between Occupy L.A.'s Mason, whose spending spree landed her in trouble, and Bouazizi is striking, to say the least.

FRIENDS AT THE TOP

THAT SAME *Time* COVER STORY SCARCELY MENTIONS THE IMPACT OF the Tea Party. Indeed, all the accusations wrongfully hurled at us were conveniently absent in the mainstream media's coverage of this pur-portedly "morally superior" protest movement. Accusations of racism, for example, were cast heavily (and unfairly) toward the Tea Party, but legitimate claims of anti-Semitism within OWS were largely ignored. Van Jones was first in line defending OWS's values, saying the move-ment's "moral clarity" excused its bad behavior and utter lack of policy clarity.

Vice President Joe Biden—who referred to Tea Partiers as "terror-ists" simply for being opposed to a bad piece of legislation—got all introspective when analyzing the OWS movement.

"What is the core of that protest?" Biden asked at a Washington Ideas Forum in October 2011. "The core is: The bargain has been breached. The core is: The American people do not think the system is fair, or on the level. That is the core, is what you're seeing with [Oc-cupy] Wall Street. Look, there's a lot in common with the Tea Party. The Tea Party started, why? TARP. They thought it was unfair." [25]

Biden voted for the Troubled Asset Relief Program when he was a senator. But now, he feels our pain.

President Obama himself is sympathetic: "I think it expresses the frustrations that the American people feel that we had the biggest financial crisis since the Great Depression, huge collateral damage all throughout the country, all across Main Street. . . . So yes, I think people are frustrated and the protesters are giving voice to a more broad-based frustration about how our financial system works." [26]

Even when the Occupiers occupied an Obama campaign rally, disrupting his speech, the president refused to distance himself from them, while they handed out a statement that read: "Over 4,000 peaceful protesters have been arrested. While bankers continue to de-stroy the American economy. You must stop the assault on our First Amendment rights. Your silence sends a message that police brutality is acceptable. Banks got bailed out. We got sold out." [27]

Obama didn't exactly defend OWS—to do so would have been to alienate the majority of Americans who find their behavior repulsive. But he did play to their complaints. "Families like yours," Obama said, "young people like the ones here today—including the ones who were just chanting at me—you're the reason that I ran for office in the first place." [28]

Obama's willingness to play ball with OWS raises important ques-tions for 2012: Should Democrats hitch their political wagon to Oc-cupy Wall Street? Can Barack Obama, the king of crony capitalism, win reelection by pandering to radical progressives after having offered his crucial vote in favor of TARP in 2008 as a U.S. senator, and after having codified "too big to fail" into law two years later as president? Can congressional Democrats, having spent the past three years attaching Republicans to so-called "Tea Party extremism," now embrace without consequence the radical demands, blatant anti-Semitism, violence, and property damage of OWS?

Who knows, maybe cognitive dissonance is a good political strategy for the Left.

But they join in common cause out of desperation. Since the first Tea Party protest, the Democratic/progressive/big government coalition has been searching for its own Tea Party. Van Jones in particular is worried that we have successfully stolen the Left's strategy playbook. OWS is just part of a broader effort by Jones to regroup after the devastating electoral repudiation of President Obama's economic agenda on November 2, 2010.

But this is Hope and Change Part II: The Empire Strikes Back. Even Jones has grudgingly conceded that we have outcrowdsourced, outorganized, and outperformed the most sophisticated community organizers on the Left, starting with the president himself. According to Jones, the Tea Party is "an upgrade on what we did":

> They have their own groups. They have their own causes. But they came up with a meta-brand too, called the "Tea Party." And they affiliated to that. . . .
>
> It's about a principle of liberty, in their mind, and their meta-brand got 3,528 previously existing groups, all with different names, all with different causes, to affiliate to something called the "Tea Party." They operate off of an operating system called the "Contract From America." The Contract From America was written by 100,000 people, as a wiki. . . .
>
> They talk rugged individualism . . . but they have enacted the most collectivist strategy for taking power in the history

of the Republic. Because they use an open-source meta-brand that they all share, they wrote their document as a wiki, and they're based on a principle and a value.[29]

Jones's new political initiative, called Rebuild the Dream, is attempting to re-create the Contract from America with his own ten-point policy platform, called the Contract for the American Dream.[30] The idea for the Tea Party's Contract from America was simple: create a web-based social media forum where anyone could submit and debate ideas. Despite a tip of the hat to the 1994 Republican Contract with America, this contract was fundamentally different. This document originated bottom-up rather than top-down, created and vetted by the people in a decentralized and transparent marketplace of ideas. Rather than being crafted by a few powerful politicians in a conference room, the planks of this political manifesto were crowdsourced—generated—by hundreds of thousands of Americans. The Contract fit perfectly within the mindset of a decentralized movement.

Between September 2009 and January 2010, hundreds of thousands of people submitted and debated more than 1,000 ideas. By February, a final online vote culled the list down to the top ten ideas. Candidates for federal office were asked to sign the Contract, just like the 1994 Republican Contract, and Mike Lee, then a little-known challenger running against incumbent senator Robert Bennett, Republican of Utah, was the first candidate to sign in April. The Contract from America ultimately played a defining role in electing a massive class of freshman legislators. A team of Brigham Young University political science professors, after conducting a statistical analysis, determined that "candidates who adopted the Tea Party label themselves by signing the Contract from America [saw] their vote shares increasing by more than 20 points" in the 2010 Republican primaries.[31]

Jones's Contract, on the other hand, is a predictably progressive wish list of big government initiatives that "fix" problems by spending more money we don't have, taxing the rich, and giving bureaucrats more control of our lives:

1. "INVEST IN AMERICA'S INFRASTRUCTURE." (Translation: Spend money we don't have on projects we may or may not need.)

2. "CREATE 21ST-CENTURY ENERGY JOBS." (Translation: Spend money we don't have on so-called "green jobs;" subsidize alternative energy that is less reliable and more costly.)

3. "INVEST IN PUBLIC EDUCATION." (Translation: Spend even more money on education, even though evidence shows declining performance from increased funding in government schools.)

4. "OFFER MEDICARE FOR ALL." (Translation: Finish the job Obamacare started; socialize all healthcare provisions.)

5. "MAKE WORK PAY." (Translation: Give labor unions more power and force businesses to pay union workers more than everyone else.)

6. "SECURE SOCIAL SECURITY." (Translation: Make future retirees pay more and more today for less and less retirement security in old age.)

7. "RETURN TO FAIRER TAX RATES." (Translation: Punish wealth and job creators by imposing higher taxes on them, even though the top 1 percent currently pay close to 40 percent of all income taxes.)

8. "END THE WARS AND INVEST AT HOME." (Translation: Savings from lower defense spending should be spent on expanding government programs. Don't even think about reducing the national debt or giving the money back to the taxpayers who earned it.)

9. TAX WALL STREET SPECULATION. (Translation: Keep taxing investors until they fail. Then, bail them out.)

10. STRENGTHEN DEMOCRACY. (Translation: Impose further campaign finance regulations that limit the free speech of individuals, but not special interests like public employee unions.) [32]

Jones thinks that he can out-Tea–Party the Tea Party because collectivists, like those drum circle protesters, are naturally drawn to a collective strategy, community-based action and, apparently, a redistribution of wealth from each according to ability, to each according to need. But there's nothing new here. Crowdsourced or not, Van Jones's progressive agenda strikes a remarkably familiar note. We've heard this tune before. In his book *Liberal Fascism*, required reading for anyone that wants to understand the roots of progressivism in America, Jonah Goldberg listed a few of the planks of the radical progressive Father Coughlin, the radio demagogue and vociferous advocate of FDR's agenda of expanded government power and executive branch control.[33] Goldberg argues that Coughlin's leftist rants often "sounded like he's borrowed Mussolini's talking points," but the radio evangelist eventually became disenchanted with the Roosevelt administration for not going far enough, fast enough down the Road to Serfdom. "Finally, on November 11, 1934, he announced he was forming a new 'lobby of the people,' the National Union for Social Justice, or NUSJ." The sixteen principles of "social justice" included:

1. That every citizen willing to work and capable of working shall receive a just and living annual wage which will enable him to maintain and educate his family . . .
2. I believe in nationalizing those public necessities which by their very nature are too important to be held in the control of private individuals.
3. I believe in upholding the right of private property yet of controlling it for the public good.
4. I believe not only in the right of the laboring man to organize in unions but also in the duty of the Government which that laboring man supports to protect these organizations against the vested interests of wealth and of intellect.
5. I believe in the event of a war and for the defense of our nation and its liberties, if there shall be a conscription of men let there be a conscription of wealth.

6. I believe in preferring the sanctity of human rights to the sanctity of property rights. I believe that the chief concern of government shall be for the poor, because, as is witnessed, the rich have ample means of their own to care for themselves.[34]

If, circa 2012, all these government-will-solve-all-your-problems platitudes seem tired, recycled, that's because they are. And they were even when Father Coughlin pitched them in 1934. Van Jones, like Father Coughlin and a countless line of political snake oil salesmen before him, is like the salesman CEO of that failing corporation described by Apple's Steve Jobs. He's trying to repackage and resell a product that no one wants to buy.[35] What is needed is a better product based on better ideas, not a slicker sales pitch. Jones's Contract for the American Dream, I predict, will work about as well as the distribution of scarce resources at Zuccotti Park among the infinite demands of the entitled.

There will be no leftist, progressive imitation of the Tea Party. There can be no real sense of cooperation, no sense of community, without respect for an individual's life, liberty, and property. You don't say "please" or "excuse me" to someone who is trying to hurt you or take your stuff.

CHAPTER 5

WHEN AMERICA BEATS WASHINGTON

Come on, this affects all of us, man.
Our basic freedoms. I'm staying.
—Walter Sobchak, *The Big Lebowski*

OUR GOVERNMENT IS HEADED IN THE OPPOSITE DIRECTION OF EVERY cultural and technological trend toward more freedom, more choice, more transparency, and more individual accountability. Those in power are not only pushing back against the liberation of individual preferences seen elsewhere in society; they are pushing back hard against anyone who wants to be let inside the castle gates, anybody who wants to be part of the process of deciding. Ensconced inside, the political class seems to be looking down from castle turrets at the rest of America.

Their disdain is palpable.

They see unwashed rubes, *amateurs* who could not possibly understand the complexities of governance. We are just too simple to understand, not quite smart enough to take care for ourselves on the big issues of the day. They, the experts, have drawn a line in the sand that you, a stakeholder in the American Enterprise, *shall not pass*.

It is said that politics abhors a vacuum. In 2008, the gap between where we stood, as Americans living in a radically decentralized world, and where government was headed, constantly imposing more top-down solutions to problems that can only be solved from the bottom up, was too large. The gap between their fantasy and our reality was a yawning expanse, and growing bigger by the day. Government was spending too much money it did not have and getting too involved in things best left to consumer-imposed accountability. Something had to give, one way or another. Something was going to fill that vacuum.

That's exactly what millions of Americans began to say in the summer of 2008. Too much spending. Too many bailouts. Too many special interests taking care of themselves first, at the expense of our families. Too many politicians thinking that they knew best. The tipping point was the Troubled Asset Relief Program (TARP), the $700 billion bailout of a select group of Wall Street investment firms. "Look," said President George W. Bush in December 2008, in defense of this extraordinary expansion of government power over market processes. "I obviously have made a decision to make sure the economy doesn't collapse. I have abandoned free market principles to save the free market system."[1] This remarkably Orwellian turn of phrase would roll off the tongues of Tea Party protesters for years to come when asked what had prompted them to first show up and fight back.

COLLUDING AGAINST US

DESPITE MASSIVE GRASSROOTS OPPOSITION TO TARP OUTSIDE THE Beltway, the leadership of both parties joined together to push it through Congress. Senator John McCain, the Republican nominee for president, and Senator Barack Obama, the Democratic nominee, both endorsed the need to bail out Wall Street, and both voted for the legislation. Either could have killed it single-handedly, and changed the course of history. But when push came to shove, they both fell in line with the establishment to prop up big banks that did not deserve taxpayer-financed propping. The Republican Bush administration worked closely with the Democratic congressional leadership, both House Speaker Nancy Pelosi and Senate Majority Leader Harry Reid, to whip the votes to jam it through the legislature, starting with the House of Representatives. On September 29, 2008, from the well of the House floor, Speaker Pelosi urged her colleagues to vote for TARP: "It just comes down to one simple thing. They have described a precipice. We are on the brink of doing something that might pull us back from that precipice. I think we have a responsibility. We have worked in a bipartisan way." [2]

Bipartisan is such a curious word. The Merriam-Webster dictionary defines the word as "relating to, or involving members of two parties (a *bipartisan* commission); *specifically*: marked by or involving cooperation, agreement, and compromise between two major political parties (*bipartisan* support for the bill)." This last usage is often invoked in Washington in lieu of a substantive argument for or against pending legislation, as if all credible legislation were bipartisan, and all bipartisan legislation were credible. Votes that should not have been cast are inevitably defended as having been a "bipartisan" imperative. "Partisanship," on the other hand, is ipso facto bad. Beltway pundits worship at the altar of bipartisanship, prioritizing the virtues of the process by which legislation is developed over the importance of substance of the legislation itself.

In reality, both parties typically *cooperate in a bipartisan manner* to grow the power and reach of government. Where do the taxpayers, back home working to put food on their table, sit at this bipartisan negotiating table? There is no third chair. Isn't this form of cooperation really just collusion by another name? In the private sector it would be. Consider a legal definition of the term:

> Collusion occurs when two persons or representatives of an entity or organization make an agreement to deceive or mislead

another. Such agreements are usually secretive, and involve fraud or gaining an unfair advantage over a third party, competitors, consumers or others with whom they are negotiating. The collusion, therefore, makes the bargaining process inherently unfair. Collusion can involve price or wage fixing, kickbacks, or misrepresenting the independence of the relationship between the colluding parties.[3]

Such behavior is illegal in the private sector, where no individual has the peculiar advantages of monopoly power granted to government agents. And yet elected representatives regularly collude, "in a bipartisan way," as Nancy Pelosi puts it, to give some an unfair advantage over others. Elected officials regularly deceive their constituents. Cabinet agency heads conspire with their allies—health insurance and pharmaceutical companies, for instance—to fix prices, limit supplies, encourage certain types of consumer behavior, construct barriers to entry, manipulate markets, and crowd out competition. Nick Gillespie and Matt Welch, coauthors of *The Declaration of Independents: How Libertarian Politics Can Fix What's Wrong with America*, refer to Republicans and Democrats as a "duopoly" that seems more intent on protecting its own interests, not ours. "Though rhetorically and theoretically at odds with one another," they write, "the two parties have managed to create a mostly unbroken set of policies and governance structures that benefit well-connected groups at the expense of the individual."[4]

TEA PARTY 1.0

YET, FOR ALL ITS BIPARTISAN GLORY, THE INITIAL VERSION OF THE TARP legislation was gloriously defeated moments after Pelosi's September 29 floor speech, against any and all expectations among Beltway interests. How was it killed? By the American people, who had simply had *enough*. They stopped yelling at the TV, got up off their couches, pushed away from kitchen tables, and started calling their representatives in Washington. Many had never called before, but they had to do something to stop the insanity. So many did so, in fact, that the Capitol switchboard was shut down, and congressional staffers were besieged by a deluge of constituent anger.

It was David versus Goliath. And it was awesome. That was the day the Tea Party was born in America. Something had to give. The fortress gates were bound to buckle, sooner rather than later. It was the emergence of the Tea Party that kicked the doors down. Activists seemed to come out of nowhere, newly armed with easy access to multiple, competitive sources of information. Enabled by the lower costs of connection and association with like-minded neighbors. Ignited by the easy availability of virtually costless technology that allowed unknown millions to coordinate plans. And fueled by the unspoken but ingrained sense of collective outrage over the violation of the principle that we shouldn't hurt others or take their stuff.

Republicans and Democrats quickly huddled, larded the bill with nongermane spending earmarks for favored constituencies—constituencies that would cooperate—and passed the bailout legislation. It passed *in a bipartisan fashion*. But they had awoken a sleeping giant, We the People.

The modern Tea Party has been widely characterized as a *partisan*—as in negative, a bad influence, *not bipartisan*—phenomenon, a Republican uprising against a newly minted Democratic administration. It is not, of course; it never has been. The Tea Party was never a political party the way Republicans or Democrats are. A party's only purpose is to get its candidates elected. Tea Partiers were bound by a set of values, not a slate of candidates. Their interest was in the ideas of freedom that formed the basis of the American experiment. Political parties are, at best, a necessary means in the cause of good ideas. More naturally, parties collude on bad ideas, with the hope that their slate of candidates wins in the next election.

The "partisan" narrative allowed the mainstream media and the political elite to ignore the emerging Tea Party uprising as it grew in strength in the early months of 2009.

The first tangible iteration of this grassroots uprising for fiscal sanity—call it Tea Party 1.0—was as a street protest, as people started to gather in town squares. This phenomenon was particularly remarkable because of an ingrained penchant of functional libertarians not to take part in the political process, wanting most of all just to be left alone to work, live, raise our families, and prosper, free from too many top-down intrusions. Why would you show up if you didn't want something, didn't expect something? Because all other options had been taken off the table. Lo and behold, as people left their homes for the streets of America, they started to discover that they were not alone in their angst over an arrogant political establishment run amok.

A February 2009 gathering of a dozen protesters in Fort Myers, Florida, grew into hundreds protesting in Seattle in March and thousands demanding accountability in Atlanta in April. All this protesting culminated in the September 12, 2009, Taxpayer March on Washington, attended by more than a million citizen activists. They put official Washington on notice: We will be ignored no more. That day was a little like karaoke night, where just about every group involved had their two minutes at the microphone. It was the biggest mutual support group ever assembled: "I am not alone, and I'm not crazy to have spent the family vacation fund to come to Washington, D.C., to petition my government for a redress of grievances."

That day, a protest movement started to morph into something else entirely. Newly minted activists went home and started organizing, community by community, town by town, congressional district by congressional district. Nobody told them to do this, but they knew that marching on Washington was just the beginning. Nothing had changed yet.

But we certainly got Washington's attention. How do I know? Because of the speed with which the political establishment went from ignoring us to attacking our motives. It was such a monumental event that former president Jimmy Carter felt called upon to impugn the motives of every single marcher, just two days after the March on Washington, with a sweeping statement on race:

> I think an overwhelming portion of the intensely demonstrated animosity toward President Barack Obama is based on the fact that he is a black man, that he's African-American. I live in the south and I've seen the south come a long way and I've seen the rest of the country that shared the south's attitude toward minority groups, at that time particularly African-Americans, that that racism still exists. And I think it's bubbled up to the surface because of belief among many white people, not just in the south, but around the country, that African-Americans are not qualified to lead this great country. It's an abominable circumstance and grieves me and concerns me very deeply.[5]

This baseless charge would seem to be the work of a partisan hack, not a former president. Why would Carter debase himself so? *Because he could see the castle gates buckling.* Something had to be done.

First they ignored us. This is a typical tactic employed by front-runners, those in charge. Never draw attention to your opponent. Never give them a space on the stage, a microphone, a platform for their agenda. But if your opponent closes in, nipping at your heels, it is time to attack. So it was with the 9/12 Taxpayer March on Washington. We got the establishment's notice. They took the threat the Tea Party posed to their power position seriously, for the first time. So they ridiculed, like the flamboyant French guard in *Monty Python and the Holy Grail*: "Now go away or I shall taunt you a second time." Then they released the attack dogs.

We were finally getting somewhere.

TEA PARTY 2.0

VIEWING EVENTS AND HUMAN ACTIONS IN REAL TIME IS INTEGRAL TO a bottom-up understanding of economic processes. Real time is constantly changing and the future is uncertain. The world we live in is not a static snapshot of any particular moment or imagined equilibrium state. People, in their purposeful actions, change along with time, new information, new circumstances, and the evolution of things based on the actions and decisions of others. In other words, things can never be exactly like they were before as humans work toward their goals. This is known as progress, but it's not "progressive" in the sense that Barack Obama might intend it to be. This is an emerging order created by free folks interacting in common purpose, not some grandiose plan conceived by a potentate with a particular goal, to be imposed from the top down.

The difference between those two kinds of "progress" is what made the second iteration of the Tea Party so unique in American political history. There was no grand plan. There was no charismatic leader. There was no particular candidate to rally around. It was a core value of the Tea Party ethos: nobody gets to tell anyone else what to do, and everyone is responsible for their own work and their own actions. We act by mutual consent based on the trader principle—value for value. It's a contract of sorts, an unspoken agreement that everyone understands. That's what makes it binding.

The conventional wisdom was that this massive uprising, now acknowledged as very real by mainstream media, would evaporate with the passage of the Democrats' government takeover of health care on March 21, 2010. After all, stopping Obamacare had become the singular focus of the grassroots movement, the raison d'être of the Tea Party, by the spring of 2010. Those in charge secretly hoped they would go away. That was part of the plan. The likely reason Obamacare actually passed was a predominant assumption among Democrats, which was aggressively promoted by their leaders, that people would go back home, passions would fade, and this formi-dable protest movement would lose cohesiveness once the bill left the headlines of the *Washington Post*. This arrogance was consistent with the by-any-means-necessary approach used to pass the $768 billion stimulus legislation in the early days of the Obama administration. Public opposition did not seem to matter, because the insiders were told that voters would shift their attentions, with the next day's above-the-fold headline.

The extraordinary tactical legislative maneuvers and procedural trickery employed by the Obama administration, Senate Majority Leader Harry Reid, and House Speaker Nancy Pelosi demonstrated this arrogance; that people would forget, or even learn to like the massive expansion of government's role in health care. That's how things had always worked in the past, after all. Crisis, and then an expansion of the leviathan state, and the ratchet effect of government control and expenditures since the halcyon days of John Maynard Keynes.[6]

Structurally, the Tea Party didn't stay a protest movement very long following the September 12 march. Certainly there were count-less additional rallies all the way until Election Day 2010. But the gatherings themselves took on a different purpose. Street protests serve a particular tactical purpose: to get the attention of the political establishment, and to build sympathy for your cause with the public. By 2010, local gatherings were taking on a different tone. Each group was now building organization at the local level. This somewhat amorphous building process is impossible to quantify, but you could literally see it happening. There were more and more local groups on the ground, and they were growing. Every group that I would visit was either built by someone or contained a substantial block of folks who had attended the March on Washington. Countless times I heard the same story that one young mom told me on August 18, 2010, as we stood on the front stairs of Sciortino's Restaurant in Brewster, New York, at a rally put together by the Hudson Valley Patriots. "I've never done this before," she told me, "but being there that day on September 12 proved to me that there were enough people out there just like me. I could do this. We just have to get organized."

Four academic researchers from Harvard University have attempted to quantify the effect that Tea Party protests had on the November elections, and other policy-making outcomes, in a paper entitled: "Do Political Protests Matter? Evidence from the Tea Party Movement." They find a positive relationship:

> How does political change come about? While freedom of speech and assembly are central pillars of democracy, recognized as intrinsically valuable, it is unclear how effective exercising these freedoms is in bringing about change. Although there are numerous historical episodes where political change has been associated with, or been preceded by, political protests and demonstrations, such as the French Revolution, the civil rights movement in the 1960s, and the recent Arab Spring manifestations, it is unclear to what extent these protests caused the change. Since protests are likely to occur during episodes when political beliefs in society change, it is difficult to disentangle whether protests cause political change, or simply reflect unobservable belief changes. Empirical evidence of the causal effects of protests therefore remain scarce.
>
> We show that larger rallies cause an increase in turnout in favor of the Republicans in the 2010 Congressional elections, and increase the likelihood that incumbent Democratic representatives retire. Incumbent policymaking is affected as well: representatives respond to large protests in their district by voting more conservatively in Congress. Finally, the estimates imply significant multiplier effects: for every protester, Republican votes increase by seven to fourteen votes. Together our results show that protests can build political movements that ultimately affect policy.[7]

By August 2010, in battlegrounds like the 19th District in Brewster, the window of opportunity provided by the 2010 midterm elections was fast approaching, and the Tea Party was quickly evolving into a powerful Get Out the Vote (GOTV) machine. The transition to Tea Party 2.0 may have seemed like an intentional, conscious rebuke to naysayers in the media who were predicting the demise of the Tea Party after the Democrats jammed Obamacare through. But it was an obvious evolution for a citizen movement that had once again been ignored by official Washington. Obama hadn't listened. Pelosi wasn't listening, and wasn't interested in the opinions of any of us, arrogantly saying, "You've heard about the controversies within the bill, the process about the bill, one or the other. . . . But we have to pass the bill so that you can find out what is in it, away from the fog of the controversy."[8]

To activists on the ground, it was painfully clear that those in charge—the *management*—were not going to listen. So activists started shifting their attention to the next logical step in institutional reform. It was time to shake up senior management. It was time to make some personnel changes. Someone needed to be fired. The American people needed to take their shareholders ballot to a vote. Like entrepreneurs responding to a shift in customer demand, Tea Partiers set out to learn effective GOTV tactics and went to the task of political accountability.

At the time of this transformation into organization building, it wasn't just the Democrats who failed to see this seismic political paradigm shift that was changing the rules of the game. The Republican ruling class—leaders within the Republican National Committee, the National Republican Senatorial Committee, and the National Republican Congressional Committee—were all proceeding as if nothing had changed since the last election. It was business as usual. Just another day at the office. "Nothing to see here." Why didn't they see it? Think about the analogy of a failing company again. Entrenched management surrounds itself with staff and a board that insulates leadership from change, from new perspectives and outside voices.

Even if someone had broken through the inner circle of yes-men and clued them in, were Republican pooh-bahs ever willing to give up some of their power for the opportunity to solve the government's spending addiction?

AT THE MARGIN

Carl Menger, one of the Austrian School economists I mentioned in Chapter 2, is best known in the economics profession as one of the first thinkers to solve the theory of value. The value of something is not intrinsic, Menger said. It is always determined "subjectively" by consumers choosing "at the margin," based on what they already have, and what they still want and need. It has nothing to do, per se, with the amount of labor that went into making something, as Karl Marx claimed. Water, for example, is a necessity of life, but succeeding buckets of water have diminishing marginal utility to the consumer. The first drink of ice-cold water on a hot day is priceless. The tenth gallon, not so much. Demand for a product is about intensity of feeling and how much you value it, at the moment you make a decision. Menger's insight was an important shift in our understanding of how the real world actually works, because he demonstrated how it was that two people could mutually benefit from an exchange. If value is based on objective inputs like labor, then trade is always, at best, a zero-sum transaction, where someone wins because someone else has lost. But exchange does not happen that way. Trading would not happen unless both parties are better off, value for value. For instance, when you go to Starbucks they want your $3 and you want that Venti brew. Trade happens and both parties are better off. It's about growing the pie, and creating more opportunity all around.

Electoral decisions, like economic decisions, are made "at the margin." In politics, this means that the last vote counted is in many ways the most important one, because it may be the vote that puts candidates over the top, particularly in tight elections in swing districts. For

Republicans and Democrats alike, they can count on a certain number of votes from their most loyal consumers—the so-called Republican and Democrat bases—who habitually vote the party line regardless of who the candidate is. In Nancy Pelosi's left-leaning congressional district, that Democratic base is enough to virtually guarantee her safe reelection. But for many political races in many congressional districts, it's the marginal vote, the so-called swing voter, that determines the outcome of elections and, typically, which party controls the House and the Senate.

How do you attract that last vote? Republican thinking on attracting swing voters is a zero-sum game, static thinking that implicitly assumes a fixed number of potential votes and that the best way for Republicans to win is to appeal to everyone. Republicans, the logic goes, could win only by peeling off enough Democrats and by embracing Democratic thinking on some issues. Like cutting taxes and then dramatically expanding Medicare Part D. Or voting for a Balanced Budget Amendment to the Constitution and then voting for a $700 billion bailout of overleveraged investment banks. It's a philosophical potpourri: a little bit of this, a little bit of that. Tea Partiers affectionately call these mixed-bag candidates RINOs—Republicans in Name Only—a term usually linked to Republican candidates who have sold out their free-market principles for the sake of reelection. But it is more likely that the recruiting and running of RINOs is the conscious operating strategy of the GOP establishment. The best candidates, according to the experts, are usually half like Them, and half like Us.

But is that how the real world works? What if the real swing voter is, in fact, motivated by a very different value calculation? What if product differentiation could create new market demand? What if the swing vote, the difference between winning and losing, is defined by a bloc of potential consumers, who might show up and vote if there is a good enough reason to stand in line at voting booths?

It's about intensity of demand. A product is worth whatever the consumer thinks it's worth, at the margin.

So, what was the Republican brand worth in early 2009, at the margin? Not that much. There were very few buyers and the words *I have abandoned free market principles to save the free market system* still hung like the Sword of Damocles over Republicans who had traded principle for the temporary security of "doing something" even though that something violated everything that they had publicly espoused. What were they thinking?

A PERFECT RECORD

Republicans seem particularly prone to doing the same thing over and over again, expecting different results. Consider the case of freshman U.S. senator Pat Toomey, Republican of Pennsylvania. The GOP famously circled the wagons around incumbent RINO Arlen Specter in 2004, with President George W. Bush, Senator Rick Santorum, and an army of party apparatchiks running to the defense of one of the most unreliable Republicans in the Senate, narrowly beating back a primary challenge by Toomey. Specter returned the favor by providing a deciding vote for the Obama stimulus in early 2009. On April 15, 2009, as Tax Day Tea Parties swept across the Commonwealth of Pennsylvania, Toomey announced a second challenge, this time focusing on Specter's vote for the highly unpopular Obama stimulus-spending bill.

Specter the defector promptly switched parties. It wasn't personal. It was political: "I've looked at the polls," Specter said. "I can't win as a Republican. I can't win as an independent. The only way I have a shot is to be a Democrat." [9]

Specter's switch ultimately gave Democrats the sixtieth vote, the vote needed to enact Obamacare. [10] Despite all this, there was no sign of buyer's remorse at the National Republican Senatorial Committee (NRSC), no acknowledgment of culpability among the GOP cognoscenti for their hand in helping President Obama enact one of the most sweeping expansions of federal government control in a generation.

Even after Specter switched parties, Senator John Cornyn, Republican of Texas, the NRSC chairman, initially refused to endorse Toomey for the Senate seat, even though he was now unopposed in the GOP primary. Republican senator-for-life and NRSC co-chair Orrin Hatch predicted, with seemingly scientific certainty, that Toomey could not win statewide in Pennsylvania, saying, "I don't think there is anybody in the world who believes he can get elected senator there." [11]

Both Cornyn and Hatch had voted for TARP. Cornyn initially opposed a strategy to run against Obamacare in 2010. "Rather than promising to scrap the bill in its entirety," the *Huffington Post* reported in May 2010, "the GOP will pledge to just get rid of the more controversial parts." "There is non-controversial stuff here like the preexisting conditions exclusion and those sorts of things," Cornyn argued. "Now we are not interested in repealing that. And that is frankly a distraction." [12]

The one thing that John Cornyn was uncertain about, it seemed, was the ability of Senate GOP candidates to win elections in 2010:

That's going to be real hard, to be honest with you. Everybody who runs could be the potential tipping point to get Democrats to 60. We've not only got to play defense; we've got to claw our way back in 2010. It'll be a huge challenge. So far this cycle, Republicans have been faced with retirements in four swing states, emerging primaries against at least three of their members and a map that, after two cycles of big GOP losses, continues to favor Democrats. [13]

Regardless of what the Republican illuminati were thinking, the rest of us were quite certain that we had to clean House. And the Senate, if we could. A growing number of Americans now understood that their country was in trouble. They had also come to the conclusion that there was no way to fix the current management team in Washington, D.C. We would need personnel changes before we could solve policy problems.

Tea Partiers knew that *we had to beat the Republicans before we could beat the Democrats.* This was the initial offer in a shareholder battle that might well determine ownership of the company. That probably explains why many of the candidates who authentically stood for something—candidates who actually believed that the government was spending too much money it does not have; candidates who actually knew that government-run health care would be disastrous to both the health of patients and the financial health of the nation—were paid little mind by top GOP strategists.

The movement focused on shifting power from the White House back to Congress, as the Constitution (which embodies the separation—and decentralization—of power) mandated. The Tea Party's approach to campaigning reflected the movement's broader philosophy of decentralization. While the Tea Party largely operated in Republican circles, having determined that there was little room for the ideas of fiscal responsibility and individual freedom in a Democratic Party now wholly owned by radical progressives, the movement and many of its candidates clearly did not have support from the Republican Party. The Tea Party looked in districts that hadn't been in play before, rejecting the old standard that money equals television and television equals victory, and replacing it with the idea that grassroots organization is infinitely more powerful.

So activists focused on truly grassroots campaigning. Eschewing traditional television ad buys—after all, there was no established organization to raise money to pay for production and airtime—the Tea Party took to social networks, technological and personal, to spread the message. As important as this strategy was, it is hard to win an election without a good, capable candidate. As it turns out, the grassroots protests were not only a good recruitment mechanism for building boots on the ground, they also created a powerful market signal to potential candidates with both the principles and the practical skills needed to win public office. This was a fundamentally different dynamic than had occurred in 1994, the last time Republicans had taken control of the U.S. House of Representatives. Then, there was no organic candidate recruitment device like Tea Party protests. As a result, many of the winners were accidental, caught in a wave of new voters opposed to President Bill Clinton's economic stimulus spending and attempted takeover of health care. Many in that freshman class were swept back out in 1996, lacking the skills to build an effective reelection campaign.

But 2010 was different from 1994, and it was going to be fundamentally different from 2008. However, the old guard didn't see it. On January 4, 2010, Sean Hannity asked Republican National Committee Chairman Michael Steele whether the GOP could retake the House. "Not this year," Steele replied.[14] In September, Cornyn told his Republican colleagues, "While we have the momentum on our side right now, it is also important to recognize that 2010 remains an uphill climb for us."[15] As late as October 2010, Pete Sessions, chairman of the NRCC, was cautious in predicting winning the thirty-nine House seats required for a majority.

UNDER THE RADAR

RATHER THAN GO ALONG WITH THE GOP'S PREEMPTIVE SURRENDER, the Tea Party set out to win elections anyway, and became the first movement to prove that the top-down method of campaigning, focused on Old Media ad buys organized by centralized clearinghouses of information and money, isn't the best path to achieve electoral success. The GOP establishment was still playing a zero-sum game, trimming their sails, preparing, preemptively, for more failure. The Tea Party was growing the pie, adding new potential voters to its ranks, voters who would potentially show up for something different than the same old, same old. Republican campaign consultant Jon Lerner reported that consistently half of Republican voters he questioned in primary polling said they aligned more with the Tea Party than with the Republican Party.[16]

In late October, the *Washington Post* published the results of a survey of hundreds of Tea Party groups, reporting, "a remarkable 86 percent of local leaders said most of their members are new to political activity." But the *Post* was skeptical of any tangible political implications. Instead, this analysis found "a different sort of organization, one that is not so much a movement as a disparate band of vaguely connected gatherings that do surprisingly little to engage in the political process."[17] Maybe this was wishful thinking? Or maybe it was an understandable inability to recognize a paradigm shift, from the bottom up, as it was actually emerging, person by person, value for value.

Many of the brightest stars in the 2010 freshman class found themselves recruited, and then organically propelled to prominence in the very emergence of this "disparate band of vaguely connected gatherings." These candidates overcame long odds—and often aggressive opposition from their own party—to make waves in Washington as prominent members of the "Tea Party Class."

One of those Americans was Mick Mulvaney. In September 2009, the South Carolina state senator attended a town hall meeting on health care hosted by his fourteen-term U.S. representative, Democrat John Spratt. Spratt was not only an entrenched incumbent; he was the powerful chairman of the House Budget Committee, a key architect in Washington's unprecedented spending spree. The GOP establishment considered him unbeatable.

In a meeting typical of so many others occurring around the country at the time, voters booed and jeered Spratt as he attempted to defend Obamacare and a government that was spending so much money that we do not have. "I decided to run while sitting in the back of that meeting," Mulvaney said.[18]

Another of those Americans who had decided to make personnel changes in Washington, D.C., was Joe Thompson. Unknown to Mulvaney, South Carolina activist Thompson was thinking along the very same lines. After holding the first Tea Party rally in the 5th District, Joe Thompson and a number of other local leaders got together to plan a campaign against Spratt. "We didn't even have a candidate yet," Thompson recalls. "Most of us are businessmen, so we looked at it from a business standpoint—what goals did we need to meet to get Spratt out of office? We knew we had to keep things simple, like a marketing campaign." Not knowing that GOP experts were counseling otherwise, Thompson "chose two issues—health care and fiscal responsibility—and highlighted how Spratt was failing to represent us on both." Thompson and his wife kept an e-mail list of several hundred activists from across the large district and corresponded with local leaders often, "to make sure we were all keeping on the same simple message. By the time the NRCC got involved with the race, we had already done much of their work for them."

At the same time, Joe was convincing many local activists to fill vacant county GOP leadership spots. "I just told them, 'we can't fix the Republican Party from the outside; we must get inside to make a difference.'"

Mulvaney was in the midst of his first term as a state senator, and had served just one term previously as a state representative, but he set out to take down South Carolina's longest-serving U.S. representative. In his first month, Mulvaney raised $53,000, all of it from individual donors.[19] While Mulvaney mobilized around Tea Party values and fiscal responsibility, Spratt used the national Democrats' talking points, running against "Tea Party extremism." Scott Huffmon, a political scientist at Winthrop University in Rock Hill, South Carolina, who moderated a debate between the two, observed "that both Mulvaney and Spratt see their chances for winning in the Tea Party—Mulvaney tapping into its conservative anger and Spratt tapping into moderates wary of its extremism."[20]

Mulvaney relied heavily on mobilizing the Tea Party, and helped turn out an unusually high number of voters for a midterm election. Poll watchers reported the number of voters ran "a close second to the number in the 2008 presidential election."[21,22] Mulvaney defeated Spratt with 55 percent of the vote.[23] (Spratt had won just two years earlier by a mammoth margin of 25 points.[24]) The hostile takeover had begun, and Mulvaney was just one example of the many Tea Party candidates who, because they actually believed what they were saying about smaller government, were sent to Washington as real agents of change.

Those responsible for breaching our constitutional contract kept hoping we would just go home. If they ignored us long enough, or attacked us viciously enough, maybe we'd go away. But there were basic freedoms, ingrained in every American, under attack. We were staying, finishing what the Founders started in the 1770s.

CHAPTER 6

SMALLER GOVERNMENT AND
MORE INDIVIDUAL FREEDOM

WHILE MICK MULVANEY AND LOCAL TEA PARTY ACTIVISTS WERE BUSY beating the conventional wisdom and the Democrats in the 5th District, Tim Scott and local Tea Party activists were beating the Republican establishment and history in South Carolina's 1st. When five-term Republican Henry Brown announced in 2009 that he wouldn't seek reelection to the U.S. House of Representatives, a door opened for Scott, then a newly minted state legislator. In the nine-candidate Republican primary, Scott campaigned hard in defense of Tea Party values, and defeated established legacy opponents like Paul Thurmond, son of longtime South Carolina senator Strom Thurmond, and Carroll Campbell III, son of a former South Carolina governor. Scott, an early signer of the Tea Party's crowdsourced Contract from America, observed the wide appeal of the movement:

> If you believe in entrepreneurship and capitalism, you believe
> in at least a third of what the Tea Party stands for. If you be-
> lieve that you ought not spend money you simply do not have,

you believe in another third. And if you believe that limiting the role of federal government in our lives is a way to return power back to the people, I think you might be a member of the Tea Party.[1]

The Tea Party's Contract became an important wedge in an aggressively contested primary fight between Scott and Thurmond. In a final debate before the primary vote, "Thurmond did stumble at one point, when the candidates were asked if they had read and signed the 'Contract from America,' a tea party manifesto," noted the Charleston *Post and Courier*. "Thurmond said he wasn't familiar with the document. Scott quickly noted that he has signed it and incorporated it into his campaign material."[2] Tim Scott won the primary overwhelmingly, by 69 percent, just a few days later.

So Tim Scott, a one-term state legislator with the enthusiastic backing of local Tea Parties in the 1st Congressional District, handily beat the son of Strom Thurmond, who left the Democratic Party in 1948 to run for president as a pro-segregation Dixiecrat.

Why does any of this matter? Because Tim Scott is African-American. Because he is the first black Republican to win a seat in the U.S. Congress in South Carolina since Reconstruction. Because establishment hacks like Jimmy Carter want to play the race card, want to change the subject, want us to believe that "an overwhelming portion of the intensely demonstrated animosity toward President Barack Obama is based on the fact that he is a black man."[3] But Scott doesn't particularly see the world as black-and-white, and he's not particularly interested in accepting the establishment's categories or the establishment's rules. "What I am eager to do is be an ambassador to all groups on my issues," he tells a reporter with the *Daily Beast*. "Sure," he will meet with "the Urban League or black business groups to talk about economic empowerment and the importance of fiscal responsibility, but I'm not going to be their black Republican."[4]

Jimmy Carter, meet Tim Scott. He's the new congressman from North Charleston, South Carolina. He thinks that "Americans need to know that the Tea Party is a color-blind movement that has principled differences with many of the leaders in Washington, both Democrats and Republicans. Their aim is to support the strongest candidates—regardless of color or background—who will fight to return our country to its Constitutional roots of limited government, fiscal responsibility, and free markets."[5]

CONSTITUTIONAL CONSERVATIVES

In Kentucky, another U.S. Senate race pitted establishment Republicans against the Tea Party. Rand Paul, son of Texas congressman Ron Paul, announced his candidacy in May 2009 and by the end of June had raised $102,000, mostly from small donors. By the end of the 2009, he'd raised almost $1.8 million, with more than half coming from small donors and less than $6,000 from committees.[6]

But Paul's popularity among donors and his dominance in the polls wasn't enough to win the support of establishment Republicans. In May 2010, Kentucky's senior senator, Senate Minority Leader Mitch McConnell, endorsed the establishment favorite Trey Grayson in the race to fill retiring senator Jim Bunning's seat. McConnell, who feared Paul wouldn't play by the establishment's rules, provided "behind-the-scenes assistance" to Grayson's traditional establishment campaign, which featured McConnell in the "largest ad buy of the campaign to date."[7]

But none of that mattered. Voters turned out in droves for the Republican primary and overwhelmingly supported Paul, who earned almost 59 percent of the vote.[8] The *Washington Post* reported that the percentage of registered Republicans voting in the 2010 Kentucky primary was the highest since 1998, and was larger than the percentage of registered Democrats for the first time since the state began collecting data, in 1982.[9]

"I consider myself a constitutional conservative, which I take to mean a conservative who actually believes in smaller government and more individual freedom. The libertarian principles of limited government, self-reliance and respect for the Constitution are embedded within my constitutional conservatism," Paul wrote in a *USA Today* editorial in August 2010. "I also believe that the common bond of liberty can unite Americans and build a winning political coalition to stand up against big government elites in both parties while reclaiming our freedom and prosperity." [10] Paul's words in effect amounted to a Tea Party manifesto, representative of what any candidate or activist marching under the Gadsden flag might say.

And Rand Paul went on to win the general election handily. [11]

TARP! TARP! TARP!

IN MAY 2010, THREE-TERM INCUMBENT UTAH REPUBLICAN SENATOR Robert Bennett, an aggressive spending earmarker on the Appropriations Committee and longtime advocate of an "individual mandate" in health care, was ousted in the second round of voting at the state Republican convention. Tea Partiers had taken over the caucus process, trumping Bennett's "support of big-name conservatives such as Karl Rove, Newt Gingrich and Mitt Romney," *USA Today* reported. [12] Bennett was eliminated in the second round of voting, finishing third to two newcomers. Caucus delegates were chanting "TARP! TARP! TARP!" as the Republican incumbent went down to defeat, bluntly eulogizing his vote in favor of the unpopular bailout. In the final statewide runoff, the Republican establishment chose Tim Bridgewater to replace Bennett, and even Bennett endorsed him. [13] But voters had someone else in mind, giving the Republican nomination to first-time candidate Mike Lee, who went on to earn nearly 62 percent of the vote in the general election. [14] Lee, the very first candidate to sign the Contract from America, was outspent by the establishment's favorite, but the young constitutional lawyer won the ground game by running on the idea that the federal government should live within its means, and within the strict limits set out by the Constitution.

At a Tea Party rally less than a month before the state convention, candidate Mike Lee argued that the U.S. Constitution had "fostered the development of the greatest civilization the world has ever known." He pulled his copy out of his pocket, holding it up as he had at every event he had spoken to across the state of Utah. "I will not apologize for this document or the country it has created—nor will I tolerate those who ignore it." As the *Deseret Morning News* would later observe, "Lee's very public embrace of the Constitution was . . . shrewd and prescient. As a candidate, he was tapping into the political zeitgeist of the time, a feeling that the nation has become unmoored from the bedrock principles outlined by the Constitution." [15]

Receiving news of the Republican incumbent's defeat, Senator John Cornyn, head of the National Republican Senatorial Committee, had this to say: "Senator Bennett has long exemplified the strong values and deep work ethic of his state, and he has fought tirelessly for lower taxes and limited government on behalf of Utah's best interests." [16]

In Florida's U.S. Senate primary, the NRSC endorsed RINO Governor Charlie Crist immediately after he announced his candidacy. The Republican Senate campaign committee had pledged to stay neutral. Cornyn justified picking winners and losers from the top down, despite the fact that Marco Rubio was already a declared candidate and the Republican Speaker of the Florida House of Representatives, by arguing that Crist "is the best candidate in 2010 to ensure that we maintain checks and balances that Floridians deserve in the United States Senate." [17] Floridians disagreed, and as Rubio's popularity grew, Crist embarrassed his establishment Republican backers by ditching the GOP primary and announcing he'd run for Senate as an independent. Rubio won decisively in a three-way race, with the enthusiastic support of Tea Partiers on the ground.

Why is it that Tea Partiers are always accused of "splitting the party," when, in practice, the only ones to split it are establishment favorites like Arlen Specter, Charlie Crist, and Senator Lisa Murkowski, who successfully ran a write-in campaign outside the party ticket after losing the Republican primary to Tea Party favorite Joe Miller?

Borrowing the Democrats' "extremist" talking points, Murkowski accused the "radical" Republican nominee of wanting to "dump Social Security, no more Medicare, let's get rid of Department of Education, elimination of all earmarks." [18] Despite breaking party ranks, Murkowski maintained her position as ranking member on the powerful Senate Energy and Natural Resources Committee.

There seems to be a double standard, just as with the duplicitous application of First Amendment rights to Tea Partiers and to Occupiers. But maybe there's an ironclad consistency to the standard being applied here as well? When is one meeting singled out of countless other meetings and arbitrarily determined by legislative counsel to be a "simulated hearing"? When are grassroots activists deemed to be "domestic terrorists"? When are Republican candidates not supported by their party's elite?

The answer to all these questions: When the established order is threatened. When senior management feels threatened by a shareholder uprising. When new people start participating in the democratic process, along with their newly elected representation in Congress, bringing to Washington, D.C., new ideas and specific plans to balance the budget, repeal government-run health care, and restore the constitutional firewall that protects the freedoms of individuals from an encroaching government.

There's an institutional hostility to change whenever the changing aims to take power and money back from the federal government. The trend seems remarkably predictable when you think about it like this.

KEYNESIAN MATH

IN SPITE OF THE ESTABLISHMENT'S ISSUE-WAFFLING, HAND-WRINGING, expectations management, and hesitancy to back Tea Party candidates, Republicans gained 6 seats in the Senate (7 if you count Scott Brown's special election in Massachusetts) for a total of 47, crushing

Democratic dreams of a supermajority. Republicans gained 63 seats in the House, for a total of 242, their largest majority since 1947. In 2009 and 2010, Republicans won 720 new seats in state legislatures, to hold a total of 54 percent of state seats, the most since 1928. After 2010, Republicans controlled both chambers in 25 states, an increase of 11 and the most since 1952.

The number of freshman winners who had signed the Contract from America: forty-five House members and eight senators.

Today, it is quite fashionable for establishment Republicans to fret publicly over how many seats the Tea Party "lost" in 2010. Republican senator Dick Lugar, who was first elected to the U.S. Senate in 1976—nearly four decades ago—blamed Tea Party activists for failing to win a Republican majority in the Senate in 2010: "Republicans lost the seats before in Nevada and New Jersey and Colorado where there were people who were claiming they wanted somebody who was more of their Tea Party aspect, but they killed off the Republican majority." [19]

Presumably, he meant to say Delaware, not New Jersey, but confusing two contiguous states is not the issue here. The question is, what majority? Before the Tea Party, Senate Republicans faced a seemingly insurmountable challenge just blocking a Democratic supermajority. "We've not only got to play defense," said NRSC chief honcho Cornyn, "we've got to claw our way back in 2010. It'll be a huge challenge." [20] Now a net pickup of seven seats was *our bad,* I suppose some bizarre form of Keynesian math in reverse.

Maybe that's the only argument an establishmentarian like Lugar has left, facing his own Tea Party challenger in 2012. Channeling onetime Republicans Charlie Crist and Arlen Specter, Lugar tells CNN he believes, "If I was not the nominee it might be lost. A Republican majority in the Senate is very important, and Republicans who are running for reelection ought to be supported by people who want to see that majority. I think the majority of Tea Party people understand that too." [21]

A SEAT AT THE TABLE

THIS INSURGENT GRASSROOTS MOVEMENT HAD OUTPERFORMED EX-
pectations from day one, accomplishing things that few within the
establishment had imagined possible. First a protest movement was
predicted to fade with the passage of Obamacare. Now an organic
GOTV machine was expected to disassemble, like a typical political
campaign, on November 3, 2010. This latest prediction was particularly shortsighted, given that many activists had first cut their grassroots teeth fighting legislative proposals like the spending stimulus
and the health care takeover.

Maybe they just wanted us to go away? But that's not what happened.

Fighting a bad idea was one thing. Coming up with better ideas
and drafting specific legislation is on a whole new level. We had a
seat at the table, but the cards were still stacked against change. The
right policies were defined by the Contract from America, creating an
incredibly cohesive set of policy priorities for the new freshman class.
But the legislative path from where we stood on November 3, 2010,
to where we need to be required a continued evolution and increased
sophistication in Tea Partier tactics.

How do we repeal and replace Obamacare? How do we cut spending and reform entitlements, balance the budget, and get our fiscal
house in order? How do we rein in the power of politicians, government employees, corporate rent-seekers, and an army of special interests that have enriched themselves at taxpayer expense?

While it is true that Republicans only controlled, in Speaker John
Boehner's words, "one half of one third of the government," [22] it is undeniable that the Tea Party started setting the agenda and shaping the
conversation even before the Class of 2010 was sworn into office. The
dominant conversation in Washington, D.C., quickly became one
about how best to cut deficit spending and get the burden of big gov-

ernment off the backs of workers and job creators. The freshman class was demanding as much because the citizenry demanded it of them.

The debate was now how much to cut; not how much more to spend. The debate wasn't about whether we should repeal Obamacare; it was now about the best way to replace it and restore individual control over your family's health care decisions.

Typically, freshman legislators are little heard from, assigned to backwater committees and expected to follow their leadership, particularly in the House of Representatives. But the sheer size of the freshman class, and the now indisputable power of the grassroots movement behind them, forced a rewriting of the rules of the game. The largest freshman class in seventy years was given unprecedented representation on the most important committees that affect spending, taxes, regulation, and new entitlements like Obamacare. "Most of the 22 House Republican freshmen-to-be selected to sit on much coveted, A-list committees won their races with Tea Party backing," the *Hill* reported. "The House Republican Steering Committee last week added the incoming members to the rosters of four powerful committees: Appropriations, Ways and Means, Energy and Commerce and Financial Services." [23]

The House leadership also decided to include two freshmen at the leadership table, and the historic class elected Tim Scott as one who would meet weekly with the Elected Leadership Committee. "In just eight months," Columbia's *State* would later report, "Rep. Tim Scott has skyrocketed from state legislator to House Republican freshman class leader who stood up to his party bosses in high-profile debt talks and is heading his party's attack on federal economic bureaucrats." [24]

Tea Party politicians were not just shaping the conversation, though. They were proposing solutions that focused on increasing freedom and putting decision-making power back where it belongs, with the people. Cutting against the progressive grain in Washington, these young legislators started asking the question: How do we move power and money back home, out of Washington, D.C.?

MIND YOUR PLACE

EVEN BEFORE THE 2010 ELECTION, AS IT BECAME CLEAR THAT THE TEA Party would have a big impact on the results and many Tea Party-aligned candidates would win, some in the media shifted the conversation away from Tea Party electoral success, and instead began to question whether elected Tea Party-aligned senators and congressmen would be effective in implementing conservative policies. Mike Lee, who would soon be elected by Utahns to the U.S. Senate, faced such a critique from his hometown newspaper, the *Deseret Morning News*. The newspaper reported that while Lee was proclaiming he would bring "radical reform," including a Balanced Budget Amendment, it was likely he would have little impact:

> Political insiders say it's unlikely [Mike Lee will] do much of significance in the Senate, at least in his first term. In the Senate, seniority governs everything: the committees you sit on, the arms you can twist to get votes, the bills you get to sponsor. "Mike will have a choice of joining with a few like-minded people to try to have more strength and power in numbers, or to work with a greater number of Republicans and Democrats on certain issues that will allow him to have a far greater influence on many more issues," says Kirk Jowers of the Hinckley Institute of Politics at the University of Utah. "I hope he chooses the latter." The question, Jowers says, is whether Mike Lee wants to make a difference, or whether he simply wants to make a point.[25]

While many in the press doubted that the new freshman class could make a difference, the Washington establishment and lobbyist class quickly began setting off alarms, manning the castle turrets, and preparing for battle as if against an invading force. Former Republican Senate majority leader Trent Lott, now a lobbyist, vividly illustrated this mind-set when he told the *Washington Post*: "We don't need a lot of Jim DeMint disciples. As soon as they get here, we need to co-opt them." [26]

This was how it had always worked in D.C., of course, and there is a natural tendency for power to corrupt, as Lord Acton famously warned. But something was different this time. The quality of the freshmen was markedly higher than average, in terms of their commitment to individual freedom and limited government. More important, there was now a constituency back home that was serving as an effective counter balance to the corrupting forces inside the Beltway. While Lott's comment reflected how out-of-touch the mainstream media and the Republican establishment were about the strength of the Tea Party movement and the conviction of Tea Party candidates like Mike Lee, it was a prediction validated by history. When Americans rose up in 1994 to throw the bums out, they promptly went back to what they were doing before, assuming that the election had fixed the problem. Lott's comment illustrates the worst kind of cynicism— that candidates like Mike Lee were just saying what needed to be said to get elected and would be malleable and could be "co-opted" once they achieved their self-interested goals at the ballot box. That, after all, is what Trent Lott had done. He came to Washington to do good, and ended up doing really well. For himself. Such a perspective fits with other establishment Republicans who did exactly that to get elected and reelected.

But Mike Lee was a different breed of political animal. As one of the senator's aides explained: "If it's perceived you're challenging authority, someone [in leadership] will put their arm around you and say, 'Hey son, that's not the way it works around here.' But Mike Lee doesn't care if that's the way it works around here." [27] Indeed, Mike Lee would politely, respectfully, directly, and publicly challenge the authority and hierarchy of the Republican establishment in his first few weeks in office. Before he was even sworn into office, Lee, a constitutional lawyer, had started drafting a Balanced Budget Amendment to the Constitution that would become the new gold standard of budget reforms, *both inside and outside the Washington Beltway.*

AMENDING THE CONSTITUTION

AS A YOUNG ECONOMIST AT THE U.S. CHAMBER OF COMMERCE IN the early 1990s, I had been in charge of federal budget policy and budget process reforms like the BBA. There was a heated debate back then about the proper structure of a BBA. Was the goal to balance at any rate of spending, even if it meant constitutionally mandated tax increases? Or was the goal to eliminate deficit spending and the unchecked growth of government, reflective of the clear intentions of the Founders? I was unambiguously in the second camp, and there was a pitched battle then between those legislators who advocated a simple BBA, which allowed a simple majority to raise taxes to balance the budget, and those of us who believed that any amendment to the Constitution had to be done right, or not done at all. We wanted "supermajority" limits on taxes, spending, and the size of government.

The simple BBA was then championed by the late Democratic senator Paul Simon of Illinois. Simon wanted to grow the size of the federal government, and he wanted the constitutional mandate to raise the taxes to finance that growth. He was an unabashed big government progressive. In his failed 1988 run for the Democratic nomination for president, Simon distinguished himself by running *to the left* of other contenders, including Jesse Jackson, Al Gore, and Michael Dukakis, by saying, "I am willing to use the tools of government to work on the problems we have."[28] According to a 1987 *Houston Chronicle* account of his campaign:

> Simon, a traditional Democratic liberal but one who has advocated a mandatory balanced federal budget, was reminiscent of unsuccessful 1984 Democratic nominee Walter F. Mondale in bringing up the politically sensitive issue of taxes. . . . Simon

said he is the only presidential candidate of either party who voted against both the federal income tax cuts enacted in 1981 and 1986. He said the tax cuts bloated the federal deficit and chiefly benefited the wealthy. . . . Simon has supported some tax increases and says more revenue increases are needed. Full employment, through a New Deal–style public works job program, is Simon's idea of one way to stimulate the economy and raise needed revenue.

Simon said in his announcement: "I stand here as one who is not running away from the Democratic tradition of caring and dreaming. I do not want the Democratic Party to forget its heritage in order to become more acceptable to the wealthy and powerful. One Republican Party is enough." . . . One of Simon's pet legislative projects is a bill to create a Guaranteed Job Opportunity Program under which public works jobs would be provided to anyone who wants to work.[29]

Oddly enough, the simple BBA long advocated by Simon was picked up by "conservative" Republican senator Orrin Hatch in 1997. His version was almost identical to Simon's progressive legislation in 1992 and 1994, requiring only a simple majority for a tax hike.[30]

On January 26, 2011, now a six-term senator from Utah and one of the most powerful and longest-serving Republicans in the Senate, Hatch introduced a new version of the Balanced Budget Amendment. This was part of a conspicuous effort to rehabilitate his conservative credentials in Utah in the wake of his colleague's defeat at the Utah Republican Convention the previous spring. Needless to say, Hatch's 2011 version was better than his 1997 version, requiring a two-thirds majority vote for a tax hike, but it was flawed in other sections. Hatch's 2011 budget amendment capped spending at 20 percent of GDP, allowing Congress to exceed this percentage with a two-thirds majority. Twenty percent is just too high, and would lock into the Constitution the expansion of government taken on under the Obama (and Bush) spending sprees. It also allowed Congress to get out of implementing a balanced budget, by raising a simple majority vote based on a vaguely defined "threat to national security." There was also no requirement of a supermajority vote to increase the debt ceiling.[31] Hatch's early list of cosponsors reads like a Who's Who of Republican establishment politicians, including Senators John McCain (Ariz.) and Olympia Snowe (Maine).

Unknown to Hatch, Senator-elect Mike Lee had chosen not to follow the *Deseret Morning News'* suggestion that he should stay quiet as a freshman, and had already drafted his own version of the Balanced Budget Amendment. I had seen a draft of the young legislative entrepreneur's amendment in December 2010, and it was the best version I had seen, much better even than the ones I had supported in the early 1990s. It was airtight. Once sworn into office, Lee introduced his own legislation—just a week after Hatch's presentation, on February 3, 2011. Like Hatch's version, Lee's Balanced Budget Amendment included a two-thirds majority for any tax hike. But that's the only major similarity. Lee veered away from Hatch's version with a much more fiscally conservative approach. Lee's version included a spending cap at 18 percent of GDP (the postwar average, prior to the Bush-Obama spending spree) and required a two-thirds majority to raise the debt ceiling.[32] Mike Lee's list of cosponsors was much shorter than Hatch's, and included Senators Jim DeMint (S.C.), Rand Paul (Ky.), Marco Rubio (Fla.), and Pat Toomey (Pa.).

Why did Lee go against conventional wisdom on what the *National Journal* called Hatch's "signature issue"?[33] Lee explained that this was what he was elected to do. "I was elected in part on [pushing the BBA]. And I think it's the most important effort of this Congress, to get something like that done."[34]

On February 14, 2011, I spoke on a CPAC panel discussion of the BBA. At the last minute, Hatch had been added to the panel. Given that FreedomWorks had come out strongly in favor of the Lee approach, it was an interesting dynamic, to say the least. I reiterated my long-held view, having watched progressives like Paul Simon corrupt the concept of the BBA, that any amendment to the Constitution needs to be done the right way. After I spoke, the senior senator from Utah leaned over to speak to me. "The problem with an eighteen percent cap on spending," he said, "is that the Democrats won't go along with it."

This logic has been the problem all along. It demanded that a BBA needed to be "bipartisan," that we needed to work across party lines to get anything done. It makes no sense. Wasn't this reaching across party lines the very form of two-party collusion that caused our government's massive debt burden in the first place? Hatch himself had collaborated with Senator Edward Kennedy, the Liberal Lion from Massachusetts, in a major expansion of government-funded health care known as "S-CHIP" in 1997, the same year he picked up the cudgel for Paul Simon's progressive BBA. It all makes your head spin.

When it comes to drafting legislation, isn't a better approach wholly nonpartisan? Shouldn't legislation be drafted based on what is needed, not just on what would be acceptable to the very political forces that caused the problem you are attempting to fix?

That's the approach Lee had taken, the one that his hometown paper considered naive. Prior to the rise of the Tea Party movement, someone like Lee bucking authority would likely have been ignored by Hatch and the Republican establishment or even punished with poor committee assignments and other repercussions.

But the rise of the Tea Party movement changed everything. As Lee noted prior to his impending election: "Can one person make a difference out of 100? No. But I won't be just one person. I'll be aligned with a number of other people who share these same principles. They can ignore one person, but they can't ignore 10." [35] Lee was right. He was not ignored. After several rounds of negotiations, Hatch accepted the major parts of Lee's Balanced Budget Amendment. The new version of the BBA, agreed to by Lee and Hatch, included Lee's 18 percent cap on spending as well as a three-fifths majority requirement for any debt ceiling increase. Additionally, Lee strengthened Hatch's waiver for vague "threats to national security." Rather than a simple majority, the newly revised Amendment required a three-fifths majority, in the event of "imminent and serious military threat[s] to national security," and permitted a waiver for "the specific excess of outlays for that fiscal year made necessary by the identified military conflict."[36] This compromise bill was fully endorsed by the forty-seven members of the Senate Republican Conference.[37] After just a few weeks in office, Lee had accomplished something that no other Republican had ever accomplished, uniting the entire Senate Republican caucus around the right BBA.

How did Lee succeed? Part of his ultimate success at the negotiating table was due to his legislative entrepreneurship. He was willing to stick his neck out and fight for what he believed in, regardless of political consequences. And by taking such risks, he forced the Republican establishment to listen. Equally important was the strength of the Tea Party movement. Not only did Lee have a number of other senators, including Jim DeMint and Pat Toomey, stand up with him, but he had the majority of American voters standing with him as well.

Of course, there was another dynamic at play. Senate Republicans, starting with Hatch himself, were worried about a possible Tea Party primary challenge against the senior senator from Utah. As *Politico* reported, "Twice [in March 2011], Hatch voted with Lee and a handful of other Republicans against short-term spending bills because their cuts weren't deep enough. Some of Hatch's GOP colleagues have watched with amusement as the veteran seemed to mimic the young senator who's gotten the attention of the base. 'You can't get a piece of paper between them,' a top GOP senator said with a laugh."[38]

Discerning the authentic from political artifice is a challenge inherent in politics. But now the facts about legislative history were available online, unfiltered, and easily accessed by mere citizens. There was a rebalancing of power going on, which was undermining the privileged access to the right information by insiders.

BY THE NUMBERS

OF COURSE, THE WHOLE DEBATE OVER A BALANCED BUDGET AMEND-
ment to the Constitution begs the question: How would *you* balance
the budget? This is a legitimate question, and many of us were rightly
skeptical about advocates of a BBA who never seemed to find specific
spending programs to cut or eliminate. The question had also taken
on a "gotcha" quality, used by reporters when interviewing grassroots
protesters, as if they were required to know the entire federal budget
chapter and verse before they could make the argument that government was spending too much money it did not have.

Indeed, every line item in the entire federal budget has a special
interest prepared to fight for a privileged position, subsidy, earmark,
or handout. Balancing the budget takes the courage of one's convictions, and the hope that the American people will stand with someone
willing to be honest, someone willing to outline priorities based on
what government can actually afford instead of the sum of all wants,
legitimate or otherwise.

The 2010 election sweep not only shifted the gavels in Congress, it also elevated a number of legislative entrepreneurs who
would transform the all-important budget debate. The young Paul
Ryan of Wisconsin now chaired the House Budget Committee. And
the new freshman class included a number of legislative entrepreneurs, eager to translate one of the key planks of the Contract from
America—"Restore fiscal responsibility and constitutionally limited
government"—into substantive, detailed legislation.

Understanding that "budget drives policy," many of the new freshman class began looking ahead to the big budget fight they knew
would take place in the spring. The new majority's first budget needed
to be game-changing. But instead of waiting passively for their leaders to come up with a plan, these entrepreneurs decided to get ahead
of the curve and shape the outcome themselves, by putting together
their own plans. They rolled up their sleeves, fired up their spread-

sheet programs, and dug into the eye-glazing minutiae of the federal budget.

Budget fights are inherently political, and budget politics isn't a game for the faint of heart. It requires courage, hard work, and discipline. Shifting the entire Washington debate from dramatic spending increases to dramatic spending reductions is a huge undertaking. You can't balance a $3.6 trillion budget, 40 percent of which is borrowed, by raising taxes, trimming around the edges, or eliminating "waste." You have to zero out dozens of agencies and hundreds of programs, and, yes, even eliminate some cabinet-level departments. You have to get Uncle Sam out of whole lines of business. Every item you identify for elimination is sure to be ringed with a bodyguard of vested interests, poised to repulse any threat. Every program, you'll be warned, is a "sacred cow" that simply cannot be touched lest the world end and the heavens fall.

A few days after the new Congress convened, Dick Armey and I took to the pages of the *Wall Street Journal* to offer our own suggestions for "What Congress Should Cut." [39] We laid out a bold agenda, specifying more than $3 trillion in immediate program cuts, reforms, and eliminations. Or at least it seemed bold at the time.

We began by pointing out that if Congress simply returned to the baseline before the supposedly "temporary" stimulus bill of 2009, $177 billion per year would be saved, and $748 billion over ten years. And if we were to go back to 2007, the beginning of the Pelosi Congress, the savings would be even bigger: $374 billion a year, or $1.56 trillion over a decade. Under realistic assumptions, repealing Obamacare would save an additional $898 billion over ten years. Still more savings, we noted, could be realized by cutting the cord between taxpayer wallets and Fannie Mae and Freddie Mac, whose bailouts had already cost taxpayers more than $127 billion and could end up costing as much as $1 trillion. Then we listed a series of additional ideas:

- Scrap the Department of Commerce and the Department of Housing and Urban Development ($550 billion). Corporate welfare agencies, HUD, and Commerce serve mostly as giant ATM machines for private interests.

- Scale back the number of government employees to fiscal year 2008 ($35 billion).
- Eliminate subsidies for ethanol and unproven energy technology ($170 billion over ten years). These wasteful subsidies merely drive up food and energy costs.
- End farm subsidies ($290 billion). Washington should never have gotten into the business of trying to manipulate crop prices and output.
- Repeal Davis-Bacon labor rules ($60 billion). These Depression-era rules require that federal contractors be paid exorbitant, union-scale wages.
- End urban mass transit grants ($52 billion).
- Privatize air traffic control, as other nations have done ($38 billion).
- Privatize Amtrak and end rail subsidies ($31 billion).
- Reform federal worker retirement ($18 billion).
- Retire AmeriCorps ($10 billion). Why are we paying people to volunteer?
- Shutter the Small Business Administration ($14 billion).

Defense, which represents a fifth of the budget, also needed to be on the table. Having been doubled in size during the Bush years, the Pentagon undoubtedly suffers from significant waste and duplication that should be cut. Our suggestion: implement the savings of $145 billion, over five years, proposed by Defense Secretary Robert Gates, who served in that capacity under Presidents Bush and Obama.

Not having room in 900 words for a comprehensive approach to entitlements (I attempt to take such an approach in the following chapters of this book)—56 percent of the annual budget and growing—we simply accepted reforms based on Paul Ryan's pathbreaking "Roadmap for America's Future." By moving toward a powerful, consumer-driven approach, we estimated that taxpayers could save $370 billion a year by 2020.

"We've identified almost $3 trillion in real spending cuts over a decade," we wrote, "and have only scratched the surface." What an understatement that turned out to be. It wasn't long before our $3 trillion in "bold" cuts was looking downright timid, next to the budget plans emanating from the eager entrepreneurs on the Hill, such as Senator Rand Paul.[40] Never having been outflanked by a sitting U.S. senator when it comes to questions of fiscal responsibility, I was slightly stunned. But I was more proud than stunned. Once again, the men and women of grassroots America, along with their new proxy representation seated at the table, had beaten expectations and Washington, D.C.

First out of the chute was the Paul Ryan budget plan, which would balance the budget over thirty years mostly by capping annually appropriated spending and reforming Medicare and other entitlements. Meanwhile, freshman Mick Mulvaney—who had just knocked off the longtime Democratic incumbent and revered Budget Committee chairman, John Spratt—was working to compile an even bolder alternative plan for the House conservative caucus, the Republican Study Committee. The RSC Plan would reach balance a full twenty years sooner than Ryan's, mostly because it cut more deeply and would slowly raise the Social Security retirement age to seventy.

Over in the Senate, Pat Toomey soon put out a plan very similar to Mulvaney's, while his fellow freshman, Rand Paul, trumped everyone with a plan to balance the budget in just five years. What distinguishes Paul's approach is that, alone among these plans, it specifies whole cabinet departments for elimination, specifically, HUD, Commerce, Energy, and Education.

All these plans would repeal Obamacare, reform Medicare, block-grant Medicaid, reduce the top tax rate to 25 percent (from the current 35 percent), shrink the government as a share of the economy, and stop the growth of the national debt. In terms of ten-year savings, the plans stacked up roughly as follows: Ryan: $6 trillion; Mulvaney: $9 trillion; Toomey: $7 trillion; and Paul: $10 trillion. Recall where we began this conversation: $3 trillion.

In April, the House passed Paul Ryan's budget after rejecting several alternatives, including Mulvaney's (narrowly). And while Harry Reid's Senate couldn't pass a budget, Paul Ryan's at least garnered forty Senate votes. Compare that to the zero that went to President Obama's. Not one Senate Democrat would vote for the Obama plan, which would have increased ten-year spending by $2.3 trillion and taxes by more than $1 trillion. By May, President Obama was demanding a massive, $2 trillion increase in the debt ceiling, without any real spending reforms.

I know what you are thinking. No one's plan was passed. So what was accomplished, exactly? Two things. First, we stopped $2.3 trillion in new spending. Second, we created a Republican consensus to fully repeal Obamacare, something that seemed implausible prior to the 2010 elections. Both accomplishments were inconceivable back in 2008 after the passage of TARP, or in the days after the Obama inauguration in 2009.

We were slowly turning the ship of state. But not quickly enough. Like the *Titanic,* we were still headed full steam toward an iceberg that could sink us all.

BUDGETING FROM THE BOTTOM UP

THAT'S ABOUT THE TIME WHEN A MEETING OF GRASSROOTS LEADERS came up with the idea of a Tea Party Debt Commission—a panel of citizens that would go out and listen to the American people and give them a sounding board on the budget and debt crises.[41] The commission's report would put to rest the argument that our movement isn't serious about specific spending cuts or that we "have no plan." The only way we will ever reduce the debt and balance the budget, we had concluded, is when America beats Washington and Tea Party activists take over the process. Real reform will only happen from the bottom up.

In late June 2011, at a Washington gathering of about 150 Tea Party leaders, we developed the commission concept. By late August, we had found a dozen volunteers to serve on the commission, at their own expense. We were in business.

The Tea Party Debt Commission was, in a sense, our answer to the "supercommittee," that unique and remarkable creature of the Beltway debt ceiling deal. While the supercommittee was composed of twelve powerful Washington insiders charged with trimming the budget around the edges, the Tea Party commission would be a dozen shirtsleeve Americans—volunteer activists and leaders from across the country—who would come together to help save our country from a Greek-style debt collapse. Whereas the supercommittee would be superprivileged—its work product would receive fast-track consideration, a guaranteed up-or-down vote in both houses, no amendments, no extended debate, and no filibusters (in other words, it would be one of the most powerful congressional committees in the history of the republic)—the Tea Party Debt Commission would succeed or fail based solely on the merits and appeal of its ideas.

As we noted earlier, the supercommittee failed to reach any agreements, and quietly slipped into obscurity. Even if it had succeeded, it would have reduced spending by a mere drop in the bucket, just $1.2 trillion over ten years, from a steeply rising baseline. The Tea Party Debt Commission, by contrast, had set for itself the much more ambitious goal of reducing spending by $9 trillion—nearly eight times as much. Why that particular target? Because that's the amount that lets you balance the budget in less than ten years while also stopping the national debt from growing as a share of the economy. Right now, the nation's accumulated debt is equal to nearly 100 percent of one year of economic output. Merely $1.2 trillion in savings does nothing to keep the debt from growing to disaster levels (for Greece, it was around 150 percent of the economy) within the next decade. Or, to put it another way, the supercommittee would have merely reduced ten-year spending from $44 trillion to $43 trillion, a mere 2.3 percent. Our $9 trillion goal, by contrast, would reduce ten-year spending from $44 trillion to $34 trillion, a *23 percent* reduction.

After four months of field hearings around the country and a massive online survey, the TPDC released its proposal, which it dubbed the "Tea Party Budget."[42] The plan achieves all its goals, and then some, incorporating good ideas from thousands of activists and survey participants, as well as some of the best ideas in the budget plans of Mulvaney, Ryan, Toomey, and Paul.

The Tea Party Budget builds on a compellingly simple framework popularized by Representative Connie Mack of Florida, who saw that by cutting federal spending by 1 percent a year in real terms, we can balance the budget within a decade. Mack's "One Percent Spending Reduction Act," also known as the "One Cent Solution" or the "Mack Penny Plan," does just what its name implies. It reduces overall federal outlays minus interest by 1 percent a year until the budget is balanced, and then caps total spending at 18 percent of national output.

Building on this simple framework, the Tea Party Budget spells out a detailed, year-by-year path to balance. The plan:

- Reduces federal spending by $9.7 trillion over ten years, as opposed to the president's plan to *increase* spending by $2.3 trillion.
- Closes a historically large budget gap, equal to almost one-tenth of our economy.
- Balances the budget in just four years, and keeps it balanced, without tax hikes.
- Shrinks the federal government from 24 percent of the economy—a level exceeded only in World War II—to about 16 percent, in line with the postwar norm.
- Stops the growth of the debt, and begins paying it down, with a goal of eliminating it within this generation.

To achieve those goals, the plan:

- Repeals Obamacare in total.
- Eliminates four cabinet agencies—Energy, Education, Commerce, and HUD—and reduces or privatizes many others, including EPA, TSA, Fannie Mae, and Freddie Mac.
- Ends farm subsidies, returns student loans to the private sector, and stops foreign aid to countries that don't support us.
- Saves Social Security and greatly improves future benefits by shifting ownership and control from government to individuals, through new personal saving accounts.
- Gives Medicare seniors the right to opt into the congressional health care plan.
- Suspends pension contributions and COLAs for members of Congress whenever the budget is in deficit.

"In short," write the citizen commissioners, "the Tea Party Budget enables us to end chronic deficits and pay down debt, while moving us back toward the kind of limited, constitutional government intended by our Founding Fathers. And it does all this without raising taxes. With these reforms," they continue, "we can unburden the productive sector and get back to robust economic growth and rising living standards for all. With this plan, everyone benefits."

How far we've come from 2009.

But for all these successes, it is painfully clear that the fight is before us, that the forces of centralized government are still playing the game in Washington from a position of strength.

All the solutions laid out in the following chapters share a common foundation: they reflect the philosophy of decentralization that will restore America as an exceptional nation based on free individuals. We need to replace top-down dictates with bottom-up control. But beating Washington is not a onetime event. If you understand and believe in the power of smaller government and more individual freedom, you know that the hostile takeover of Washington requires continued vigilance of the people, for the people.

CHAPTER 7

LOOTERS AND MOOCHERS

When you see that money is flowing to those who deal,
not in goods, but in favors—when you see that men
get richer by graft and by pull than by work . . . you
may know that your society is doomed.
—Ayn Rand, *Atlas Shrugged*

ONE OF THE MOST PERSISTENT MYTHS IN MODERN POLITICS, CONSID-
ered by the mainstream media to be as reliable as the laws of gravity, is
the belief that corporate America is a staunch defender of free markets
and unfettered entrepreneurship. A corollary of this lie is a second one:
Republicans, as advocates of limited government, are "pro-business,"
and Democrats, as defenders of the common man, are populist watch-
dogs against corporate greed.

These lies may be politically convenient to those who employ
them, but they are lies nonetheless.

Do you believe these lies? I wouldn't really blame you if you did,
because they are reinforced daily in the news. Today, this precon-

ceived storyline substitutes for hard-earned investigative journalism. Likewise, you would be hard-pressed to find a single speech by Barack Obama that did not set up these caricatures and then knock them down. For our progressive president, public policy always involves more benevolent government, selflessly implemented by better bureaucrats, to stop the greed and excesses of corporations in unregulated markets. But for Republicans in bed with business interests, the story goes, President Obama would lead us to the promised land of limited corporate power and honest government guardians of "the little guy."

Great story, but it's never true.

I learned the hard way about my own naïveté when I worked as a budget economist at the U.S. Chamber of Commerce in the early 1990s. When I took the job, I assumed that the world's largest business organization, with "The Spirit of Enterprise" emblazoned across the top of its logo, was just that: an unwavering defender against the encroachments of big government on free enterprise. I suppose I knew better going in, but conventional wisdom sometimes gets the best of all of us. I left the Chamber several years later with a more realistic view of how the world works, soon after that supposedly staunch defender of free enterprise endorsed President Bill Clinton's attempted government takeover of the health care system. As I watched in disbelief, many of the biggest member corporations saw an opportunity to shift their costs onto someone else—consumers, taxpayers, and smaller upstart competitors. Pharmaceutical interests and health insurance companies saw a competitive advantage in rewriting the rules of the game to their advantage. All this was a noxious stew of "rent protection" and shameless "rent-seeking." These interests dominated the Chamber's health care policy-making process, pushing the "spirit of enterprise" to endorse a government takeover of one-sixth of the U.S. economy.

In 2009, those same corporate interests would shift their policy-making influence from 1615 H Street, the Chamber of Commerce headquarters, and migrate across Lafayette Park to 1600 Pennsylvania Avenue, where they would help a Democratic president write the provisions in Obamacare to their own benefit.

In truth, the struggle of individual freedom against the power of big government has never been about Republicans versus Democrats or big corporations versus the public good. It has always been about Them versus Us: insiders in charge, ensconced behind closed doors, versus the shareholders, outside. From the time of the East India Company and entrenched New York business interests in bed with the British Empire in the 1770s, it has been a struggle between the insiders who conspire against our freedoms, and the working folks on the streets of Boston, who will always pay the price.

The Founders were keenly aware of these facts of life. Sam Adams had targeted the New York delegation of the Continental Congress with grassroots pressure from their constituents, literally goading them into signing the Declaration of Independence. They didn't want to, because New York had made its comfortable accommodations with the British Parliament, but grassroots power from the bottom up made them feel the heat of accountability. They were the crony capitalists of the day, growing fat on government-granted monopoly power.

Adam Smith, ably representing the ethos that defined America's founding in 1776's *The Wealth of Nations*, wrote of the tendency of those in business to conspire. It's human nature. But the real danger, he warned, was the potential of "the law" to "facilitate" the collusion of businesses:

> People of the same trade seldom meet together, even for merriment and diversion, but the conversation ends in a conspiracy against the public, or in some contrivance to raise prices. It is impossible indeed to prevent such meetings, by any law which either could be executed, or would be consistent with liberty or justice. But though the law cannot hinder people of the same trade from sometimes assembling together, it ought to do

nothing to facilitate such assemblies; much less to render them necessary.[1]

AN OFFER YOU CAN'T REFUSE

WASHINGTON, D.C., IS THE TOWN OF "GRAFT AND PULL," AND ITS reach is expanding. What Ayn Rand understood, and what the Left would rather have the masses forget, is that when government becomes a favor factory—doling out exemptions, stimulus funds, and tax breaks—the private sector will come. As long as government remains in the business of redistributing wealth—hurting other people and taking their stuff—business interests will find it irresistible to come to the seat of power, find "a man in Washington," and compete through the political process instead of delivering the best product to consumers.

Rand called those who engaged in these cozy relationships "looters and moochers." The moochers are the corporate bigwigs who feed from the public trough of political largesse that the looters in government have stolen from the people. In other words, while the heroes in *Atlas Shrugged* are indeed the entrepreneurs who "carry the world," the villains are also industrialists who know that the best way to beat their competition when they fail to meet the demands of consumers is to go to Washington.

Like characters in Rand's novel, modern-day corporate executives ply their trade in the political arena, beating a path to Washington, D.C. Once inside the Beltway, CEOs and their armies of lobbyists collude with committee chairmen for mutual gains, writing regulatory barriers to entry to boost both the bottom line and government power. And while I'm about to blast them for doing so, why shouldn't they? Washington politicians—in both parties—have essentially put up an Open for Business sign to companies willing to deal. There are strings attached. A partner in Washington is like a business partnership with Don Vito Corleone in *The Godfather*: sometimes the committee chairman comes calling on you and sometimes you go, hat in hand, to see the chairman. Either way, expect someone to make an offer you can't refuse.

IMAGINATIVE MOOCHING AT WORK

EXHIBIT 1: JEFF IMMELT, CEO OF GENERAL ELECTRIC, PRESIDENT Obama's "jobs czar," and corporate rent-seeker. Soon after Barack Obama was sworn in as president in 2009, Immelt informed his shareholders that the economics of the future had shifted fundamentally, away from freedom and the accountability of competition to serve consumer needs, toward something else entirely. "The interaction between government and business will change forever," said the CEO. "In a reset economy, the government will be a regulator; and also an industry policy champion, a financier, and a key partner."[2] This from the storied American company founded by Thomas Edison, inventor of the incandescent lightbulb. In 2007, the struggling corporation had successfully lobbied for a government ban of that ubiquitous bulb. The company wanted to shift consumer demand to its compact fluorescent bulbs made in China, which was part of its big political bet on green energy—or as its message shop put it, GE's "ecomagination." Eventually, the company hoped to force consumers to buy a far more expensive, higher efficiency incandescent bulb.[3]

The "reset" GE business model includes a staff of over 900 tax experts and corporate lobbyists, who scour the tax code, support expansive new government regulations, and pursue lucrative government contracts to fatten their bottom line. Judging by the results, all those extra paychecks pay for themselves.

A 2011 ABC News report noted that GE had spent over $238 million on lobbying since 2000, more than any other company: "money that has helped GE gain access to the corridors of power and some of the most remote crevices of the governing process."[4] Between 2008 and 2010, GE was the top spender on lobbying, at over $84 million.[5]

And like so many companies, many GE employees have gone through the "revolving door" between lobbying and politics. Interestingly, a number of their employees made the somewhat more unusual move of leaving GE to take lower-paying public-sector jobs. What are they doing there?

And what does GE get for all this money and influence in the nation's capital? More business and a competitive edge in the marketplace. GE received more than $140 million in stimulus funds under 88 separate contracts.[6] And one-third of the 100 initial "smart-grid" grant recipients under the stimulus were GE clients.[7] As *Washington Examiner* columnist Tim Carney has noted, "Look at any major Obama policy initiative—healthcare reform, climate-change regulation, embryonic stem-cell research, infrastructure stimulus, electrical transmission smart-grids—and you'll find GE has set up shop, angling for a way to pocket government handouts, gain business through mandates, or profit from government regulation."[8]

In 2008, the GE political action committee contributed more than $1.5 million to federal campaigns, with 60 percent of it going to Democratic candidates.[9] This bias has nothing to do with ideology or party affiliation. What it means is that in 2008, GE made the smart bet that Democrats, and in particular Barack Obama, had a good chance of gaining power. And if you want a place at the table, you'd better put your money down.

All told, in 2010 corporate America spent more than $3.5 billion on hiring nearly 13,000 lobbyists,[10] whose main job is to secure tax breaks, regulatory waivers, contracts, and congressional investigations to tilt the market for those who hire them: Wall Street, Big Pharma, Big Insurance, and Big Business. For all these industries, good business leads through Washington. Rather than create products that better serve consumers, these companies spend valuable resources trying to sway policy in ways that hurt their consumers and their competitors while boosting their own position in the marketplace. Economists call this behavior rent-seeking. But let's call it what it is: crony capitalism. If you wonder why young people hold "capitalism" in such low regard, perhaps it's this low life trough feeding that the word now invokes in people's minds. Americans rightly hate what capitalism in America is becoming: an unholy alliance between big government and big business.

DUDE, WHERE'S MY BAILOUT?

THE TROUBLED ASSET RELIEF PROGRAM BAILOUT WAS PERHAPS THE most egregious example of this behavior, with the big banks foisting their losses onto taxpayers. This hit a nerve with the American public, waking them up, and ultimately creating the movement that became the Tea Party. Indeed, if one looks at the more recent protests of Occupy Wall Street, the root frustrations are the same—namely, Wall Street's cozy relationship with the government and the multimillion-dollar bonuses for corporate executives who have used Washington to force taxpayers to subsidize their losses.

The problem is that Occupy Wall Street learns the wrong lessons from this arrangement. What they don't see is the root cause of the problem: too much government. As monetary economist Gerald O'Driscoll argues, there is now an incestuous relationship between the two: "Business succeeds by getting along with politicians and regulators. . . . We call that system not the free-market, but crony capitalism. It owes more to Benito Mussolini than to Adam Smith." [11] The trend is global. *The Economist* calls "State Capitalism" the new way of economic organization, one that squeezes individual freedom out of the equation. How ominous is this trend? "A striking number of governments, particularly in the emerging world, are learning how to use the market to promote political ends. The invisible hand of the market is giving way to the visible, and often authoritarian, hand of state capitalism." [12]

The proliferation of words to describe what's going on is bewildering, but also enlightening. Mussolini sought government control of the means of production, a textbook definition of "fascism." One man's "state capitalism" is another's definition of "progress." "Socialism" replaces private ownership with government ownership of the means of production. Today we call all this "progressive."

Call it whatever you want. Me, I'm still clinging to my freedom.

The Occupy Wall Street movement ignores the political power of big business to effectively lobby government for favors. Their solution—placing more power in the hands of government and more economic decisions in Washington—will only encourage more bad behavior. When politics, rather than individuals freely acting in a marketplace, is used to make important economic decisions, those with the most political power win. And it is clear that those with the power in Washington are those who can afford to hire the lawyers and lobbyists needed to twist legislation and regulation in their favor.

Are you like GE, with 900 tax experts and lobbyists acting on your behalf in Washington? The business of government, unlike the private economy, is booming. There are endless examples of corporate interests evading market forces through government protection. As the housing market unraveled, Fannie Mae chose Franklin Raines, former Office of Management and Budget chief under President Clinton, to be its CEO. Clearly, political pull was more important than addressing the structural problems in the government-induced housing bubble. Ultimately, Fannie Mae and Freddie Mac were bailed out, with estimates of the final price tag topping one trillion taxpayer dollars.[13] And that's how political markets work: it's all based on your pull in Washington, not on your economic performance.

These days large swaths of the economy are in the hands of the government, including such critical sectors as health care, energy, and financial services. The Obama administration's response to the jobless economy has been to expand government control even further. As Robert Higgs has documented, every crisis provides government an opportunity to grow. Unfortunately, the size of government rarely recedes to pre-crisis levels.[14] Businesses, in turn, simply follow the money. With government's hands in so many sectors, corporate America couldn't ignore Washington even if it wanted to.

But, at a fundamental level, this transition toward a more expansive government does little to alter the inherent behavior of individuals; self-interest is an aspect of human behavior, and there is no reason to assume that it evaporates when a government entity supplants the market in various sectors of the economy. Given the track record of government action—from campaign contributions that shaped legislative outcomes to the blatant misuse of government funds as in the Solyndra case—greed feeds on the benevolent claims of progressive policies. Only the decentralized nature of the market mitigates and minimizes the corrosive aspects of greed in ways that centralized authority never could.

Occupy Wall Street and others calling for greater government control ignore this fundamental aspect of human nature and somehow assume that government officials are selfless arbiters of the public good. Call it the myth of the benevolent bureaucrat. Occupy Wall Street constantly points to market failure, while ignoring any potential for government failure. Economist Harold Demsetz calls this the Nirvana fallacy, when a real, imperfect market is compared to an imaginary but ideal government.[15]

Remember that government power is, at best, a zero-sum game. Resources are allocated by taking from one group to give to another. Taxes collected are spent by the government on particular programs that benefit particular people, usually to satisfy a particular interest. When we turn to the government for resource allocation, we leave the world of voluntary transactions and turn to a world where political power and special interests determine outcomes. And in this world, the lobbyists and corporate deal makers—the moochers—have every incentive to seek favors from the central planners—the looters.

CARTERNOMICS

Unfortunately, government planning in practice is seldom a zero-sum game. Because of unseen consequences, the lives of people, like those who heat their homes and drive to work every morning, are diminished by misallocations caused by the collusion of public and private interests. Energy markets in the United States, for instance, have long been plagued by government intervention, with little benefit to show for it. Consider this: the U.S. Department of Energy was created in 1977 with an explicit mandate to make America energy independent. President Jimmy Carter, presuming that government oversight, from the top down, could better manage the problem, famously lectured the American people in a televised address that year:

> Our decision about energy will test the character of the American people and the ability of the President and the Congress to govern. This difficult effort will be the "moral equivalent of war"—except that we will be uniting our efforts to build and not destroy.
>
> The oil and natural gas we rely on for 75 percent of our energy are running out. In spite of increased effort, domestic production has been dropping steadily at about 6 percent a year. Imports have doubled in the last five years. Our nation's independence of economic and political action is becoming increasingly constrained. Unless profound changes are made to lower oil consumption, we now believe that early in the 1980s the world will be demanding more oil than it can produce.[16]

How did it turn out? The only thing that this government plan and the Department of Energy have succeeded in creating is more politicized energy markets. Federal energy policy today is a train wreck of tax credits, mandates, regulatory roadblocks, and subsidies, all guided by business interests looking to game the system, distorting the marketplace, and making it difficult to expand the nation's energy supplies and deal with the energy demands of the future. But one thing is certain. If you want to produce energy, you will need to catch a flight to Washington first to talk to the man in charge.

By any standard, federal energy policy has been ineffective in promoting a diverse portfolio of abundant and reliable energy. Today the United States imports nearly half of its petroleum.[17] The price of gasoline has reached record highs and domestic oil production, which fell 17 percent during the Clinton years, remains weak because vast areas of the United States have been deemed off-limits to exploration. The development of natural gas and deposits of low-sulfur coal has been prohibited because of National Park designations and other federal land-use restrictions. Meanwhile, the Environmental Protection Agency has declared war on coal, one of the nation's most abundant energy resources.

Rather than removing government barriers to new energy innovations, the Obama administration continues to use government to promote a particular vision of energy. In this case, it is so-called green energy, an attempt to supplant carbon-based fuels with green technologies such as solar power and wind power. Remember Van Jones? He was, briefly, the man in charge, the "green jobs czar" responsible for planning, from the top down, a transition to "green-collar jobs." To achieve these goals, the administration is aggressively pursuing rules and regulations that will artificially increase the price of carbon-based fuels while providing subsidies to greener fuels. In fact, Obama's stimulus bill triggered what one reporter termed a "gold rush" for energy subsidies.[18] One renewable energy executive said, "I have never seen anything that I have had to do in my 20 years in the power industry that involved less risk than these projects," in an interview with the *New York Times*. "It is just filling the desert with panels."[19]

Of course, this means that government has to choose which businesses are worthy of its largesse. "The government support—which includes loan guarantees, cash grants and contracts that require electric customers to pay higher rates—largely eliminated the risk to the private investors and almost guaranteed them large profits for years to come," reported the *New York Times* in November 2011. "The beneficiaries include financial firms like Goldman Sachs and Morgan Stanley, conglomerates like General Electric, utilities like Exelon and NRG—even Google."[20] Money was moving out the door as fast as it could be processed. Which brings us back to Solyndra.

The Solyndra fiasco is a clear case of what happens when government tries to pick winners and losers. But it's also an example of what happens when government does the bidding of business. In the novel *Atlas Shrugged*, Ayn Rand describes the underhanded machinations of a failing industrialist, Orren Boyle, a steel producer who cannot compete with his more efficient rivals. Boyle seeks, and receives, favored treatment from Wesley Mouch, lobbyist turned administration bureaucrat at the Economic Planning Bureau. With Solyndra, a corporate insider manages to convince a White House insider—such as Valerie Jarrett—that you have the solution to the nation's energy woes. The Solyndra debacle so perfectly captures this crony capitalism that it sounds almost fictional—unfortunately, it was very, very real.

The solar panel company from Fremont, California, filed a loan application with the Department of Energy during the Bush administration, but the application was rejected because there was a lack of evidence that the project would be financially sustainable.[21] Rather than shelve the project, Solyndra redoubled its efforts in Washington.

Despite government officials having already raised concerns that Solyndra could run out of cash by September 2011, the company pursued an aggressive campaign in Washington to obtain federal funding.[22] The Obama administration was enamored of the company, citing it as the perfect example of building green jobs that expanded the economy while promoting the administration's vision of cleaner energy. Vice President Biden touted the program, while Energy Secretary Steven Chu talked about how the company was providing the kind of jobs that America needs for the future. President Obama visited the plant, and Solyndra was even featured in a video as the example for the success of the economic stimulus.[23]

In the end, politics trumped markets and concerns over the company's financing; in September 2009, Solyndra was awarded $535 million in stimulus funds, the first company to receive Department of Energy funding under the stimulus package.[24] The unsavory episode was emblematic of a Democratic White House doing the bidding of business. As we now know, the company failed to produce any permanent jobs, green or otherwise. In the end, the company shuttered its doors, laid off its workers, and filed for bankruptcy under Chapter 11, while a new facility it built in Fremont sits idle—waiting, apparently, for all those "green-collar jobs."

Why did Solyndra receive the expedited loan for a questionable product? Lobbying. Solyndra spent $1.8 million on lobbying during 2008 and 2009, and subsequently received both the first loan approval from the Department of Energy as well as the largest loan. None of the other companies that received loans early on had spent money on lobbying.[25]

Two major Obama fund-raisers were tied to Solyndra. One, George Kaiser, owned the fund that held the largest investments in Solyndra. The other, Steve Spinner, was one of the main decision makers for the loan approval process in the Department of Energy. Spinner had to recuse himself from the final decision on Solyndra "because his wife's law firm represented the company."[26]

E-mails revealed that Kaiser's connections had discussed Solyndra with administration officials in March 2009, well before the contract was awarded by the Department of Energy. Later in the year, when the contract application was under way, one e-mail to Kaiser declared that the White House "has offered to help in the past and we do have a contact within the WH that we are working with."[27] They had their guy in charge.

Kaiser himself appears to have been careful, never actually approving direct lobbying or influence-peddling for Solyndra in his e-mails with his fund managers. However, Kaiser did visit the White House a number of times, including right before the loan was approved. He claimed that Solyndra itself never came up.[28]

Solyndra was far from the only company to receive stimulus funds just before heading into bankruptcy.[29] Predictably, both the vetting process and the enforcement of the loan terms failed. In fact, Solyndra actually violated the terms of its loan because it was running out of money, but the Energy Department changed the terms of the loan so that the company would remain eligible for taxpayer money,[30] restructuring the loan in a way that put the taxpayer funds second in line to claim a lien on the loan money, despite warnings from officials that endangering taxpayer money in such a way was likely illegal.[31] After it became apparent that Solyndra was going under, the administration actually considered bailing out the company under a GM-like plan that would make the government a 40 percent owner of the company. This plan was eventually rejected.[32]

Solyndra may be the most infamous example of a company buying access to taxpayer funds, but it's hardly the only one. According to Peter Schweizer, author of *Throw Them All Out*, "about 75 percent of the loans and grants doled out by the federal government has gone to 'Obama-connected companies' even though the acceptance rate in the program is less than 10 percent."[33]

After Solyndra went bankrupt in August 2011, a DOE spokesman, Damien LeVera, said, "The project that we supported succeeded," adding that "the facility was producing the product it said it would produce, and consumers were buying the product."[34] Of course they blamed market conditions, which had "changed dramatically." So much for the government's ability to grasp the decentralized knowledge that was behind those changes.

But the story doesn't stop there. Once the doors closed and the production stopped, Solyndra went to bankruptcy court seeking $500,000 to be used for bonuses to retain valuable employees—valuable employees for a company not producing anything. As a final injustice to the taxpayer, the company began destroying the high-grade glass that it produced because it was cheaper to trash than to store.[35]

Solyndra's last act of glass smashing was a bitterly fitting end to an insanely expensive Keynesian experiment—the philosophy of the "broken window" after all being a tenet of Keynesian economics. Producing and then smashing solar panels, like burying and then digging up banknotes, ought to have produced new economic growth, according to the theory. Maybe all that broken glass was simply an elaborate Keynesian ploy to stimulate aggregate demand, like so much OWS-trampled, government-funded sod in McPherson Square?

In the end, Solyndra proved to be a scandal that epitomizes the absurdity of government efforts to supplant markets in resource allocation. Despite the Obama administration's rhetoric and rosy scenarios, the plan ultimately led to layoffs and FBI investigations. Markets may make the same mistakes, with entrepreneurs backing the wrong horse, but the dollars at risk are private, and investors soon learn which investments are profitable and which are not. In cases like Solyndra, the dollars at risk are taxpayer dollars, and the venture is directed by a coterie of lobbyists and government officials in collusion to allocate government largesse.

SPUTNIK MOMENT

SINCE SOLYNDRA COLLAPSED, OTHER BAD GOVERNMENT INVEST-ments have been revealed, and the crony capitalists behind taxpayer losses exposed. The latest failed government plan is Ener1, a producer of lithium-ion batteries for electric cars that went bankrupt on January 26, 2012. Just a year earlier, Vice President Joe Biden visited the production facility in Indiana, and was particularly bullish on the Obama administration's ability to set a better course for the U.S. economy and a clear path to green job creation. He told attendees that the government was "not just creating new jobs, but sparking whole new industries that will ensure our competitiveness for decades to come—industries like electric vehicle manufacturing. . . . Ener1, Inc. was awarded a $118.5 million grant from the Department of Energy—part of a $2.4 billion Recovery Act investment nationwide—to expand its production of advanced batteries for hybrid and electric vehicles." Biden predicted job creation "from 336 workers at its Indianapolis manufacturing and assembly facilities, to over a thousand by the start of 2013." [36]

Vice President Biden was certain about the future of electric vehicle manufacturing. How could he have been so wrong? In early March 2012, GM announced that it would be halting production of the Chevrolet Volt[37] despite receiving heavy state and federal subsidies for the vehicle, upwards of $3 billion.[38] Despite an aggressive sales pitch by the Obama administration and *Government Motors*, consumers were not interested in buying the electric car. In 2011, the Volt barely reached 75 percent of its projected 10,000 sales and was on track to only meet 15 percent of its target sales in 2012.[39] This, despite a big order from General Electric, which committed to purchase a total of 12,000 of the electric vehicles by 2015. "By electrifying our own fleet, we will accelerate the adoption curve, drive scale, and move electric vehicles from anticipation to action," said GE CEO Jeff Immelt.[40] The initial halt in production will result in the layoff of roughly 1,300 employees at one of GM's Detroit area factories. [41]

The political penchant for choosing winners and losers, and getting it dead wrong, is hardly exclusive to one political party. Another example is Raser Technologies in Utah. Home-state Republican senator Orrin Hatch, a longtime supporter of Raser, had attempted to secure seven earmarks—worth over $20 million—for the company's automotive wing.[42] None of these earmarks went through, however, and the plant moved on to bigger and better things when it was approved for a $33 million Treasury grant in 2010 to build a geothermal plant.[43] Hatch was present at the groundbreaking ceremony for the plant, which Raser later renamed after the senator.

The plant was approved despite being built on ground that was known to have less geothermal energy than would ordinarily be necessary to run steam turbines, and despite the fact that Raser was massively in debt before it ever broke ground on the plant. Raser received the loan via a "blind application process" that did not take the company's finances into consideration, and Raser even used a portion of the grant money to pay its debts.[44] Predictably, the geothermal plant failed and Raser went bankrupt, but not before wasting millions in taxpayers' money.

BAPTISTS AND BOOTLEGGERS

CONTRARY TO THE SILLY PREDICTIONS OF JIMMY CARTER, DOMESTIC exploration could provide significant amounts of new oil and natural gas. In fact, proven reserves of domestic natural gas and oil have increased significantly.[45] New technologies and new discoveries in Pennsylvania, Texas, Oklahoma, and elsewhere have provided the potential for the United States to become a much larger player in global energy markets, with access to reliable and affordable energy here at home. In fact, one study found our federal lands alone, hold enough energy to fuel 65 million cars for 60 years and heat 60 million households for 160 years.[46] Yet we have been a net importer of energy since the 1950s and in January 2012 imported on average 11,050,000 barrels a day.[47]

Access to energy requires a large and vibrant global market, as well as the ability to utilize domestic energy resources. Yet regulations continue to restrict domestic exploration and the Obama EPA has unleashed an outbreak of new regulations—from greenhouse gas rules to new rules on cross-state pollution—that will cost consumers billions in higher energy costs while impeding efforts to access domestic energy resources.

Indeed, the decline of domestic production tracks well with the rise of radical environmentalism. The first Earth Day in 1970 marks the beginning of a steady decline in domestic production. Today, domestic production is at levels similar to those of 1950, despite the fact that population has increased by 104 percent, the economy has expanded by 553 percent, and the Department of Energy has been around for over 30 years.[48,49] Some of this shift is due to cheaper offshore alternatives; however, the domestic regulatory environment has made it almost impossible to access our nation's abundant energy resources.

The energy sector is plagued by an array of subsidies, taxes, spending programs, government-created monopolies, trade barriers, and mandates. Federal mandates have shuttered smaller refineries and made many areas of the country more vulnerable to price shocks following rapid shifts in supply or demand. Mandates that require specific fuels, such as the heavily lobbied ethanol program, are extremely destructive, with impacts felt not only in the energy sector but also in agriculture as cropland is shifted from the production of food to energy.

In fact, regulatory barriers inhibit the expansion of energy markets, from hydroelectric power to nuclear power. Even clean renewable energies such as wind face challenges from environmentalists. And as exploration takes natural gas companies beyond producer-friendly states such as Texas, energy companies are running into challenges from environmental groups and state and local governments that delay or actually deter energy production. Producers in Colorado, in particular, have faced significant political opposition to expanded oil shale exploration, and the Marcellus Shale formation in Pennsylvania faces both environmental and political opposition.

Duke Energy is a power company headquartered in Charlotte, North Carolina. In a move that has virtually nothing to do with providing consumers with affordable and reliable power, Duke Energy's CEO, Jim Rogers, guaranteed a $10 million line of credit to the DNC for hosting the Democratic National Convention in Charlotte in 2012.[50] Clearly, Duke's largesse has more to do with securing an advantageous position with the power brokers in Washington than it does with serving consumers.

This is nothing new for companies like Duke, which are creatures of regulation and thrive on government policy. In fact, Duke Energy is a member of the U.S. Climate Action Partnership, a business group dedicated to promoting costly cap-and-trade programs that would impose significant new economic burdens on businesses and consumers.[51] As Holman Jenkins noted about Rogers in the *Wall Street Journal*, "No executive has lobbied as noisily or consistently for a national price on carbon output."[52] Duke Energy also accepted $204 million in stimulus funds for "smart grid" projects.[53]

While support for cap-and-trade may appear to some as a noble effort, it is perhaps a better example of a rent-seeking phenomenon economist Bruce Yandle referred to as "Baptists and Bootleggers." Both groups supported Prohibition, but for clearly different reasons. The bootleggers were simply using the Baptists' opposition to alcohol to protect a government-created black market. Given Duke's particular portfolio of fuel sources, it would benefit relative to its competitors from cap-and-trade regulation.

Rogers gambled a lot of money on cap-and-trade passing, building a huge coal gasification plant in Indiana, which he presumably expected would give Duke Energy a huge break under a carbon tax system. But only the regulatory apparatus made such a venture possible: "Without regulators around to guarantee a return on such a risky and pioneering investment, Duke likely would have sat on its hands and let rising electricity prices take care of any gap between demand and supply while waiting for the country to make up its mind about global warming."[54] Another article noted that "Duke embarked on this venture only after securing a government subsidy of $460 million."[55]

Duke was open about its lobbying for cap-and-trade, and tried to play it off as an attempt to create a better version of the bill that would cost its customers less.[56] In fact, Eileen Claussen, a former climate change czar and now head of the leftist Pew Center on Global Climate Change, noted, "It's fair to say that we wouldn't be where we are in Congress if it weren't for [Rogers]. He helped put carbon legislation on the map."[57] The lobbying paid off, as the cap-and-trade bill passed by the House "gave Duke most of the credits it will need for 15 to 20 years for free."[58] Fortunately, the bill never made it through the Senate. While this was a victory for consumers, Duke's shareholders are not quite as fortunate. "Not only did Rogers' legislative gambit fail to become law, but he wasted years and significant shareholder money chasing legislative windmills," says Tom Borelli, a free-market shareholder activist.[59]

Duke Energy is clearly in the camp of businesses that curry favor and seek profits through government favoritism. Again, it doesn't really matter who's running the government; what matters is that government is dictating the terms of exchange. As Borelli notes, "Cap-and-trade is an example of the coordinated effort of big business and big government pursuing their agendas. Obama establishes a massive government program to control energy and big business hopes to make a quick buck while Americans pay for it all in terms of higher energy prices."[60] It should be clear that Duke Energy is the bootlegger, not the Baptist, in this tragic tale. As Frank O'Donnell, president of Clean Air Watch, commented, "Duke is in favor of carbon controls as long as they are the carbon controls that Duke is comfortable with. No one is going to mistake Duke for Greenpeace."[61]

Unfortunately, Duke is not an isolated case. GE just as aggressively pursued cap-and-trade legislation. GE, like Duke Energy, is a member of the U.S. Climate Action Partnership (USCAP). GE's Ecomagination program, one of Immelt's marquee assets, reportedly earned the company more than $85 billion in revenue from "products and solutions" through 2010.[62]

Immelt backtracked on his support for cap-and-trade after he received backlash from company shareholders and grassroots activists at a GE board meeting where Tom Borelli presented Immelt with poll results that showed GE's favorability declining among conservative-leaning consumers when they were told of his lobbying for carbon caps. Not long after the shareholder meeting, Immelt backed off. "If I had one thing to do over again I would not have talked so much about green," he said. "I'm a businessman. That's all I care about, is jobs. . . . I'm kind of over the stage of arguing for a comprehensive energy policy. I'm back to keeping my head down and working."[63]

GE remains a member of USCAP and in active pursuit of the renewable energy markets created by government regulation. As the *New York Times* noted, "G.E., for example, lobbied Congress in 2009 to help expand the subsidy programs, and it now profits from every aspect of the boom in renewable-power plant construction."[64] In fact, GE managed to secure the contract for the largest wind farm in the United States, Shepherds Flat, Oregon. The generous loan guarantee from DOE even raised eyebrows within the Obama administration. Economic adviser Larry Summers, environmental czar Carol Browner, and Vice President Biden adviser Ron Klain penned a memo to the president that raised serious concerns about the project. They were particularly concerned that the project might have moved forward even without the federal dollars, because state regulations and mandates already provided a return on the project. This led to concerns that GE was double-dipping, pulling in federal grants, state tax credits, state and federal tax benefits, and a healthy loan guarantee. Because of mandates requiring the use of renewable energy, ratepayers would be paying higher-than-market rates for the electricity generated by the wind farm.[65] All this government largesse raised concerns. Of the $1.9 billion project, "the government would provide a significant subsidy (65+%), while the sponsor [GE] would provide little skin in the game (equity about 10%)."[66]

For General Electric, business is good. Good for them, bad for us.

UNHEALTHY BEHAVIOR

LIKE CAP-AND-TRADE, CORPORATE CRONYISM PLAYED A KEY ROLE IN the passing of Obamacare. What was sold to the public by many progressives on the Left as an effort to help the helpless and fight back against the evil, out-of-control health insurance industry was in reality one of the biggest corporate boondoggles in history.

One *Forbes* analyst noted that Obamacare is "very likely to be the greatest boon for lobbyists ever conceived. . . . In the health care field, the Holy Grail of rent-seeking is to get one's medical device, drug, or procedure added to state health insurance mandates." Obamacare created a one-stop shop for lobbyists by centralizing health care decisions.[67]

Of course, Obamacare wasn't the first time this collusion occurred. During the Bush administration, the Pharmaceutical Manufacturers Association's efforts to pass a new Medicare Part D drug benefit went as far as offering rides in private jets to Senate Majority Leader Bill

Frist and Speaker of the House Dennis Hastert, at steeply discounted fares. They also made enormous campaign donations to many of the key health care committee members.[68] The pharmaceutical lobbies particularly dreaded the repeal of laws barring U.S. prescription drugs from being reimported from other industrialized nations, as the lower prices of drugs from Canada and elsewhere would force them to dramatically reduce their profit margins in order to compete.

Billy Tauzin, the former congressman who had played a large role in drafting Medicare Part D, was the head of the pharmaceutical makers' trade association, whose acronym is PhRMA, when Obamacare was being crafted. He left his chairmanship of the health care committee of jurisdiction to become Big Pharma's top lobbyist shortly after Part D passed.[69] Obama actually pointed to Tauzin as a bad actor in a campaign ad in 2008, promising not to take lobbyist money or be part of the lobbyist-induced culture of corruption once in Washington.[70] Only moments after being sworn into office, Obama reconsidered his campaign promise, and he soon began "cutting deals to neutralize would-be antagonists." Embracing industry demands early "was one of the Democrats' key takeaways from the failed 'Hillary-Care' effort."[71]

One such deal came on prescription drug reimportation. Obama had promised during his campaign that he would allow the reimportation of prescription drugs, and in 2007, Obama voted twice to allow it. When pharmaceutical companies became concerned about the potential for reimportation ending up in Obamacare, they were directed to meet with Democratic senator Max Baucus, chairman of the powerful Finance Committee.[72] Baucus initially asked the drug industry to contribute $100 billion in cost reductions in return for concessions in the bill, but the industry balked at the high cost.[73]

The *Wall Street Journal* reported in July 2009 that PhRMA reps met with the White House and received some assurances that prescription importation would not be allowed by Obamacare, in spite of Obama's campaign promises to the contrary.[74] The *Los Angeles Times* also reported that the White House protected pharmaceutical companies by blocking access to generic and imported drugs—in exchange for drug company backing of Obamacare.[75]

A memo obtained by the *Huffington Post* broke down the eventual deal reached between PhRMA and Baucus, approved by the White House. Drug companies agreed to chip in $80 billion in cost reductions. The White House, not eager to be seen as colluding with pharmaceutical lobbyists, lest it expose the lie, initially backed away from the memo.[76]

Many Democrats in Congress were furious at the concessions and accused Obama of caving to the drug companies. Nervous that the White House might go back on their deal, Tauzin publicly acknowledged the veracity of the numbers in the memo and called upon the White House to do the same. The White House had no choice but to confirm the deal.[77]

Senator Bill Nelson proposed an amendment to the bill that would have obliged drug companies to lower prices even more, to fill in the "doughnut hole" (a large coverage gap) in Medicare Part D, but under pressure from drug companies, a number of key Democrats voted with Republicans to kill the amendment. Similarly, Senator Byron Dorgan, Democrat of North Dakota, introduced an amendment to allow the reimportation of drugs, but the amendment was defeated "with numerous Democrats previously in support of re-importation switching to 'no' votes."[78]

The drug companies also committed up to $150 million to run ads in support of Obamacare, a remarkable number, more than John McCain spent on his entire 2008 presidential campaign.[79]

In February 2010, after the election of Scott Brown in Massachusetts to fill Ted Kennedy's old seat, the health care bill appeared dead. Pharmaceutical industry leaders became worried that Tauzin "had gone too far giving concessions" to the White House for too little return, and Tauzin was pressured into resigning as head of PhRMA.[80]

Examples of health care rent-seeking are everywhere. Obama had promised that he would prohibit agencies from issuing large contracts without a competitive bidding process,[81] but that is exactly what occurred with New York–based Siga Technologies, which successfully negotiated a contract to sell the government $433 million worth of smallpox vaccines. After Siga was awarded the initial contract, another company complained that the contract was designated for a small company and that Siga was well above that threshold. A new contract was then written, which only Siga was allowed to bid on.[82]

Even worse, these vaccines weren't even necessary, by the reckoning of medical and defense experts. Various experts on smallpox and epidemiology voiced concerns that the expense of procuring this particular vaccine was unjustified, since another vaccine already exists with more proven effectiveness and a longer shelf life than Siga's new version. Moreover, the vaccine has not even been approved by the FDA, and with no real way to test it on human subjects (since smallpox has been eradicated in the U.S.), there is no sure way to know whether the vaccine is effective.[83]

What stake did the Obama administration have in the vaccine? Siga's controlling shareholder is "Ronald O. Perelman, one of the world's richest men and a longtime Democratic party donor."[84] Perelman donated "$130,000 mostly to Democrats over the last two cycles alone" and contributed $50,000 for Obama's inaugural parties. Another member of Siga's board: Andrew Stern, former head of the Service Employees International Union (SEIU) and one of the most frequent visitors to the Obama White House.[85]

According to the Center for Responsive Politics, "The pharmaceutical and health products industry . . . is consistently one of the top industries for federal campaign contributions." The center's number crunching reveals that drug companies traditionally favored Republican candidates but began to donate more to Democrats after the balance of power shifted in 2006. They also note, "The [pharmaceutical] industry's political generosity increased in the years leading up to Congress' passage in 2003 of a prescription drug benefit in Medicare."[86] Indeed, drug company donations and independent expenditures for campaigns more than doubled, from $13 million to $27 million between 1998 and 2000, and they increased from $20 million to $31 million between 2006 and 2008.[87]

The evidence of lobbyists' influence is clear in the aftermath of a major victory. After Medicare Part D passed, numerous members of Congress and staff involved in its drafting left "public service" for lucrative careers with pharmaceutical lobbies. "Every time a major bill passes, there is an exodus of Hill staffers," one former staffer told ProPublica. "In many cases, they have worked for 2–3 years on the legislation and then they go to work for firms with a stake in the implementation. These staffers, obviously, have a unique understanding of the issue and people are willing to pay a premium for that knowledge—even more so than for their so-called 'connections.' "[88]

WHAT WOULD REAGAN DO?

SUMNER KIBBE—HE WAS POPS TO MY BROTHER, MARK, AND ME— worked for General Electric most of his adult life. In Erie, Pennsylvania, he helped build locomotive engines. Sometime in the early 1960s he discovered a former actor named Ronald Reagan, the host of General Electric Theater. My dad would eventually become a Reagan delegate to the 1968 Republican National Convention in Miami Beach, a brokered convention that was the beginning of the Reagan Revolution, an earlier hostile takeover bid against the Republican establishment.

Pops stood with Reagan long before it was considered cool.

Today, General Electric celebrates its affiliation with Reagan, and it spent lavishly on Reagan's centennial celebration throughout 2011. From the GE website:

Long before he changed the world, or led a nation, or governed a state, Ronald Reagan inspired our company with his optimism, entrepreneurial spirit and belief in innovation. From 1954 to 1962, Ronald Reagan served as host of a popular Sunday evening television program called General Electric Theater. During that time he also spent ten weeks each year traveling the country as GE's roving ambassador. By the time the show concluded its eight-year run, Ronald Reagan, by his own account, had visited 139 GE research and manufacturing facilities. He walked the plant floors, toured offices and met over 250,000 individual employees, honing his renowned communications skills and leaving a unique legacy that continues to inspire our company today.[89]

Critics of GE's trough feeding, including yours truly, wondered about the company's real motives. Was their renewed interest in associating with Reagan's legacy just a convenient way to repair their public image?

You can't find it on their website, but GE fired Reagan at the peak of the show's popularity. Why would they do that? "Dad explained that CBS hadn't canceled the highly rated show," says Reagan's son Michael. "Instead, GE had pulled the plug. As the company was negotiating some government contracts, Bobby Kennedy, the attorney general of the United States, bluntly informed GE that if the company wished to do business with the U.S. government, it would get rid of 'General Electric Theater' and fire the host."[90] Reportedly, the dispute was over Reagan's harsh criticism of the Tennessee Valley Authority.

In April 2009, President Obama rolled out yet another "stimulus" project, $13 million in federal money for high-speed rail. "There's no reason why the future of travel should lie somewhere else beyond our borders. Building a new system of high-speed rail in America will be faster, cheaper and easier than building more freeways or adding to an already overburdened aviation system—and everybody stands to benefit." Sure enough, Lorenzo Simonelli, CEO of GE Transportation, announced a month later that GE was standing "ready to partner with the federal government and Amtrak to make high-speed rail a reality."

The locomotives needed for the job would be produced in Erie at the same plant my father used to work at, and were introduced "before a crowd of employees and public officials," according to the *Erie Times-News*. "This was typical," says Tim Carney in his book *Obamanomics*, "an Obama policy pronouncement in close conjunction with a GE business initiative. It happens across all sectors of the economy and in all corners of GE's sprawling enterprise." [91]

Typical, maybe. But one thing's for sure. That's not my father's GE.

CHAPTER 8

SCRAP THE CODE

WARREN BUFFETT WANTS YOU TO KNOW THAT HE THINKS THAT THE rich don't pay their fair share.

Buffett is the third richest person in the world. He had a net worth of $39 billion in 2011.[1] That's probably about 406,250 times your net worth.[2] But it matters to him that you know that his enormous wealth and good fortune do not mean he is a selfish man, uncaring about the plight of the American people during a time of economic turmoil. He is so generous, in fact, that he wants the government to force "the rich"—those filthy wealthy one-percenters—to bear the cross of economic self-sacrifice for the good of society and the government coffers.

In a 2011 *New York Times* op-ed piece, Buffett proclaimed that he wanted to pay higher taxes for the purpose of "shared sacrifice." How altruistic. He argued for a tax hike for those making more than $1 million a year and an even higher hike for those making more than $10 million. Buffett argued that new social engineering through the tax code—selectively applied tax hikes—was necessary because "so many . . . citizens are truly suffering." He noted that he and his rich friends have "been coddled long enough by a billionaire-friendly Congress" that applied low capital gains and dividends tax rates, leading to Buffett himself paying a lower effective income tax rate than "the other 20 people" in his office. He finished with a rhetorical flourish: "It's time for our government to get serious about shared sacrifice."[3]

WARREN BUFFETT'S SECRETARY

PRESIDENT OBAMA, NEVER ONE TO MISS AN OPPORTUNITY TO RAISE taxes and draw a line in the sand for people who "make too much money," quickly heralded the op-ed and called for the implementation of a "Buffett rule" that would "rais[e] some revenue from folks who've done very well."[4] We are not allowed to say "tax hike" in Washington, D.C. "Enhanced revenue" is the preferred nomenclature. (The list of politically approved jargon can be exhausting for the layman, but there are a few simple rules: "New revenue" does not mean higher taxes; "quantitative easing" is not the printing of new money out of thin air; and de facto government ownership of a bank or a car company is absolutely, positively not "socialism." It's just "progressive.")

Buffett engaged in a whirlwind tour of Washington, meeting with President Obama, Nancy Pelosi, and other insider luminaries.[5] The president went so far as to seat Warren Buffett's secretary next to Michelle Obama for the 2012 State of the Union Address, and reiterated in that speech, in case you didn't hear it before, that "right now, Warren Buffett pays a lower tax rate than his secretary."

What exactly are Buffett and Obama talking about? So far, the president's prop for higher taxes has not released her own tax returns, so no one really knows what that actually means. Is that the marginal or effective rate? Does that include payroll taxes? The employer's share of payroll taxes? Does the AMT apply? State taxes? How many deductions? No one knows exactly what President Obama, Warren Buffett, or his secretary is actually talking about, because of an enormously complex tax code where everyone is treated differently from everyone else.

If our government were to get serious about shared sacrifice, it seems like we might start with some serious belt-tightening in Washington, D.C. But that's not how things are done inside the marble walls of Congress. Adding another layer of complexity to our incomprehensible tax code is anything but fair. Such changes are inevitably gamed by insiders, tax lawyers, and lobbyists who will make it very difficult to accumulate wealth if you are not already rich. Complexity ensures, by definition, that those who are politically connected will always get a better deal. Might that be the real agenda here?

The real battle in America is not between the 99 percent versus the top 1 percent. The fight is between the privileged insiders with pull, who have rigged the tax code to their advantage, and the rest of us, who foot the bill. Buffett's proposal simply to raise taxes on the wealthy is anything but simple, and it would only exacerbate the problem of an overly convoluted tax code. The only way to achieve true fairness is through fundamental tax reform, including a flat tax and a massively simplified tax code.

COMPLEXITY IS THE ENEMY

CONSIDER WARREN BUFFETT ONCE MORE. JUST A COUPLE OF DAYS after his benevolent-sounding *New York Times* op-ed, Buffett's company and chief asset, Berkshire Hathaway, was in the news for admitting in its 2010 annual report that it likely owed more than $1 billion in back taxes.[6,7] This revelation was not the first time Buffett and Berkshire squabbled with the IRS over taxes. They had also previously fought and won a 2002 dispute with the agency over $23 million in deductions denied by the IRS from 1989 to 1991.[8] Despite the minuscule dollar amount of the tax challenge compared to the assets of the multibillion-dollar company, Buffett argued that the protracted litigation was worth pursuing.[9]

His assertion that the tax code allows the privileged elite to avoid taxes is correct. Our current tax code, weighing in at 3.6 million words, is filled with deductions, credits, penalties, and loopholes, and provides some with a massive advantage in minimizing their taxes—opportunities to game the system unavailable to the average American.[10] As President Obama's commissioner of the IRS noted in a speech, there were "an astonishing 4,400 legislative changes to the Code" between 2000 and 2010 alone.[11]

Buffett can afford an army of accountants to seek out every deduction and loophole and an army of lawyers to engage in protracted litigation with the IRS to ensure that he pays the least amount possible every year. He employs an army of lobbyists (Berkshire Hathaway spent almost $9.5 million on lobbying in 2010)[12]—to influence politicians to create additional tax deductions, loopholes, and carve-outs for his businesses.

Most Americans can't afford such armies. We end up doing our own taxes, wading through 161 pages of instructions to do so, triple the page total in 1985 and four times more than in 1975.[13] The IRS itself reported to Congress in 2010 that the complexity of the tax code is "the most serious problem facing taxpayers."[14] It's no wonder Americans spend about 7.3 billion hours per year complying with the filing requirements of the Internal Revenue Code.[15] How can an untrained individual who has to wade through a morass of rules and regulations compete with teams of sophisticated accountants and lawyers?

Now, what about Buffett's tax-hike solution? Would the code be fairer if we imposed additional, targeted tax hikes on the rich? In a word, no. Buffett, in his *New York Times* op-ed, played fast and loose with the truth regarding his tax burden. His argument that he pays a lower tax rate than all his employees because of low dividends tax rates ignores the fact that our tax code already double-taxes such capital income. Buffett and others who pay such taxes first pay a corporate income tax on capital income before facing the dividends tax for that same income. When this is taken into account, Buffett likely faces a tax rate of almost 45 percent, higher than that of any of his employees.

Among the ultrarich, IRS statistics show that the top 1 percent of earners pay 36.73 percent of all income tax revenue, and the top 5 percent pay 58.66 percent.[16] How much more does Buffett expect such Americans to give to a perceived "shared sacrifice"?

The president and his friends like to throw around words like *fairness*. But I think most of us think about the rules of fair play, particularly when it comes to the laws of the land, as treating everyone the same. The idea that government can benevolently pick the right winners and punish the bad actors is utterly contrary to our sense of justice and common sense.

I say let's scrap the tax code altogether. Let's put the professional tax lobby and army of tax lawyers *out of business*. A tax code that is simple, low, fair, and honest means that workers and capitalists, and even Warren Buffett, can spend their time working to put food on the table and, with a little luck and hard work, create wealth and jobs and opportunities outside Washington, D.C.

SIMPLER TAXES MEAN MORE FREEDOM

THE CONTRACT FROM AMERICA CALLS ON CONGRESS TO "[A]DOPT A simple and fair single-rate tax system by scrapping the internal revenue code and replacing it with one that is no longer than 4,543 words—the length of the original Constitution."[17] There's a reason nearly half a million Tea Party activists around the country decided to include fundamental tax reform as one of the top planks of the Contract, and it's not that they're all super-rich and looking for an easy way to avoid paying taxes. I would argue that though the economic benefits of such reform are important, the passion of grassroots activists for fundamental tax reform is driven primarily by a set of simple values:

Treat everyone the same as everyone else; don't punish success; and simplicity equals transparency—so everyone knows that there isn't a better deal to be had if you can afford a lobbyist or a lawyer. In other words, simple, low, fair, and honest.

When policy wonks like me talk about tax policy, we often remove the moral component. We crunch a lot of numbers and discuss end results (which I'll do later in this chapter, so be prepared). But the elegance of our modeling of distributional effects is secondary to the ideological foundation of a certain and clear policy, especially when such a policy is in line with simple fairness and the values espoused in our Constitution.

Fundamental tax reform is necessary because it is the only solution that fully ensures our individual liberty as human beings. The Declaration of Independence recognizes our "unalienable rights" of "life, liberty, and the pursuit of happiness." This means that a just government cannot take our liberty or the fruits of our labor from us just because it thinks that the end result will be beneficial for "society."

Why is our liberty so important? It seems like a silly question, but it's crucial, since our government is violating our liberties every day, especially through the crazy quilt of tax code regulations. Liberty is important to us because it gives us the opportunity to fully define ourselves. No committee chairman or IRS bureaucrat can regulate that with a better set of preferences and choices, imposed from the top down. No president, no matter how confidently he asserts it, knows at what point you have "earned too much money."

If a system of taxation is not fair, and government can create arbitrary rules and laws that hinder your ability to earn and produce, it infringes on your ability to express yourself as a human being and live your own life. And it's not just the government taking away our money that erodes our ability to define our own lives; the arbitrariness and inconsistency of government rules also negatively impact our life, liberty, and pursuit of happiness.

FOUNDING FAIRNESS

THE FOUNDING FATHERS CLEARLY UNDERSTOOD WHY EXCESSIVE AND unfair taxation directly harms our liberty. Thomas Jefferson, in an 1816 letter, described in detail his belief that government must choose "economy and liberty" over "profusion and servitude," as excessive taxation would lead to "wretchedness and oppression."

> To preserve [the] independence [of the people,] we must not let our rulers load us with perpetual debt. We must make our election between economy and liberty, or profusion and servitude. If we run into such debts as that we must be taxed in our meat and in our drink, in our necessaries and our comforts, in our labors and our amusements, for our callings and our creeds, as the people of England are, our people, like them, must come to labor sixteen hours in the twenty-four, give the earnings of fifteen of these to the government for their debts and daily expenses, and the sixteenth being insufficient to afford us bread, we must live, as they now do, on oatmeal and potatoes, have no time to think, no means of calling the mismanagers to account, but be glad to obtain subsistence by hiring ourselves to rivet their chains on the necks of our fellow-sufferers. . . . And this is the tendency of all human governments. A departure from principle in one instance becomes a precedent for a second that second for a third and so on till the bulk of the society is reduced to be mere automatons of misery and to have no sensibilities left but for sinning and suffering. . . . And the fore horse of this frightful team is public debt. Taxation follows that and in its train wretchedness and oppression.[18]

Jefferson perfectly encapsulated why unfair taxation directly impacts our liberties. If we are taxed too heavily and unfairly, we cannot truly live our lives, and we will have "no time to think."

Jefferson was not alone in his fears about taxation. James Madison too saw the impact of unfair and inconsistent taxation on individual liberty.

> In a word, as a man is said to have a right to his property, he may be equally said to have a property in his rights. . . . A just security to property is not afforded by that government, under which unequal taxes oppress one species of property and reward another species: where arbitrary taxes invade the domestic sanctuaries of the rich, and excessive taxes grind the faces of the poor; where the keenness and competitions of want are deemed an insufficient spur to labor, and taxes are again applied, by an unfeeling policy, as another spur; in violation of that sacred property, which Heaven, in decreeing man to earn his bread by the sweat of his brow, kindly reserved to him, in the small repose that could be spared from the supply of his necessities.[19]

Madison, like Jefferson, described with great clarity how unfair and unequal taxes can destroy society, deprive us of our right to "sacred property," and inhibit the pursuit of our happiness.

How did we get here from where the Founders stood? The tax code distorts important decisions that people make about investing and saving money. High marginal rates and double taxation reduce incentives to invest, while special-interest tax policies push resources toward politically favored investments rather than toward the most efficient ends.

All of this social engineering and special interest politics have generated inequities in the tax code that leave individuals paying taxes not based on income but on how that income is used. Neighbors with the same income can pay vastly different taxes based on whether they own their house, if they give to charity, or where they invest their money. Someone else is deciding. Individuals whose pursuit of happiness lines up well with the goals of lobbyists and the politically powerful receive unfair advantages. Such inequality is anathema to our Founders' demand for economic liberty.

1913

THE ARTICLES OF CONFEDERATION, ADOPTED IN 1781, LEFT THE AU-thority to levy taxes with the several states, with the national government having to request funds from the states. Even when the Constitution was adopted nine years later, with a stronger federal government authorized to tax individuals directly, the power to tax remained limited by Article I, Section 2, requiring any direct tax to be "apportioned." (Under U.S. law, a "direct" tax is one levied directly on *persons* or *property*, such as a head tax or real-estate tax. An "indirect" tax is levied on an *event*, such as when a good is sold, imported, or manufactured.) This constitutional limitation meant that the federal government could not impose a direct tax without first determining a specific sum to be collected from within each state in proportion with the state's congressional representation. So, for example, if New York had 9 percent of the representatives in Congress, 9 percent of the revenues produced by the tax would have to come from New York. If Rhode Island had only 1 percent, then only 1 percent could come from Rhode Island. But since population density and property values vary widely across states, to get the "portions" right the tax *rate* must also vary from state to state, sometimes wildly so. A wealthy state would actually have to have a lower tax rate than a poor state to satisfy the apportionment requirements, making it practically impossible for Congress to secure the votes to pass a direct tax. This impediment may have been intentional. While the Founders clearly didn't want to forbid direct taxes, they also seem to have disfavored them, perhaps because such taxes offer a very convenient tool for politicians to redistribute wealth among classes, states, and regions—and thus sow the seeds of corruption. As a result, for most of the nation's early history, Congress avoided direct taxes. Instead, indirect taxes such as tariffs and excises (which the Constitution only requires to be "uniform throughout the United States") produced the vast bulk of federal revenue.

Up through the early twentieth century, taxes tended to be low. Wars did, of course, lead to higher taxes, but typically the war debts would be paid down quickly and the temporary taxes eliminated. The system tended to minimize the burden of government and maximize individual liberty.

Everything changed in 1913.

To be fair, the radical transformation that began in the fateful year of 1913 did not occur immediately. Like many bad public policies, taxes crept up over time, the result of a gradual process that, like so much bad public policy, had its roots in war—the Civil War, to be exact. That conflict produced the first tax on personal income. The Revenue Act of 1861 established an income tax to fund the Union war effort. Although this first income tax was potentially the sort of engine for wealth redistribution that the Founders had clearly disfavored, it was deemed an indirect tax (a tax on the "event" of receiving income) and therefore not "apportioned" but rather imposed uniformly throughout all areas of the country "not in rebellion." The rate was moderately progressive, 3 percent on all income over $800, which meant most workers did not pay the tax.[20]

The following year, with the war proving to be neither as brief nor as cheap as originally assumed, Congress increased both tax rates and progressivity, with the exemption lowered to $600, a tax rate of 3 percent for incomes up to $10,000, and a new 5 percent tax for income over $10,000. Thus was born the first graduated (i.e., not flat) income tax—the first "progressive" tax. Rates were increased again in 1864, and an emergency bill that same year added an additional 5 percent surtax on all income over $600.[21]

And so began the centralized establishment's long love affair with tax code meddling. After the war, Congress moved to lower the income tax when surpluses began to emerge, because the majority of Americans viewed it as a temporary measure needed for the war effort. Rates were lowered and exemptions were increased, and in 1872, the tax was abolished. But for many in Congress, the urge to spend was irresistible. They'd had a taste of funding whatever their hearts desired by a well-manipulated tax code, and would stop at nothing to taste that sweet nectar again. Politicians' insatiable desire for more taxpayer money led to more than sixty bills over the next twenty years seeking to reinstate the income tax.[22]

For the emerging Socialist, Populist, and Progressive movements— then gaining ground—the lure of "taxing the rich" to spend more taxpayer money was irresistible, and in 1894, Congress, controlled by the Democrats, passed a bill that included a flat federal tax on income. However, the portion of the new tax that touched income from real estate and personal property was challenged in court as a direct tax that ran afoul of the Constitution's apportionment rule, and in 1895 the Supreme Court agreed, striking it down 5 to 4.[23]

This came as a surprise to everyone, since the earlier income tax adopted during the Civil War had reached all income "from any sort of property . . . or from any other source whatever" and been upheld by the Supreme Court as an indirect tax.[24]

Progressives were horrified, seeing their chance to force the "moneyed class" to pay "in proportion to their ability to pay"[25]— the first half of *From each according to his ability, to each according to his need*—forever barred by five unelected judges. At once, they launched a campaign to reverse the decision, culminating with the ratification of the Sixteenth Amendment in 1913. This amendment ended the convoluted legal debate over the metaphysical nature of the income tax by clearly granting Congress "power to lay and collect taxes on incomes, from whatever source derived, without apportionment among the several States, and without regard to any census or enumeration."[26] In the parlance of our times: Boom. End of discussion. Let the redistribution begin.

This contorted legal history raises an important point for today's tax debate. Simply abolishing the Sixteenth Amendment does not necessarily eliminate the threat of an income tax. Past Supreme Courts have been on both sides of the issue, and there is no guarantee that a future Court will again rule against the income tax. To truly end the income tax, we would need an amendment that not only repeals the Sixteenth but also positively prohibits such a tax in the future.

After the 1895 ruling, Progressives and politicians, drawn by the siren call of spending, promptly redoubled their efforts to adopt a federal income tax via an aggressive campaign. A series of tax bills by Democrats failed, and in a case of Republicans trying to out-Democrat the Democrats, President William Howard Taft joined efforts to amend the Constitution. In a letter read to Congress on June 16, 1909, Taft wrote: "I therefore recommend to Congress that both houses by two-thirds vote shall propose an amendment to the Constitution conferring the power to levy an income tax upon the National Government without apportionment among the States in proportion to population."

Congress moved quickly on this advice, and by 1913, thirty-six states had approved the Sixteenth Amendment, which was declared ratified on February 3, 1913. The language of the amendment is, of course, intentionally very broad, to allow for lots of flexibility (i.e., control) in the future.

Washington wasted little time, with newly elected President Woodrow Wilson signing the 1913 Revenue Act in October.[27] The new tax was progressive, with rates starting at 1 percent for income greater than $3,000 ($4,000 for a married couple)—a very good income in those days—and rising to 7 percent for income greater than $500,000.[28] At most 1 percent of the population (2 percent of households) would have to file a return. In retrospect, it seems almost quaint. This new tax also spawned the first Form 1040, the bane of taxpayers to this day.

Richard E. Byrd, Speaker of the Virginia House of Delegates, had argued against the Sixteenth Amendment with chilling prescience:

A hand from Washington will be stretched out and placed upon every man's business; the eye of the Federal inspector will be in every man's counting house. . . . The law will of necessity have inquisitorial features, it will provide penalties, it will create complicated machinery. Under it men will be hailed into courts distant from their homes. Heavy fines imposed by distant and unfamiliar tribunals will constantly menace the tax payer. An army of Federal inspectors, spies and detectives will descend upon the state. . . . Who of us who have had knowledge of the doings of the Federal officials in the Internal Revenue service can be blind to what will follow? [29]

With the amendment's ratification, federal coffers—and the federal appetite for more spending—swelled. Initially, only 1 percent of the population paid income taxes, but that would change quickly. World War I saw a significant jump in taxes and expansion of the tax base. As recounted by the Department of Treasury, which has in obvious ways benefited from this whole mess, "By 1917 the Federal budget was almost equal to the total budget for all the years between 1791 and 1916. Needing still more tax revenue, the War Revenue Act of 1917 lowered exemptions and greatly increased tax rates. In 1916, a taxpayer needed $1.5 million in taxable income to face a 15 percent rate. By 1917 a taxpayer with only $40,000 faced a 16 percent rate and the individual with $1.5 million faced a tax rate of 67 percent." [30] Washington's insatiable appetite for revenue was fully whetted. Income tax revenue jumped from $761 million in 1916 to $3.6 billion in 1918—almost a fivefold increase. [31]

With the end of the war in November 1918, surpluses began to build, reaching a high of $6.7 billion. Progressivity also increased dramatically in the 1920s, with upper-income groups moving from 30 percent to 65 percent of the total tax burden. [32] The surpluses and excessive tax burdens eventually led to a series of tax reductions, but the income tax was here to stay. Washington had a new tool that would fuel the spending binge of the twentieth century.

FEEDING THE BEAST

POWERFUL SPECIAL INTERESTS BEGAN TO MANIPULATE THE TAX CODE almost immediately upon its creation. Senator Nelson Aldrich, the powerful, progressive Republican who proposed an amendment to establish the income tax, worked to provide tax-exempt status to foundations, something of interest for those trying to protect their fortunes, such as the Rockefellers (into which family Senator Aldrich's daughter had married), the Morgans, and the Carnegies. In other words, an aggressive advocate of taxing the rich had proceeded immediately to create a shelter for those with the pull and influence to reshape things.

Sounds very modern and familiar, doesn't it? Such efforts by special interests to shape the tax code have unfortunately plagued politics in Washington ever since. It is inevitable, like water running downhill, when the founding notion of fairness—treating every single American the same under the laws of the land—is corrupted. It is guaranteed that well-heeled favor seekers will show up outside the committee rooms of the House Ways and Means Committee and lobby for a better deal.

Despite the persistence of the Great Depression, the Democratic Congress and Republican White House passed the Tax Act of 1932, the largest peacetime tax increase up to that time. President Franklin D. Roosevelt pushed for even higher taxes in 1934, raising taxes on both businesses and individuals (which were also made more progressive). With the budget still not balanced, additional tax increases were introduced in 1936, when the top rate reached 79 percent. An undistributed profits tax was added and in the next two years, payroll taxes (i.e., taxes on wage income) were also introduced, to cover unemployment insurance and Social Security and railroad retirement. In 1939, Congress codified the tax code, giving lobbyists and lawyers a specific target for future tax battles.[33]

World War II saw a surge in spending that led to the introduction of an "excess profits" tax, higher corporate taxes, and increased personal income taxes. To increase revenues, the tax base was expanded by reducing the number of exemptions available. In fact, at that point the personal income tax began to hit the general population, which had previously been mostly exempt. Withholding—collecting taxes at the source of the income—was also introduced as the tax base expanded, to combat rising problems with tax avoidance. In fact, the tax industry by this time was in full swing, creating early tax shelters and working its way around the emerging tax code.[34]

Unfortunately, the end of World War II did not usher in a return to earlier levels of government spending and lower revenues. In fact, even before the war in the Pacific ended, domestic spending was rising. Congress had become addicted to spending, and taxes were needed to keep the pork-barrel machine running. Indeed, as Congress tweaked the tax code in search of more and more revenues, marginal rates rose, with the top rate reaching its wartime high of 94 percent in 1944 and remaining at 91 percent for the next two decades. Both President Dwight D. Eisenhower and President John F. Kennedy pushed some tax reductions through, but the call for more revenue kept rates relatively high for most of the 1960s and 1970s. The top rate stood at 70 percent from 1965 through 1981.

Unbridled spending in Congress also fueled inflation, as spending outpaced revenues, and monetary policy was used to monetize the federal debt. Spending problems came to a head in the 1970s, as the nation experienced an era of stagflation, characterized by both high unemployment and high inflation.

The Reagan Revolution reduced income tax rates to their lowest levels since the 1920s. The top rate fell from 70 percent to 50 percent in 1982, and by 1988 it was just 28 percent.[35] Based on the results of previous rate cuts under President Calvin Coolidge in the 1920s and President Kennedy in the '60s, the results of the Reagan tax reforms should be unsurprising—federal income tax revenue increased by 25 percent from 1980 to 1990, and real economic growth increased from 1.6 percent in 1983 to 3.5 percent in 1990.[36] Tax rates went down, growth and revenues went up.

Unfortunately, despite all the evidence that the lower tax rates of the Reagan era had worked, a sharp but brief recession in 1990–91 prompted President George H. W. Bush to raise top income tax rates in 1991 (the infamous "read my lips" tax hike), followed by an even larger tax hike by President Bill Clinton in 1993. Clinton's abrupt increase in the top marginal rate, from 31 percent to 39.6, slowed economic growth coming out of the recession, and even as growth continued, real wages fell. Notably, after relatively small tax cuts resulting from a 1997 compromise between Clinton and the Republican-controlled Congress, GDP and real wages both began to grow at a significantly higher rate.[37]

Clinton's successor, George W. Bush, delivered on his campaign promise to lower taxes, passing major tax cuts in 2001 and 2003, which reduced the top tax rate to 35 percent. Unfortunately, though the Bush tax cuts did give tax relief to a large percentage of Americans, they were also made temporary, creating economic uncertainty because the rates would automatically increase again in 10 years without congressional action. In addition, the Bush tax cuts shrunk the tax base considerably and greatly increased progressivity. By 2003, the Joint Economic Committee reported that not only did the top 50 percent of earners pay 96.5 percent of all income taxes, but 11 million of the lowest income earners actually paid a "negative income tax"; that is, they received more in refunds from the IRS than they paid in taxes.[38]

Looking back at the last quarter-century of bipartisan tax rate fiddling, we find ourselves stuck with a progressive tax system that destroys wealth and prevents job creation and economic growth. This is true not only for the personal income tax but also for the corporate income tax, which drives businesses away from our shores.

Though the United States once may have been the premier location for doing business worldwide, that image has been tarnished, in large part, due to a tax code that puts American businesses at a competitive disadvantage. Rates that were low relative to other nations are no longer a draw to businesses. As of April 1, 2012, when Japanese tax cuts took effect, the United States will have the highest corporate tax rates in the developed world.[39,40] Since 1960, the number of the world's twenty largest companies headquartered in the United States has been in steep decline, from eighteen in 1960, to just eight in 1996, and only six in 2010.[41]

The result of decades of meddling is a system so complex that only the most resourceful can navigate it. According to the U.S. Government Accountability Office, the lawyers have a field day with the tax code: "Tax avoidance has become such a concern that some tax experts say corporate tax departments have become 'profit centers' as corporations seek to take advantage of the tax laws in order to maximize shareholder value."[42] Indeed, General Electric, with its team of well-heeled lobbyists drawn from the ranks of the IRS and the congressional tax-writing committees, filed a 57,000-page tax return.[43] The massive tax return is a symptom of a broken tax code that has long been a tool of political influence, with Congress setting policies based not on efficiency or fairness but "by graft and by pull."

The picture is no better for individual tax filers. The tax code itself has more than 693 sections applicable to individuals, and 1,501 sections applicable to businesses. The IRS has issued more than 20,000 pages of regulations, according to Congress's Joint Committee on Taxation.[44] And even the IRS may not be able to help you understand it. Numerous studies have found that, when called for advice, the IRS has provided the wrong answer up to 35 percent of the time. Filling out IRS Form 1040 takes taxpayers an estimated 2.4 billion hours.[45]

Complexity does more than just increase compliance costs. It also increases the deadweight costs in the economy, when resources are diverted from productive to less-valued uses. This includes resources paid to accountants and lawyers to decipher the tax code as well as the more significant costs of lobbying and campaign spending as various interests pursue favorable changes to the tax code. Quite simply, the tax code has become an awkward, inefficient political tool for redistributing income to favored political interests. Tax credits, tax breaks, earned income credits, and deductions are used to reward or promote everything from renewable energy to child-rearing. Far from simply raising revenue, the tax code has become a favored target of lobbyists and others seeking special benefits or social goals.

SIMPLE, LOW, FAIR, HONEST

At the most basic level, a tax code should be designed to collect revenues fairly, efficiently, and in a way that does not promote corruption, encourage tax avoidance, or hamper economic growth. In short, if we are going to have an income tax, it should be a flat tax, period.

It is time to scrap the code and replace it with a simple, fair, flat tax, which would greatly ease the burden of compliance and, with it, the need for an intrusive IRS. A flat tax would make the process of paying tax far less painful, while at the same time stimulating the economy. The average American would benefit; all individuals would be treated exactly the same as everybody else, and the average taxpayer would no longer be at the mercy of special-interest lobbyists who constantly seek to shift the tax burden to others.

How would it work?

Step one. Scrap the existing code.

Step two. Establish a single, flat rate on personal and business income.

These steps would massively shrink the current tax code, replacing hundreds of pages of tax forms with one postcard-size return. Taxpayers would calculate their income (salary and wages plus pension and retirement benefits), subtract their personal allowances based on marital status and number of dependents, and pay a flat rate on the rest. In one popular flat tax proposal, a family of four would have the first $40,000 of its income tax free, $10,000 per person; any amount above this would be taxed at 17 percent.

Step three. Do the same thing with corporate taxes.

These would also be simplified tremendously, reducing compliance costs and allowing businesses to invest in job growth while also lowering costs to consumers. Like the individual flat tax, with the business flat tax income would be taxed once and only once. Businesses would calculate total revenue, subtract total expenses, and pay a flat tax on that amount. Expenses would include purchases of goods and services, wages, salaries, and pensions, as well as capital expenditures such as land and buildings. The people or businesses that profited from those expenses would pay those taxes. Businesses making a profit, therefore, would pay a flat rate on those profits, while businesses with no profits or losses would pay nothing.

Step four. File your taxes on a postcard.

Step five. Use all the time and money you've saved in the full pursuit of life, liberty, and happiness.

Under real tax reform, everyone will understand the tax code, and clever lawyers or lobbyists will have no influence over how America pays its taxes. All taxpayers would be treated equally—imagine that—and the tax code would no longer discriminate against individuals based on how they spend their income. At the same time, generous personal allowances would assist those families struggling to make ends meet, by reducing their tax burden.

In addition, American taxpayers can reclaim the billions of hours they spend trying to comply with the current code. By eliminating the confusing and confounding layers of credits, deductions, and penalties that have been carved out by special interests over the years, taxpayers will reclaim the high ground, paying taxes simply and efficiently, without the painful, contorted maneuvers foisted on them by special interests.

While this is great news for the taxpayer, it is bad news for the lobbyists who curry favor in Washington. The tax code is arguably responsible for the majority of lobbying activity in Washington. One measure of this activity is that members of the congressional tax-writing committees are the most heavily lobbied. According to data from the Federal Election Commission (FEC) compiled by the Center for Responsive Politics, during the 2009–2010 congressional cycle, the thirty-nine members of the House Ways and Means Committee received a total of $31,473,562 in contributions from various political action committees (PACs). During this same period, the twenty members of the Senate Finance Committee received a total of $59,285,173 in PAC contributions.[46] Under a flat tax, this growth industry and its backroom deals would evaporate.

A simple flat tax thus offers a number of advantages over the existing tax code. The fixed rate exercises a real restraint on government growth. Politicians who try to raise it would likely face universal opposition. And the flat tax is much more transparent than the current code, allowing taxpayers to keep a much closer watch over the spending proclivities of Congress.

Under existing tax law, interest, dividend income, and capital gains are taxed at both the corporate and the individual level, meaning investors are double-taxed. With the flat tax, however, this income would no longer be taxable, ending the excessive double taxation of investment income.

Additionally, rescinding the capital gains tax removes negative incentives for investment, since returns would be greater with lower taxes. Improved gains from investments would encourage more savings, through stocks, bonds, and bank accounts. Savings plans like IRAs would have no caps and all returns would be tax free. By encouraging savings, the flat tax would fuel economic growth, as savings prompts capital formation, which increases productivity, lowers costs, and increases wages.

Adopting a flat tax will also boost economic growth by increasing take-home wages, which will increase incentives to work and expand economic output.[47] Additionally, removing punitive taxes on capital gains and interest would promote greater investment in the economy. In other words, hard work and success would be rewarded. Economist Lawrence Kotlikoff found that within ten years, the capital stock would increase an estimated 17 percent, which would help to fuel an initial increase in the national output of 4 percent.[48] If GDP does grow immediately by 4 percent, and over the next ten years the capital base increases by 17 percent, this would greatly promote long-term fiscal health, as wages, profits, dividends, and consequently, incomes would increase rapidly.

This all sounds great, you might say, but the federal government still needs to function. Won't lowering tax rates prevent the government from providing essential services? In fact, historical data shows that lowering tax rates can *increase* government revenue by growing the economy. According to economist Veronique de Rugy, when President Coolidge slashed tax rates for the highest bracket of taxpayers (from 60 to 25 percent), their share of the overall tax burden actually doubled.[49] Tax rate cuts by President Kennedy (one of the original supply-siders?) similarly saw revenues from the wealthy climb by 57 percent, while the Reagan tax rate cuts saw the revenues from the top 1 percent increase from 17.6 percent of the totals to 27.5 percent, according to Cato economist Dan Mitchell.[50]

Why did this happen? Because freedom works. When individuals and entrepreneurs pay less in taxes, they can spend more on developing their businesses, investing in expansion, and hiring new workers. Lower rates unlock wealth and capital that otherwise sits idle and protected in tax shelters and havens. More wealth creation means more income being taxed and more government revenue. So we can have both economic growth and sufficient revenue to fund the constitutionally appropriate functions of government.

Such a healthy, growing economy is obviously not only good in the abstract; it has real-world impact. It means more jobs, more wealth creation, and more opportunities for Americans of all backgrounds to assert their economic liberty and pursue their happiness. Indeed, economic growth is important to all Americans and provides the engine for families to live the American dream. To shackle growth with a tax code that is inefficient, complex, and unfair makes no sense.

I STILL HAVEN'T FOUND WHAT
I'M LOOKING FOR

INCENTIVES MATTER, AND SO DO TAX SYSTEMS. AS WITH ANYTHING else, if you punish wealth creation (through the tax code), you will get less of it. If you punish the capital that drives innovation, and the wealth that rewards successful innovation, you will get less of it. Barack Obama and Warren Buffett apparently don't buy into this economic law. But U2 certainly does. Wildly successful, the band U2 is known as much for the advocacy by its leader, Bono, on behalf of third-world debt relief as it is for its music. In 2006, the band responded with their feet to what would have amounted to a massive tax increase imposed by the government of Ireland on the group's royalty payments (*profit* is such a dirty word I won't employ it here). As you might expect, U2 picked up and moved a good portion of its business interests, reincorporating as U2 Ltd in the Netherlands. The shift, according to the band's manager, Paul McGuinness, made economic sense. "Like any other business," he said, "U2 operates in a tax-efficient manner." [51]

Democratic senator John Kerry of Massachusetts, who along with his wife, Teresa Heinz Kerry, is estimated to be worth a total of $1 billion,[52] also seems to understand the importance of tax systems. At least when it comes to protecting *his* family's fortune, that is. In 2010, the Massachusetts resident registered the new family yacht in Rhode Island, which had repealed the Boat Sales and Use tax in 1993. According to the *Boston Herald,* "*Isabel*—Kerry's luxe, 76-foot New Zealand–built Friendship sloop," features "an Edwardian-style, glossy varnished teak interior, two VIP main cabins, and a pilothouse fitted with a wet bar and cold wine storage." Here's the catch: "Cash-strapped Massachusetts still collects a 6.25 percent sales tax and an annual excise tax on yachts. Sources say *Isabel* sold for something in the neighborhood of $7 million, meaning Kerry saved approximately $437,500 in sales tax and an annual excise tax of about $70,000." [53]

Soon after the senator's "tax-efficient manner" of registering his new 76-foot toy was discovered by the press, the progressive, tax-loving Democrat agreed to "voluntarily pay $500,000 to Massachusetts tax collectors on his luxury yacht, a pledge made hours after state officials had begun inquiring into whether he had attempted to evade the payment by docking the boat in Rhode Island." [54]

Senator Kerry is one of President Obama's most reliable votes in the U.S. Senate. Bono, meanwhile, should "count himself as one of President Obama's unofficial foreign policy advisers," according to *Politico*.[55] At a 2010 sit-down with the president at the White House, Obama got a download on the rock star's vision for third-world economic development:

> A recurring theme was innovation. We agreed that there are simple technologies that need to be made more available to transform not only public health, but also agriculture, helping farmers check prices and weather patterns. While acknowledging these are difficult times for donor economies, we discussed the President's food security initiative and agreed to encourage other countries who signed up to keep their commitment to invest $22 billion over 3 years.[56]

Perhaps "tax efficiency" and the need for simple, low, fair, and honest tax systems could be added to the next briefing agenda? After all, a number of struggling nations—twenty-three at last count—have scrapped their punitive tax systems for a simple, low flat tax on income, and the results have been exactly what you might predict: more economic growth, more tax compliance, more freedom. To be sure, tax reforms do not substitute for sound money, strictly enforced property rights, and the rule of law that ensures other people won't hurt you or take your stuff. But the simple logic of a tax system that does not try to socially engineer preferred behavior from the top down is undeniable.

Back here in the United States, too many wealthy, well-connected people are perfectly comfortable with big, expensive government and a tax code that punishes accomplishment, because they know, when push comes to shove, that their tax lawyer will find a way to work around it, or their man in Washington will just draft a brand-new carve-out.

The political marketplace for special provisions in the tax code is a particularly brazen example of the insider trading that takes place within the walls of the political establishment. Every year, a pitched battle over temporary, one-year tax provisions—so called "tax extenders"—becomes the most important occasion in Washington. There is no economic logic for the permanent uncertainty of not knowing, from one fiscal year to the next, what your personal or company tax treatment will be. It's not the logic that matters here. The purpose of an annual battle over tax extenders is to sustain the symbiotic culture of members of Congress who sit on the right committee, feeding off the PAC dollars of any interest needing an extender, while the well-heeled interests most skilled in manipulating the tax-writing process feed off the political pull of the politicians whose attentions they just bought.

Days after the president's massive health care bill passed in 2010, one lobbyist explained to me why it was that small businesses that own tanning beds ended up, at the eleventh hour, becoming a "pay for" revenue offset for new Obamacare spending. What on earth do tanning beds have to do with the funding of government-run health care? "They didn't show up," she said. The message is clear: Play the game, write the checks, feed the beast, or someone who is playing the game better might just put you out of business.

That tanning-bed tax, by the way, has so far only raised one-third of the revenue officially projected when it was proposed, as local salons shut down and customers seek out cheaper alternatives—like sunbathing.[57]

How do we break the cycle? *You have to show up.* Government goes to those who show up. We will only succeed in scrapping the tax code and replacing it with a simple, honest system when America beats Washington and all the interests aligned against honest tax policy. Once, this was a pipe dream. But today, all the tax lobbyists lined up outside the House Ways and Means Committee or the Senate Finance Committee do not have the privileged vantage of a closed system where the only people who know what is being drafted and debated and voted on are those inside the process. We the People now have millions of freedom-loving eyeballs and an army of citizen reporters who get the facts first and distribute them through chosen pathways and social-media outlets online. The lowered cost of the right information at the right time takes away much of the strategic advantage once enjoyed by the swarm of interests inside the Washington Beltway.

At some point, Thomas Jefferson believed, you have to choose "between economy and liberty, or profusion and servitude." You have to show up. Otherwise, you might become the next "pay for" dropped into the small print of the next "shared sacrifice" tax hike legislation ostensibly targeting those among us who have been deemed, from the top down, to have already "made enough money."

CHAPTER 9

A STANDARD OF VALUE

Freedom of our currency is the fundamental
issue; it is the keystone of a free society.
—Hans Sennholz, *Money and Freedom*

DR. HANS SENNHOLZ WAS THE CHAIRMAN OF THE ECONOMICS DE-
partment at Grove City College when I was a student there. He was
an intellectual mentor and his Austrian approach to economics was an
important influence on my own way of thinking. Sennholz's thought,
in turn, was shaped by the work of Ludwig von Mises, Sennholz having received his doctorate in economics under Mises at New York
University soon after the Viennese expat had arrived in the United
States. Both Mises and Sennholz were known for their students' as
well as their own scholarly work in economics.

Before reading this book, you may never have heard of Sennholz or
even Mises. But one of Sennholz's most successful "students" is someone you probably do know. That's Congressman Ron Paul, M.D., of
Texas, who says that Sennholz's ideas on money and the business cycle
were "a tremendous influence." [1]

I think it's safe to say that we would not be talking about the failures of top-down monetary policy in the United States without the uncompromising determination of Dr. Paul, and the attention he has brought to the issue of sound money through his presidential campaigns. We would not have access to revealing new information produced by the first public audit of the Fed. We would not be debating, in the mainstream media, the massive damage, from the top down, that the government's grossly irresponsible manipulation of the dollar has wrought on our economy.

INFLATED SCRUTINY

THE GENERAL PUBLIC OFTEN VIEWS MONETARY POLICY AS A COMPLEX, technical field that is better left to the experts. That's exactly how the Washington establishment and its czar culture like it. But monetary policy came into the spotlight in 2008, when the financial collapse revealed, as long-battling reformers like Paul had been warning for years, that the "experts" were more concerned with protecting their interests and the interests of the crony capitalists of Wall Street than in defending the taxpayers. Suddenly the American people became interested in the complicated world of monetary policy, learning how it has been used over the years to manipulate markets for the benefit of big banks and big government. They're focusing, correctly, on the Federal Reserve, demanding that the agency come under greater scrutiny, and that we abandon policies that use money as a tool for the elites, and instead pursue alternative monetary policies that focus on creating a standard of value.

Just a few short years ago, hardly anyone except Paul was questioning the Federal Reserve. The financial meltdown of 2008, and the decentralization of information, changed that, and not a moment too soon.

In the wake of a secretive trillion-dollar bailout by the Fed, where the central bank purchased toxic assets at home and abroad to save certain favored banks and shift the burden to taxpayers (and anyone who holds dollars, for that matter), the American people started to take notice. Congress ordered an audit—albeit a watered-down one. Suddenly the Fed saw the political need to be—or at least appear to be—more transparent, and Fed chairman Ben Bernanke claimed that increasing transparency and accountability would be the highlights of his chairmanship.[2] This was a response to public pressure, but it smacked of damage control, not a shift in policy. Regardless, the American people are now paying attention to the elephant in the room, Fed responsibility for the boom and bust of financial crises and the bailout culture that has grown over the past century.

The expansive monetary policies of government central banks have reaped disastrous consequences for both the U.S. and global economies. Europe, in particular, faces serious economic challenges brought on by an attempt to set monetary policy without regard to fiscal differences among member nations. Unfortunately, many U.S. banks have risky exposures in these debt-strapped countries and many are now hoping that the Fed and the International Monetary Fund will bail out their bad bets. Haven't we been here before? Easy money and too much government spending and meddling and another financial crisis that will surely rival the 2008 meltdown. The boom and the bust, and American taxpayers are once again left holding the bag.

WHERE DOES MONEY COME FROM?

THOUGH WE ALL USE MONEY EVERY DAY, MOST OF US PROBABLY DON'T often sit down and think about what makes money work. If you are like most folks, you might never have thought to ask the question until you saw Keynes and Hayek rap on YouTube. Or maybe you just knew, without anyone needing to point out the obvious, that creating trillions in money and credit out of thin air to pay for bailouts and unfunded government promises was a really bad idea. Something didn't add up.

Against all plausible expectations, Ben Bernanke made it cool to debate monetary policy. Go figure.

Money comes from the same process of people acting and interacting that generates knowledge, coordination of plans, and societal progress. In order to understand the extent of the damage done by the Fed and our national monetary policies, we have to answer a seemingly simple question: "What is money?" The answer to this question immediately revisits a now common theme you will immediately recognize. Sound money emerges freely, from the bottom up. The destruction of sound money, and the collateral damage that ensues, is inevitably imposed from the top down.

At the simplest level, money is a medium of exchange. Forms of money used by different societies have changed over time, but the basic goal of money is to facilitate transactions in the market. You can trace the origins of money (and virtually every other good) back to the subjective values of individuals interacting in the marketplace. In essence, money is an unintended consequence of individuals pursuing their self-interest. Its use and purpose is defined from the bottom up, by people trading and interacting. We need money for markets to work. Remember that the Marxist conception of socialism was the complete elimination of money and exchange.

The first thing to notice about money is that it's different from many other elements of the market in that it permeates the whole market order. Any changes in the money supply will have an impact on the entire economy. If an imbalance between supply and demand for money arises, the effect is upon the economy as a whole. This is different from the case of a commodity, where supply and demand can be adjusted by the individuals engaged in exchange without disturbing other markets. To use an example, a shortage of steel would lead to an increase in its price, signaling consumers to reduce their use, while encouraging producers to identify additional sources of steel or cheaper substitutes. The price mechanism forces people to adjust their behavior. An imbalance between the supply and demand of money, on the other hand, has far more significant implications for the economy, with the potential for creation of depressions or hyper-inflations that dramatically affect economic output.

For Carl Menger, Ludwig von Mises, and others in the Austrian School, the value of money is determined in the same way the value of other goods is determined—subjectively. Individuals desire money because it facilitates the exchange process. Other standard character-istics of money—a unit of account, a store of value—are secondary to the importance of providing a medium of exchange. Money is valued for its ability to be exchanged for final goods. This poses a challenge for economists, because how I value money will rely on how others value money. I will value money because I know that others value it and will exchange goods and services for it. It appears that individuals value money because the group values money, but the group values money because individuals do. It's a chicken-and-egg question with far-reaching ramifications.

So where does money get its value? For Mises, the individual's subjective evaluation was the source of all value for all goods, includ-ing money.

To solve this quandary, Mises developed a "regression theorem," drawing from Carl Menger's insight into the origins of money.[3] Menger proposed that money emerged from a barter society, an inef-ficient process that forced people to seek out commodities that were highly tradeable.[4] In effect, money solves the problem of the double "coincidence of wants." That is, in a barter system, I must find some-one who has what I am seeking and who is also interested in obtaining my goods. But what if I can't find such a person? It can be very incon-venient. But if there is some other thing that many people are willing to use as a medium of exchange, and if I have enough of that thing, then I will find it easier to obtain what I'm seeking. I should be able to find someone who will gladly accept *that* thing, in exchange for the thing I want. As a result of this indirect exchange process, eventually one commodity emerges as the dominant and most readily accepted commodity, and thus becomes a form of currency, or money, for the society. Thus, the ultimate source of value for money can be found by examining the original use value. For example, cattle were a form of money for many centuries. But cattle, though they make good wallets, unfortunately don't fit into very many. Can you imagine buying a plane ticket with a cow? It could prove cumbersome.

While Menger claimed that money evolved from the bartering process, Mises worked backward, looking at the value of money today, and tracing its value back to when the money was traded as a commodity. Mises observed that we only know about money based on what it was worth yesterday. So, instead of a circular flow between objective exchange value and subjective use value, we have a spiral that goes back in time. Fortunately, this spiral does not regress infinitely; the spiral stops when a stage is reached where money has a use value other than as money. Gold, for example, may be used in jewelry and industrial processes, and is exchanged as a commodity for such purposes. This exchange process is where the value of money is generated.

In his classic book, *The Theory of Money and Credit,* Ludwig von Mises wrote that money is the most marketable commodity.[5] Many societies somehow found commodities that everyone accepted in exchange for whatever was sold. Throughout history, people have used countless commodity items as money, such as shells, beads, rice, and even alcohol. Cigarettes are still used as commodity money in U.S. prisons.[6] The most popular form of commodity money has always been precious metals.

The free market has repeatedly chosen gold and silver as money. These precious metals are seen to have value, and people easily accept gold or silver as payment. Gold and silver have been used as money for at least four thousand years.[7] One of the most attractive characteristics of gold and silver is that they cannot be manufactured on demand by government. "The amount of gold in the market is limited by the profitability of mining it out of the ground," writes economics professor Richard Ebeling of Michigan's Northwood University. When linked to gold, "the quantity of money, therefore, is controlled by the market forces of supply and demand." This means that governments cannot manipulate the quantity or value of money as a means of financing more government.[8]

This original use value and the spontaneous emergence of money solves the so-called circularity problem—money has a value that originates historically from the point where the commodity was used for other things. Money is a spontaneous order that evolves over time arising purely from free exchange among individuals as they pursue their self-interest. No government mandates or decrees are required to create money to facilitate exchange. Money is the unintended consequence of individuals all pursuing their self-interest.[9]

THE BOOM AND BUST

LIKE ALL ECONOMISTS, AUSTRIANS AGREE THAT AN INCREASE IN THE money supply can generate an increase in the price level; however, unlike monetarists, Austrians do not believe in a strict, mechanical relation between the price level and the money supply. There is a causal relationship, but that is all we can say. This difference leads to important divergent views on inflation. For monetarists, the money supply and money demand are aggregates, so their description of inflation leads monetarists to assume that a change in the money supply leads to a uniform change in the price level, affecting all market participants equally.

The Austrians offer a different view of the impact that changes in the money supply can have on economic decisions; this view examines the transmission mechanism for changes in the money supply. When new money enters the market, it is not introduced evenly across the board. There is an injection effect, with money entering the market at certain points and then spreading throughout the economy. Individuals close to the source of the injection will see the effects first, providing them with definite advantages. It is as if they are receiving new money for nothing. In turn, the spending patterns of these individuals will determine the next round of recipients, as the expansion pushes through the economy. These subsequent individuals may benefit from the "new" money as well, but as the process continues, prices are eventually bid up by people who believe that they are wealthier than they really are. Unfortunately, those at the bottom of this process will be paying higher prices without receiving any new money. Ultimately, everyone is paying higher prices and no one is better off, because the currency has been artificially inflated.

In other words, when the Fed creates money out of thin air, it corrupts the primary function of money as a standard of value. It violates an implied contract across society that a dollar is worth a dollar. These distortions send bad price signals, encourage bad investments, and create bubbles. Take, for example, the artificial boom in housing prices of the past decade. Many people at points of entry, such as mortgage bankers and investment banks that bet big on mortgage-backed securities, cashed in. Many homeowners, herded into inflated mortgage contracts by Fed-expanded credit, tax incentives, government-subsidized loans through Fannie and Freddie, and mandates like the Community Reinvestment Act, were left holding the bag. The "bag," as it were, was filled with phony government money.

"True," says Mises, "governments can reduce the rate of interest in the short run. They can issue additional paper money. They can open the way to credit expansion by the banks."[10] These are all ways that the Federal Reserve injects new money into the economy. "They can thus create an artificial boom and the appearance of prosperity. But such a boom is bound to collapse soon or late," he predicts. The inevitable corrections are painful, leaving people poorer. More often than not, the first victims of this boom and bust are those on the lower rungs of the economic ladder. Like so many self-professed "well-meaning" public policies, the net effect of government "help" aimed at allowing the working poor to own homes leaves them worse off, stripped of their savings. But some savvy, well-connected mortgage banker, positioned at a privileged "injection point," and armed with a long contact list of friends in high places in Washington, D.C., comes out of the crisis fat and happy. In fact, he may even receive a bonus for the misery he helped create.

Attempts by government to inject still more money into the economy, to prop up the bad decisions created by the last cycle of easy money and to repair the real economic pain caused by the boom-bust cycle, leads to more sustained pain, inflation, and economic stagnation. To quote Rick Santelli's famous Rant Heard 'Round the World, "Did you hear that, President Obama?" How about you, Chairman Bernanke?

PROGRESSIVELY CENTRALIZED

MONEY DOES NOT ORIGINATE WITH GOVERNMENT. IT ARISES NATU-rally from market forces. But power-hungry governments invariably come along and try to take control of money creation. For example, Executive Order 6102, signed by President Franklin D. Roosevelt in early 1933, made it a criminal offense for an individual to own large amounts of gold.[11] With this step—monopolizing gold—the federal government effectively made itself the creator and controller of our money supply. A dollar is, in effect, a contract between you and the federal government. The government issued the contract. In the past, the government promised you an amount of gold for a piece of paper, and vice versa. Now, unfortunately, the government has breached the contract (by breaking the link to gold) and is controlling the value of money to support its own spending binges, bailouts, and manipulations of markets.

We are required by law to use the paper dollar as money. Thus the U.S. dollar has become a "fiat currency," meaning that it is backed by absolutely nothing but the government's promise, potentially worth nothing more than the paper it's printed on. Unlike gold or other currencies whose value is based on supply and demand, the U.S. dollar has value only because the government says it does. The value of that little green piece of paper is guaranteed by the "full faith and credit of the United States." Or in other words: "Trust us."

History demonstrates that fiat currencies typically fail, with an average life expectancy of just twenty-seven years.[12] In the words of Detlev Schlichter, author of *Paper Money Collapse—The Folly of Elastic Money and the Coming Monetary Meltdown*: "Complete paper money systems are always creations of the state, never the outcome of private initiative or the free market. All paper money systems in history have, after some time, experienced growing financial instabilities, economic volatility, and an accelerating decline in money's purchasing power. All of them ultimately failed."[13]

Although FDR broke the link between the dollar and gold for U.S. citizens in 1933, the U.S. government continued to back the dollar with gold in transactions with other nations. In the midst of World War II, with the help of John Maynard Keynes, governments came together in Bretton Woods, New Hampshire, to plan for postwar currency stability through a system in which all currencies would be linked to the U.S. dollar via fixed exchange rates, and the dollar would be backed by U.S.-held gold. Central banks could come to the U.S. "gold window" and trade pieces of paper for little bits of yellow metal, just as citizens could once do.

But the gold-based Bretton Woods system only lasted till 1971, when it utterly collapsed, never to rise again. Why? Because the United States had been running a serious deficit, due to a massive surge in government spending. Uncle Sam had been using the privileged position in the global economy given him by Bretton Woods to spend like a drunken sailor in an upscale brothel. The costly Vietnam War and President Lyndon Johnson's Great Society programs drained the gold from Fort Knox. To avert the crisis, on August 15, 1971, President Nixon defaulted. He radically changed the global monetary system by suspending the convertibility of the U.S. dollar into gold. He shut the "gold window" to the world's banks, and thereby severed the final link tying the U.S. dollar—and the global economy—to anything more valuable than a promise. He should have made an effort to dramatically cut government spending. Instead, he opted for what turned out to be a colossal monetary error.

Since that day four decades ago, the U.S. dollar has been a pure fiat currency. The decision to end the gold exchange standard is remembered as the "Nixon Shock," and it still holds enormous ramifications for every single American today. Separating the link between U.S. dollars and gold eliminated important restraints on the government's ability to manipulate the money supply. Nixon made other mistakes that cemented a different legacy in Americans' minds. Otherwise, he'd be getting much of the blame for our current problems.

Fiat currencies grant central bankers and politicians flexibility and discretion—a veritable blank check. This is not a good thing for the American people, because more flexibility means more power for the central authority. Unlike the gold exchange standard, there is no limit on the amount of money the government can print. As a result of the government's abuse of this power, the dollar has lost 80 percent of its value since 1971, meaning today's dollar is worth less than 20 cents compared to the stronger pre-Nixon dollar.[14] The price of gold, which is essentially a reflection of the dollar's weakness, has risen to all-time highs.[15]

Here's the rub. The government has zero money of its own. It's not Santa Claus with a Midas touch. It can't replenish Fort Knox on command. The government has to go out and get money from those who produce the things that make money valuable. When it wants to spend money that it does not have, it can do but three things. 1) It can raise taxes. 2) It can borrow money through the selling of government securities (i.e., promises to repay in the future). Or 3) it can simply print more dollars. Given his penchant for new spending, Barack Obama has gone for the full Monty. But even with all the administration's new taxes and massive borrowing, printing money is the most destructive practice. It's also the easiest, essentially a form of taxation without legislation and, at least until recently, little noticed by the public. The inherent complexity of currency manipulation through monetary policy makes it a tempting vehicle for government growth.

Enter the Federal Reserve, a quasi-governmental bank that controls the amount of dollars in the economy. Created in 1913, the Fed has a seven-member board of governors, appointed by the president and confirmed by the Senate. In addition, there are twelve regional Federal Reserve banks. The Federal Open Market Committee (FOMC) is the arm of the Fed that controls monetary policy. It is comprised of the seven members of the board of governors and the presidents of five of the regional reserve banks. The New York Fed is a continuous member of the FOMC; the other reserve banks rotate one-year terms. The FOMC influences interest rates by either buying or selling government bonds. When it wants to increase the money supply, it purchases long-term treasury bonds, which lowers interest rates and pumps more dollars into the economy. When it wants to decrease the money supply, it sells these bonds, which raises interest rates and reduces the number of dollars in the economy.

Most of the time, the denizens at the Fed's grandiose headquarters on Constitution Avenue in Washington don't like to admit that their manipulation is essentially a sneaky way to print more money, but occasionally they let the truth slip. In a March 15, 2009, interview on *60 Minutes*, picked up by the researchers at Comedy Central's *The Daily Show*, Federal Reserve Chairman Ben Bernanke—who now regularly denies that the Fed is printing money—admitted that "to lend to a bank . . . it's much more akin to printing money than it is to borrowing." "You've been printing money?" *60 Minutes* asks. Bernanke replies: "Well, effectively." [16] This unchecked power gives the Fed monopoly control over our money supply. The more dollars we have in the circulation, the less valuable our money becomes; they are essentially stealing our hard-earned money through a hidden tax.

On the Federal Reserve's main website, it says that the bank was founded "to provide the nation with a safer, more flexible and more stable monetary system." [17] The Fed's original mandate was to establish a monetary system and furnish an "elastic currency." But, as with every government creation, the scope of its power increased over time. In 1977, Congress passed the Federal Reserve Reform Act, which established the Fed's "dual mandate": maintaining stable prices and maximum employment. It has failed miserably at both of these stated missions. One reason is that neither mission can be reliably achieved with a printing press. Another is that the dual mandate is premised on faulty economics, introduced at a time when many economists thought there was a trade-off between unemployment and inflation that could be used to guide policy. However, the stagflation of the 1970s and early 1980s proved this theory wrong, as the era was plagued by both high inflation rates and high unemployment.

The goal of the Progressive Era was to increase government control over the economy, replacing the dispersed wisdom of free people with a government of experts empowered to plan a better society from the top down. The creation of a central bank was a key piece of the puzzle, along with a federal income tax. The fateful Federal Reserve bill was passed on the evening of December 22, 1913, when many congressional members were home on Christmas break. This sounds a lot like the dirty tactics used to pass Obamacare in 2010, doesn't it? It concluded a terrible year for individual liberty, with the Progressive movement achieving some of the most destructive pieces of legislation in American history, including the federal income tax and the creation of the Federal Reserve.

SEXTILLIONS

LONG BEFORE HE WOULD CONTRIVE NOTIONS LIKE "AGGREGATE DE-mand," even John Maynard Keynes understood that allowing governments to inflate the money supply unchecked would be devastating to a free economy. In by far his best book, *The Economic Consequences of the Peace*, Keynes wrote that "Lenin is said to have declared that the best way to destroy the Capitalist System was to debauch the currency. By a continuing process of inflation, government can confiscate, secretly and unobserved, an important part of the wealth of their citizens. By this method they not only confiscate, but they confiscate arbitrarily; and while the process impoverishes many, it actually enriches some. . . . Lenin was certainly right. There is no subtler, no surer means of overturning the existing basis of society than to debauch the currency."[18]

It is beyond dangerous for the government to have monopoly power over money creation. Consider Zimbabwe. Back in 1980, one Zimbabwe dollar equalled a U.S. $1.47. Beginning in the early 2000s, the Reserve Bank of Zimbabwe fired up the printing presses to pump massive amounts of new Zimbabwean dollars into their economy to pay off debts to the International Monetary Fund.[19] You can guess what happened next. Correct: rampant hyperinflation. In November 2008, Zimbabwe's annual inflation rate was 89.7 sextillion percent.[20] Does that sound like a made-up number? For future reference, it goes trillion, quadrillion, quintillion, sextillion. The last term is a 1 followed by 21 zeroes. Written out, 89.7 sextillion is 89,700,000,000,000,000,000,000. The inflation rate was so overwhelming that Zimbabwe's chief statistician, Moffat Nyoni, declared it impossible to calculate.[21]

In 2008, the *Los Angeles Times* reported that, "Zimbabwe is about to run out of the paper to print money on."[22] Zimbabwe printed its first 100-trillion banknote, worth roughly $30 USD, in early 2009.[23] Can you imagine walking around with a $100 trillion bill in your pocket? Zimbabwean children would traverse the streets with wheelbarrows full of cash. Tragically, the wheelbarrow was worth more than the mound of money it carried.

The Zimbabwean dollar officially collapsed in April 2009.[24] That month, the Freakonomics blog at the *New York Times* reported that "Zimbabwe's currency has been essentially worthless in-country for months. Now the Zimbabwe dollar is officially worth more on eBay, where collectors can snap up a few trillion-dollar notes for less than $25."[25] Zimbabwe had to ditch its currency and start all over again.

Another example of hyperinflation was in Germany's Weimar Republic. Before World War I, Germany had a fairly strong currency backed by gold, called, conveniently, the gold mark. About four or five marks could be exchanged for a dollar in 1914.[26] That year, Germany abandoned the gold backing of its currency.[27] Just as with Zimbabwe, it did this on purpose: to evade the repayment of massive debts. The Treaty of Versailles that ended World War I required Germany to pay heavy reparations to the Allies. The defeated Germans were on the hook for 132 billion marks, then worth $31.4 billion.[28] That's roughly equivalent to $442 billion in 2011. Critics argued that it would take a whopping 59 years to pay off the reparations, putting the final payment around 1978. They were wrong. It took Germany until October 3, 2010, to make its last payment.[29]

Most of the debt, however, was paid off in the first few years—with worthless paper. The Germans may have been beaten on the battlefield, but they knew how to evade their peacetime obligations. They just fired up the printing press. The consequences for the German people were disastrous. In 1923, 4.2 trillion marks could be exchanged for just one dollar.[30] An automobile full of cash could not have bought a newspaper. The mark became so worthless that the German people used it as wallpaper, toilet paper, and a substitute for firewood.[31]

We are not experiencing a devaluation of currency that rivals Zimbabwe or the Weimar Republic yet. But it's foolish to ignore the monetary policy mistakes they made, which left their money virtually worthless. Printing excessive amounts of money out of thin air to pay off debts has harsh consequences.

Our national debt is more than $15 trillion, making the United States not only the most indebted nation in the world but the most indebted nation in the history of the world.[32] But fear not; like Zimbabwe and Germany, we can just print more money to pay it off. Confirming this in an August 2011 *Meet the Press* interview, former Federal Reserve chairman Alan Greenspan said, "The United States can pay any debt it has because we can always print money to do that. So there is zero probability of default."[33] It's certainly true that the

Federal Reserve can just print more money, or add a few more zeros on a balance sheet to create money out of thin air—but not without trashing our currency and our economy.

SEND IN THE CLOWNS

THE FEDERAL RESERVE'S MAIN WEBSITE SAYS THAT "OVER THE YEARS, its role in banking and the economy has expanded." It now includes "maintaining the stability of the financial system and containing systemic risk that may arise in financial markets."[34] In practice, the Fed's machinations have produced systemic *instability*.

The Great Depression is a classic example of a Fed-generated boom and bust. The 1920s saw real economic growth with the nation's return to a peacetime footing plus the Coolidge pro-growth income tax-rate cuts. But it also saw a stock market bubble fueled by Fed policy. In late 1929, that bubble gave way to what should have been a sharp, but short correction. Fed intervention (compounded by the big-government, redistributionist policies of FDR) turned it into a decade-long economic nightmare. Some of its political aftershocks are still being felt even today. Global depression helped to fuel global destabilization, war, and a resurgence of socialist regimes across the world.

The Fed hasn't ended the business cycle; arguably, it has made it worse. According to George Mason University economist Lawrence White, "the classical gold standard of 1879–1914 functioned quite well without a central bank in the U.S., thank you very much. Despite the financial panics, which could have been avoided with banking deregulation, the business cycle wasn't worse than under the Fed's watch."[35]

Many Americans likely believe that continuous boom and bust cycles are natural occurrences, part of the inevitable "business cycle." But it's not true. We would not experience such dramatic economic swings were it not for monetary policies that distort real prices and encourage bad investment decisions. Boom and bust cycles are inevitable, though, when government interventions confuse consumers and producers.

The single greatest contributor to financial crisis is the Fed's manipulation of interest rates in ways that distort the true price of capital. When the Fed artificially lowers interest rates, it creates a false boom somewhere in the economy. The low cost of credit and unsustainable increase in money supply encourages businesses to greatly expand at the same time. It may seem as if businesses are overinvesting, but they are simply responding to false economic signals sent by the Federal Reserve. In retrospect, the businesses' decisions are seen as a bad allocation of resources.

The Federal Reserve cannot continue the boom permanently. An inevitable bust will always follow. The malinvestments fed by easy money are revealed, and wasted capital and economic losses incur as these misdirected investments are liquidated. In his classic book *Human Action,* Mises wrote:

> the popularity of inflation and credit expansion, the ultimate source of the repeated attempts to render people prosperous by credit expansion, and thus the cause of the cyclical fluctuations of business, manifests itself clearly in the customary terminology. The boom is called good business, prosperity, and upswing. Its unavoidable aftermath, the readjustment of conditions to the real data of the market, is called crisis, slump, bad business, depression. People rebel against the insight that the disturbing element is to be seen in the malinvestment and the overconsumption of the boom period and that such an artificially induced boom is doomed. They are looking for the philosophers' stone to make it last.[36]

Peter Schiff draws a perfect analogy between an artificial boom and a circus that comes to a small town for a short time. During this time, the circus attracts a large crowd, which is a boom to local businesses. Now imagine that a local businessman mistakenly believes that the upturn in his business will endure permanently. He responds by greatly expanding his business, hiring new workers or opening a second location. All is well until the circus leaves town and the businessman is left with a large surplus of workers and capacity. He finds out he miscalculated when all the bad investments are exposed.[37]

The last decade in America has been a textbook example of a boom and bust cycle. Between 2001 and 2004, the Federal Reserve injected new credit into the economy, pushing interest rates to their lowest level since the late 1970s.[38] The economy boomed as a result of the false economic signals to businesses with respect to demand for their products. These businesses responded by hiring more staff, buying more resources, investing in capital, and so forth.

The early 2000s marked the boom phase. Between September 2003 and December 2007, we experienced fifty-two months of uninterrupted job growth.[39] Treasury Secretary Henry Paulson in March 2007 said that "the global economy is more than sound: it's as strong as I've seen it in my business career."[40] He was certain it was true. On October 9, 2007, the Dow Jones Industrial Average closed at a record level of 14,164.53.[41] Federal Reserve Chairman Ben Bernanke seemingly concurred, saying in January 2008 that "the Federal Reserve is not currently forecasting a recession."[42] At the time he spoke, the recession had already begun.

Just as Austrian business cycle theory predicts, the boom was followed by the bust, when the stock market crashed in October 2008.[43] Some were quick to wrongly blame free market capitalism for the economic downturn. As economist Henry Hazlitt once said, "in a crisis and a slump . . . worse than the slump itself may be the public delusion that the slump has been caused, not by the previous inflation, but by the inherent defects of 'capitalism.' "[44]

Ted Forstmann, a private equity pioneer, gave a concise, perfectly "Austrian" explanation of the damage caused by easy money in a July 5, 2008, interview with the *Wall Street Journal*. Predicting the financial train wreck that was just months away, Forstmann said that he did not "know when money was ever this inexpensive in the history of this country. But not in modern times, that's for sure." Banks had "tons of money left," after making loans and investments based on proper risk assessment and a reasonable expectation of returns. That's when banks went into "such things as subprime mortgages." About a year before he died, I had the opportunity to ask him if he had read any Austrian business cycle theory, referencing this interview's foresight. I was sure he had. "No," Forstmann said, with a somewhat mystified look on his face. He just understood a top-down corruption of market signals when he saw one.

The Federal Reserve has repeatedly attempted to "fix" the problem that it created. The official unemployment rate has hovered around 9 percent for the past two years.[45] The central bank devised QE1 and QE2, which stands for quantitative easing parts 1 and 2, which is a more polite way of saying "printing money and then printing some more money." As economist Thomas Sowell says, "When people in Washington start creating fancy new phrases, instead of using plain English, you know they are doing something they don't want us to understand."[46] And the Fed has been busy; since 2007, their balance sheet has increased from roughly $850 billion to $2.7 trillion, which includes all the mortgage-backed securities and questionable assets the Fed has purchased—and you can be sure that any risk posed by these purchases will be borne by the taxpayer.[47]

"FULL FAITH AND CREDIT"

When the Federal Reserve was established, many championed the fact that the new regime was creating an independent body that could establish monetary policy without influence from political interests. This fantasy—centralized power without the undue influence of special interests—is the political unicorn of progressivism. It's never, ever true. The 2008 bailout, and the various tranches of "quantitative easing" since, ably demonstrate just how responsive the Fed is, in fact, to political pressure. The facts were hard to ignore when the Federal Reserve used the full "faith and credit" of the United States to rush to the aid of the big banks on Wall Street.

Simon Johnson and James Kwak report in their book *13 Bankers*:

> Any modern economy needs a financial system, not only to process payments, but also to transform savings in one part of the economy into productive investment in another part of the economy. However, the Obama administration had decided, like the George W. Bush and Bill Clinton administrations before it, that it needed *this* financial system—a system dominated by the thirteen bankers who came to the White House in March. Their banks used huge balance sheets to place bets in brand-new financial markets, stirring together complex derivatives with exotic mortgages in a toxic brew that ultimately poisoned the global economy.[48]

As the housing bubble burst and the house of cards collapsed, Wall Street was on the first train to Washington. Treasury Secretary Paulson, a former Goldman Sachs chairman, and the then-chairman of the New York Federal Reserve and soon to be Treasury Secretary Timothy Geithner rushed to prop up their Wall Street allies: first through the $700 billion Troubled Asset Relief Program, then through the Fed's special lending facilities, quantitative easing 1, quantitative easing 2, and other actions, the Fed propped up the failing banks, shifting their "troubled assets" over to the taxpayers. Since September 2008, when the crisis erupted, the Fed's security purchases increased from $3.7 billion to $1.97 trillion. This pushed the Fed's excess reserves up from $68.7 billion in 2008 to $1.47 trillion today.[49]

Despite the fact that trillions of dollars in questionable assets were sloshing through the system, it was virtually impossible for the public to access any information on what the Fed was up to. Even Neil Bartofsky, the Special Inspector General assigned to TARP, served up harsh criticism of the Treasury Department and the Fed in his testimony before Congress, where he estimated that the taxpayer liability for bailing out Wall Street reached more than $27 trillion. TARP was only the tip of the iceberg. In all, there were roughly fifty programs working furiously to stabilize Wall Street. While the liability figure is a worst-case scenario that would see none of the Fed's loans paid back, even a small percentage of it would be a significant burden for taxpayers.

The Fed's actions have done little to spark economic growth. Excess reserves—resources that banks are holding that could be lent to new ventures—increased by $490 billion, bringing the total to $1.5 trillion in 2011.[50] In other words, banks sat on the cash, facing gross uncertainty about the rules of the game as the Obama administration continued to change them, ad hoc. What, exactly, will a dollar be worth tomorrow? Will the government honor contracts? With a dragging economy and huge new, unquantifiable risks from forthcoming health care, financial services, and environmental regulations, many businesses faced too many uncertainties to make the investments necessary to spur economic growth. Nobel economist Robert Lucas compared economic growth in the United States to growth in Europe, which has typically had a larger regulatory state. Growth rates in Europe have lagged behind those of the United States, and Lucas noted that increases in the size of government and the regulatory state in the U.S. could mean that our growth rates will be more like those in Europe and we may never return to the pre-2008 growth path.[51]

Further, the Fed's spending binge may have paved the way for a next financial disaster. To date, inflation has remained low, ending 2011 at around 3.4 percent.[52] But that does not mean there is no threat of inflation. The Fed has to determine how to clear out its own balance sheet, which includes trillions in assets of questionable value. Will it choose Zimbabwe's path?

FATAL CONCEIT

BERNANKE HAS SUGGESTED THAT THE FED HAS THE SKILL TO FINE-tune monetary policy at the first hint of inflation, but again, this places the fate of the nation's economy in the hands of the experts—experts whose track record does not inspire confidence. Does the czar of the federal bank really have complete knowledge of the countless millions of bits of information dispersed throughout the economy? Does he know for certain both the seen and unseen consequences of his actions from the top down? I doubt it. Allan Meltzer, a professor of political economy at Carnegie Mellon University, wrote in 2009 that "the enormous increase in bank reserves—caused by the Fed's purchase of bonds and mortgages—will surely bring on severe inflation if allowed to remain." [53]

Despite lack of evidence to suggest that the Fed's actions are boosting economic growth, Bernanke is expanding its efforts to bail out banks—even European banks. Given the adverse publicity associated with the Fed's previous bailouts, the organization has taken a slightly different approach. Rather than directly bailing out the struggling European banks, the Fed is engaged in currency swaps with the European Central Bank, which can then use the dollars to extend loans to failing banks. As Gerald O'Driscoll noted, "This Byzantine financial arrangement could hardly be better designed to confuse observers, and it has largely succeeded on this side of the Atlantic, where press coverage has been light." [54]

The Federal Reserve is the most secretive and least accountable operation of the federal government. Bureaucrats at the bank are unelected and unaccountable to the American people. The first audit ever of the Federal Reserve was conducted in July 2011, almost 100 years after the secretive institution was founded. We finally have a sense of what the Fed has been hiding all these years. The Government Accountability Office conducted a onetime, watered-down audit of the central bank, and it gave the American people their first peek into the Fed's books but prevented investigators from peering into their deliberations on interest rates and other crucial transactions.

The central bank handed colossal amounts of cash to its Wall Street cronies without a single vote in Congress. In less than three years, unelected bureaucrats at the Fed "lent" out $16 trillion at 0 percent interest to corporations and banks around the world.[55] To help put that massive number into perspective, the national output of the U.S. is only about $14 trillion. Some observers speculate that billions of dollars may even be missing from the bank's released records.[56]

The Federal Reserve was ordered through a Freedom of Information Act request to release 28,000 pages of documents in March 2011, after fighting tooth and nail for more than two years to keep their actions hidden from the American people. Top Fed officials claimed that releasing their loan information to the public would cause "severe and irreparable competitive injury" to borrowing banks.[57] What were they hiding in there?

THE BUFFETT RULE

THE DOCUMENTS REVEALED THAT FOREIGN BANKS WERE AMONG THE largest recipients of the Fed's money during the 2008 meltdown. *Bloomberg News* reported that "the biggest borrowers from the 97-year-old discount window as the program reached its crisis-era peak were foreign banks, accounting for at least 70 percent of the $110.7 billion borrowed during the week in October 2008 when use of the program surged to a record."[58]

The top foreign banks that received money included the Brussels- and Paris-based Dexia SA, Dublin-based Depfa Bank Plc, the Bank of China, and Arab Banking Corp., which received seventy-three different loans in spite of the fact that it was 29 percent owned by the Libyan central bank at the time.[59]

The released documents revealed that the Federal Reserve had committed $7.77 trillion to "rescuing" the financial system as of March 2009, according to a study from *Bloomberg News*.[60] The Fed also kept secret which banks were in trouble during the height of the financial crisis while bankers were raking in tens of billions of dollars in emergency loans. *Bloomberg* has calculated that the secret Fed loans helped banks net a whopping $13 billion.[61] All these numbers are staggering—but not exactly surprising. The unelected bureaucrats at the Federal Reserve have fought to keep their dealings behind closed doors for a reason—some of those dealings help their politically connected friends.

The bailouts of 2008 and 2009 created a fantastic opportunity for moochers to profit from government-backed loans. Among those who lobbied for the bailouts and then profited from them was none other than Warren Buffett. As the markets tumbled and Congress was discussing a bailout, he took to the media to push the plan, calling the financial crisis an "economic Pearl Harbor."[62] While he claimed that the bailouts would be the right thing for America, the Oracle of Omaha also foresaw a massive business opportunity, in the form of government-backed loans. As several news sources later reported, Buffett's company, Berkshire Hathaway, had the fifth largest total of investments in companies receiving bailout money,[63] and its investment in TARP-backed companies reflected "at least twice as much dependence on bailed-out banks as any other large investor."[64]

Like many others who bet on the government bailouts, Buffett profited handsomely, making over $3.6 billion in profits from his investment in Goldman Sachs. And that wasn't his only winning bet on crony capitalism: Buffett has also profited by $1.2 billion from investments in—why does this not surprise?—the king of all government-subsidized corporations, General Electric.[65] More recently, Buffett appears to have placed another bet on the government's too-big-to-fail policies, sinking $3 billion into the struggling Bank of America. As Tim Carney of the *Washington Examiner* noted, Buffett's Bank of America bailout coincided with an announcement that he would be hosting another fund-raiser for President Obama's reelection campaign.[66] America's wealthiest financier certainly knows how to protect his investments.

The Federal Reserve is a prime player in the growth of our bailout culture. Fiat money enables the Fed to bail out its friends with little risk, but with massive ramifications for the rest of us. To make matters worse, *Bloomberg* has reported that we haven't been told the whole truth about the bank bailouts: "While Fed officials say that almost all the loans were repaid and there have been no losses, details suggest taxpayers paid a price beyond dollars as the secret funding helped preserve a broken status quo and enabled the biggest banks to grow even bigger."[67]

A prime example of the Fed's close ties to the banking industry it supposedly oversees is reflected in the bailout of the American International Group. When AIG's credit lines dried up after being downgraded in September 2008, Ben Bernanke decided that the insurance titan was simply "too big to fail." With the blessing of Treasury Secretary Hank Paulson, Bernanke allowed the New York Federal Reserve Bank (headed by the future Treasury secretary, Timothy Geithner) to extend a credit line of over $80 billion to bail AIG out, and AIG eventually put taxpayers on the hook for over $182 billion.[68]

Secretary Paulson justified the decision by saying, "An AIG failure would have been devastating to the financial system and the economy,"[69] yet the deal that was reached seemed to have more to do with protecting the assets of certain banks. Beyond putting taxpayers on the hook for a company that had overloaded its holdings with toxic housing securities, the deal negotiated by the Fed allowed companies with significant interests in AIG to recoup 100 percent of their investments instead of the fraction they would ordinarily receive from a bankruptcy settlement. So, instead of protecting AIG's ability to pay back taxpayers by liquidating its assets, the Federal Reserve protected these outside companies, which included Wall Street giants like Goldman Sachs and Merrill Lynch, essentially granting them a "backdoor bailout."

As is so often the case, the story itself is not as interesting as the ensuing cover-up. E-mails disclosed during a congressional inquiry revealed that the New York Fed told AIG officials to keep quiet about payments to the other banks.[70] While Tim Geithner, in his testimony before Congress, denied any involvement in the decision making, his evasive answers merely infuriated congressmen of both parties. As Representative Dan Burton told Geithner, "It stretches credulity for us to believe that you had no role in this and didn't know anything about it when your attorneys and people that worked for you were sending e-mails all around the place."[71] More curious was the fact that former executives from various banks that profited from the bailout were scattered throughout the Federal Reserve system and the Treasury, including Secretary Paulson, who had been the CEO of Goldman Sachs.[72]

BAILING OUT THE WORLD

Now the Federal Reserve and the International Monetary Fund (IMF) are working together to bail out spendthrift European countries and banks. With your money. The IMF receives a lot of American cash; U.S. taxpayers contribute an estimated $55 billion, or 17.09 percent of the bank's total funding.[73] The IMF recently borrowed from the Federal Reserve to bail out Greece, Ireland, and Portugal.[74] Meanwhile, the Fed may be lending money to the IMF to bail out Italy and Spain in the near future.[75]

The Fed's activities, at home and abroad, pose significant threats to American taxpayers. As John Cochrane of the Hoover Institution noted, "The guarantee/regulate/bailout regime ends eventually, when the needed bailouts exceed governments' fiscal resources. That's where Europe is now. . . . And the U.S. is not immune. Sooner or later markets will question the tens of trillions of our government's guarantees, on top of already unsustainable deficits."[76]

All these nations have been living beyond their means for too long. According to the Organisation for Economic Co-operation and Development, total government expenditures in Greece were 44.8 percent of GDP in 2008.[77] Greece's failure to cut its bloated public sector and lavish welfare programs left it bankrupt. And we were forced to pay for their errors, leaving one to wonder who will be around to pay for our forced errors when they come to fruition. Who will bail out the bailers of last resort?

Taxpayer-subsidized bailouts to countries with bad economic policies and banks that make risky loans only encourages more reckless behavior. It inflames what economists call moral hazard. To instill greater caution in the bankers who invest, and the politicians who spend, other people's money—our money—we need to make sure they can fail. We need to expose them to the full costs of their potential mistakes. We need them to live in the same world you and I do.

FREE MONEY

"THE CURE FOR INFLATION, LIKE MOST CURES, CONSISTS CHIEFLY IN removal of the cause," wrote Henry Hazlitt in *What You Should Know About Inflation.* "The cause of inflation is the increase of money and credit. The cure is to stop increasing money and credit. The cure for inflation, in brief, is to stop inflating."[78]

Remember, in complex market economies, would-be planners never know nearly as much as they think they do. To assume that they do is fatally conceited. So top-down monetary policy cannot be an effective economy management tool to be used by governments. Ideally, there should be no policy aimed at increasing objective exchange values (inflation) or decreasing objective exchange values (deflation). No federal reserve or central bank is required, and many monetary economists endorse competing currencies, the gold standard, and other tools that would provide a stable currency while removing the government's ability to manipulate the money supply. Whatever the preferred solution, there's no intrinsic need for a central authority to "manage" the system.

George Mason University professor Lawrence White advocates a system of competing currencies, which societies have used throughout history. "Much more competition in money has existed in the past," he writes. "Under 'free banking' systems, private banks routinely issued their own paper currencies, or 'banknotes,' that were redeemable for underlying 'real,' or 'basic,' monies like gold or silver. And competition among those basic monies pitted gold against silver and copper."[79]

A sure way to stop inflating would be to end the Federal Reserve. The case for top-down control of something as vital as our medium of exchange has long since lost all credibility. But ending the Fed will happen only when America beats Washington and shreds the cozy web of interests that enjoy a taxpayer-financed safety net for their bad behavior. To be sure, replacing the Federal Reserve with a competitive system that protects the value and stability of our currency is no small task politically. Expect current management to react with unfettered hostility to a shareholder proposal to eliminate their monopoly power over the printing press.

At the same time, we need to pursue a realistic strategy that forces more transparency and accountability and less self-anointed bureaucratic discretion at the Fed. This is the strategic tack Ron Paul has pursued. A big step in the right direction would be to audit the Fed fully, as Paul advocates. While the results of the limited audit were disturbing enough, just imagine what kind of mischief we would find through a true, comprehensive audit where nothing is off-limits. The Federal Reserve lending trillions to foreign banks may be just the tip of the iceberg.

Auditing the Fed would inform the American people about what the central bank is doing behind closed doors. The information revealed would likely help convince more Americans that the Fed has done more harm than good. An overwhelming 75 percent of Americans want a comprehensive audit of the Federal Reserve, according to a Rasmussen poll.[80] This is a transparency issue that has transcended left-versus-right politics. Fiscal conservatives like Senator Jim DeMint of South Carolina, and a self-identified Democratic socialist, Senator Bernie Sanders of Vermont, have joined the libertarian Ron Paul in these efforts. A true audit should be one of the first things Congress pursues in January 2013.

The next step would be to downsize the Fed's mission from "full employment" to a simple mission of stable money. The Fed has expanded its own job description to include maximizing employment, "supervising" banking institutions, "maintaining the stability of the financial system," and "providing financial services to depository institutions."[81] Congress should direct the Federal Reserve to abandon its dual mandate and focus solely on providing a stable dollar. As should be painfully obvious, Ben Bernanke is not omnipotent, and the manipulations he has presided over are only making things worse. Much worse.

And then we should allow for the accountability and discipline that always arise from competition. "Immediately allow private individuals to put themselves on a parallel gold standard if they so choose," proposes Larry White. "Ron Paul's HR 1098, the Free Competition in Currency Act of 2011, is one approach: ensure the enforceability of contracts denominated in units other than fiat dollars, remove taxes on gold and silver coins that [Federal Reserve] notes do not face, and remove federal statutes that criminalize the victimless activity of minting distinctive private pieces of metal intended to circulate as money."[82]

Relinking dollars to a valued commodity, preferably gold, would allow the free market to harness the forces of competing currencies to promote stable money. Under the gold standard, it becomes obvious when politicians spend way beyond their means, because they simply run out of gold reserves. Relinking the dollar to gold would decentralize the authority to determine the value of money, which in turn would *limit the amount of money that Congress can spend*. The Treasury and the Federal Reserve would no longer be able to create money out of thin air, preventing runaway inflation and rising prices of goods.

Winston Churchill famously said of democracy that it is "the worst form of government, except for all those other forms that have been tried from time to time." In the same way, no monetary system is flawless. But, as Lewis E. Lehrman, senior partner at L. E. Lehrman & Co., has written, "empirical evidence of two hundred years of American monetary history shows that the true (or classical) gold standard has the least imperfect record as a stable monetary standard, because the dollar convertible to gold acted as the stable gyroscope of rapid economic growth."[83]

TRY FREEDOM

"THE ESSENTIAL ELEMENT OF THIS REFORM IS FREEDOM," WROTE MY professor and mentor Hans Sennholz. "U.S. currency must be freed from government monopoly."[84] We have tried everything else. Why not try freedom? I think he would be proud to know that you and I, along with untold millions of Americans armed with better information and a newly democratized power to reform our government's mistakes from the bottom up, are intent on doing exactly that.

CHAPTER 10

A TEACHING MOMENT

Why can we afford wars and Wall Street bailouts
but our education system is broken?
—Occupy Los Angeles Banner

I ATTENDED GROVE CITY COLLEGE, A PRIVATE LIBERAL ARTS SCHOOL
in Western Pennsylvania that accepts no federal funding. By the time I
had enrolled, the U.S. Department of Education had already initiated
legal action against the college for having refused to sign a Title IX
"Assurance of Compliance." Title IX of the Education Amendments
of 1972 requires that "No person in the United States shall, on the
basis of sex, be excluded from participation in, be denied the benefits
of, or be subjected to discrimination under any education program or
activity receiving Federal financial assistance." [1]

Oddly, this costly legal action was aggressively pursued by the
federal government, despite the fact that Grove City never violated
Title IX—there was never any suggestion by anyone in or out of the
federal government that Grove City had in fact broken either the
spirit or the letter of the law. Grove City did not discriminate against

women or anyone else. It was a coed school, and had been since its founding in 1869. Half of the student population at GCC was female, and so were many of the professors.

Grove City is where I met my wife, Terry. Thank goodness for coed institutions.

The case made its way to the Supreme Court, which in 1984 ultimately sided with the Department of Education in its argument that Grove City students accepting financial aid through the Stafford Federal Loan Program (now called Pell Grants) constituted federal funding, even though the school had always refused direct federal funding. In his concurring opinion, Justice Lewis Powell notes that the Department of Education "has prevailed, having taken this small independent College, which it acknowledges has engaged in no discrimination whatever, through six years of litigation with the full weight of the Federal Government opposing it."[2] The decision was limited, however. "According to the Court's decision, only the financial aid/admissions office was subject to federal regulation, not the entire College," according to David Lascell. "The *program* receiving federal assistance was subject to regulation, not the entire institution."[3]

CONTROLLING THE CLASSROOM

NOT SATISFIED WITH THIS COURT-IMPOSED LIMIT ON THE FEDERAL government's reach into the operations of private educational institutions, Senate Judiciary Committee Chairman Ted Kennedy put the Civil Rights Restoration Act of 1988 on President Reagan's desk, and then the Democrat-controlled Congress overrode Reagan's veto of the legislation. Kennedy's legislation to "restore" civil rights was a congressional response to a case where no civil rights were actually broken based on the government's own standard. But the net result was more federal control over higher education.

For me, the Department of Education's legal mugging of my alma mater was a teaching moment. Maybe federal control of education wasn't about educational quality at all? It certainly wasn't about civil rights. Maybe more government involvement in education is always all about the protection of the power of insiders, quality be damned?

How is it that a small college in Western Pennsylvania triggered such a massive response from the federal government? *Because it refused to subjugate its independence to a federal blank check—submission to any and all of the government's regulations of its operations now and in the future.* Having done so would have undermined Grove City's ability to determine the school's programs and curriculum free of federal meddling. It would have limited their ability to respond to their customers—the needs of students and their parents. Conceding control to federal bureaucrats would inevitably have increased operating costs (and ultimately the tuition paid by students) by forcing GCC's administration to respond first to regulatory compliance and relegating the efficient delivery of education to a lower position on a list of actionable priorities.

The fight over Grove City's refusal to fill out the required paperwork was not about the efficient delivery of education, and it wasn't about the needs of students and their parents. It was about the ability of Washington, D.C., and certain special interests, to control education from the top down.

Today, the human costs of more centralization are easy to see, from kindergarten through twelfth grade, and in higher education. Like all centralized systems, top-down education has produced skyrocketing costs and falling quality. But the social costs of the government's failures are far greater.

In few other realms of our society is the destructive power of centralized government more obvious—and tragic—than in public education. Obvious, because few topics have been discussed more extensively over the past several decades than the decline of U.S. education. Tragic, because we're talking about the futures of our children, and because we've known the primary cause of the decline of education in this country for many years, but have yet to fix it.

Just as Milton Friedman predicted fifty years ago, education's failure is the direct result of too much government. "Formal schooling is today paid for and almost entirely administered by government bodies or non-profit institutions," he wrote in *Capitalism and Freedom*. "This situation has developed gradually and is now taken so much for granted that little explicit attention is any longer directed to the reasons for the special treatment of schooling even in countries that are predominantly free enterprise in organization and philosophy. The result has been an indiscriminate extension of government responsibility."[4]

The Department of Education has sought to improve what its own report described as "the mediocrity" of the educational system in 1983, but the response since has been more government solutions to government-caused problems. Centralized authority sees itself as the solution to all problems, so government's role in public education—and increasingly higher education—has grown exponentially since 1983. Meanwhile, American students are paying the price as the system grows fatter on government-funded largesse.

U.S. students trail most industrial nations, particularly when it comes to math and science. Chinese, Japanese, and South Korean students are leading the way in the technological fields. The well-respected Program for International Student Assessment (PISA), given to fifteen-year-old students around the world, found that U.S. students place twenty-third and thirtieth in science and math, respectively.[5] American students scored slightly better in reading, ranking seventeenth in the world.[6]

The quality of American education has been declining rapidly for the past several decades, in inverse proportion to increased government funding. Student academic test scores have hit all-time lows. In the high school graduating class of 2011, only 31 and 32 percent of students test *proficient* in reading and math, respectively.[7] Just 20 percent of fourth graders, 17 percent of eighth graders, and 12 percent of high school seniors demonstrate proficiency on the U.S. history exam, according to the National Assessment of Educational Progress.[8] In other words, the average American student becomes *dumber* on the subject of U.S. history as he works his way through the system.

BLAMING PARENTS FIRST

PARENTS TRUST THAT WHEN THEY HAND OVER THEIR CHILDREN TO government-run schools—for which they pay ample taxes—they are at the very least in good, safe hands. But even this assumption is proving wrong. Inner-city schools are particularly plagued with violence, gangs, and disruptive behavior. The *Philadelphia Inquirer* found that more than 30,000 serious violent incidents have taken place in the Philadelphia school system over the past five years. On any given day, the newspaper found, 25 students, teachers, or staff members were beaten, robbed, or sexually assaulted in the 155,000-student school system.[9]

Districting requirements designed to prop up the centralized model force many parents to send their child to a dangerous public school just because it's close to where they live. Some have taken desperate measures to ensure that their child goes to a safe school. But, just like any top-down model, the system punishes those who disobey. Ohio mom Kelley Williams-Bolar was sentenced to ten days in a county jail and three years of probation for the heinous crime of registering her two daughters at her father's suburban Ohio address to get them out of a failing Akron school and into the successful Copley-Fairlawn district.[10]

Akron city schools are some of the worst schools in Ohio. Nearly every school within the system is dangerous and underperforming. The Ohio Department of Education reported that the Akron system failed to make Adequate Yearly Progress, receiving passing ratings on only four of twenty-six state benchmarks. The Copley-Fairlawn district, however, achieved Adequate Yearly Progress and had passing ratings in all twenty-six indicators.[11] Williams-Bolar was trying, as any mother might, to help her daughters get a good, safe education; and the state threw her in jail for it.

Can you blame her? Williams-Bolar says that she decided to enroll her daughters in a better school district after her home was burglarized. She is a single mother who wanted her daughters to have a better life filled with more opportunities for success. The sobbing mom told the court, "I was just trying to keep my kids safe. That was my objective." [12] Put yourself in her shoes for a minute; wouldn't you do the very same thing?

Violence is hardly exclusive to inner-city schools. It affects every school district nationwide. Schools are failing to provide a safe learning environment for children. A survey conducted by the U.S. Centers for Disease Control and Prevention found that 11.1 percent of youth nationwide report having been in a physical fight on school property within the last year.[13] The study also revealed that 5 percent of students admitted that they did not go to school for one or more days within the past thirty days because they felt unsafe at school.[14]

Poor results and an unsafe learning environment might help explain America's troubling high school dropout rate. An estimated 1.3 million young Americans drop out every year.[15] More than one in ten U.S. high schools is considered a "dropout factory," which means that no more than 60 percent of high school freshmen make it to their senior year.[16] Only 25 percent of high school students in Detroit public schools graduate within four years.[17] Loretta Singleton, who dropped out of her Washington, D.C., public school, described it as violent and dull. She says that "girls got jumped. Boys got jumped, teachers (were) fighting and hitting students. . . . They were teaching me stuff I already knew . . . basic nouns, simple adjectives." [18]

The high school dropout phenomenon has major economic and social implications. On average, a high school dropout will earn about $260,000 less than a high school graduate in his or her lifetime.[19] Dropouts are also more likely to be incarcerated, unemployed, or dependent on government social programs. Seventy-five percent of state prison inmates are high school dropouts.[20] This ultimately results in higher taxes to pay for the rising costs of social programs and prisons.

The sad truth is that public schools are even more segregated by race and class than they were four decades ago.[21] This is because our communities are still largely divided by these two demographic factors, and the centralized model depends on a rigid location-based approach. Education is generally regarded as the best way out of poverty, but children in poor areas are trapped in failing schools that aren't teaching what they should. Many parents in the inner cities cannot afford to send their child to a high-quality private school or move to an area with better public schools. This makes it extremely difficult for a child to break the cycle of poverty.

It's not untypical of teachers and others who work inside the system to blame parents for many of the failures of that system. *Parents don't take enough interest in their child's learning,* they complain. But the reality is far more complicated. Certainly, there are bad parents, and their lack of interest contributes to the problem. But the centralized system, bristling at unwanted interference, tells parents: "Don't worry; we'll take care of everything." As with health care decisions, and saving for retirement, we are constantly told that some third party will take care of it. If you want a better choice, if you want to be part of the decision-making process, if you want to see your options, you are typically greeted with silence. "We have this. We are the professionals," parents are told. When parents get desperate for a better choice, the system comes down on them.

Just ask Kelley Williams-Bolar. She went to jail for taking an active interest in her daughters' education.

SPEND MORE, GET LESS

Since as far back as Milton Friedman's time, the government's answer to poor public education results has been the same: spend more money. We've been told for decades that "properly funded," monopoly schools would yield better results. It's the taxpayers' unwillingness to spend what is required that is to blame for the fact that Johnny can't read. But the more we spend, the less the system seems to yield.

The national price tag to educate one student for one year averaged $10,499 in 2009—a 2.3 percent increase over the previous year.[22] Public schools collectively spend a whopping $605 billion every year. Several states spend more than $15,000 per student every year, including New York ($18,126), Washington ($16,408), New Jersey ($16,271), Alaska ($15,552), and Vermont ($15,175).[23] Pennsylvania taxpayers pay $14,420 per student, yet only about half of eleventh graders are proficient in math and reading.[24,25]

The dollar amounts are even more staggering in inner-city schools. Los Angeles spends more than $25,000 per student. However, only 10 percent of black male eighth graders are proficient in reading and fewer than 1 percent are advanced readers. Only 41 percent of black males end up graduating from high school in Los Angeles.[26] New York City spends about $21,500 per student,[27] but more than two-thirds of fourth-grade students and three-fourths of eighth graders in New York City are not proficient in math or reading.[28]

Education spending has skyrocketed over the past few decades. After adjusting for inflation, total education expenditures per pupil are nearly two and a half times higher today than in 1970.[29] But has the increased spending improved academic achievement? Of course not. For instance, reading and math scores for seventeen-year-olds have remained stagnant for four decades. Science scores for these seventeen-year-olds have slightly declined since 1970.[30]

Compare that to what happens with private spending. Washington, D.C., spends an average of $28,170 per student annually, yet only 12 percent of eighth graders are proficient in reading, only 8 percent in math.[31,32] Meanwhile, the average tuition for a private school in Washington, D.C., is about $10,000 *less* than what the public schools spend, per pupil.[33]

THE UNION LABEL

WHERE IS ALL THE MONEY GOING, IF IT'S NOT BEING USED TO IMPROVE educational outcomes? To government employees. The number of public school employees has exploded. The ratio of staff to students has gone up by 70 percent since 1970. Concurrently, the number of teachers' union members has increased by an incredible 4.5 million people,[34] even as unions nationwide have continued to bleed membership.[35] Why hasn't the hiring of more public school staff improved academic achievement for students? Well, to whom do public employees answer?

Teachers' unions exist to protect teachers, not students. Government employees are "the customer" in a top-down school system. And the customer is always right. As Albert Shanker, the late president of the American Federation of Teachers, once put it, "When schoolchildren start paying union dues, that's when I'll start representing the interests of schoolchildren." Shanker supporters dispute that he said this,[36] but its staying power hints of the indisputable truth at its core.

One clear goal of teachers' unions is the hiring of more dues-paying teachers to feed the system. A total of twenty-eight states are forced-unionism states, where workers have no choice but to join if they want a job.[37] So in the majority of states, teachers in public schools are also forced to join a union and pay dues as a condition of employment. Why don't they get a choice? The freedom to associate necessarily means also the freedom not to associate.

More teachers hired means more dues-paying members. The more dues-paying members, the more money for the union bosses. The money is invested in politics, to pump more taxpayer dollars into the system and maintain the status quo by blocking any meaningful educational reforms—so as to keep up the number of dues-paying members. It's a business.

When it comes to raw political muscle, two national education unions, the American Federation of Teachers (AFT) and the National

Education Association (NEA), are formidable forces. Since 1990, the NEA has contributed more than $30 million to Democrats (82 percent of its total), while the AFT has contributed more than $28 million to Democrats (91 percent of its total).[38] Regardless of political affiliation, few state or federal legislators are willing to risk provoking the unions, in order to push through the needed fixes to our broken school system.

These unions strongly oppose education tax credits, school vouchers, merit pay, charter schools, or, for that matter, any meaningful educational reform. As former top officials at the NEA's Kansas and Nebraska state chapters now admit, "The NEA has been the single biggest obstacle to education reform in this country. We know because we worked for the NEA."[39]

BAD APPLES

THE UNIONS' GREATEST ACHIEVEMENT FOR TEACHERS—TENURE—IS among the worst things perpetrated on students. Public school teachers typically get tenure after they have taught for only three years,[40] practically guaranteeing educators a job for life. Teachers' unions have imposed these burdensome rules to ensure that all teachers keep their jobs, no matter what. After all, as we've seen, an employed teacher is a dues-paying teacher, and the teacher (not the parent) is the union's customer, and the customer is always right. Parents come and go, kids age out, but a (tenured) teacher is forever.

It is almost impossible to fire a bad teacher because of how costly and time-consuming unions have made the process. In major cities, only 1 out of 1,000 teachers is fired for performance-related reasons.[41] In Chicago, for instance, only 28.5 percent of eleventh graders in Chicago are proficient in reading and math, but only 0.1 percent of teachers were dismissed for bad performance between 2005 and 2008.[42] Something doesn't add up here.

Some school districts have nearly given up. Over the past three years, New York City has fired only 88 out of about 88,000 school teachers for poor job performance.[43] That's better job security than even incumbent members of Congress enjoy. Instead of attempting the long and costly process of firing a bad teacher, New York City used to put these teachers in so-called "rubber rooms." At any given time, about 700 New York City schoolteachers were paid not to teach. They sat all day in the rubber rooms and read magazines and chatted. These teachers didn't do any work and still drew full salaries, at a cost to New York taxpayers of $20 million a year.[44]

The rubber rooms were ended after taxpayers got wind of the practice. Now New York City teachers accused of wrongdoings are assigned to do administrative work or "nonclassroom" duties. But the dismissal process for bad teachers has not improved. On average, a failing New York City teacher, when successfully fired, will have spent nineteen months in the disciplinary process.[45] It cost an average of $163,142 to fire one teacher in New York City, according to *Education Week*.[46]

The costs and legal hoops associated with firing a teacher prevent school districts from getting rid of the bad apples, even if they are accused of inappropriate behavior with a student. It took six years to fire one New York City teacher who admitted to exchanging sexually explicit e-mails with a sixteen-year-old student. Even though he didn't teach during those six years, he still got paid more than $350,000.[47] It took four years and $283,000 to fire a New Jersey teacher who hit kids.[48] The news is filled with disgusting stories of teachers sexually assaulting or physically abusing students. It shouldn't take several years and hundreds of thousands of dollars to get them out of the classroom and off the taxpayers' dime.

Public schools have many great teachers who are model educators. These teachers go the extra mile to inspire and enrich the lives of their students. Great teachers should be rewarded for all their hard work. Private-sector companies generally give bonuses and salary increases to excellent employees. Why should teaching be an exception? Yet it is often just as difficult to reward good teaching as it is to punish poor performance.

As Friedman wrote in 1962, "With respect to teachers' salaries, the major problem is not that they are too low on the average—they may well be too high on the average—but that they are too uniform and rigid. Poor teachers are grossly overpaid and good teachers grossly underpaid."[49] Yet union rules often dictate that teacher raises be based on seniority rather than actual performance.

NO BUREAUCRAT LEFT BEHIND

JIMMY CARTER CREATED THE DEPARTMENT OF EDUCATION IN 1977 AS a political quid pro quo for the teachers' unions' endorsement the previous year.[50] Over the last thirty-plus years, unions have continued to pump money into Democratic political gains, and the money has provided a substantial return on their investment. For Democrats, federal interference in education is now an article of faith.

Education was not considered by the Founders to be a federal responsibility, and it is not specifically listed in the Constitution. It should be left to the states and the people, in accordance with the Tenth Amendment. Eliminating the Department of Education *used* to be a standard Republican talking point. Ronald Reagan ran on abolishing it in the early '80s. For years after he left office, it remained GOP orthodoxy. The 1996 GOP platform declared: "The Federal government has no constitutional authority to be involved in school curricula or to control jobs in the market place. This is why we will abolish the Department of Education, end federal meddling in our schools, and promote family choice at all levels of learning."[51]

But after the government shutdown fight of 1995 and 1996, Republicans began to lose stomach for the task and no more was heard of abolishing Jimmy Carter's Education Department. By 2001, President George W. Bush had partnered with Ted Kennedy to enact a massive expansion of the Department of Education's funding and reach. The legislation—No Child Left Behind—*was passed in a bipartisan fashion.*

The U.S. Department of Education is, at best, a counterproductive waste of money. Like all federal agencies and virtually everything government does, federal education spending costs taxpayers dramatically more than initially predicted. The department's 2011 budget is nearly six times greater than its first. It has increased from $13.1 billion (in 2007 dollars) in 1980 to $77.8 billion in 2011.[52] All that money to prove what we already know: that a group of federal bureaucrats in Washington, D.C., cannot possibly design a curriculum that meets the unique needs of the millions of individual schoolchildren across the nation.

Just ask the parents. Only 55 percent of parents whose children attend an assigned public school reported being "very satisfied" with their child's education (and satisfaction is far lower in inner-city public schools), compared to 82 percent of parents whose children attend a private, nonreligious school.[53]

We have tried top-down management of education for a generation. We've tried top-down union control. The test was taken; the results posted. Government monopoly schools have failed to make the grade. We need to try a bottom-up approach, one that restores control over education to the local level, where parents are put back in charge.

Parents and students should be free to choose a secular or religious school, a traditional or progressive school, an arts school or one focused on technology. Where there is market demand, options will be supplied. A one-size-fits-all educational approach in public schools meets no one's particular needs. Every individual child is unique. Each has a different learning style and interests, which the centralized model either fails to recognize or is incapable of responding to.

Throwing more money at the problem is not the solution. Hiring more teachers hasn't increased educational outcomes. Schools are not "out of money," as the education establishment would have us believe. The solution is to break down the centralization of control. The union monopoly has to go. So does the Department of Education. So does No Child Left Behind, with all its mandates and meddling and throwing good money after bad.

THE CORRECT ANSWER IS FREEDOM

WHY SHOULDN'T PARENTS BE FREE TO CHOOSE? SCHOOL CHOICE PROgrams grant parents more control over their child's education, empowering them to choose the best educational option for their child. Just as competition and choice has improved everyday products, school choice produces better-performing schools. Two of the most popular proposals are school vouchers and education tax credits.

It was in fact Milton Friedman, while a professor at the University of Chicago, who first introduced the idea of school vouchers. As he wrote in *Capitalism and Freedom,* "The parent who would prefer to see money used for better teachers and texts rather than coaches and corridors has no way of expressing this preference except by persuading a majority to change the mixture for all. This is a special case of the general principle that a market permits each to satisfy his own taste—effective proportional representation; whereas the political process imposes conformity."[54]

Since he proposed the revolutionary idea in 1955, school vouchers programs have been implemented in a handful of states, despite what can only be termed *unyielding* resistance from teachers' unions and the political establishment. Parents are granted a voucher worth a predetermined amount of money to help them pay for the school of their choice. School vouchers have boosted student achievement, graduation rates, and parental satisfaction. In state after state, freedom is working.

Milwaukee's Parental Choice program is a widely popular school voucher program that has been proved to increase math scores and raise high school graduation rates.[55] The cost of educating one student in Milwaukee public schools is $14,011 every year. The Milwaukee

Parental Choice program provides up to $6,501 to eligible students, saving taxpayers' money and increasing parents' freedom of choice.[56]

School vouchers have helped turn tragedy into triumph in New Orleans. Before the devastation of Hurricane Katrina in 2005, New Orleans public schools were some of the worst in the nation. The city had only a 40 percent literacy rate, and 50 percent of black students did not graduate from high school in four years.[57] In 2008, Louisiana enacted the Student Scholarship for Educational Excellence Program, which gives low-income students a tuition voucher to attend the school of their choice.[58] The New Orleans school district now has an open choice policy that allows students to attend any public school regardless of their geographical location.

The results of Louisiana's scholarship experiment have been outstanding. On the first day of the voucher program, parents were lining up around the block for a chance to get their child out of failing New Orleans public schools. Sherri Thomas, a parent with two children, who lined up for a chance to receive a voucher, said that "it gives my children, in particular, stability for the first time since Katrina has hit. The school that they are in is not up to standards, academically. And this program, of course, is, and that's my main reason for being here this morning."[59] The combined district test scores have risen 24 percent since 2005, according to Louisiana Superintendent of Education Paul Pastorek.[60]

The District of Columbia Opportunity Scholarship Program was authorized by Congress in 2004. Drafted and championed by House Majority Leader Dick Armey, the legislation allowed students to take some of the dollars that would have been spent on their education at the local school they would have been forced to attend and freed them to choose their own school. The program cost an average of $6,620 per student—one-fourth of the cost that the District pays for K–12 schooling.[61] (Constitutional note: While education is one of the areas reserved to the states under Tenth Amendment, the Constitution gives Congress "power to exercise exclusive Legislation in all Cases whatsoever"—that is, to operate like a state or municipal government—within the federal District.[62])

The D.C. scholarship program has also been responsible for increasing student achievement and parental satisfaction.[63] The Department of Education found that 91 percent of voucher students graduated, compared to 70 percent of nonvoucher students.[64] Parents of students in the voucher program were more likely to describe their child's new school as "orderly and safe."[65] Students who were in the D.C. Voucher Program when it first started had a nineteen-month advantage in reading compared to their public school counterparts.[66]

A young student named Mercedes Campbell was one of the 1,700 D.C. voucher students. The voucher money enabled her to escape the failing D.C. public school system to attend Georgetown Visitation Prep. "It's different, now that I go to Visitation," said Mercedes. "I approach things differently. It's like a whole new world, basically."[67] Unfortunately, the program is a perennial target of entrenched union interests. With the election of Barack Obama, these interests asked for a return on the millions of dollars in campaign cash they had dished out to Obama and the Democrats.

Despite the substantial and verified benefits to the children of D.C., President Obama and the Democrat-led Congress obliged, ending the D.C. Opportunity Scholarship Program in 2009. This was nothing short of tragic for the thousands of children who had no choice but to be "educated" in one of the nation's worst-performing, most expensive, and most violent school systems. After the Tea Party sweep in 2010, the House of Representatives restored the program, but congressional Democrats will surely kill it again, if given the chance. In a brazen display of servitude to the education unions, President Obama again zeroed out the program in his 2013 budget—even while calling for more education spending.

Elsewhere, states are experimenting with personal education tax credits, which allow taxpayers to subtract educational expenses from the total amount of taxes that they owe, enabling parents to afford a better education for their child. A similar idea: donation education tax credits, which allow individuals or businesses who donate to non-profit scholarship-granting organization to subtract the contribution from the total amount of taxes they owe. These ideas are catching on. Illinois, Minnesota, and Iowa provide personal tax credits to families to offset education costs. Meanwhile, Florida, Pennsylvania, Arizona, Indiana, Georgia, Rhode Island, and Virginia provide tax credits to those who donate to nonprofit scholarship organizations.[68]

The Florida Tax Credit Scholarship Program has been widely successful and popular. The program provides businesses with a dollar-for-dollar tax credit for donating to Scholarship Funding Organizations. Students receive scholarships equal to $3,950, or the actual tuition and fees charged by the private school, whichever amount is less. More than 23,000 Florida students attend private schools using these generous scholarships. A study by the Friedman Foundation for School Choice found that 80 percent of parents are "very satisfied" with the academic progress their children are making, compared to 4 percent in their previous public schools.[69]

Pennsylvania's Educational Improvement Tax Credit has enabled hundreds of thousands of students to escape failing public schools. Over the past ten years, the program has awarded more than 284,000 scholarships to students, worth $335 million. The Keystone State's EITC program has saved taxpayers millions of dollars and boosted parental satisfaction.[70] It's a huge win for students, parents, taxpayers, and businesses.

THE STUDENT LOAN BUBBLE

BUT IT'S NOT JUST K–12 EDUCATION THAT NEEDS DRASTIC REFORM. America's higher education system is in crisis as well. Many colleges aren't preparing their students for their future careers. The price of college is skyrocketing, but educational quality hasn't improved. More and more college students are trapped with massive student loan debt once they graduate from expensive schools. And in this economy, many can't find a job that will enable them to pay off the debt.

The cost of higher education has become outrageous. In the 2011–12 school year, public four-year colleges charged, on average, $8,244 in tuition and fees for in-state students. Out-of-state students spent $12,526 to go to these same schools.[71] Taxpayers subsidize a large portion of the tuition costs at public colleges. By comparison, private nonprofit four-year colleges charge, on average, $28,500 per year in tuition and fees.[72]

Since 1982, the cost of attending college has risen by 439 percent—more than four times the rate of inflation.[73] And the price of attending public colleges has risen faster than that of private colleges. In the 2010–11 school year, the average increase in tuition and fees at public four-year colleges was 8.3 percent for in-state students and 5.7 percent for out-of-state students, compared to an average 4.5 percent increase in the tuition and fees for private nonprofit colleges.[74] From 2001 to 2011, the average annual increase in the cost of public four-year institutions was 5.6 percent, compared to 2.6 percent for private schools.[75]

Where does all the money go? A lot of it goes to professors, who, like their counterparts in primary and secondary education, are protected by tenure. Colleges are *supposed* to be about educating students and preparing them for success in their careers, but many professors believe that their research is more important than actually teaching a class. Some even consider teaching to be a burden. A Texas Performance Review found that the average professor at a research university teaches only 1.9 courses per semester. About 22 percent of faculty members do not teach a single class.[76]

Tenure at the college level has been destructive to higher education. Tenured professors are guaranteed their jobs for life and generally only teach a few hours a week, if they teach at all. Most tenured professors make well over $100,000 a year, often producing research that has little to no direct value to students.[77]

Most colleges are also suffering from administrative bloat. The number of administrative employees at leading colleges is rapidly growing. Between 1993 and 2007, the number of administrators per 100 students at leading universities grew by 39 percent, while the number of employees dedicated to teaching and research grew by only 18 percent.[78]

Despite the ever-rising cost, college represents a low return on investment. The class of 2010 has faced the highest unemployment rate in recent years, at 9.1 percent.[79] A survey found that 56 percent of 2010 graduates have not found a job within a year.[80] Another study, conducted by Rutgers University, found that the median salary for students graduating in 2009 and 2010 was $27,000—down from $30,000 in 2006 and 2008.[81] Many students who graduated with degrees in biology or English find themselves bartending or waiting tables.

At the college level, too, the problems can be traced back to a centralized approach to education policy. The federal government's financial aid programs are largely responsible for higher tuition costs. These loans and grants increase demand for college, which translates to higher tuition costs for all. Ironically, some are unable to afford college because government has artificially increased the price by trying to make it possible for more people to attend college.

And you wonder why the Millennial Generation is pissed off and pessimistic about the future?

One of the most common government financial aid programs is Pell Grants. These taxpayer-funded grants are given to low-income students and do not need to be paid back. Approximately 8.3 million college students received an average of $3,865 in Pell Grants during the 2010–11 school year.[82] Hillsdale College professor Gary Wolfram found that "private four-year colleges increased listed tuition prices by more than two dollars for each dollar increase in Pell Grants, and public four-year colleges increased their listed tuition by 97 cents for every dollar increase."[83]

Only a small handful of colleges in the United States have taken the principled position of not accepting any form of federal funding. The earliest and still the most outspoken of these are Hillsdale College in Michigan and my alma mater, Grove City College in Pennsylvania. Since the enactment of Senator Ted Kennedy's Civil Rights Restoration Act of 1988, both Hillsdale and Grove City have said, "No, thanks" to any federal student aid—forced by the government to refuse students who accept federal government loans or grants.

As I recounted earlier, it was Grove City's refusal to sign a Title IX compliance form that led to the Education Department lawsuit that led to the Supreme Court decision that led to Senator Kennedy's legislation mandating still more sweeping federal regulation and top-down control, under the guise of "civil rights."

"We did not withdraw from these programs out of caprice or just for the sake of independence," wrote the former president of Grove City, Jonathan Moore. "Nor did we do it because of the compliance costs (although they can be steep). We did it because we want to be free to pursue our mission." [84] Grove City established an entirely private student loan program with PNC Bank.

The tuition costs at Hillsdale and Grove City have risen slower than at other private schools whose students receive federal funding. In the 2011–12 academic year, the cost of tuition and fees at Grove City and Hillsdale rose by only 3.9 percent and 4 percent respectively, compared to the average 4.5 percent rise at private schools[85] and the 8.3 percent increase at public colleges.[86]

The increased cost caused by inflated demand means that many recent college grads have massive student loan debt. A report by the Project on Student Debt concluded that students who graduated in 2010 owed an average of $25,250—up 5 percent from the previous year.[87] A study by Moody's Analytics found that student loan debt has surpassed $750 billion in the United States,[88] and the volume of student loan debt now exceeds credit card debt in the U.S.

The stories of young people trapped under student loan debt are heartbreaking. Northeastern University alum Kelli Space, 23, is $200,000 in debt because she took out student loans to finance her sociology degree.[89] That means she owes $1,600 per month for the next twenty years of her life. The government easily granted her a student loan without caring about her major, her grades, or how much money she would be able to make. A private lender operating in a free market would have never given out a loan so carelessly. Like so many recent college graduates, Kelli Space had to move in with her parents after she finished college.[90]

About 17 million college-educated Americans are doing jobs that require less than the skill levels associated with a bachelor's degree, according to the U.S. Bureau of Labor Statistics.[91] There are more than 5,000 janitors in the United States with Ph.D.s, other doctorates, or professional degrees.[92]

When did the federal government determine that everyone should go to college? How could they possibly know the dreams and aspirations of so many unique individuals? Talk about a presumption of knowledge. Peter Thiel, a cofounder of PayPal, strongly doubts that government bureaucrats know best when it comes to higher education. He is actually paying college students big bucks to drop out and develop business ideas instead.[93] His idea is that a college education— given the standards and costs today—is not a prerequisite if you have the right talent and ideas. Thinking of extremely successful college dropouts like Bill Gates, Mark Zuckerberg, and Steve Jobs, Thiel is definitely on to something important. While not everyone with a good idea should drop out of college, we need to get away from the one-size-fits-all notion that a college education is "required" for success of any kind.

But don't dare raise the issue with the centralized elite of the education establishment. For them, a college education is a "right," and like any positive right proposed by the Left, it must be financed with taxpayer dollars. Who benefits from this arrangement? Mostly politicians, college administrators, and tenured professors. For them, persuading society that a college degree is a "right" is a shrewd investment. Facing a guaranteed supply of new, subsidized customers every year, the higher-ed establishment can simply raise its prices. It's a great business model, if you care more about the sustainability of the system than about the future indebtedness of your customers.

OCCUPY THE EDUCATION INDUSTRIAL COMPLEX

REMEMBER SARAH MASON? HER FACE IS THE COMPOSITE IMAGE OF *Time* magazine's Person of the Year dedicated to "The Protestor." The Occupy L.A. activist attended Northern Arizona University. Now she works at an art gallery, and the debt payments from her student loans are the real reason she feels so disenfranchised from the system. "I really don't know what the system is because if you accumulate billions of dollars in debt like Washington Mutual or the Greek or Irish government, apparently you just get a clean break," she says. "It's like, we'll just lend you our tax revenues so you can turn this mess around."

Sarah, like many Millennials saddled with the skyrocketing costs of a top-down education establishment, wonders where her bailout is. "I think the Occupy Wall Street Movement has shown that a lot of attention has been going to the fact that students have made an investment in their educations, then they come to the real world and they realize that that investment is essentially worthless." [94]

In many respects, the student loan crisis looks remarkably similar to the subprime mortgage crisis. Both involve easy and readily available credit made possible by government policies that sounded too good to be true. *Everyone who wants to should go to college. Everyone who works hard has a right to their own home.* In the mid-2000s, government-sponsored enterprises Fannie Mae and Freddie Mac encouraged lenders to hand out mortgages to countless people who should never have gotten them in the first place. [95] But when these borrowers began to default en masse on their mortgage loans, the whole financial sector nearly collapsed, and taxpayers were forced to pick up the tab. In the same way, the government's grants and loans have increased the number of students who go to college. College enrollment has surged in the past decade, sure; but the government-backed student loans have driven up the cost of education, essentially flipping on its head the economic rationale of higher education. The promise was a better future, not insurmountable debt. But more students than ever before are defaulting on student loans, up to 8 percent in 2011.[96]

Taxpayers will instantly be on the hook for hundreds of billions of dollars when this bubble does indeed burst. But many taxpayers are not college-educated—only about 27.5 percent of Americans have a college degree.[97] So, just like the apartment-renting taxpayers who had to bail out people who purchased homes they could not afford, the majority of Americans who did not go to college will likely bail out the Sarah Masons of the world.

The only ones untouched by this vicious cycle are the insiders: politicians, the Education Department *educrats*, the teachers' unions collecting ever more mandatory dues to feed the beast, abusive teachers in broken schools who cannot be fired, and tenured professors who find the actual process of teaching students beneath their stature. For them, business is booming.

Don't you think it's high time that parents and taxpayers educate the insiders, remind them who they work for, and teach them about customer service, from the bottom up?

CHAPTER 11

LOSING PATIENTS

ROBERT REICH IS RILED UP. "WE CANNOT, SOME PEOPLE SAY, ANY longer afford as a nation to provide the safety nets for the poor and the infirm or for the people who fall down for no fault of their own," he declares, incensed. "But how can that be true if we are now richer than we have ever been before?"[1] His audience clearly agrees with the sentiment, cheering and applauding. It is November 15, 2011, and Reich is addressing an Occupy Cal protest on the Mario Savio steps at the University of California, Berkeley. "We are losing the moral foundation stone on which this country and our democracy are built," he continues. *Applause.*

A key member of the Obama campaign's policy transition team, and labor secretary in the Clinton administration, Reich is now a tenured public policy professor at UC Berkeley. He wants the Occupiers gathered in Sproul Plaza to know that he cares. In fact, he cares far more than *some people.* "Now, there are some people out there who say we cannot afford education any longer, we cannot afford, as a nation, to provide social services to the poor." (He regularly employs President Obama's favorite rhetorical device, the straw man.)

Applause.

Reich also wants Occupy Cal to know that he stands with them. He is proud of the Berkeley tradition "of free expression, of social justice and of democracy."

> You must also—and in fact I'm sure you do—feel in your gut that the Occupy movement—the Occupy Cal, the Occupy Oakland, occupations are going on all over this country—are ways in which people are beginning to respond to the crisis of our democracy. And I am so proud of you here today. Your dedication to these principles, your willingness to be patient, your willingness to spend hours in general assemblies, your willingness to put up with what you have put up with is already making a huge difference.

Applause.

Reich is simpatico with their sense of "moral outrage" over the failures of the system to take care of the "infirm." "The days of apathy are over," he says. *Applause.*

You may wonder what exactly the *moral foundation* is, according to Professor Reich, if you care about *social justice*? What does a proper government-run *safety net* look like when it comes to caring for the *infirm*? These questions were at the heart of the debate over the signature progressive accomplishment of Obama's first term, and it is important that we get to the answers unclouded by political hyperbole.

WHOSE CARE?

DEBATE OVER HEALTH CARE REFORM IS BY DEFINITION A MOST PERsonal argument. After all, it's about your health, and the well-being of you and those you love. The decisions we make about our health are personal, informed by our right to life and liberty, and by the personal knowledge that only we have about the needs and circumstances of those closest to us. Patients should come first. Patients should decide. Patients, the customers in health care, should be in charge. Health care decisions are best made individually, from the bottom up.

The idea that someone else would decide for us is downright un-American, a moral breach of a sacred boundary. And that, in its essence, is what the battle over Obamacare was really all about.

You will recall the unified sense of outrage expressed by advocates of Obamacare when opponents claimed that the legislation would lead to "death panels" staffed by government bureaucrats empowered to determine for you, from the top down, which treatments you might qualify for based on some kind of cost-benefit to society, within the constraints of some politically determined global budget. In August 2009, in the heat of the national debate over his plan—his fellow Democrats were on the defensive in town hall meetings across the country, struggling to defend their health care bill amidst a citizen outcry—President Obama himself sought to step forward and de-bunk the notion:

> The rumor that's been circulating a lot lately is this idea that somehow the House of Representatives voted for "death pan-els" that will basically pull the plug on grandma because we've decided that we don't—it's too expensive to let her live any-more. . . . Now, in fairness, the underlying argument I think has to be addressed, and that is people's concern that if we are reforming the health care system to make it more efficient, which I think we have to do, the concern is that somehow that will mean rationing of care, right?—that somehow some government bureaucrat out there will be saying, well, you can't have this test or you can't have this procedure because some bean-counter decides that this is not a good way to use our health care dollars.[2]

The president denies any such motive or outcome under his plan to manage health care, based on the best knowledge of the brightest health care planners, from the top down. "I recognize there is an underlying fear here that people somehow won't get the care they need," he assured a crowd of supporters that day at a Portsmouth, New Hampshire, town hall meeting designed by his staff to stanch criticism of his plan. "You will have not only the care you need, but also the care that right now is being denied to you—only if we get health care reform."

There are no explicit "death panel" provisions in the bill, of course. Legislation is never named for what it really is, and the "Patient Protection and Affordable Care Act" is no exception. In reality, *patients* are not *protected*. It's not *affordable*. It's not *care*. Nancy Pelosi understood this from day one, and she knew that the vivid imagery of health care rationing was the Achilles' heel of any government takeover of health care. But facts are stubborn things, and the legislation that Pelosi passed and Obama signed *will in fact* shift power over important matters affecting people's lives and health by injecting a bureaucrat into the sacred doctor-patient relationship. When the supporters of Obamacare talk about "controlling costs," they are speaking euphemistically about using their new bureaucracy to deny certain treatments deemed "too costly."

WE'RE GOING TO LET YOU DIE

BACK IN 2007, SENATOR OBAMA WAS CAMPAIGNING FOR PRESIDENT on a platform of "universal coverage"—who could be against that? Robert Reich, meanwhile, was giving another speech to another UC Berkeley audience, and the seasoned Democratic apparatchik who would be appointed to President-elect Obama's transition team had somehow wandered off the party message. Way off message.

Remember Berkeley, the epicenter of *social justice* where they defend a *safety net* for the *infirm* as a moral right? Well, it turns out that there are exceptions to your rights. There is fine print in the social contract. Here, according to Reich, is

> what a candidate for president would say if that candidate did not care about becoming president. In other words, this is what the truth is, and a candidate will never say, but what candidates should say if we were in a kind of democracy where citizens were honored in terms of their practice of citizenship, and they were educated in terms of what the issues were, and they could separate myth from reality in terms of what candidates would tell them.
>
> [W]hat I'm going to do is I am going to try to reorganize it to be more amenable to treating sick people. But that means you—particularly you young people, particularly you young, healthy people—you're going to have to pay more.
>
> *Applause.*
>
> Thank you.
>
> And by the way . . . if you're very old, we're not going to give you all that technology and all those drugs for the last couple of years of your life to keep you maybe going for another couple of months. It's too expensive, so we're going to let you die.
>
> *Applause.*
>
> Also, I'm going to use the bargaining leverage of the federal government in terms of Medicare, Medicaid—we already have a lot of bargaining leverage—to force drug companies and insurance companies and medical suppliers to reduce their costs. But that means less innovation, and that means less new products and less new drugs on the market, which means you are probably not going to live that much longer than your parents.
>
> *Applause.*
>
> Thank you.[3]

Pay more. Innovate less. Die sooner. *Applause. Applause. Applause.* Did he really say that? Did they really applaud? And he thanked them?

You and I would not believe such a thing could be true except for the decentralized transparency of YouTube. Listen for yourself, and tell me if you are not totally creeped out.

Barack Obama, by the way, has never disassociated himself from Reich's views on health care.

But you have to give Reich credit: he understands what he is proposing and he is willing to admit the logical consequences for patients, at least among friends.

BAD MEDICINE, UNIVERSALLY

BUT DON'T TAKE REICH'S WORD FOR IT. GOVERNMENT-RUN HEALTH care has been tried already. Britain offers one of the best examples of centralized medicine in practice. Since 1948, the United Kingdom has had a true "single payer" health care system. The British government purchases and distributes 95 percent of all medical items and services in the country. One global budget, fixed by Parliament and distributed by Her Majesty's Health Ministry, provides for virtually the entire health care sector of the economy. Most hospitals are publicly owned, and most health care professionals are, in effect, public employees.

American progressives like President Obama openly admire this sixty-year experiment in government medicine. They like its simplicity and what they imagine to be its superior efficiency and social equity. Indeed, Obamacare clearly draws its inspiration, if not all its details, from the British model. U.S. progressives hope it is but the first step toward bringing that model to America.

If you want to see the future they're bringing us, consider this fact: the British National Health Service is one of the world's five largest employers, with no fewer than 1.6 *million* employees.[4] That's not a typo. If the NHS were an army, it would be the second largest on earth, behind only that of the People's Republic of China. Yet the NHS serves an island population of just 62 million people, compared to China's more than 1,200 million. NHS employees now represent more than one-quarter (26.7 percent) of all public employees and more than 1 of every 20 workers employed in the U.K.—and a substantial majority are not health care providers but administrative personnel.

"If the quality of British medicine were uniformly high," reports a Joint Economic Committee study, "there might be no good argument for reducing [the NHS] bureaucracy or liberating [British] doctors and patients. But the quality of British medicine is not uniformly high," JEC notes. "In fact, the U.K. has a poor record relative to other European nations and the U.S. on several measures, including specialty access, cancer outcomes, patient-centeredness, life expectancy, and infant mortality for socially deprived populations." [5]

These dismal results confirm what Milton Friedman called Gammon's Law, named for a British physician named Max Gammon, who studied the NHS in England closely in the 1960s and '70s. Dr. Gammon measured the Service's productivity by comparing two simple variables: inputs (defined as the number of employees) and output (measured as the number of hospital beds). His finding: while inputs had increased sharply, output had actually fallen. This led him to formulate the rule that now bears his name: "In a bureaucratic system, an increase in expenditure will be matched by a fall in production. Such systems act rather like 'black holes' in the economic universe, simultaneously sucking in resources and shrinking in terms of 'emitted production.'" [6]

In other words, the more the government spends in a top-down system, the less care patients receive.

NOT SO NICE

IN THE U.K., THE RATIONING PROCESS IS QUITE TRANSPARENT. IT puts a remarkably specific monetary value on human life, expressed in pounds sterling. The Quality Adjusted Life Year, or QALY, is the amount of money that NHS experts have determined an additional year of a human life is worth, based on various factors, such as one's current age, medical condition, and the likelihood of benefiting from the treatment. Generally, if a treatment costs more than £20,000 to £30,000 per additional QALY gained through the treatment (an arbitrary limit determined by budgetary constraints), then it is deemed "not cost effective," and individuals and families who want those treatments are left to pay for them entirely out-of-pocket, sometimes by traveling abroad.[7]

The name of the agency that crunches the Quality Adjusted Life Years to determine if you are worth treating? The National Institute for Health and Clinical Excellence, NICE.

Just to prove how not-so-nice NICE is, the bureaucracy has rejected the use of the often life-extending drug Avastin (bevacizumab) for use in shrinking cancerous intestinal tumors, because "the cost . . . at about £21,000 per patient, does not justify its benefits." Avastin is used in the U.S. and across Europe, but will now be effectively unavailable in the U.K. NICE's decision, which came after a year of internal deliberation, will affect an estimated 6,500 NHS patients.[8]

Nice.

In Canada—which in the 1970s adopted a variant of the "single-payer" model (the rationing decisions are made in the provinces rather than in Ottawa)—the national median waiting time from the moment you see a doctor to the time you actually receive your treatment was, in 2010, a brisk 9.3 weeks. That's the median. If you were a woman in need of gynecological help, your median wait was 15.5 weeks. Had a brain problem? Canadian neurosurgeons were able to see you in just 29.7 weeks. Orthopedic surgery? 35.6 weeks. Urological treatment? 13.5 weeks.[9]

Those are statistics. But the tragedy of government-run health care is best understood by looking into the faces of the suffering. Canadian newspapers are filled with horror stories of citizens suffering while standing in line. The following item from the *Toronto Star* December 2010 is just a typical example:

It's no surprise to Thelma Lee that emergency room wait times are not meeting provincial targets.

Lee said her 41-year-old daughter, Marlene Stephens, died Saturday after waiting nearly 90 minutes at the William Osler Health Centre's Etobicoke campus emergency room with breathing problems.

Lee feels her daughter was not seen fast enough by medical staff.

"They didn't touch her," said the grieving Lee. "She was crying out, 'I can't breathe, I can't breathe.' . . . Nobody attended to my daughter." [10]

Somebody should be fired, you say. Heads should roll. How could this happen in socially progressive Canada, the land of free universal health care? Well, read on:

On Monday, Auditor General Jim McCarter released his annual report which found that despite putting an extra $200 million into shortening emergency room wait times over the last two years, "significant province-wide progress has not yet been made."

Emergency room waits for people with serious conditions sometimes reached 12 hours or more, the report said. That is far greater than the province's 8-hour wait time target, the report found.

And for emergency patients who need a hospital bed, they waited on average for about 10 hours but some waited 26 hours or more, according to the 2010 Annual Report. . . .

"This should not be happening in Canada," Lee told the Star. [11]

This should not be happening anywhere. But it does happen, where the system is more important than the customer, where health care is a "right," too important to be left to market forces.

Canadian Dr. David Gratzer learned the hard way about the gap between the legend of centralized health care and the reality. In fact, he was mugged by that reality, and became a convert to health care freedom.

> My health-care prejudices crumbled not in the classroom but on the way to one. On a subzero Winnipeg morning in 1997, I cut across the hospital emergency room to shave a few minutes off my frigid commute. Swinging open the door, I stepped into a nightmare: the ER overflowed with elderly people on stretchers, waiting for admission. Some, it turned out, had waited five days. The air stank with sweat and urine. Right then, I began to reconsider everything that I thought I knew about Canadian health care. I soon discovered that the problems went well beyond overcrowded ERs. Patients had to wait for practically any diagnostic test or procedure, such as the man with persistent pain from a hernia operation whom we referred to a pain clinic—with a three-year wait list; or the woman needing a sleep study to diagnose what seemed like sleep apnea, who faced a two-year delay; or the woman with breast cancer who needed to wait four months for radiation therapy, when the standard of care was four weeks.[12]

As in Canada, Obamacare doesn't contain explicit rationing. But it does establish the basic building blocks of a rationing infrastructure eerily similar to Britain's. The law creates a new Patient Centered Outcomes Research Institute (PCORI) to determine the comparative cost effectiveness of medical treatments and therapies.[13] Meanwhile, a new Independent Payment Advisory Board (IPAB), an unelected panel of fifteen health industry experts, will be using that cost-effectiveness data to impose hundreds of billions of dollars of Medicare "savings," which can only be stopped by a majority vote in both Houses of Congress.[14] IPAB will be one of the most powerful boards ever created. For now, its reach only extends to Medicare. But as the largest health care system in the country, Medicare's coverage and payment policies—and price controls—have an enormous influence on private-sector health care delivery. And President Obama has already signaled a desire to extend IPAB's reach to cover the private sector directly, through the bureaucratic apparatus established under Obamacare, if he can't hit his budgetary targets otherwise. If these two new agencies (PCORI and IPAB) are allowed to go into operation in 2014 as planned, they will constitute an American version of NICE. They create the machinery of care denial.

But don't call them death panels.

Anyone who doubts that Obamacare paves the way to bureaucratic rationing should consider the public statements of Dr. Donald Berwick, who served as the president's Medicare chief until forced to step down last year after Congress declined to confirm his appointment. Dr. Berwick, who was knighted by Queen Elizabeth for his outspoken admiration for the NHS, lauds Britain's rationing of medical care and even more loudly defends the practice as unavoidable in America.[15] "The social budget is limited," he argues. "We have a limited resource pool," and "the decision is not whether or not we will ration care. The decision is whether we will ration with our eyes open."[16]

Whose life is it, anyway? And what exactly is a *social budget*? The *real* decision, the only one that really matters in health care, is *Who will decide?* Who will decide how scarce resources are to be allocated: patients or bureaucrats?

ARE PATIENTS CUSTOMERS?

HEALTH CARE IS THE ONLY INDUSTRY THAT DESCRIBES ITS CUSTOMERS as "patients." Think about that. We don't think of the consumer of medical goods and services as a customer. We think of him, rather, as the passive recipient of care provided by somebody else. And that somebody else, we don't call a "seller" but a "provider." We even prefer to speak of medical goods and services by the more soothing term: *care*.

Patients. Providers. Care. Clearly, we view health care as *different* from other industries. And the sanctity of the doctor-patient relationship really is a key to personalized care. But viewing health care as *different* from other industries has opened the door for drastic centralization, which has led to many of the problems rampant in our system today: endemic medical inflation, widespread lack of coverage, limited access to vital new therapies, and people losing coverage when they change jobs.

These are all relatively recent developments. Before the twentieth century, nobody ever thought of the doctor-patient relationship as something that should include a bureaucrat. Bureaucratic health care—by whatever name we call it, be it "national health insurance," "socialized medicine," "single payer," "Medicare," "Medicaid," "managed competition," the "Affordable Care Act," or whatever—is a recent innovation, historically speaking. There was a time, not all that long ago, when government bureaucracies didn't bother to take any notice of the doctor-patient relationship, let alone try to meddle with it.

But meddle they have. And do. And will. Until we stop them. And the first step to stopping them is acknowledging that the provision of health care is, in reality, a marketplace like any other.

The ancient code of the physician famously begins, "First, do no harm." But the oath of the bureaucrat can be summed up as "First, obey the rules." The doctor begins with his patient; the bureaucrat, with his orders. The physician's oath reminds him that, in using his knowledge and skills, he is acting with a responsibility to an individual. By contrast, the bureaucrat is, by law, to enforce a "system" from the top down. The loftier the goals of that system—the broader its scope, the more ambitious its promises—the more sweeping must be the bureaucracy's powers. And when that system is premised on an asserted universal "right" to health care, then the bureaucracy's powers must grow beyond mere administration of "benefits"—it must place the bureaucrat more and more in the shoes of the physician himself.

For the doctor, when he and his patient are acting freely in a kind of medical marketplace, the patient is also a *customer* whose needs and wants *must* necessarily come first. For the public employee, acting within an elaborately constructed "system," the patient must always come second, if he is thought of at all. The *rules* come first. The *system* is what matters: there is a *social budget*, after all.

What's at stake in the health care debate is nothing less than whether we, as patients, will be free to choose our doctors and medical treatments or have them chosen for us—and potentially denied to us—by bureaucrats. Either we will choose, or some third party will choose for us. There is no middle ground. There is no room for a bureaucrat between you and your doctor.

HEALTH CARE AT THE TIPPING POINT

MOST OF THE PROBLEMS OF THE U.S. HEALTH CARE SYSTEM ARE symptoms of a single underlying disease: centralization from the top down.

Even before Obamacare, government's share of the health care sector was large and growing. Health care expenditures currently represent about 17 percent, or one-sixth, of total national output. Nearly 40 percent of the health care sector (or about 10 percent of the whole economy) is controlled by government at the federal, state, or local level. Health care is growing as a share of the economy, which can be a good thing, if it means medicine is getting better. But government's share of health care is also growing, which is a bad thing, because government involvement is always a drag on efficiency and innovation. With the enactment of the Patient Protection and Affordable Care Act, the distinction between public and private is effectively at an end. The federal government has effectively nationalized one-sixth of our economy.[17]

The relative inefficiency of the government, compared to the private sector, combined with government's proneness to cause inflation and retard innovation, means the growth of government health care is inevitably driving costs up while driving quality down. And these destructive effects will only worsen if Obamacare is allowed to come fully online, on New Year's Day 2014.

Remember when Nancy Pelosi said we needed to pass the bill to find out what was in it?[18] Well, I have read it. Besides creating two massive new entitlement programs (Obamacare and CLASS, a Medicare-like entitlement to nursing-home care), the 2,801-page bill establishes 159 new bureaucracies. These remote and faceless entities include: 47 new agencies, boards, and commissions; 68 new grant programs; 29 new demonstration and pilot programs; 6 new regulatory systems and compliance standards; 4 new loan forgiveness and easy loan-repayment programs; and 3 reforms to existing Medicare reimbursement policies.[19]

The legislation includes such promising new entities as the Commission on Key National Indicators, the Private Purchasing Council for State Cooperatives, the Consumer Navigator Programs, the Exchange Grants Program to Establish Consumer Navigator Programs, the Independent Payment Advisory Board, the Consumer Advisory Council to the Independent Payment Advisory Board, the Program for the Use of Patient Safety Organizations to Reduce Hospital Readmission Rates, and the Pregnancy Assistance Fund.[20] Regarding that last one, I will resist the urge to speculate as to what exactly our government has planned.

The secretary of health and human services has already begun to wield the 1,968 new powers delegated to her under the law.[21] And if you've been concerned about the nation's high unemployment rate since 2008, you'll be happy to hear about the 16,500 new IRS agents[22] they'll be hiring to collect the law's $569 billion in new taxes they're levying on everything from upper-income folks (of course) to tanning beds.[23] Another count, by the experts at the Congressional Research Service, declares the number of new bureaucracies created by Obamacare as essentially "unknowable."[24]

Conservatively speaking, this alphabet soup of new government bureaucracies will cost $2.6 trillion over the first ten years of full operation.[25] And that's with optimistic assumptions. Recall that back in the 1960s, official government projections underestimated the initial ten-year cost of Medicare by *700 percent*.

In ramming this unpopular monstrosity through Congress, on a strictly partisan basis, Harry Reid had to twist arms, bend rules, and buy votes with a series of astonishingly large earmarks. One can't help but enjoy the colorful nicknames bestowed by the press on some of these legislative bribes, like the "Louisiana Purchase" (given for the vote of Louisiana's Mary Landrieu, who actually took to the Senate floor to celebrate and defend her bribe), the "Cornhusker Kickback" (which bought the vote of Nebraska's Ben Nelson), the "Gator-Aid" (given to Florida's Bill Nelson, to help get the bill out of committee), and the "Conn-U" (the payoff dramatically held out for by Connecticut's Hamlet-like Joe Lieberman).

The Democrats calculated that, once their unpopular bill had become law, public opposition would subside, as voters finally "found out what was in it." But it hasn't played out that way. One of the reasons is the hundreds of "waivers for favors" bestowed after the fact on the administration's friends and supporters. True to Gammon's Law, this massive new regulatory scheme has "customers" attempting to escape the bureaucratic "black hole" like rats fleeing a sinking ship. HHS documents show that the administration has been granting waivers from the law's more onerous requirements hand over fist— especially to its friends. A total of 1,625 groups representing 3,914,356 individuals are now exempt from some of Obamacare's more onerous mandates.[26] Recipients include large corporations, health insurance companies, and even whole states. By far the biggest beneficiaries? Labor unions, representing 543,812 workers.[27]

Welcome to the government system, where who's in and who's out and what care you get and don't get is based on your political "graft and pull" in the system. Lost in translation: patients, and *their* intentions and choices.

YOU WILL PAY

ONE OF THE MANY TRAGEDIES OF OBAMACARE IS THE SO-CALLED "IN-dividual mandate" to buy a government-defined benefits package that you may not want, may not need, or cannot afford. No matter. You will buy it, or you will pay dearly. Polls show this mandate to be the single most unpopular aspect of the entire scheme: two-thirds of Americans oppose it, and 72 percent think it's unconstitutional.[28] But this will never stop its supporters from clinging to it, to the bitter end. By their own repeated admissions, the mandate is the law's linchpin. Without it, their whole scheme unravels.

The mandate, in its essence, asserts a power on the part of the federal government to regulate you *simply because you live and breathe.* Think about the implications of such government powers over your individual freedoms.

So where exactly does the Constitution grant Congress the author-ity to tell us to buy health insurance? The law's defenders point to the power to regulate interstate commerce . . . or wait, is it the General Welfare Clause? . . . the taxing power? . . . well, um, it's probably in the Fourteenth Amendment somewhere. Hmm. Okay, they're not re-ally sure by *what* authority they've mandated it, but they just *know* it's constitutional. In February 2012, Congresswoman Kathy Hochul, Democrat from the 26th district of New York, committed a classic gaffe—let the truth slip out—when she admitted to an astonished group of her constituents: "Well, basically, we're not looking to the Constitution on that aspect of it."[29]

Arguably the most victimized constituency under Obamacare—and there are many potential victims—is the Millennial Generation, young people who showed up in droves to vote for Obama. They worked for hope and change, but what they got was the short end of a typical collusion between health insurance interests and the Obama administration that forces younger, healthier, poorer people to sub-sidize the health care consumption of older, sicker, wealthier folks.

Young people, already saddled with record joblessness and unprecedented debt from student loans, will be forced into the system to prop up a financial house of cards. But hey, at least they'll now get a free ride on their parents' insurance policy until they're twenty-six.

Know who deserves a waiver? All 310 million of us.

GOVERNMENT FAILURE, MARKET SUCCESS

ADVOCATES OF CENTRALIZED MEDICINE ARGUE THAT MARKETS HAVE failed to meet people's needs, and (because, they're always telling us, health care is *different*) government must step in to do it. But this argument never holds up. Every alleged instance of market failure turns out, upon examination, to be an example of government failure. Whether it's railroads, energy production, or health insurance, the culprit behind the flaws in the system will invariably be a misguided government regulation or benefit scheme that impedes competition and keeps consumers from making the right choices.

The price-signaling system works to allocate resources to those who need and want them. Where the price system appears not to be working, look closer: you'll find the government behind the curtain, pulling levers and pushing buttons, trying to displace the personal knowledge of millions and millions of Americans regarding the best decisions for their families.

In top-down systems run by third parties who don't know you and will never care about you, patients get lost, subjugated to someone else's purposes.

HEALTHY COMPETITION

SURE ENOUGH, THERE IS AT LEAST ONE AREA IN HEALTH CARE TODAY where we *can* see patient freedom working effectively: cosmetic surgery. That's because insurance companies don't typically cover it; it's a "self-pay" market. So third parties like insurers, employers, and governments aren't meddling in the doctor-patient relationship. The result? Continuously falling prices and continuously rising quality. Exactly what we'd expect in freely operating markets where the patient (the customer) controls the dollars.

One of the best examples is laser eye surgery, more commonly called LASIK. At the time of its approval in the 1990s, it cost upwards of $2,000 per eye.[30] Today you can get it done for $1,800 per eye, on average,[31] and as low as $500 in some cases, with success rates approaching 100 percent. Faster lasers, larger spot areas, bladeless flap incisions, intraoperative pachymetry, and "wavefront-guided" techniques have significantly improved the speed, reliability, and comfort of the procedure for patients. That record of increasing value compares extremely favorably with other areas of health care that are typically covered by insurance. In areas dominated by third-party payment, it's not the value that goes steadily up, year after year, but the cost.

The paternalist types will protest: well, maybe economic freedom works for *optional* services like cosmetic surgery, but surely we can't trust people to be in the driver's seat for their own care when it comes to *serious* ailments like cancer and heart disease! Actually, we can. It's true most of us have never been to medical school. But when it comes to making health care decisions for ourselves, there's no reason why we can't make prudent choices with the help of our doctors, without interference by third parties.

When you walk into a typical modern grocery store, what do you see? An incredible, almost bewildering array of products. How did that remarkable cornucopia come into existence? Who decided how much shelf space to devote to tomato soup, as opposed to candy bars? Why does one brand get more space than another? Why are some products not offered at all? *Who planned all this?*

The answer, of course, is no one planned it. The miracle of the grocery store is generated out of the trillions of small decisions made by millions of individual shoppers every day. These choices are constantly shaping and refining what you find when you walk into Safeway or Wal-Mart. We aren't all farmers or chefs, and most people don't even pay that much attention to what groceries they buy. But driving up the quality of choices doesn't require everyone to be an expert, nor does it take every single shopper scrutinizing every product carefully. Even if just a small handful of smart shoppers make careful discriminations between products, favoring those of highest value and eschewing those of lower value, the effect is sufficient to be transformative. These informed consumers' choices signal to the grocer: stock more of this, less of that; provide more shelf space for this, less for that. It's awesome. Especially for us lazy shoppers, who get to glide along in the wake of our neighbors who are more aggressive discriminators of price, quantity, and quality.

FOOD FOR THOUGHT

WHAT'S TRUE OF GROCERY STORES CAN ALSO BE TRUE OF HEALTH care. In fact, as it happens, one great example of health care innovation based on putting patients first can be found at Whole Foods Market. The chain's cofounder and CEO John Mackey has empowered "team members" at Whole Foods to voluntarily choose high-deductible insurance plans coupled with Health Savings Accounts. The result has been better choices at lower costs. According to Mackey,

> The combination of high-deductible health insurance and HSAs is one solution that could solve many of our health-care problems. For example, Whole Foods Market pays 100% of the premiums for all our team members who work 30 hours or more per week (about 89% of all team members) for our high-deductible health-insurance plan. We also provide up to $1,800 per year in additional health-care dollars through deposits into employees' Personal Wellness Accounts to spend as they choose on their own health and wellness.
>
> Money not spent in one year rolls over to the next and

grows over time. Our team members therefore spend their own health-care dollars until the annual deductible is covered (about $2,500) and the insurance plan kicks in. This creates incentives to spend the first $2,500 more carefully. Our plan's costs are much lower than typical health insurance, while providing a very high degree of worker satisfaction.[32]

John Mackey is an interesting cultural mash-up, best understood by imagining what might have happened if Ayn Rand and Jerry Garcia had procreated. Mackey would surely be their love child—half organic-food-obsessed, crunchy vegan hippie; half Declaration of Independence–reading, freedom-loving rugged individualist. On the one hand, Mackey is an advocate of what he calls Conscious Capitalism, through which he means to debunk the caricature of the revenue-maximizing-at-any-cost businessman. He believes that "every business has the potential for a higher purpose. And if you think about it, all the other professions in our society are motivated by purpose, beyond a narrow interpretation of purpose as restricted to maximizing profits."

Mackey notes that "doctors are some of the highest paid people in our society and yet doctors have a purpose—to heal people—and that's the professional ethics taught in medical school."[33] On the other hand, Mackey has become famous for saying things that could never pass Barack Obama's lips: "America became the wealthiest country because for most of our history we have followed the basic principles of economic freedom: property rights, freedom to trade internationally, minimal governmental regulation of business, sound money, relatively low taxes, the rule of law, entrepreneurship, freedom to fail, and voluntary exchange."[34]

Some progressives don't quite get it. Describing Whole Foods' founding grocer, *The New Yorker* observed, "The right-wing hippie is a rare bird."[35] Capitalists who care about their fellow man? *Crazy!* They react to Mackey in much the same way Al Sharpton does to *black conservatives*. What exactly is the Left afraid of—a little diversity?

That certainly explains the far Left's unchecked aggression against what Mackey wrote against Obamacare in a *Wall Street Journal* op-ed in 2009.

> While we clearly need health-care reform, the last thing our country needs is a massive new health-care entitlement that will create hundreds of billions of dollars of new unfunded deficits and move us much closer to a government takeover of our health-care system. Instead, we should be trying to achieve reforms by moving in the opposite direction—toward less government control and more individual empowerment.[36]

His critique of Obamacare was followed by an eight-point health care reform plan based on the company's own experience. First, he recommended, government should "[r]emove the legal obstacles that slow the creation of high-deductible health insurance plans and health savings accounts (HSAs)." Daring to take this real-world experimental data to its logical conclusion, he went on to recommend other, even bolder ideas, such as equalizing the tax treatment of health insurance, regardless of whether you get it from your workplace or the yellow pages; increasing competition among insurers; repealing costly, unnecessary mandated benefits on insurance policies; tort reform; Medicare reform; and greater price transparency for consumers.

But what really got Mackey sideways with some was his willingness to address the wholly contrived point of faith among progressive Democrats that health care services are a government-granted right:

> Many promoters of health-care reform believe that people have an intrinsic ethical right to health care—to equal access to doctors, medicines and hospitals. While all of us empathize with those who are sick, how can we say that all people have more of an intrinsic right to health care than they have to food or shelter?

Health care is a service that we all need, but just like food and shelter it is best provided through voluntary and mutually beneficial market exchanges. A careful reading of both the Declaration of Independence and the Constitution will not reveal any intrinsic right to health care, food or shelter. That's because there isn't any. This "right" has never existed in America.[37]

Unforgivable! The greengrocer's apostasy against the Chosen One's plan to take over our health care system was greeted by an organized boycott of Whole Foods. That boycott was in turn offset by a Tea Party counterprotest—a "buy-cott."

PAGING DR. PAUL

EVERYONE KNOWS RON PAUL IS AN OUTSPOKEN LIBERTARIAN, BUT many aren't aware that the Texas congressman is also a physician who has helped deliver 4,000 babies. Dr. Paul shares Mackey's rejection of "health care as a right." He also points out the silliness of the idea that a lack of government-promised care means that people should or would go without. At a Republican presidential candidates' debate in 2011, Paul shared what would become a notorious exchange with moderator Wolf Blitzer of CNN. Blitzer asked a hypothetical question about a thirty-year-old man caught without health insurance when calamity hits, and he goes into a coma. "Who pays for that?"

"In a society where you accept welfarism and socialism," responds Paul, "he expects the government to take care of it." Responding to multiple follow-up questions, Paul explains that what this hypothetical man "should do is whatever he wants to do and assume responsibility for himself. . . . That's what freedom is all about, taking your own risks."

Blitzer: But Congressman, are you saying that society should just let him die?

Paul: No. I practiced medicine before we had Medicaid in the early 1960s when I got out of medical school. I practiced at Santa Rosa Hospital in San Antonio. And the churches took care of 'em. We never turned anybody away from the hospital. [*Loud applause.*] And we've given up on this whole concept that we might take care of ourselves and assume responsibility for ourselves—our neighbors, our friends, our churches would do it. This whole idea—that's the reason the cost is so high. The cost is so high because we dump it on the government, it becomes a bureaucracy, it becomes special-interest, it kowtows to the insurance companies and the drug companies, and then on top of that you have the inflation. The inflation devalues the dollar. We have lack of competition. There's no competition in medicine.[38]

This episode is a classic example of Bastiat's "seen and unseen" in the debate over who gets what in the provision and allocation of health care services. Is "health care" an objective good that exists outside of the incentives to provide it, a fixed pie of treatments, medications, and services that can be reallocated, from the top down, by the smartest, most benevolent bureaucrats? Government promises, empty as they are, are seen as doing something for this hypothetical (and irresponsible) man in need of health services. What goes unseen is the destruction of the social contract between free people living in a community where you are expected not to hurt others and not to take their stuff. Free people support and help each other. Where health care is a government-imposed "right," someone else will take care of it, so there is little responsibility for yourself or others in a bind. One thing that history teaches us is that a contrived right to everything in theory amounts to exactly nothing in practice.

But a right to health care prompts key questions: What standard of care? Do you get access to the latest innovations and treatments? Will there be new innovations, or will the government deem them too expensive? Will a competent doctor be available when your government-imagined right to see him discourages young people from becoming doctors in the first place?

Who decides these questions? In a government-run system, the patient certainly will not.

The news stories of the Blitzer-Paul exchange focused exclusively on a single rude audience member who screamed "yeah" when the CNN reporter asked if "society should just let him die." Who might have that individual have been? We will never know. Maybe Robert Reich slipped past security?

THE UNSEEN

ALL OUR SYSTEM'S PROBLEMS—INFLATION, JOB LOSS, EXCESSIVE PA-perwork, 47 million uninsured—are symptoms of an underlying disease. The disease has a name: centralization. In the health care system, that's usually referred to as "third-party payment." Too much of our health care is paid for by third parties. Too much control has been taken away from *us*, the patients, and is being wielded by others.

No one spends other people's money as wisely as he spends his own. That insight is as true in health care as it is everywhere else. And in health care, the negative effects of letting other people spend our money have encouraged more centralization of the system, away from patients. It's as tragic as it was foreseeable, and preventable.

Happily, it's also reversible.

The most common form of health benefits coverage today is a fairly comprehensive insurance plan covering most hospital costs and doctor bills, as well as any medically necessary prescription drugs and medical devices. For most folks, the benefits also tend to be rich in terms of cost-sharing. The deductibles and co-pays—the portion of the bill we pay before our insurance kicks in—tend to be relatively low. That means our premium payment—the amount we make each month to keep our coverage in effect—must be relatively high. This is the basic trade-off with health insurance: we can have higher premiums with lower cost-sharing, or lower premiums with higher cost-sharing.

The lower-deductible kind of coverage so widespread today is great for those who want "more" benefits and don't mind paying extra for them, up front. The higher-deductible kind is more economical; it makes more sense for people of lesser means. More important, the higher your deductible, the more of a role you'll tend to take in your own care—because, in keeping with human nature, we tend to spend more carefully when, by doing so, we can save money for something else we'd rather have more.

The downside of the more generous, lower-deductible sort of coverage prevalent today is that it tends to encourage medical inflation. People consume more than they otherwise might—demand rises unchecked—because, once their insurance kicks in, any additional costs feel "free" to them. *An extra test? Another office visit? Name brand instead of generic? Don't worry, your insurance will cover it!* Americans have become disconnected from the cost of their own health care. And it's why in health care, unlike most other areas of the economy, prices always go up; they never remain flat or go down. We're spending what feels to us like "other people's money."

How did things get like this? The answer lies in the tax code, specifically in section 106. That provision excludes health benefits from the income and payroll taxes—which is very generous treatment—but only *if* those benefits come from your employer. As a result of this government policy, more than half of Americans get their health coverage through the workplace. Which is odd, if you think about it, since no other country on earth does it that way.

The downside is that Americans without access to job-based coverage don't get the tax break. They pay full freight. The 15 percent of the population that goes without coverage, either voluntarily or involuntarily, is, in a sense, the price we pay for having this peculiar system. To be sure, some of the uninsured have sufficient resources to protect themselves, out-of-pocket. But for most, coverage is simply too expensive, relative to its value for them personally.

Section 106 is one of the great examples of how a seemingly small, "altruistic" change in the law can have massive negative repercussions over time.

Historically, this policy was a bureaucratic response to the *unseen* economic consequences of wage and price controls imposed by FDR during World War II. Bureaucrats at the War Labor Board were charged with enforcing a complicated system of wage and price controls, and faced pressure from employers and labor unions eager to get around those controls. The board decided to embrace the idea that fringe benefits up to 5 percent of wages shouldn't be deemed "inflationary" and could therefore be excluded. That fateful 1942 decision was followed the next year by an IRS ruling that employer-provided health insurance, already tax-deductible as a business expense, didn't have to be declared as income by workers. Employers seized on this new tool for attracting workers in a competitive labor market, and workers readily accepted the tax-free fringe benefits in lieu of cash compensation. By 1946, enrollment in employer-sponsored group health benefit plans had more than tripled, from 7 million to 26 million members.[39] In 1954, Congress codified the new policy in the tax code.

With the advent of Medicare and Medicaid in the Lyndon Johnson Great Society years, the entire system began to evolve into one of reliance on third-party payers. By the 1990s, national health spending, public as well as private, had almost tripled, to 13 percent of the economy. Today, two decades later, health spending represents about 17 percent of output, or more than one-sixth of our entire economy, and it's still rising.[40] Now, by itself, that increase might not be a bad thing, if it simply means medicine provides more value than it did in the past. After all, who's to say how much health care is "too much"? But while overall spending was going up, the share of health spending paid for by individuals out of pocket was falling dramatically, from close to half of all health spending in the early '60s to only about one-quarter today.⁴¹ Meanwhile, government's share is growing; today, it represents nearly two-thirds of all health spending.⁴²

Value has been rising, to be sure. Medicine can do all sorts of things it couldn't in our grandparents' time. But medical inflation has been rising too. Indeed, it's plagued health care for half a century now, and has reached the point that it's the single largest driver of federal debt and deficits. It's not as if the government hasn't been trying to fight rising costs. Bureaucrats have come up with every solution you can think of—from local restrictions on the number of hospital beds to repeated attempts to impose price controls. Nothing has worked. The one solution that hasn't been tried is the only one that *can* actually work: abandoning the centralized model and returning power to patients.

PROGRESSIVELY WORSE

SO FAR, I'VE BEEN TELLING ONLY THE DOLLARS-AND-CENTS PART OF the story. There's also the political story, the long twilight struggle of ideas between top-down government and individual freedom.

That struggle can be traced all the way back to Teddy Roosevelt's Progressive Party platform of 1912, which—stealing an issue from the then-rising Socialists—included a promise of national health insurance. Democrats under Woodrow Wilson picked up the idea, and every Democratic president since has attempted to make it a reality. Franklin D. Roosevelt tried it in his Social Security plan in 1935, but had to back off under pressure from the medical community. John F. Kennedy and Lyndon Johnson tried again in the '60s, falling back to a "seniors and poor people first" strategy, and succeeded with enactment of Medicare and Medicaid in 1965. Jimmy Carter tried for the whole kahuna again in the late '70s, only to fail miserably. Bill Clinton picked up where Carter left off, and almost secured passage of Hillarycare in 1994, but was famously foiled by a united GOP and a handful of centrist Democrats. That plan, however, hadn't smoldered on the ash heap of history for very long before a fallback plan known as Kids First was picked up in 1997 by a senatorial duo: Ted Kennedy, the famously progressive Massachusetts Democrat, and Orrin Hatch, the Utah Republican. It soon became law as the State Children's Health Insurance Program, or S-CHIP.

Essentially a big Medicaid expansion, S-CHIP revived the Left's fortunes after their disastrous repudiation in the '94 elections. Ever since, they've been on the offensive, pushing incremental initiatives, like HMO reform and a Medicare prescription drug benefit, waiting patiently for the day when yet another Democratic president and Congress could resume the fight. And of course, it finally happened, in March 2010, when President Obama and a Democratic Congress managed to ram Obamacare into law, on a strictly party-line basis.

With this last step, the Left's nearly century-old dream is almost realized. All that remains is for Democrats to stave off repeal of their handiwork until 2014, when the machinery of centralized medicine will finally roar into full operation.

The history of the past seventy years is a history of a steady loss of patients' freedoms. The consolidation of ever more power in Washington spells destruction for what remains of individual choice in our health care system. This is why we must repeal Obamacare and replace it with policies that focus on patients first, promoting price transparency and portability, and ultimately getting at the root cause of our current ailments: section 106 of the tax code. We must decouple health care from third parties payers.

PATIENT-CENTERED CARE

IN THE WORDS OF RONALD REAGAN, "THERE *ARE* SIMPLE SOLUTIONS, just no easy ones."

Let's begin by asking ourselves: What would health care look like if we reversed the mistakes of the past seventy years? What if we put patients first? The answer is: We would have a health care system where patients are truly in charge and the rest of the system exists for *their* benefit.

A key way to measure progress in this effort is by how many millions of people move from centralized to decentralized sources of health coverage—how many Americans obtain good, private health insurance from the private market, or what I call "true insurance," as compared to the number who rely on "government-based" coverage. Unlike group health benefits, whether public or private, true insurance is personal, portable, and individually owned and controlled.

Here are some general strategies that can help make this vision a reality:

1. Focus on reducing costs and expanding freedom, not on "expanding coverage."
2. Reduce reliance on third-party payment.
3. Promote price transparency for all consumers.
4. Equalize the tax treatment of health benefits (don't discriminate in favor of job-based coverage).
5. Defend true insurance and promote access to the individual market (as opposed to favoring the group market).
6. Make participation in all federal health care programs, especially Medicare, truly voluntary.
7. Increase consumer choice and competition within federal health benefits programs.
8. Convert all federal health care subsidies into defined contributions, including Medicare and tax code section 106 (the exclusion from tax, for employer-sponsored health benefits).
9. End Medicare price controls. Let doctors charge more than the Medicare rate, and allow private agreements between doctors and patients.
10. Prevent rationing by letting Medicare beneficiaries voluntarily add their own money on top of what Medicare pays.
11. Until the income tax is abolished or replaced by a flat tax, give

individuals greater control and security through strengthened Health Savings Accounts.

12. Call for state-based medical-malpractice reform.
13. Permit insurance to be purchased across state lines.

Earlier, I quoted a Canadian doctor who was awakened to the brutal reality of centralized medicine. Health care, he realized, is a serious business—and should be treated like one. Dr. David Gratzer has emigrated to the United States to practice medicine more freely, and offers Americans a hard-earned perspective:

> American health care is expensive. And Americans aren't always getting a good deal. . . . True, government bureaucrats would be able to cut costs—but only by shrinking access to health care, as in Canada, and engendering a Canadian-style nightmare of overflowing emergency rooms and yearlong waits for treatment. America is right to seek a model for delivering good health care at good prices, but we should be looking not to Canada, but close to home—in the other four-fifths or so of our economy. From telecommunications to retail, deregulation and market competition have driven prices down and quality and productivity up. Health care is long overdue for the same prescription.[43]

As I've said, before any positive steps toward patient-centered care can be made, we must fully repeal Obamacare—scrap it and start from scratch. A majority of the public is with us. So are a majority of the states; more than half have sued to overturn the law in court.[44] So is a majority of the current House, which has passed a full repeal bill. So is a near-majority of the Senate, including every single Republican. Voters have approved repeal wherever the idea has appeared as a state ballot initiative, including in Missouri, Arizona, Oklahoma, and Ohio.

Voters have made up their minds. They want Obamacare pitched into the dustbin of history, right along with eight-track tapes and Marxism. In November 2010, the president's health care law was the top policy issue for voters, well ahead of others. Supporting the unpopular law played a big role in the defeats of scores of Democratic candidates, incumbents and challengers alike. Seven of the eight House Democrats who switched their position on the bill from "no" to "yes" in March of that year were defeated by Republicans in November. Before the election, Democratic candidates were spending more money on advertisements *opposing* the health care bill than for it. Among that rarest of species, the incumbent who bravely defended his pro-Obamacare vote, two were especially vocal: Senator Russ Feingold of Wisconsin and Congressman Earl Pomeroy of North Dakota. Both lost.

FIGHT FOR YOUR RIGHTS

LIKE SO MANY IDEAS IN THIS BOOK, OUR SUCCESS IN MOVING AWAY from an imposed, top-down health care bureaucracy requires that each of us must rise up, from the bottom up, and take our rights back from the insiders in Washington. As we move to get government out of the exam room and out of our hospital bed, we also have to build up a strong and flourishing market for patients—health care's customers—that can never again be colonized by political agendas and industry interests from the top down.

The problem with reliance on third parties—whether it's your employer limiting your choice of health care plans or your government limiting your access to treatment—is that the decision-making power is concentrated in a central location and managed by someone who isn't you and doesn't know or care about you.

A "patient-centered" approach, by contrast, means the customer is always right and the folks who undergo treatment also control the dollars and make the important decisions about their own care. After all, shouldn't those decisions *always* be made by the people who are sick, along with their loved ones, their doctor, and other trusted advocates?

Here are seven principles that might constitute a new Patient's Bill of Rights. Note that not one of these rights is protected under the government takeover. In fact, most are violated by it.

1. Every intelligent, adult human being has a right to make his or her own health care choices.
2. Patients have a right to shop around and take their business elsewhere.
3. Health care professionals have a right to be paid for their services, at market rates.
4. Doctors and patients should have the right to freely enter into contracts with each other.
5. Individuals should bear the consequences of their own free choices.
6. Taxpayers should be free to opt out of government insurance programs.
7. Communities should be free to help those who are less fortunate through private charity, unencumbered by federal mandates and regulations.

These are rights worth fighting for; rights consistent with the right to "life, liberty, and the pursuit of happiness." I am losing patience with the status quo. After all, someday any one of us might be lying in that hospital bed. That is not the time to discover that someone else, someone from the government, whom you do not know and will never meet, has determined that treating you, or your wife, or your mother is, in the words of Obama adviser Robert Reich, "too expensive, so we're going to let you die."

CHAPTER 12

A Time for Choosing

WHO WILL CONTROL YOUR FINANCES IN RETIREMENT, YOUR HEALTH
care and your savings? Who decides—you and your family, or politicians and bureaucrats? Bottom up, or top down? These are questions
every American must answer as we inevitably confront the future of
entitlement spending in America.

They're not easy questions; but not choosing is still a choice. Not
choosing relegates our progeny—your children and grandchildren—
to a dark economic future of more debt, less opportunity, and no
security in their retirements. Refusing to answer, letting politicians
continue to kick the can down the road, is exactly the head-in-the-
sand strategy that put Greece and Italy at the mercy of foreign lenders. Are Americans willing to prop up a welfare state mentality like
the one in those bankrupt countries? There, because of a national
sense of entitlement, it was assumed that someone else would keep
paying for cradle-to-grave government support programs even as the
demographic shifts in those countries—fewer young workers paying

for more and more retirees—made default inevitable. It was always a question of when, not if.

Entitlements are a problem. They're a problem because they're budget-busters, to be sure. But the deeper problem is that they threaten your freedom. Why, after working so hard to be financially independent our entire lives, do we accept total dependency in retirement, letting someone else decide for us what we have earned, what we deserve?

The good news is that there is a proven better way to manage our health and retirement needs in later years. In private enterprise, employers have moved away from old top-down pension systems, so-called "defined benefit" systems, where someone else determines what you will get in retirement. Now more and more employees are freer and less dependent on the goodwill and long-run financial viability of employers; you can invest in your own future every week with "defined contribution" plans that belong to you, are controlled by you, follow you wherever you go and wherever you work, and stay with you and your family forever.

So you have to choose. Not choosing means that some politician or some gray-suited bureaucrat will choose for you. Whose best interests do you suppose he has in mind?

A BLACK HOLE

Dependency on government is reaching a tipping point. The Tax Foundation estimates that 60 percent of Americans receive more in benefits and services from the government than they pay in taxes.[1] Another analysis predicts that, even without counting Obamacare, by 2018 two-thirds of the population will be dependent on the government.[2]

It's no coincidence the three largest entitlements—Medicare, Medicaid, and Social Security—are the most challenging to reform.[3] Today, more than one in six Americans depends on at least one of

these three massive programs as an important part of his livelihood—
nearly 60 million people in a population of 310 million.[4]

More than 53 million Americans rely on Social Security. Their
retirement checks are modest, averaging just $1,200 a month, or
$14,400 a year. But, for a majority of the 40 million recipients who are
65 or older, Social Security provides the majority of their cash income;
for one-quarter of seniors, it provides more than 90 percent of their
income; and for 15 percent of them, 6 million people, Social Security
is their sole source of income.[5]

Medicaid, which started out as an additional source of support for
people on welfare, has become the sole source of health coverage for
50 million Americans, including an increasing share of the middle
class.

Medicare, meanwhile, is now the sole source of health coverage
for 48 million elderly and disabled Americans, because participation
in it is effectively mandatory and private-sector alternatives (choice, in
other words) aren't permitted. And it's the future that awaits us all, if
yet another federal health entitlement—Obamacare—isn't repealed.

The growth of these programs, measured by rising costs, is breath-
taking. In 1970, the big three consumed about 20 percent of the federal budget[6]; by 2010, their share had doubled, to 40 percent[7]; and
by 2020 they're likely to consume more than half the budget.[8] If we
do nothing, by 2050 the big three will consume 100 percent of all
expected tax receipts, forcing Congress to either eliminate all other
spending or borrow to pay for it.[9]

And by the way, don't forget that $100 trillion in additional future
entitlement obligations that Washington intentionally keeps off the
books. As I mentioned in the first chapter, these are promises that
politicians have written into law but haven't provided any way to pay
for. We would have to put $100 trillion in the bank today to cover all
that future exposure. (Remember, our entire annual national product
is only about $15 trillion.) In the private sector, there's a term for keep-
ing books the way Uncle Sam does: illegal. When private companies
hide their long-term unfunded liabilities, people go to jail.

If it weren't for grassroots Americans willing to rise up and question our senior management on issues like the growing national debt, Washington wouldn't even be discussing the entitlement problem. The focus would still be on spending still more money we don't have, like Greece, on stimulus, bailouts, and creating new entitlements.

Now that we have their attention, the heavy lifting of cleaning up the company books can begin in earnest. Don't expect this to be easy.

LOSING OUR WAY

IT HASN'T ALWAYS BEEN THIS WAY. BEFORE 1935, THERE WERE NO FEDeral entitlement programs, unless you counted things like veterans' hospitals and civil service pensions, which are basically compensation or rewards for past services rendered. During the vast bulk of the republic's history—more than a century and a half—the idea that the government would dole out direct financial aid to large numbers of individuals was unthinkable.

In the Founders' day, essentially local or domestic functions were the province of states, towns, households, extended families, and private associations. Nobody imagined the federal government had any business meddling in such matters. Indeed, the Founders feared that if the federal government did meddle, if it tried to become a continental municipality or charity, national politicians, acting under the guise of compassion, would find ways to redistribute wealth and buy votes at election time, spawning dependency and centralizing power in the nation's capital.

The past seventy-five years have seen their fears realized. Since the Progressive Era, we've seen every constitutional barrier preventing Congress from getting into the charity and wealth transfer business systematically dismantled. The walls of federalism and enumerated and separated powers have been breached. Our traditional aversion to a steeply progressive income tax has been sapped. Our resistance to unearned welfare benefits and mass dependency has been overcome.

The result is the modern entitlement state, something that looks more like the European model, top-down and "progressive."

The reach of the federal government has grown in three big waves: the 1930s, the 1960s, and our own day. Entitlements now represent more than half of federal spending. They've become the main engine of the national power structure. Walk down any city block in downtown Washington and you'll see whole office buildings filled with people whose jobs basically depend on protecting and expanding existing entitlements and thinking up new ones. Those people include armies of lawyers and lobbyists who do nothing but monitor and think about entitlements for their clients' financial benefit. And then there are the pressure groups like AARP and the National Committee to Protect Social Security and Medicare. These political "entrepreneurs" spend hundreds of millions each year trying to elect politicians who will protect and expand the entitlement state.

On Capitol Hill, in marble hearing rooms that invoke the architecture of the kingly Palace of Versailles, the Democrats and the Republicans have colluded, *in a bipartisan fashion*, to continually grow "mandatory spending" and to saddle our children with top-down systems that they must fund but that will likely not still exist when they themselves retire.

FOR FUTURE GENERATIONS

IN A BETTER WORLD, THIS WOULD NOT BE. WASHINGTON WOULD BE A much smaller town. We would be a much freer and more self-reliant people. Unfortunately, that isn't the world we live in. A century ago, the experiment commenced, and today we still grapple with the profound results.

The questions that should occupy our thinking are simple. How do we get back to real retirement security that is independent of a top-down entitlement mentality? Is there a better way to do things from the bottom up, a better way more consistent with our founding principles? Government, speaking for us, has made promises it cannot possibly keep. Implicitly, our political leaders have appropriated the logic of John Maynard Keynes when he said of the long-run consequences of stimulating "aggregate demand" by spending money we didn't have: "In the long run, we are all dead."

Well, nobody lives forever, but the question weighs heavily on our minds: What country will we leave to our children and grandchildren? Will they be better off, with more economic opportunity than we had? Will they be freer? Or will they be indentured servants, paying for a broken entitlement binge we refused to take responsibility for, refused to fix? The Democrats, as I mentioned, now seem to exist solely to protect and expand the entitlement state; and many Republicans—including a lot of self-described "conservatives"—are all too comfortable with that state, so long as it's "well managed."

What no one can deny is that the major entitlements are unsustainable. The math is remorseless. The question is no longer whether but *when* we will reform entitlements.

The good news is there is still time to reform them in a way that can benefit everyone. We can make these programs affordable to taxpayers, without hurting those already dependent on them, and in ways that reduce Washington's control over our lives and increase our freedom. We can also restore the Founders' vision of decentralized government, personal freedom, and self-reliance.

I'm going to focus on Medicare and Social Security. There are plenty of others, of course: Medicaid, food stamps, student loans, farm subsidies, all manner of bailouts and giveaways. But these two are the biggest and most important, from the standpoint of their cost and the dependency they foster.

What we're going to find, in looking at all entitlements (not just these two), is that while each is unique, at root, they're all basically the same, and that means the basic remedy for each is the same: 1) Make it voluntary. 2) Make it individually owned and controlled. That's it.

ONE MAN'S ENTITLEMENT

ENTITLEMENT. IN MY TRAVELS AROUND THE COUNTRY, I'VE NOTICED that what Washington means by this important word—*entitlement*—isn't always the same thing that Americans hear. There's a disconnect, because the word has several different meanings. Webster's gives three definitions:

a) A belief that one is deserving of or entitled to certain *privileges*.
b) A government program providing *benefits* to members of a specified group.
c) A *right* to benefits specified especially by law or contract.[10]

Benefits and *privileges* are both granted by government, and can therefore be taken away by government without just compensation. A *right*, by contrast, can come either from government (such as a "right" to "free" health care)—in which case it's really just a benefit or privilege by another name—or from somewhere *other than government*, such as (to use the Founders' terms) from "Nature" or from "Nature's God." When we have a right that comes from somewhere beyond government, we think of it as *unalienable*. We think of it as our *property*.

So "entitlement" can basically mean either of two opposite things, *property* or *privilege*, and this helps clear up the mystery. Americans distinguish between "entitlements" they regard as essentially their own money coming back to them (property), and those they don't (privileges). They like and will defend property. They are less willing to defend privileges. The word "entitlement" confuses and sometimes irritates them. Many of them think: *Don't confuse my hard-earned retirement with some damn welfare program.*

Why is this important? Because the confused language muddles discussion and impedes honest debate. As a legal matter, all our federal entitlements are welfare programs, including Social Security and Medicare: they're privileges, not property. Congress could vote to abolish them tomorrow, and no one would have any legal recourse. But that's not how most Americans understand the situation. The popular perception, reinforced by the advocates of the entitlement state, is that these programs are basically "insurance" contracts, and this perception has become so deeply rooted, it's taken on a life of its own. But it's simply not true. The Supreme Court has repeatedly made clear these programs are not "property" in any enforceable legal sense.[11]

Before we can begin to reform entitlements, we have to overcome the myths surrounding them. Clearly, they've corrupted our politics. Americans have been told, from day one, and believe, that Social Security and Medicare are "insurance"; that the payroll taxes that "fund" them are "contributions"; that there is an "account" with your name on it in Washington; that the government is really just holding your money in trust for you until you retire. All those notions are false, part of an elaborate myth—a web of lies—perpetuated by politicians to make it as hard as possible for us to change these programs.

Where did the myth begin? How has it persisted for so long?

A LIVING DOCUMENT

IN 1934, PRESIDENT FRANKLIN D. ROOSEVELT'S ADVISERS STRUGGLED to identify the constitutional basis for their envisioned social security program, which would involve forcing workers to pay a tax on their wages to fund a welfare benefit for the aged. There's no mention in the Constitution of any power to undertake a national program of social insurance or a power to compel citizens to "save" for their own retirement or pay taxes for other people's. Additionally, the Tenth Amendment declares: "The powers not delegated to the United States by the Constitution, nor prohibited by it to the States, are reserved to the States respectively, or to the people."[12] So without a clear basis in the Constitution, Roosevelt's proposal could have been struck down by the Supreme Court.

Two bases, however, seemed at least plausible to Roosevelt's team. The first was the tax-and-spend power, more commonly known as the General Welfare Clause, which declares: "The Congress shall have Power to lay and collect Taxes, Duties, Imposts and Excises, to pay the Debts and provide for the common Defence and general Welfare of the United States." [13] The second was the Commerce Clause: "The Congress shall have Power . . . to regulate Commerce . . . among the several States." [14]

Whichever basis they chose would affect the program's structure and how it would be sold to Congress and the courts.

From the beginning of the republic, the tax-and-spend power had been the subject of a fierce debate between the so-called Madisonian and Hamiltonian interpretations. Alexander Hamilton famously read the words "to provide for the general Welfare of the United States" as a distinct grant of power *in addition* to the other enumerated powers of Congress. Madison, however, read it as a general rule of construction intended to *limit* those powers. The latter reading left no room for a federal social insurance scheme.

Up until the 1930s, congresses and presidents went back and forth, with Madison's more restrictive view tending to prevail before the Civil War, and Hamilton's more expansive one after it. But there was no consistent winner; and all the time, the Supreme Court carefully avoided choosing sides. Now, in 1934, with New Deal legislation falling left and right at the hands of a seemingly Madisonian Supreme Court, basing Social Security on the tax-and-spend power seemed risky. [15]

And yet the Commerce Clause seemed even less promising. How could the administration claim with a straight face that old-age benefits are a "regulation" of interstate "commerce"?

The problem seemed insoluble. But then FDR and his team came up with an idea. They would have it both ways. They would take their chances in court with the tax-and-spend power, but in order to get it through Congress and make it politically untouchable, they'd also couch it, outside the courtroom, as mandatory insurance authorized under the Commerce Clause. Armed with this legal rationale, the team in January 1935 unveiled the president's Social Security plan, describing it from the beginning as insurance, the benefits of which would come "as a matter of right." Later, when defending the enacted legislation in the Supreme Court, they would declare just the contrary: that the Act "does not constitute a plan for compulsory insurance within the accepted meaning of the term 'insurance'"; rather, it is a mere "bounty" to which the pensioner "has no legal right." [16]

In other words, it would be either property or a privilege, depending on who was being lied to.

To bolster the impression that Social Security payroll tax payments were insurance, they were publicly (though not in the bill) called "contributions." To bolster the opposite impression—that the program was *not* mandatory insurance—the amount of an individual's payroll tax payments was not tied to the amount of his benefits. Instead, eligibility was determined simply on the basis of one's age, industry, and having a minimum number of work years; the amount of the benefit was determined by one's average earnings. For additional security, the draftsmen of the Act carefully placed the payroll tax and old-age benefit elements in two widely separate titles of the bill. The payroll tax, they would tell the judges, was merely to "raise a revenue," while the old-age benefit was simply a spending program to promote the "general welfare" in the current crisis. Each part, viewed by itself, would appear to be well within Congress's powers to tax and spend for the general welfare.

BACK TO THE FUTURE

THE COURT BOUGHT IT. THE TWO-FACED STRATEGY WORKED. THE justices not only upheld Social Security as a valid exercise of the tax-and-spend power, but in what is today remembered as the "revolution of 1937," the Court also took the opportunity to come down firmly on the side of the Hamiltonian interpretation of the General Welfare Clause, while giving up on any further attempts to enforce limits on the Commerce Clause.[17] With these revolutionary changes, the Court effectively liberated the elected branches—the politicians—to spend, tax, and regulate to their hearts' content. The modern welfare state had received judicial clearance for takeoff.

The FDR strategem worked so well that Democrats would follow a very similar path seventy-five years later, with Obamacare.

Although President Obama's health care mandate is enforced by a fine collected by the IRS, Democrats took care to call it a "penalty." After enactment, when ABC commentator George Stephanopoulos said the mandate met the dictionary definition of a tax, President Obama testily replied: "I absolutely reject that notion." [18]

Yet as soon as the case went to court, it seems, the president had a change of heart. Now the mandate *was* a tax. As the *New York Times* reported: "When Congress required most Americans to obtain health insurance or pay a penalty, Democrats denied that they were creating a new tax. . . . But in court, the Obama administration and its allies now defend the requirement as an exercise of the government's 'power to lay and collect taxes.'" The *Times* added: "in a brief defending the law, the Justice Department says . . . Congress can use its taxing power 'even for purposes that would exceed its powers under other provisions' of the Constitution." [19]

And even as Team Obama was attempting to bamboozle the Court, it was *still* making the opposite argument right across the street, in the Capitol—unashamed, apparently, to be speaking out of both sides of its mouth.[20]

"NO DAMN POLITICIAN"

But back to Social Security. Years after upholding the Act, the Court would clarify a vital point, initially obscured by Roosevelt's clever approach: No one is *entitled* to Social Security benefits as a legal matter. Congress can change or eliminate them at any time, like any other welfare program.[21] That important clarification came a generation later, however. In 1935, the myth was off and running while the truth was still tying its shoes. In a 1936 pamphlet, the Social Security Administration declared:

> Beginning November 24, 1936, the United States Government will set up a Social Security account for you, if you are eligible. . . . The checks will come to you as a right. . . . [Y]ou and your employer will each pay 3 cents on each dollar you earn, up to $3,000 a year. That is the most you will ever pay. . . . Meanwhile, the Old-Age Reserve fund in the United States Treasury is drawing interest, and the Government guarantees it will never earn less than 3 percent. . . . What you get from the Government plan will always be more than you have paid in taxes and usually more than you can get for yourself by putting away the same amount of money each week in some other way.[22]

Every claim made in this excerpt is either a lie or an exaggeration. But that didn't stop the New Dealers, who were only warming up. A pamphlet published the following year went even further: "[Your payroll tax] payments are like premiums paid for fire insurance or accident insurance" or "saving for a rainy day."[23]

President Roosevelt would later confirm the duplicitous nature of the "insurance" line:

> [Regarding the payroll taxes being regressive,] I guess you're right about the economics, but those taxes were never a problem of economics. They are politics all the way through. We put those payroll contributions there so as to give the contributors a legal, moral, and political right to collect their pensions. . . . With those taxes in there, no damn politician can ever scrap my social security program.[24]

Though, as we've seen, the payroll taxes aren't a "legal" right in the property sense, all those decades of politicians lying to us have indeed made collecting government retirement benefits a "moral" and "political" right that "no damn politician" dares to touch without fear.[25]

The trouble is that the irresistible force of political reality is now coming up against the immovable object known as math. The big entitlements are unsustainable in their current form. They must be changed.

The beautiful thing here is that we know recovery is possible, even at this late date. We can make the big entitlement programs live up to the actual promises made for them by the "damn politicians" of the past. We can make them sources of security *through* rather than *in lieu of* liberty. We know this, because we know that freedom works. Freedom, and the power of individual ownership, offer a road map to ensure that our children and grandchildren will live in a better, wealthier, and more secure world in retirement. Freedom, and the decentralization of information, will ensure that the political lies of the past will not work on future generations. The gig is up, and the people now have access to the facts.

"#SUCKS"

As I noted earlier, more than 40 million Americans depend on Social Security to provide a significant share of their retirement income. But Social Security is going bankrupt, and absent reform, sometime in the next three decades the benefits will have to be cut, or taxes will have to be raised.

The basic design of the program is modeled on the original "social insurance" plan adopted in Bismarck's Germany in the late nineteenth century. The Iron Chancellor created "social security" to help him control the people and protect his position of power. Under his model, which American Progressives fell in love with, today's workers pay taxes to support today's retirees, and each successive generation supports the generation that came before it. This is often described as a "social contract" or "intergenerational compact." What that means in practice: people aren't really saving for their own retirement; they're paying for their parents' or grandparents'. And the promise is that their children and grandchildren will come along and do the same for them, ad infinitum. That's why they have to call it "social" insurance. As far as the math goes, it's a model that works, as long as each generation that comes along is about the same size as the one that came before it and the benefits stay about the same in real terms.

But that never happens.

The twentieth-century "baby boom" has thrown the worker-to-retiree ratio out of whack. In 1935, there were about forty-two working-age Americans for each retiree. By 1950, that number had fallen to sixteen workers per retiree. Today, there are just three workers; and by 2035, the program's centennial, there will be only two workers for every retiree. To be clear, those two workers are your children, laboring under a yoke of debt that they are not responsible for creating.

The share of the U.S. population over sixty-five is growing, while the share represented by workers aged twenty to sixty-four is shrinking.[26] Meanwhile, the burden on those workers is growing, because our politicians have continually voted major benefit hikes for their constituents. For the program's first three decades, Congress would come back every two years, like clockwork, and vote higher benefits for retirees. In the early 1970s, when inflation was taking off, Congress decided to switch to automatic cost of living increases, but for good measure they also supercharged the basic benefit so each new generation's retirement checks would be substantially bigger than those of the previous generation. They did this by having the amount people receive when they first retire grow over time, at the same rate as workers' wages, rather than with general inflation (prices). So the benefits, rather than just retaining their existing purchasing power, grow in real terms over time.[27]

Social Security was initially a great deal, so long as we willfully ignored the declining returns for future retirees. At the very beginning, in the 1940s, for the initial generation of retirees who had paid little into the system, it was almost entirely gravy. Over time, each generation of workers has gotten a worse return on "investment." In fact, the real return for today's workers is only about 1 to 2 percent, and the expected return for today's children is expected to fall below 1 percent. For some individuals, particularly younger ones, it will be negative. For them, simply stuffing the money under the mattress is literally an attractive investment alternative.

That Social Security trust fund you've heard all about? It's filled with IOUs, because every year Congress spends all the revenues that come in from the payroll tax, and any surplus besides. The trust fund is a fiction. But even if we accept its actuarial legitimacy, it's still broke. The demographic problem I mentioned earlier, combined with the big benefit hikes of the '70s, almost exhausted the trust fund in the mid-'70s and again in the early '80s. The response? Raise taxes and cut benefits. But mostly raise taxes. Since the 1983 bipartisan "reform," which combined an increase in the retirement age (from sixty-five to sixty-seven for people born after 1960) with a large and immediate payroll tax hike, the fund has run substantial cash surpluses. More money has come in than has been needed to pay benefits. Guess what Congress has done with these surpluses? That's right, it has "borrowed" them to finance other government programs. But don't worry, that money has been replaced by "completely reliable" government "bonds" that promise the borrowed money will be returned when needed, "with interest." And where is the government going to get the money to pay back all those "bonds," with "interest"? By taxing young people, or else debasing the value of the dollars in their paycheck through inflation.

As it happens, the cash surpluses ended last year, and now the Social Security "trust" fund is having to borrow back from the general fund by redeeming those "bonds." Eventually, when those IOUs are all redeemed—and current projections put that date in the 2030s, but it could easily come sooner—the program will be legally unable to pay all promised benefits. To keep the system going as promised, retiree benefits will have to be cut by about a fourth and/or workers' payroll taxes will have to be raised by about a third. But continued borrowing is the more likely path.

Remember how they told us our benefits would come to us "as a right" and that the current payroll tax level would be "the most we will ever pay"? Remember how they were going to safeguard our money in an account with our name on it, and guaranteed a minimum 3 percent rate of interest on our money? Is it any wonder young people nowadays are more likely to believe in UFOs than that Social Security will keep its promises and be available to them when they retire?

But there's an even bigger problem with Social Security: *You don't own it.* You pay a big chunk of your wages, paycheck after paycheck, over your whole working life, and then you die and they won't let you pass your benefits on to your loved ones. If you die before you reach retirement, your spouse or kids get nothing. Oh, they may qualify for their own modest "survivor's benefit," plus 250 bucks to bury you with. But all that money you paid in, all those years? They'll never see it.

Turns out the "intergenerational compact" is a recipe for intergenerational resentment and a massive wealth transfer from younger, less-wealthy Americans. The Millennial Generation, already saddled with inflated education debts and lousy job prospects, bears *this* growing financial burden as well. That, as the Twitter generation might put it, "#sucks."

REAL RETIREMENT NEST EGGS

ON PAPER, IT'S EASY TO MAKE SOCIAL SECURITY SOLVENT OVER seventy-five years, which is the traditional time horizon by which actuaries judge the program's fiscal health. Just change the base benefit amount so it grows with inflation instead of wages, and bump up the eligibility age to seventy from the current sixty-seven. And if those fixes aren't enough, there's always means-testing, which means denying the benefit to wealthier folks, even though they "paid in," too.

In other words, we could keep asking people to pay more in to fund someone else's retirement, and then get less and less back out of the system when their turn comes.

If retirement security were just an accounting problem, the solutions would be that easy. But all these conventional Washington "reform" ideas would actually worsen the program's rate of return. And, more important, none of them would give young people any personal control they could believe in.

Freedom offers a better way—one that doesn't make unreliable promises, one that gives you, the individual who actually has to live your life, ownership and control of your own retirement. A "defined contribution" approach differs from the traditional, Bismarckian, top-down "defined benefit" approach in the same way that relying on somebody else differs from relying on yourself, or that an easily broken promise differs from real money in the bank. With a defined contribution, you have a real retirement account, and the money in it belongs to you. It's your property. American employers have largely switched to defined contributions from old-fashioned pension schemes, and a number of countries around the world have done the same for their workers, with much success. Uncle Sam should follow suit.

What makes defined-contribution programs work, both actuarially and politically, is that they can produce better returns, thanks to the power of compound interest. Social Security offers around a 1 percent return, but the average rate of return from the stock market since 1926 has been at least 7 percent, even taking into account significant stock market declines such as those that famously occurred in 1929, 1987, and 2008. Defined contributions also provide something truly priceless: real ownership.[28]

Do you remember during the Republican presidential primary debates when Herman Cain talked about the "Chilean model"? No, he was not referring to the *Sports Illustrated Swimsuit Edition*, but to a remarkable example of freedom at work. Three decades ago, Chile embarked on a bold transformation of its public pensions. Today the Chilean system is the envy of the world, giving seniors far better benefits than its old, government-run system. Here's how it works. Let's say you're a worker in Chile. Upon entering the workforce, you're given an account into which you must contribute 10 to 20 percent of your income. These contributions are your property, not the government's.

The amount you opt to contribute determines the age at which you can retire. At retirement, your private fund is converted into an annuity offered by a private, government-regulated insurance company. You choose your insurance company and the kind of annuity plan you want. If you're not satisfied with either, you can make a switch.

For those workers who were under the older, traditional pension system, they were given a choice to stay in that system or enter the new one. The biggest challenge for the reformers: every worker in the old system who switches to the new system creates a problem for the government, a "transition cost," since that worker is now saving for himself instead for paying the benefits of a previous generation. But Chile financed these transitional costs by selling off state-owned enterprises. The program has been so successful that 93 percent of Chilean workers have switched to the new program.

The whole system is based on the principles of voluntary choice and personal ownership, and the positive effects have been remarkable. The new accounts offer benefits 40 to 50 percent higher than the traditional "social security" pensions. Disability and survivors benefits are 70 to 100 percent higher. Meanwhile, significant decreases in the payroll tax have contributed to the country's low unemployment rate, which is under 5 percent. Savings rates have soared. Investment has gone up. Economic growth rates have more than doubled over the past ten years. And the reform has helped generate government budget surpluses without raising taxes, inflation, or interest rates. Does that sound like something we might want to try in America?

EVERYTHING'S BIGGER IN TEXAS

ABOUT THE SAME TIME THE CHILEAN PENSION REFORMS WERE GETting under way, a telling experiment began in three U.S. counties that took advantage of an opportunity to opt out of Social Security in favor of offering their public employees personal retirement accounts. (The option has since been rescinded, and those three jurisdictions—

Galveston, Matagorda, and Brazoria Counties, in Texas—are grand-fathered.) Thirty years later, the verdict is in, and the experiment is a smashing success.

County workers under the "Galveston model" retire with more money and have better death and disability supplemental benefits than do retirees in traditional, defined-benefit Social Security. In fact, many of them end up with more than twice the money they'd get under Social Security. And more important, because it's a defined contribution, that money is their *property*. No damn politician can take it away on a whim. When a worker enjoying this plan dies, his entire account belongs to his estate and can be passed along to his heirs.

The money in the account isn't immediately spent and "credited" to a phony "trust fund" full of IOUs; it's actually invested in safe instruments by a real financial institution under contract to the county. Not surprisingly, when it comes to returns, these investments invariably beat the pants off the old FDR, pay-as-you-go model.

And here's the kicker: These three counties—unlike almost all others in the United States—face *no long-term unfunded pension liabilities*. How is that possible? Because of the model. Just like the rest of us, the employee under the Galveston plan contributes 6.2 percent of his income while the employer (the county) matches the contribution. But, as policy expert Merrill Matthews explains, "once the county makes its contribution, its financial obligation is done—that's why *there are no long-term unfunded liabilities*."[29]

Better benefits. Personal ownership. A more secure retirement. Zero public debt. Do we need more proof that freedom works better than government?

GET SMART

IN THE FIRST CHAPTER, I MENTIONED THE TEA PARTY DEBT COMMISsion, which has put forward a comprehensive plan to cut spending, *balance the budget in four years*, and stop the growth of the national debt. Among other reforms, the commission found that America could achieve all of those goals *and* fix Social Security by adopting the Chilean model, even after accounting for transition costs. The commission embraced a modified version of Rep. Jeff Flake's Strengthening Medicare and Repaying Taxpayers (SMART) Act. This bold reform, first offered by the Arizona Republican in 2005, would allow young people to opt out of traditional Social Security into a personally owned and controlled account. In the Tea Party Budget variant of this idea, the accounts would be phased in. New workers born after 1981 would be allowed to invest half of their payroll taxes (7.65 percent of their wages) in a SMART account, which they could use to fund their retirement and health care costs in retirement. It would be their property, and, unlike the traditional program, they could pass it on to their heirs. (To get program costs back under control, the future growth of the guaranteed benefit amount under the traditional program would be slightly reduced for upper-income folks. But this change wouldn't affect the accounts.) The accounts are purely optional. You could have one all your life, and then switch back to the traditional system on reaching retirement age, though you'd have to relinquish the money in your account at that point—something I suspect very few would do. As happened in Chile, the SMART accounts will offer better benefits and more financial security. And all of this, without eat-your-spinach reforms like means-testing or raising the retirement age.

One of the more Orwellian aspects of federal budgeting is the fact that more than $100 trillion in long-term unfunded liabilities is not on the accounting books, but the "cost" of taking those liabilities— young people—off the government's obligations by allowing them to save for themselves with their own earnings is scored as a "cost." And you wonder how Jon Corzine—Obama confidant, former Democratic senator and governor, former Goldman Sachs head, and now disgraced MF Global CEO—managed to misplace $1.2 billion in customer funds? He said, "I simply do not know where the money is, or why the accounts have not been reconciled to date." Apparently he was used to government math.

SMART accounts would, over the first decade, have a net budgetary "cost" of about $500 billion, but in the long run would eliminate Social Security's unfunded liability. That $500 billion "cost" would be "an excellent investment on a better system, and one that is fully paid for in this plan."[30] How can we fund the "transition" costs? By cutting federal spending and selling off certain government-owned assets.

BROKEN PROMISES

WHEN IT WAS CREATED IN 1965, MEDICARE PROMISED OLDER AMERI-cans the peace of mind that comes from having guaranteed access to medical expense coverage. Seniors, it was alleged, were exhausting their savings due to high health expenses and finding it too expensive to afford private health insurance. This "crisis" would now be over. As President Johnson described it in 1965:

> Through this new law . . . every citizen will be able, in his productive years, to ensure himself against the ravages of illness in his old age. . . . [N]o longer will older Americans be denied the healing miracle of modern medicine. No longer will illness crush and destroy the savings that they have so carefully put away over a lifetime so that they might enjoy dignity in their later years. No longer will young families see their own incomes, and their own hopes, eaten away simply because they are carrying out their deep moral obligations to their parents, to their uncles, and to their aunts.[31]

And to reassure doctors and patients that the doctor-patient relationship would never be infringed by Medicare bureaucrats, the very first section of the law promised: "Nothing in this title shall be construed to authorize any Federal officer or employee to exercise any supervision or control over the practice of medicine or the manner in which medical services are provided . . . or to exercise any supervision or control over the administration or operation of any [health-care] institution, agency, or person." [32]

Today, it's clear that Medicare has broken all these promises and will never be able to deliver on them in its current form. In that way, it's like the health-insurance equivalent of a politician's campaign promises.

The second largest federal program, Medicare is also one of the fastest growing. Currently comprising 13 percent of the budget, this program is also the most important single factor in future deficits and debt. You can't realistically balance the budget without rethinking Medicare for future generations.

Today the nation's single largest health insurance benefit plan, covering more than 40 million elderly and 8 million disabled persons, or 1 out of every 8 Americans, Medicare's rolls are currently growing at the rate of 10,000 people a day, and will continue to do so for the next two decades. In 1967, Medicare covered 9 percent of the U.S. population; today it covers about 15 percent; and by 2030, that figure is expected to be 20 percent.

Medicare spending has grown at an average rate of 9 percent a year over its forty-five-year history (10 percent in 2009) and is projected to grow by "only" about 7 percent a year during the coming decade, or more than twice as fast as the economy. The cost of Medicare has always been orders of magnitude higher than expected. For example, in 1965, its official projected cost for 1990 was $12 billion; the actual 1990 cost was $110 billion.

The official underfunding of Medicare's hospital insurance trust fund is $2.4 trillion. The comparable figure for its other trust fund, the one for physician services and prescription drugs, tops $35 trillion. Combined, that's nearly *$38 trillion* in future promises no one has figured out how to pay for. In fact, Medicare's unfunded liabilities are so obscenely high that they are not really even a topic of polite discussion in Washington. No one wants to even think about it—after all, *in the long run we're all dead.*

Beyond its fiscal impact is its enormous effect on the entire health care sector. Medicare controls one out of every four dollars spent on health care in America. The open-ended, blank-check nature of the Medicare system fuels a persistent health care inflation that has, on average, exceeded economic growth by 2.4 percentage points a year since 1970. Medicare's inefficient design and price-controlling bureaucracy drive up the costs of care in the private sector, while also retarding medical innovation and diminishing quality and access to care.

And on top of all that, Medicare has the highest fraud rate of any health insurer. In 2009, fraud in this program cost taxpayers somewhere between $60 billion and $100 billion, or between 12 and 19 percent of the program's total spending. Essentially a giant check-writing operation, Medicare audits fewer than 1 percent of the billions of claims it pays annually. Its ability to recoup stolen funds is weak. Horror stories abound.

The Medicare bureaucracy focuses all its efforts on trying to control medical prices, rather than on preventing fraud—and by every measure fails miserably at both.

Designed in the mid-1960s, Medicare has never been adequately updated to reflect changes in medicine. Medicare offers seniors and the disabled a benefit that is poorly designed, wasteful, and in many ways inadequate. Despite popular perception, Medicare covers only about half of the average senior's expected annual health costs, and has never offered any protection against catastrophically high medical costs, the most basic purpose of insurance.

BETTER THAN MEDICARE

THE CHALLENGE IS TO FIND WAYS TO SLOW MEDICARE'S UNSUSTAINable growth rate without rationing patients' access to care or stifling medical progress and innovation.

The three conventional options for Medicare reform are: a) increase the retirement age; b) means-test the premiums; and/or c) ration benefits through lower reimbursement rates. None of these ideas put patients in charge of their health care.

It's a fact of life: scarce goods must be allocated. The question is not whether, but how: via individual choices, or bureaucracy? Government-run health care always favors bureaucracy. And it shows. For example, the reimbursement rate for doctors under Medicare is typically around 15 percent below the private sector. Medicaid's rates are notoriously lower than that, so low, in fact, that 28 percent of doctors won't take Medicaid patients, and an additional 32 percent will take them only under certain conditions.[33] Studies show Medicaid patients get substandard care and have worse health outcomes than others.[34] Because Obamacare is funded in part by reducing Medicare payments by $500 billion over ten years, Medicare is on track, by the end of this decade, to pay doctors even less than Medicaid does. This is a bureaucratic form of rationing care, and it the inevitable result of a centralized system.

True reform will occur only when we return the focus to individual patients. Medicare is simply too bureaucratic, top-down, and government-centric. We need to give patients more choice and control. We must make it patient-centered. It's not about national health; it's ultimately about *your* health.

From this perspective, an obvious question is why the government would force anyone to participate in the program we can't afford. If Medicare is a good system, it should survive and thrive being chosen by individual patients.

First and most important, then, we need to let individuals opt out of Medicare. This is currently prohibited, and that is simply outrageous in America.

Second, let seniors who opt out of Medicare buy private insurance in the open market. This, too, is effectively banned today, because private insurers aren't allowed to compete with the Medicare bureaucracy.

Third, allow individuals to opt into the popular and successful Federal Employees Health Benefit Program. This is the same program enjoyed by current and former members of Congress. The congressional health care program relies on competing private insurers to provide benefits, and as a result has a better record than old-fashioned Medicare, in terms of cost control, quality of benefits, and customer satisfaction. It also has very little of the fraud and waste that plague old-fashioned Medicare. This reform would also make the system more patient-centered. It would give beneficiaries more modern insurance plans with more rational cost-sharing and co-payments. This idea, the "Congressional Health Care for Seniors Act," was first proposed by Senator Rand Paul of Kentucky. Senator Paul estimates the change would save about $1 trillion over its first ten years and cut Medicare's $38 trillion unfunded liability nearly in half.[35]

Fourth, eliminate IPAB, the Independent Payment Advisory Board. That's the Obamacare care rationing panel consisting of fifteen unelected bureaucrats, whose job will be to squeeze savings out of Medicare through formulaic rationing. Government functionaries should never have the power to determine what you should or should not receive, especially care that could determine whether you live or die. You don't have to call the IPAB a "death panel" to know it is morally wrong.

This plan doesn't means-test the premiums, doesn't raise the retirement age, and most important, it doesn't ration. Instead, it ends the *current* rationing and reduces costs by putting seniors in charge of their health care dollars.

CONTROL YOU CAN BELIEVE IN

IN JULY 2009, PRESIDENT OBAMA TOOK GREAT JOY IN MOCKING ONE lady who was upset with his plan to divert $500 billion from Medicare into a new government-run health care entitlement. He was speaking to a group hosted by the AARP, the massive interest group whose aggressive advocacy for new entitlement spending has been instrumental in creating the daunting unfunded spending liabilities faced by future taxpayers. Business, for the AARP, is great. Their Washington, D.C., headquarters has been referred to as the Taj Mahal.

"I got a letter the other day from a woman," Obama told the crowd. "She said, 'I don't want government-run health care. I don't want socialized medicine. And don't touch my Medicare.' I wanted to say, you know, that's what Medicare is: a government-run health care plan," Obama said as he smiled.[36] The AARP crowd laughed, with the President of the United States, at the author of the letter. The joke, it seemed, was on her.

He might as well have said, "I've got you now."

The principles to fix the two biggest entitlements, Social Security and Medicare—choice, individual control, ownership, self-sufficiency—are quintessentially American ideas as old as our founding. They are the same principles that a young Ronald Reagan applied to the question of how to fix these top-down programs. In 1964, in what became one of the most important political speeches Reagan would ever give, he declared in "A Time for Choosing":

They've called it 'insurance' to us in a hundred million pieces of literature. But then they appeared before the Supreme Court and they testified it was a welfare program. They only use the term "insurance" to sell it to the people. And they said Social Security dues are a tax for the general use of the government, and the government has used that tax. . . .

A young man, 21 years of age, working at an average salary—his Social Security contribution would, in the open market, buy him an insurance policy that would guarantee 220 dollars a month at age 65. The government promises 127. . . . Now are we so lacking in business sense that we can't put this program on a sound basis, so that people who do require those payments will find they can get them when they're due—that the cupboard isn't bare? . . .

At the same time, can't we introduce voluntary features that would permit a citizen who can do better on his own to be excused upon presentation of evidence that he had made provision for the non-earning years? Should we not allow a widow with children to work, and not lose the benefits supposedly paid for by her deceased husband? Shouldn't you and I be allowed to declare who our beneficiaries will be under this program, which we cannot do? . . .

I think we're against forcing all citizens, regardless of need, into a compulsory government program, especially when we have such examples, as was announced last week, when France admitted that their Medicare program is now bankrupt. They've come to the end of the road.[37]

France "saved" its Medicare program with tax hikes and borrowing—massive borrowing.

What Reagan could not have known then, in 1964, was that Americans would one day rise up off of our couches, stop yelling at their TVs, and demand accountability from their government. We are armed with facts from a multitude of sources online and offline. We know that our government has lied to us. We know that it makes no sense to shift $500 billion from a program that is already trillions in debt to create yet another new government takeover of health care. We know that this is the inevitable price for letting government control our destiny. And sometimes they even come armed with actuarial spreadsheets demonstrating, beyond a reasonable doubt, that our children and grandchildren will pay an unconscionable price if we do not act to take control of our government back.

A CEO would never make fun of a stockholder. It might cost him his job. But top-down government in the United States has sought to turn stakeholders into wards of the state. But that was then. Now is a new *time for choosing*.

CHAPTER 13

DISINTERMEDIATION POLITICS

Let your life proceed by its own design.
—John Perry Barlow

IT SEEMS AS IF EVERYWHERE YOU LOOK, EVERYTHING IN MODERN LIFE is becoming more about the individual. Everything has become personal, more individualized. More to *your* liking; what *you* need. Consumers are finding and buying what they want, not what some commercial on daytime TV told them they wanted. We are now used to rating products and celebrities by voting online, thumbs up or down. Markets and services have been radically democratized, providing every individual with a voice, an opinion, a say in what happens, what comes to market, and what is ingloriously pitched into the dustbin of history.

We answer to no single boss because, unlike our parents and grandparents, we typically do not work at one job for most of our lives. We search, we compete, and we explore options at Monster.com; we can reach hundreds of "friends" on Facebook and "followers" on Twitter in the time it takes to read this sentence. Sometimes we exploit our new mobility and move to a new locale and a new opportunity. We look out for ourselves instead of expecting some mother ship corporation and its underfunded pension system to tend to our family's needs from the first day at work to the day we receive the gold-plated watch at our retirement.

We now get our information on the day's events from a multitude of sources. We control our own newsfeeds and follow our own favored citizen-journalists. We can choose to get the latest happening, fact, breaking story, or career-wrecking, 140-character rant via Twitter. Bloggers in basements with personal agendas and ideological axes to grind get the story first while the Old Media monopolists struggle to keep up with yesterday's news. We don't need Dan Rather or the *New York Times* telling us what to think anymore.

We have access to goods and services that meet our unique—some might say weird—tastes and preferences. Much to my wife's chagrin, I can buy the entire seventy-two-disc collection of the Grateful Dead's Europe '72 tour, browse an original printing of F. A. Hayek's *Road to Serfdom*, and download the fourth season of *Breaking Bad* to my iPad, all before breakfast. Decentralization at least creates a *perception* of more freedom for husbands about to be reined back to reality by their loving wives.

Chris Anderson, editor-in-chief of *Wired*, put it well:

> Our culture and economy is increasingly shifting away from a focus on a relatively small number of "hits" (mainstream products and markets) at the head of the demand curve and toward a huge number of niches in the tail. As the costs of production and distribution fall, especially online, there is now less need to lump products and consumers into one-size-fits-all containers. In an era without the constraints of physical shelf space and other bottlenecks of distribution, narrowly-targeted goods and services can be as economically attractive as mainstream fare.[1]

Anderson nailed this trend in 2004 and coined the term *the long tail* for it. He predicted something that was not so obvious then, but today is so ubiquitous that we almost don't even notice it, like gravity or the air we breathe.

We Americans are free, opinionated, and utterly mobile. We are not to be controlled, not to be dictated to, not to be restrained in our opinions or consumption habits. Each individual in this radically decentralized world is, in effect, the fearless "Honey Badger" of You-Tube fame—27 million hits and counting, no corporate sponsorship, unstoppable.

This democratization of information and choice is global. Everything is rapidly progressing away from top-down hierarchies toward bottom-up decisions driven by individual preferences.

Freedom is "trending," as they say of dominant topics that emerge spontaneously, by choice, on Twitter. Everything is disintermediating. The middleman has been sent—mercilessly—to the back of the line.

Except government. Government is trending toward more centralization, more gray-suited middlemen dictating—usually unknown to you—what you may or may not do. More and more choices are being made for you, using your money, the money of your neighbor, and the money of someone you don't know. Tellingly, the trends toward more centralized government seem to accelerate with the declining state of government balance sheets. From Brussels to Berlin, from Athens to Rome, from Harare, Zimbabwe, to Washington, D.C., insolvency and old welfare-state habits are being propped up with other people's money and money that is being created, out of thin air, by government central banks.

Here in the United States, once the Land of the Free, the contrast is the most striking. What was once a "shining city on a hill" for freedom-loving people across the world, an example to be emulated and sought after, is now a quagmire of debt, bureaucracy, economic stagnation, and government failure. When it comes to the federal government of the United States, everything is trending toward more. More spending. More debt. More control. More one-size-fits-all. More "I'm from the government and I'm here to help"—a phrase

Ronald Reagan famously called the "nine most terrifying words in the English language."

As we become more independent, Washington, D.C., is growing, with increasing velocity, to inhibit our freedom. Everything coming out of the nation's capital is more centralized, more command-and-control, more distrusting of our ability to live the lives we choose, to pursue the happiness we desire. The Obama administration and its growing legion of "czars" has been feverishly building more top-down structures to make more choices for us, and using our money to do it. Rather than creating an open-ended, transparent approach to health care to be molded by you, by your needs and preferences and demands, the government chooses a single approach to which you must conform. The pretense of knowing better what you need is then corrupted, "in committee," by the favored interests, trough feeders, and crony capitalists that grow fat on a special diet of your hard-earned substance. When it comes to power, someone else is always getting privileged treatment different from what you will, or could, receive.

POLITICAL INDULGENCES

You are required under Obamacare—by "individual mandate"—to buy a one-size-fits-everyone benefits package you may not want, need, or be able to afford. The primary beneficiaries just happen to be the health insurance companies who provide that benefits package. The rest of us are screwed. But if you happen to be an insider, if you know someone special who knows someone in Washington, you might just receive a waiver from that someone with the power and the discretion to grant special dispensation—an indulgence—from Obamacare. That someone might have been Nancy-Ann DeParle, described by *Time* magazine as "Obama's Health Czar: Behind the Scenes but Leading the Charge." She reports to President Obama; is immune from congressional oversight; and has been "tasked with what she has always done best, working behind the scenes to improve the health-care system." [2]

One waiver recipient—the Robert Wood Johnson Foundation, an aggressive advocate of government-run health care, as it happens—has friends in high places. And Czar DeParle "sits on the foundation's board of trustees." [3]

If you didn't know someone with the cell phone number of Czar DeParle, maybe you could get an in with the now-more-powerful head of the U.S. Department of Health and Human Services, Kathleen Sebelius. If you're reading this book, it is highly unlikely that either DeParle or Sebelius will take your meeting, or will bless you with indulgences from the government's rules. Because the rules are for your own good, except if you "know a guy"—then they're for suckers.

Someone in the Obama administration did, however, take the meeting with Big Labor. As I noted earlier, labor unions have received a disproportionate allocation of waivers from the costly health care mandate. Almost half of the waivers distributed involve employees of unions even though union workers are only about 12 percent of the workforce. [4,5]

At a rally in Detroit on Labor Day 2011, Jim Hoffa, president of the International Brotherhood of Teamsters, made a point of expressing his appreciation for the favor. He pledged his unconditional fealty to the man in charge of things: "President Obama, this is your army," Hoffa declared. "We are ready to march . . . and when he sees what we're doing here he will be inspired. But he needs help and you know what? Everybody here's got to vote. If we go back and we keep the eye on the prize, *let's take these son of a bitches out* and give America back to America where we belong!" [6]

"These son of a bitches" Hoffa is referring to are the men and women of the Tea Party, of course. (Don't dwell on the bad English. Let's assume for the sake of argument that the head of the Teamsters is a victim, like I am, of the government's education monopoly.) Hoffa deeply resents that these citizens might want a say, too; that taxpayers may want a voice in how their tax dollars are spent. They might even insist that everyone in America, regardless of who you know, is treated equally under the laws of the land. Those "son of a bitches." A quick search of waiver recipients posted by the Sunlight Foundation in a comprehensive spreadsheet reveals that no fewer than twenty-one state and local Teamster unions have been blessed with waivers from the Obama administration.[7]

QUID PRO QUO, MR. HOFFA?

DIDN'T WE DECLARE OUR INDEPENDENCE FROM THIS TYPE OF FEALTY-to-a-king servitude some 236 years ago? Didn't our Founders pledge "our Lives, our Fortunes, and our sacred Honor" to ensure that no American citizen would ever act as vassal to some self-anointed government overlord? The Declaration of Independence and the Constitution are binding contracts that have as the basis of their power *the consent of the governed*; not to be ignored, renegotiated, or broken.

The centralized control of health care is just the beginning of the story. Our government is centralizing the banking system, too. One of the main drivers of the financial collapse of 2008 was too much concentrated risk in the banking industry, which was incentivized by past bailouts. Banks deemed "too big to fail" still existed because of past government interventions. Fannie Mae and Freddie Mac, the oxymoronic "government-sponsored enterprises," centralized financing of the mortgage industry, driving the writing and signing of bad loans. Both actions socialized risk, leaving you, Joe and Jane Taxpayer, on the hook if something went wrong. And it went really, really wrong.

Later, the same legislators most culpable for this concentration of banking power "fixed" the system again by turning an implicit guarantee of taxpayer bailouts into an explicit socialized risk pool that punishes sound banks and is too shallow to protect from another raid on the public treasury. Dodd-Frank, the shorthand for this legislative train wreck, was authored by then Senate Banking Committee Chairman Christopher Dodd (D-Countrywide Financial) and then House Financial Services Chairman Barney Frank (D-Fannie Mae and Freddie Mac). This is what President Obama refers to, in a mirror image of the truth, as "Wall Street reform." No, Mr. President, it's the protection of bad actors on Wall Street, retrenching the status quo.

How do we fund centralized health care and centralized investment banking? With centralized money, arbitrarily printed, more and more, to monetize bad judgments.

What could possibly go wrong?

DECLARING INDEPENDENCE

IN 1996, JOHN PERRY BARLOW, A ONETIME CAMPAIGN COORDINATOR for Dick Cheney in his first run for Congress, a lyricist for the Grateful Dead, and cofounder of the Electronic Frontier Foundation, posted "A Declaration of the Independence of Cyberspace" on the Web. Channeling a young Thomas Jefferson, it read in part:

> Your increasingly obsolete information industries would perpetuate themselves by proposing laws, in America and elsewhere, that claim to own speech itself throughout the world. These laws would declare ideas to be another industrial product, no more noble than pig iron. In our world, whatever the human mind may create can be reproduced and distributed infinitely at no cost. The global conveyance of thought no longer requires your factories to accomplish.
>
> These increasingly hostile and colonial measures place us in the same position as those previous lovers of freedom and self-determination who had to reject the authorities of distant, uninformed powers. We must declare our virtual selves immune to your sovereignty.[8]

Barlow's declaration became a manifesto of sorts for cyberlibertarians who believed that the spontaneous spread of information could create, in Barlow's words, "a right to know." The liberating forces of knowing, at diminishing marginal cost to the end user, had implications for individual freedom, politics, and the functioning of democracy. Beyond even Barlow's futuristic optimism, the free flow of information online was breaking down barriers and leveling the playing field between mere citizens and the insiders who had always exploited special access to information to fix the game, concentrate benefits for a select few, and disperse costs outside the walls of the establishment.

In a 2008 speech before the Icelandic Digital Freedom Society's conference in Reykjavik, Barlow anticipated the coming clash between bottom-up freedom and top-down control in the name of intellectual property.[9] He quotes Jefferson, the radical democrat, from an 1813 letter to Isaac McPherson:

If nature has made any one thing less susceptible than all others of exclusive property, it is the action of the thinking power called an idea, which an individual may exclusively possess as long as he keeps it to himself; but the moment it is divulged, it forces itself into the possession of every one, and the receiver cannot dispossess himself of it. Its peculiar character, too, is that no one possesses the less, because every other possesses the whole of it. He who receives an idea from me, receives instruction himself without lessening mine; as he who lights his taper at mine, receives light without darkening me. That ideas should freely spread from one to another over the globe, for the moral and mutual instruction of man, and improvement of his condition, seems to have been peculiarly and benevolently designed by nature, when she made them, like fire, expansible over all space, without lessening their density in any point, and like the air in which we breathe, move, and have our physical being, incapable of confinement or exclusive appropriation.[10]

Only too much meddling and rearranging by government could imperil the potential of the Internet to liberate information and knowledge and the decentralized spirit of the American idea.

Barlow's cyberspace declaration of '96 also portended—sixteen years after it was posted—an important tipping of the insiders' apple cart and a disruption in the collusive and symbiotic relationship between big government and big business. An attempt to give the federal government sweeping discretionary control over content on the Internet through the Stop Online Piracy Act (SOPA) and the Protect IP Act (PIPA) managed to bring grassroots forces from across the political spectrum together against this Washington power grab.[11] Adding to the drama, the legislative bum's rush on Internet freedom had been orchestrated by a trifecta of powerful Washington insiders: Democratic chairman of the Senate Judiciary Committee Patrick Leahy (PIPA), Republican chairman of the House Judiciary Committee Lamar Smith (SOPA), and disgraced senator-turned-*über*-lobbyist Chris Dodd, now head of the Motion Picture Association of America (MPAA). That's right, *that* Senator Dodd, who once received a sweetheart mortgage deal from Countrywide Financial and who, once outed, ignominiously retired in 2010 rather than face voters looking to hold him accountable for the Dodd/Countrywide/housing bubble nexus.

Julian Sanchez of the Cato Institute argues that these proposed bills would have put government bureaucrats into a new and dominant position to control online speech, not just blocking legitimate free speech and undermining the inherent openness of the Internet. "The practical effect of SOPA," Sanchez says, "will be to create an *architecture for censorship*—both legal and technological—that will radically alter the costs [to government] of engaging in future censorship unrelated to piracy or counterfeiting."[12]

Micah Sifry with Personal Democracy Media argues that the opposition coalition of interests and activists that coalesced is something new, representing a shift from traditional defense of parochial interest politics to something broader and bigger. "[T]he bills have backfired on Hollywood, fostering the emergence of a significant new force: a civic-business alliance to defend the freedom of online speech and sharing and to protect the basic values and structure of the open Internet . . . This is the first time," he says, "we've seen a wave of nonprofit and for-profit sites that exist primarily to serve their users openly choose to use their platforms to interrupt their users—without asking for permission—and implore them to take a stand." [13]

According to *Talking Points Memo*, every bit as left-leaning and progressive as Sifry and PDM, "The clearest turning point was surely 'Blackout Day,' Wednesday, January 18, [2012] which saw coordinated online protests by upwards of an estimated 115,000 websites, coupled with physical protests by hundreds on the ground in five cities. Throughout the day, 19 senators and numerous other representatives—many of them Republicans—came out in opposition to SOPA and PIPA or renounced their former support for the bills." [14]

In case anyone was missing the point—the potential for this government power grab to create the essential architecture to censor political speech—Senator Mike Lee tweeted the following on January 18: "Here are my thoughts on #SOPA #PIPA: ██ ███ ██ ██ ███ ████ ://ow.ly/8ynx4 Please RT to ████████ ██████ Internet." [15]

What's interesting about this is the strange bedfellows who united against the establishment's coalition of insiders. Against SOPA and PIPA was everyone from presidential candidate Ron Paul (and eventually, all Republican candidates for president in a January 2012 South Carolina debate hosted by CNN), Senator Rand Paul, *RedState*, and FreedomWorks to the Electronic Frontier Foundation, *Talking Points Memo*, Personal Democracy Media, Google, and Wikipedia, to name just a few. Even the diametrically opposed groups MoveOn.org (for the Left) and the National Taxpayers Union (for the Right) were against it. Without hyperbole, it was the greatest display of *nonpartisanship* in Washington since September 11, 2001.

Dodd, who was not "lobbying," because he is still legally prohibited from doing so, proffered something far more blatant than the mutually beneficial payoffs between Big Labor and the health care czars of the Obama administration.

"Candidly, those who count on quote 'Hollywood' for support need to understand that this industry is watching very carefully who's going to stand up for them when their job is at stake," Dodd pronounced on Fox News. "Don't ask me to write a check for you when you think your job is at risk and then don't pay any attention to me when my job is at stake. . . . I would caution people don't make the assumption that because the quote 'Hollywood community' has been historically supportive of Democrats, which they have, don't make the false assumptions this year that because we did it in years past, we will do it this year."[16]

We sent our "*quid*," Dodd was saying. Lots and lots of quid, in fact. Where's my "*quo*"?

Usually, such threats are delivered with a modicum of subtlety and panache. You just don't discuss political bribery in public like that; it's really not polite. Save it for the back rooms. But Hollywood insiders were caught flat-footed, flummoxed because their major investment in politics was not paying the proper financial returns. And Dodd—the epitome of Washington insiderdom if there ever was one—couldn't contain his frustration. At least he was honest.

HOPE AND CHANGE

OF COURSE, THIS WAS NOT THE FIRST TIME THAT THE INTERNET HAD disintermediated legislative horse-trading and disrupted the comfortable relationship between committee chairmen and rent-seekers out to protect or grow their share at someone else's expense. It happened when grassroots America defeated Nancy Pelosi's first TARP bill, in 2008. It was happening with more and more frequency throughout the Obama administration, forcing a monumental clash between the regular pathways of legislative fixes crafted behind closed doors and the new transparency and "the right to know" inherent in the decentralized nature of the Internet.

In reality, it was as much about the rushed, secretive, and cobbled-together nature of the Obama stimulus boondoggle, which generated such a visceral grassroots response among fledgling Tea Partiers. The same was true with Obamacare, a massive undertaking that sought to redesign one-sixth of the American economy, all before the August recess. It seemed like they were jamming it through—hiding something—because they were in fact jamming it through in order to hide something from the public.

The onslaught of grassroots activist opposition to these big-government power grabs in early 2009 caught Team Obama totally by surprise, just as flat-footed as Big Hollywood's Chris Dodd. People caught off guard often say dumb things, because they never plan to be asked questions like the one asked by disillusioned Obamanista Lydia DePillis by the *New Republic* on October 29, 2009: "What happened to Obama's massive network of grassroots activists?" [17]

"It wasn't supposed to be this way," wrote DePillis. "The reason was Organizing for America [OFA]. Last year, after winning the presidency, Obama decided to keep intact the backbone of his stunningly efficient, innovative campaign. . . . OFA was supposed to be a new kind of permanent campaign: a grassroots network wielding some 13 million e-mail addresses to mobilize former volunteers on behalf of the administration's agenda (and keep them engaged for 2012)."

Frustrated and panicked, the response of partisans in and around the Obama administration was to attack the motives of the Tea Party. They were *racist*! They were angry! They were *domestic terrorists!* The name-calling was a Saul Alinsky–inspired diversionary tactic, but it only thinly veiled an internal debate among the newly triumphant axis of the mainstream media, the progressive movement, and the Democratic political establishment. Obama had toppled the Democrats' establishment candidate, Hillary Clinton, by rewriting the rules of politics, replacing top-down money bundlers and paid media consultants with a whole new, bottom-up grassroots political machine. Right?

The reality of Organizing for Obama (OFO) was a mixed bag, part bottom-up and part top-down. Clearly it was more decentralized than the McCain campaign, which was seemingly indistinguishable from Bob Dole's failed 1996 effort. It is true that the Obama campaign took a fundamentally different strategic tack by fighting in more states, not just the big prizes like California. The slow accumulation of delegates in caucus states, favorable territory for the motivated grassroots troops of OFO, proved to be an essential tactic for the Obama campaign, allowing the candidate to eke out victory before the Democratic National Convention. OFO's formidable e-mail database allowed the campaign, to a certain extent, to end-run the Democratic establishment's bundlers, who were by and large standing with Hillary and Bill Clinton. But, as it turns out, the decentralized nature of the Obama campaign was much more about optics and message.

Was the actual campaign structure bottom-up? The campaign was still about a single charismatic leader, and the grassroots activists were still tightly controlled from Obama headquarters. "The truth is that Obama was never nearly as free of dependence on big money donors as the reporting suggested, nor was his movement as bottom-up or people-centric as his marketing implied," argues Micah Sifry in a must-read post on TechPresident. "And this is the big story of 2009, if you ask me, the meta-story of what did, and didn't happen, in the first year of Obama's administration." [18]

Why didn't the grassroots machinery of the Obama campaign sustain itself after President Obama was sworn into office? "The answer, ultimately," says Sifry, "is that [Obama campaign manager David] Plouffe and the rest of Obama's leadership team, wasn't really interested in grassroots empowerment. Instead, they think they've invented a 21st century version of list-building, and to some degree they're right." To prove his point, Sifry quotes directly from Plouffe's book *The Audacity to Win*:

Our e-mail list had reached 13 million people. We had essentially created our own television network, only better, because we communicated with no filter to what would amount to about 20 percent of the total number of votes we would need to win. . . . And those supporters would share our positive message or response to an attack, whether through orchestrated campaign activity like door-knocking or phone calling or just in conversations they had each day with friends, family, and colleagues.[19]

Plouffe ultimately wanted control of every aspect of the campaign, and the need to run things from the top ultimately undermines decentralized networks, whether the spontaneous emergence of knowledge, the dissemination of information online, or local grassroots organization. "We wanted control of our advertising, and most important, we wanted control of our field operation," says Plouffe of the Obama campaign. "We did not want to outsource these millions of people, and these hundreds of thousands of full-time volunteers to the DNC or any other entity."[20]

In other words, the Obama campaign wanted to control things, from the top down. Progressive politics, like progressive solutions to economic and social problems, is always that way. Political power and the freedom to let things emerge, by choice, just don't seem to mix. But they also were smart about it. Plouffe and the rest of the Obama brain trust knew what was happening out there. They knew the popularity of social networks. They knew people wanted to believe they were in control. Most of all, they knew that Obama's appeal as a candidate could not stand on Obama's accomplishments as a politician. Obama needed something else: And that something else was the *appearance* that Obama was the candidate of the people.

It was an illusion.

This is the cognitive dissonance on the Left that I will simply never grasp. Government power must be checked, strictly limited, as Jefferson and Madison insisted, or it will always end up getting in lines of business you never intended it to get into, like censoring speech on the Internet. Centralized health care and centralized education must always lead to less individual autonomy, less freedom. More government is just about less of everything else. It is not possible for the federal government to take over one-sixth of the economy without the undue influence of interests who have something to gain (and much to lose). The loser will always be the least connected among us, the ones with the least pull, in this particular case the patient most in need of a functioning health care system that treats patients individually, not special interests collectively.

CULTURE CLASH

HISTORICALLY, THERE IS A BOOM AND BUST IN POLITICS. THE DEMO-crats who held control of the House of Representative uninterrupted for forty years were thrown out by Republicans in 1994, who were, in turn, turned out in 2006. Political fortunes rise and fall. The media seems to expect this to happen to the Tea Party as well. And it may. But the problem with this narrative is that it has failed as a predictive model for explaining the future behavior of the Tea Party, which hasn't ebbed with the natural flow of the political cycle.

The Tea Party was supposed to disappear after the 800-plus Tax Day rallies on April 15, 2009. It was supposed to dissipate after the passage of Obamacare in 2010. "The air is out of the tea party balloon," said one DNC operative on March 16, 2010. "Today's dismal showing on Capitol Hill coupled with the turnout we're seeing at health reform rallies across the country where supporters are outnumbering opponents by three to one and four to one clearly demonstrates that the momentum is squarely on the side of those who support reform."[21] Grassroots opposition to legislation could not translate into an effective GOTV machine, everyone predicted.

But, like a community trying to solve a problem, the Tea Party continued to evolve, reflecting changing circumstances, different challenges, and the inevitable momentum of an organic movement that is not directed by any single mind.

We no longer have to gather in D.C. en masse to get the establishment's attention. We did that in 2009, with more than a million activists choosing to squeeze their family budget and put aside, for a few days, the obligations of everyday life. But remember Saul Alinsky's seventh "rule for radicals": "A tactic that drags on too long becomes a drag." It wouldn't make sense to gather en masse in D.C. anymore. We're beyond that.

Protesters protest because they have no better avenue to vent their dissatisfaction with the status quo.

"Tea Party activists who were protesting outside their Statehouses two years ago have now grown more sophisticated," writes Matt Bai. "They're quietly organizing through social media, running local candidates and pressuring lawmakers in private meetings." Bai is a *New York Times Magazine* political reporter, and author of *The Argument: Inside the Battle to Remake Democratic Politics*. The Democrats went through their own hostile takeover bid leading up to the defeat of Hillary Clinton in the 2008 primaries. More recently, he wonders: "Does anybody have a grip on the G.O.P.?"[22]

Bai sees some significant analogies between what happened to the Democratic Party then and the Republican Party today. There is a culture clash going on, at this moment, between the entrenched management of the Republican establishment and grassroots insurgents— both inside the legislative bodies of the House and Senate, and back home, across America.

The question is, who will co-opt whom? Many on the elite management team hope, like former Senate majority leader Trent Lott, that the new Tea Party class and the grassroots that elected them will be absorbed into the system with as few ruffled feathers as possible. "But there is another interpretation," argues Bai. Maybe "the movement is actually starting to alter the makeup of the party from the bottom up, and it only appears to be losing intensity because its leaders are no longer interested in shouting into bullhorns. If that's true, and if more Tea Party members start streaming into Washington in the years head, then the next chapter of Republican politics in Washington could look less like 'The Empire Strikes Back' and more like 'Attack of the Clones.'"

One thing is certain: things will never go back to the way they were before. The system has been democratized in ways that Thomas Jefferson could only dream of in 1776. "There are practical explanations for why both party establishments have undergone some version of this same devolution," writes Bai. "The most important, and most obvious, is the proliferation of broadband Internet and the way it has redefined, within the space of just a few years, the very concept of a political movement." The hurly-burly of millions of people seeking information, connecting with one another, organizing groups of never-met-before cyber-brothers and cyber-sisters who share facts and correct the record, countless times daily.

This beautiful chaos is an emergent order that creates "a right to knowledge." But "knowledge" is a negative right, like "the pursuit of happiness." You are free to seek information, to hold elected officials to account, to fact-check, and to know new things unencumbered by some top-down government bureaucracy that would block your pursuit. But no one is going to do it for you. No one is going to deliver to your door, as an entitlement, a positive right, the knowledge you need to participate in this new democratized, disintermediated world of politics.

That's up to you. Government will go to those who bother to show up.

You are in charge. For the first time in recent memory, the American people are poised to enact change from the ground up, in response to their own feelings and desires, not those that have been crafted and force-fed by political parties. The political status quo has enjoyed incredible stability. Past political movements like the Reagan Revolution relied on the system itself to enact change, and in the years since, many of Reagan's accomplishments have been slowly rolled back.

As for Alexander the Great, the empire could not survive the death of its creator; the generals, freed from the hypnotic power of their leader, ran amok. The same is true of the Republican Revolution in 1994—another example of reform from within the system, managed by the system, and ultimately controlled (and lost) by the system. A good effort that was ultimately doomed to fail. In 2006 and 2008, the Left tried to send "agents of change" to Washington, but ended up getting more of the same.

But real change isn't really about political power anyway. Political power corrupts and unchecked political power disappoints absolutely. It's about the paradigm shift, from the top-down to the bottom-up. Real impact, if and when it manifests itself, will be from sustainable, ever-present pressure from the bottom up, to do things differently in Washington, D.C. Different than they've been done in the past.

The power of our community, what sets us apart, is back home: neighbor to neighbor, street by street, town by town, district by district. Think nationally, act locally.

The genie is out of the bottle. The toothpaste won't go back in the tube. As much as incumbent CEOs might try, there is no returning to the old politics of closed systems. The hostility and disdain with which the establishment attacks is just a reflex, like the headless chicken that keeps running. They think things can go back to the way they were before. But they won't. Just ask former president-for-life Zine El Abidine Ben Ali of Tunisia. Or ask former House Budget Committee chairman John Spratt of South Carolina. A hostile take-over, by the people, replaced both through the power of information and decentralized social media, and through a willingness of the human spirit to say, "Enough!"

The liberalization of political markets through easy-to-access information and social media—and the narrowing of the gap between concentrated benefits and dispersed costs via the Internet—has fundamentally changed politics forever. If you believe in freedom and government accountability, then this is a fundamentally good thing for the human condition and poses a fundamental threat to tyrannical government. Information *is* power. Social media like Facebook and Twitter have had this effect because these networking tools eliminate the middleman—in most cases, the government bureaucrat—and we should jealously guard political conversations that are intermediary-free.

FREEDOM IS OUR STRATEGY

FOR ALL THE HYPE ABOUT THE OBAMA MACHINE AND THE TAKEOVER of the Democratic establishment, I don't think that the contemporary Left has a real grasp of the implications of political disintermediation. The problem for them is that you can't ever really control, from the top down, spontaneously organizing social movements. You can't outadjust markets; you can't outprice the price system. You can never know as much as can be known through the process of discovery and adjustment to change that produces "a greater social intelligence." And you can't outorganize, from the top down, what people might do of their own free will, toward a set of goals based on a set of values determined by them, not you, the government official.

Left free, people can accomplish great things, working together on a voluntary, value-for-value basis. Not free, they will seek, like water finding its own level, any opportunity to break their bonds.

This is the dilemma confronted by the coalition that elected Obama in 2008. This is why Van Jones, former Obama green jobs czar, is spending so much time studying what Tea Partiers did to outorganize the community organizers in the 2010 elections. The assumption of Plouffe and others involved in Organizing for Obama was that you needed a leader, someone at the top of a hierarchy. Progressives, it seems, pine for leaders. According to Jones:

> So we had Obama the meta-brand, and then we all affiliated to it. And that's why 2008 felt so great. You know why? Because you didn't have to quit your labor union to be a part of this meta-brand. You didn't have to leave your lesbian rights group

to be a part. You got to keep everything you ever had, you got to keep your identity, everything you were passionate about. You could still put on that baseball cap and be a part of something bigger: That's a meta-brand. And we thought "Well, you could only do that if you got a presidential candidate." [23]

But the Tea Party emerged as a leaderless movement, and changed everything. Tea Party 2.0, the spontaneous evolution of the movement into a Get Out the Vote machine, was unexpected by just about everyone, simply because such a thing had never happened before. It was a fundamentally bigger step toward the disintermediation of politics than anything the Obama machine had built in 2008.

"We can no longer rely on a single charismatic individual," says Van Jones, referring to their now tarnished political messiah of hope and change. Why? Because "people let you down."

But principles are enduring. And values are enduring. And it's time for us not to just have a charismatic leader, but a charismatic network. That's the genius of the Tea Party. They have charismatic leaders . . . of a certain kind. But if Michele Bachmann and Sarah Palin and Glenn Beck and Dick Armey had a press conference tomorrow and said, "The Tea Party is over," it wouldn't be over. Because the values and the network wouldn't let it. They built a starfish and not a spider, and that is the next challenge for our movement. [24]

Ultimately, Van Jones won't get it right, because he doesn't comprehend how freedom works. He was a czar, after all, hardwired to assume that someone else—namely himself—is better suited to make decisions than free people choosing for themselves. He doesn't understand how millions of people located in disparate places—each individual with unique knowledge of their community and circumstances—can voluntarily cooperate and coordinate plans to create something far greater and more valued than any individual could have done alone.

This is the miracle of the market, what Hayek called the spontaneous order. The basis of Hayek's critique of central government planning and Keynesian attempts to "stimulate" the economy through new spending is this understanding of the market process of discovery. Even the most benevolent czar or the smartest bureaucrat rationing health care on the Independent Payment Advisory Board in the bowels of the Department of Health and Human Services could not possibly know better than free people acting to better themselves and their communities.

"Spontaneous order" equally describes the emergence and power of the citizen protest against big government that we now commonly refer to as the Tea Party. Tea Party values are based on a fundamental belief in freedom, and so is our strategy. There is no leader; no one is in charge. Our movement is fueled by the decentralization of information on the Internet and the ease of connecting with like-minded citizens through social networking tools like Facebook, Twitter, and FreedomConnector. We have evolved, spontaneously, from a protest movement to a GOTV machine. No one knows exactly what is next, but there can be little doubt that the Tea Party is now one of the most important nonviolent social movements in American history.

The future now depends on a continued commitment to the ethos of decentralization, the idea that even in politics, the customer is always right. Intermediaries, be they politicians or organizations like FreedomWorks, exist only as servants to this cause. Do what you say you will do. Add value. Don't take credit for work that someone else performs. Don't hurt other people and don't take their stuff. These are values that defined America's founding. They can define our future, too.

Too many worry about the limits of decentralization—that eventually the whole leaderless bubble will pop—and the elite will reassert their centralized control. But the best way to beat the entrenched looters and moochers, the powerful public employees unions and the billionaire progressive elites clamoring to spend your paycheck on their grand designs, is by fully embracing the beautiful chaos of this citizen revolt against big government. That's how we have accomplished so much in such a short period of time, and it is the only practical way that we will ever beat the well-financed special interests that comprise the big government coalition.

If we try to match them toe to toe, dollar for dollar; if we fight them on their field, with their referees and their rules; if we concede the eventuality of our own grassroots demise and look for someone else's "support" and "know-how," we will lose. But, as we have seen again and again, the Left intrinsically believes in order from the top down. They believe someone needs to be in charge: a czar, a better benevolent bureaucrat who knows better than you do, a messiah who will heal the planet with a global plan. They can't help but build hierarchical structures, because that's what they believe in. This is our strategic window. Embrace the beautiful chaos of citizen action and, by our own movement's success, prove that freedom works.

CHAPTER 14

THE REVOLUTION WILL BE CHOSEN

Don't follow leaders. Watch the parking meters.
—Bob Dylan

"WHERE IS THE NEXT RONALD REAGAN?" IT SEEMS THAT A DAY CAN-
not pass without someone, deeply concerned for the future of our
country, asking me the question. *The Next Ronald Reagan* serves as a
conceptual proxy for a jumble of aspirations, but when someone poses
the question, they are likely on a personal quest to find a better president than the one we have now—someone principled, *who can take
charge* and fix things in Washington, D.C.

Are you looking for the next Reagan? Finding that guy is the Holy
Grail of American politics. In your search, you will quickly discover
that virtually every politician fashions himself or herself, at one time
or another, as The Guy. A quick Google search reveals that virtually every potential political challenger to the sitting president is, it
is hoped, the "Next Ronald Reagan." In 2008, Fred Thompson was
supposed to be The Guy. Mitt Romney may turn out to be in 2012,

according to some. Bobby Jindal, Sarah Palin, Newt Gingrich, Michele Bachmann, Chris Christie, and Herman Cain have all been, at one time or another, heir apparent to the NRR title.

According to the *Huffington Post,* the real Next Ronald Reagan isn't even a Republican; it's Stephen Colbert. The popular Comedy Central host, argues Jordan Zakarin, clearly has what it takes:

> A mildly successful actor who spent years researching and refining his political beliefs, he reached a new level of fame and success after beginning a career of frequent, thinly-veiled activist speeches on the dime of a major corporation. During a time of national upheaval, he decided to take the next step, launching a campaign for office predicated on disciplining young protesters and preserving states' rights to curtail progressive social progress.
>
> Stripped of specific details, the political beginnings of Ronald Reagan and Stephen Colbert are remarkably interchangeable.[1]

Even Barack Obama, whose conviction that history holds a special place for his presidency seemingly knows no bounds, sometimes sees himself as the next Reagan. "I think Ronald Reagan changed the trajectory of America in a way that Richard Nixon did not and in a way that Bill Clinton did not," candidate Obama told the *Reno Gazette-Journal* in early 2008.

> He put us on a fundamentally different path because the country was ready for it. They felt like with all the excesses of the 60s and the 70s and government had grown and grown but there wasn't much sense of accountability in terms of how it was operating. I think he tapped into what people were already feeling. Which is we want clarity, we want optimism, we want a return to that sense of dynamism and entrepreneurship that had been missing.[2]

Admit it. You, or someone in your family, or one of your dearest friends, voted for Barack Obama, wanting to believe the sales pitch. Everybody wanted to believe the unbelievable when the young, good-looking, half-a-term senator from Illinois told us, "I want to make government cool again."[3] No one particularly knew what that even meant, but we didn't dig too deep beneath the surface to figure it out, because it sounded like a step up from the Bush years. And we were desperate. We hoped against history that Obama meant it when he promised to kink the fire hose of new spending and impose accountability on the insiders in Washington. "The only way you can control [the out-of-control spending]," he said while soliciting your vote, "is if there is some sense of shame and accountability. The more we increase accountability the more we reduce the special interests in Washington."

He sounded like the next Ronald Reagan, for sure.

WHAT WOULD GEORGE WASHINGTON DO?

WHY DO WE, IN THIS DAY AND AGE, KEEP LOOKING TO A BETTER CHIEF executive officer to solve our problems for us? We keep pursuing the quixotic hunt for a better benevolent dictator, hoping for change that we know can never come from the top down. Who is elected president matters, no question about it, but we will never restore liberty and the proper limits of government in America through a more "enlightened" implementation of the expanded powers, real and contrived, of the executive branch of government.

Isn't top-down executive power exactly what the Sons of Liberty were fighting against in 1773?

Americans have always jealously guarded against the natural urge of those in power, and those in cahoots with those in power, to seize our liberties. It's encoded in our moral DNA. "The ideology of the Revolution, derived from many sources, was dominated by a peculiar strand of British political thought," writes historian Bernard Bailyn in his seminal work, *The Ideological Origins of the American Revolution.* "It was a cluster of convictions focused on the effort to free the individual from the tyranny of the state. But the spokesmen of the Revolution—the pamphleteers, essayists, and miscellaneous commentators—were not philosophers and they did not form a detached intelligentsia." [4]

In other words, the values and principles of our founding spontaneously came from, and were defended by, the people for the people. From the bottom up.

No one understood this better than our first president, who was a humble embodiment of the uniquely American ethos of bottom-up governance by the people. Time after time, George Washington would resist the temptations of more centralized authority centered in the executive branch of the federal government. He is reported to have turned down requests by members of his own army that he become king of America. Instead, he voluntarily resigned his commission as commander-in-chief. According to historian Paul Johnson, no one was more surprised by Washington's decision than King George III. When told by American painter Benjamin West that Washington would "return to his farm," the British emperor was incredulous. "If he does that," said George, "he will be the greatest man in the world." [5]

Washington strongly resisted serving a second term as president of the United States. He finally refused a third term, declining to run for office in an open letter to the American people, what became known as his Farewell Address, first published in the *American Daily Advertiser* on September 19, 1786. His final missive reflected his belief that the people should be eternally wary of encroachments in the exercise of power by the branches of government:

> It is important, likewise, that the habits of thinking in a free country should inspire caution in those entrusted with its administration, to confine themselves within their respective constitutional spheres, avoiding in the exercise of the powers of one department to encroach upon another. The spirit of encroachment tends to consolidate the powers of all the departments in

one, and thus to create, whatever the form of government, a real despotism. A just estimate of that love of power, and proneness to abuse it, which predominates in the human heart, is sufficient to satisfy us of the truth of this position. The necessity of reciprocal checks in the exercise of political power, by dividing and distributing it into different depositaries, and constituting each the guardian of the public weal against invasions by the others, has been evinced by experiments ancient and modern; some of them in our country and under our own eyes. To preserve them must be as necessary as to institute them.[6]

Washington worried about conflict between opposing political parties; what he did not anticipate was their collusion, together, in a bipartisan fashion, to expand the power of government beyond the bounds of the Constitution. But he was particularly aware of the threat that the "spirit of encroachment" and the consolidation of power would lead to "a real despotism."

SUBTERRANEAN HOMESPUN VALUES

I AM FROM THE *REPUBLICAN WING* OF THE REPUBLICAN PARTY. MY loyalty is not to a political party; I am committed to a set of values: *Jeffersonian republicanism.* I am this type of *republican* who, in the words of Senator Rand Paul, "actually believes in limited government and individual freedom." Is that radical? If it is, that radicalism is deeply rooted in America.

America's exceptionalism was never dependent on the wisdom and generosity of our chief executive officer. Our greatness never came from the beneficence of an exclusive board of directors—the "different depositaries" and departments, cabinet secretaries, senators, congressmen, and even Rules Committee staffers—that would guide the operations of the American enterprise from inside closed doors, armed with the best data provided by the most knowing experts, and vested with the responsibility to make budget allocations and production decisions for us.

No, the American spirit was different.

"What reasonable social and political order could conceivably be built and maintained where authority was questioned before it was obeyed, where social differences were considered to be incidental rather than essential to community order, and where superiority, suspect in principle, was not allowed to concentrate in the hands of a few but was scattered broadly through the populace," asks Bailyn, referring to the Whig mash-up of republicanism, ideas from the Scottish Enlightenment, and the inherently stubborn independence of people who had by and large chosen to be free by traveling at great sacrifice to the New World.[7]

> The details of this new world were not as yet clearly depicted; but faith ran high that a better world than any that had ever been known could be built where authority was distrusted and held in constant scrutiny; where the status of men flowed from their achievements and from their personal qualities, not from distinctions ascribed to them at birth; and where the use of power over the lives of men was jealously guarded and severely restricted. It was only where there was this defiance, this refusal to truckle, this distrust of all authority, political or social, that institutions would express human aspirations, not crush them.[8]

The intellectual foment of the 1760s, with its pamphleteers and grassroots rallies under the Liberty Tree, is not so different from the happy mob of Tea Partiers that gathered by choice in Washington, D.C., on September 12, 2009, to petition the government in defense of their liberties.

From beautiful chaos emerges an essential order. We don't follow leaders. But we jealously watch the "parking meters"—the rules of the game, the limits on authority We the People temporarily grant to the government monopolist, and the nonnegotiable principle that everyone be treated exactly like everyone else under the laws of the land. If you choose to park here in America, you put in your quarter just like the next guy. But the meter maid cannot—will not—shake you down for tribute, steal your fruit scale, and slap your face, simply because she can, and simply because she works for the government.

THE HOSTILE TAKEOVER

OUR NATION HAS ALWAYS BEEN ABOUT THE AUTONOMY OF THE SHAREholders, stakeholders with an unalienable property right in their shares of the company. Our nation is about the men and women in the streets, in their hometowns, lacking the proper lineage, having no family connections, and absolutely no pull with the man in charge. The citizenry is free, operating outside the top-down structures of hierarchical decision-making; independent of royals, emperors, kings, and czars.

Is it possible that George Washington's distaste for unfettered executive power, for kings and permanent presidents alike, was part and parcel of this bottom-up, uniquely American ethos? Was he, too, responding to how his fellow citizens might judge him? Did he value, as Adam Smith believed we all do, the positive judgments of others?

Did peer pressure from the public square, from the homespun values of grassroots America, make even George Washington more accountable?

Each of us is endowed by our Creator with certain unalienable rights to life, liberty, and the pursuit of happiness, and the wildly radical notion that potentates, governors, crony corporatists, and any and all manner of rent-seekers, lever-pullers, influence-dealers, and earmarking hucksters shouldn't get special privileges. The elites have to drop a quarter in the meter just like the rest of us. No cutting in line, and no jetting to Washington in your Gulfstream V when your customers have deemed both your business model and your product unwanted. The insiders don't get to decide, for you, how to spend your tax dollars, the value of those dollars, or even whether or not birth control pills will be included in your mandated, government-dictated health insurance benefits package.

Who do they think they are? Better yet, who do you think it is that's going to stop them?

We know that politicians can't be trusted with power; that, once in office, they will collude with other powerful elites to the betterment of their interests, not ours. But you want to believe it, knowing that the alternative would shift the blame of failure squarely back on your shoulders—the shoulders of the shareholders, of We the People.

All of them, the Republican and Democratic parties, the teachers' unions, the crumbling media cartel, each and every one of them wants you to fail. They, the insiders, are hoping you will do what you did before, after rising up to demand accountability and throw the bums out. Last time, after you won, you went home, thinking that politics can be left to better politicians. Maybe a better president.

But that's not the deal. It never was the deal. "The people," said Jefferson, "are the only sure reliance for the preservation of our liberty." He's talking to you. You want it fixed? So fix it.

It won't be easy, and it won't always be fun. Senior management has circled the wagons. The board of directors has kicked you out of the company headquarters even though your investment helped build the building. The CEO refuses to even consider our shareholders resolution, a commonsense proposal that says government ought to clean up its books, eliminate money-sucking lines of business, and modernize lines of production for its core competencies. They need to get back to a business model—explicitly narrow in scope—that made the American enterprise great in the first place. But they won't. They need to listen to their customers again. But they are certain that we are all wrong. They need to let the customer choose. But they've brought on the very best management consultants, and they say they already know what you want, what you need.

They still don't think you matter, because they know that all those unanswered questions from the last annual meeting will fade with your interest in them. Sure, you elected new board members in a heroically successful challenge to the chairman, but the people's seat at the table is a minority position. You could do it again, they know, but they are betting their privileged positions that you won't.

However, if you don't lose interest, if you continue to show up, if you push the matter, things will most certainly get hostile. They will call you names. Nasty names. They will respond to your request for equal treatment with a tax audit from the city of Richmond.

But you are not alone. Like the pamphleteers of the Spirit of '76, a community of bloggers is there with you to get the story first and turn an infinite sea of facts into the knowledge required of citizens to hold their government accountable. You can connect almost instantly will millions more through a multitude of social media outlets. You can join together, based on a common set of values, toward a mutually agreed-upon purpose.

So, what are you going to do to take our country back?

Acknowledgments

TRUE TO THE BOTTOM-UP, SPONTANEOUS NATURE OF THE GRASSROOTS community known as the Tea Party, this book would have never been possible without the unplanned participation of millions of known and unknown partners across the nation. Our joint efforts are an historic venture in shareholder accountability; together, we are putting timeless principles into practice. Hopefully my work is a true reflection of, and a constructive contribution to, the work of the community.

Terry, my awesome wife of 25 years, served as an essential source of new ideas, and as a listener and a critic. She also let me work through the Christmas holiday to meet overly ambitious deadlines without sacrificing the demands of my day job. She's my Honey Badger; more honey than badger.

Peter Hubbard, Senior Editor at HarperCollins, has been a great business partner, advocate, bullet-catcher and risk-taker on behalf of this project.

There are a number of colleagues at FreedomWorks whose hard work also made this book a reality. Adam Brandon, Agitator-in-Chief, got this project off the ground as he always does, by committing to the impossible. Dean Clancy, Wayne Brough, Julie Borowski, Laura Howd, Josh Withrow, and Ryan Hecker all contributed substantial research and thinking on the "policy" chapters, often putting in late hours to make good, better. Patrick Hedger, Michael Duncan and Max Pappas provided detailed copy edits to the final draft.

Since 2003, I have been the lucky beneficiary of the wisdom and mentoring of my colleague Dick Armey, a real life hero who has consistently put his principles and his commitments first, even when doing so was costly. There are few people who have accomplished what he has in Washington, D.C. for whom I can say the same. Similarly brave support has come from my Board of Directors, who have stood with the staff of FreedomWorks through thick and thin.

I have also benefited from the reactions, the insights and the fearlessness of Glenn Beck. He is inspiring. The same can be said of Judge Andrew Napolitano and Senator Mike Lee of Utah.

Chapter Thirteen and Fourteen would not have been possible without an open bar stool at Russian River Brewing Company and the insight-inducing nature of their best brew, Pliny the Elder. Other chapters drew unsanctioned inspiration from Bob Dylan, Ludwig von Mises, John Coltrane, F.A. Hayek, Jerry Garcia, Ayn Rand, *The King of Limbs*, and Roark the cat.

The crazy exaggerations, unhealthy obsession with Austrian economics, obtuse Big Lebowski references, and any and all errors are my responsibility alone.

NOTES

Prologue: The Hostile Takeover

1. Walter Isaacson, *Steve Jobs* (New York: Simon & Schuster, 2011), pp. 568–69.
2. Dick Armey and Matt Kibbe, "A Tea Party Manifesto," *Wall Street Journal,* Aug. 17, 2010.

Chapter 1: The Central Problem

1. United States Senate website, "The Kennedy Caucus Room." Accessed Dec. 18, 2011. http://www.senate.gov/artandhistory/history/common/briefing/Caucus_Room .htm#3.
2. FreedomWorksAction, "Senator Schumer Shuts Down Tea Party Debt Commission." Last modified Nov. 18, 2011. http://www.youtube.com/watch?v=lKCnz_RgIOE.
3. MichelleMalkin, "Who's Afraid of a Tea Party Panel?, Part II: What the Fishwrap of Record Didn't Tell You," MichelleMalkin.com Nov. 18, 2011. http://michellemalkin .com/2011/11/18/whos-afraid-of-a-tea-party-panel-part-ii-what-the-fishwrap-of -record-didnt-tell-you/.
4. Global Security.org, "Forum on National Security Implications of Disclosing the Identity of a Covert Intelligence Officer—Committee Hearing," July 22, 2005, CQ Transcriptions. http://www.globalsecurity.org/intell/library/congress/2007_hr/070316 -transcript.pdf.
5. "A Tea Party 'Hearing' in the Senate That Wasn't," The Caucus Blog, Nov. 17, 2011, first posted at 4:09 p.m. and "corrected" at 5:12 p.m. http://thecaucus.blogs.nytimes .com/2011/11/17/a-tea-party-hearing-is-blocked-in-the-senate/.
6. U.S. Capitol Police, e-mail to reporters, Nov. 17, 2011, as shared with the author by the *New York Times.*
7. Lynden Armstrong, e-mail to Spencer Stokes, Nov. 17, 2011, 1:03 p.m., quoted in Ben Howe, "Was the Tea Party Kicked Out of the Capitol By Former Bennett Staffers Mad at Mike Lee?"
8. Spencer Stokes, e-mail to Lynden Armstrong, Nov. 17, 2011, 1:05 p.m., quoted in ibid.
9. Ryan McCoy, e-mail to Lynden Armstrong, Nov. 17, 2011, 1:10 p.m., quoted in ibid.
10. Lynden Armstrong, e-mail to Spencer Stokes, Nov. 17, 2011, 1:11 p.m., quoted in ibid.
11. U.S. Capitol Police Command Center, e-mail to all Senate staff, Nov. 17, 2011, 1:31 p.m., quoted in ibid.

12. *Ibid.*

13. Jeff Zeleny, "Thousands Rally in Capital to Protest Big Government," *New York Times*, Sep. 12, 2009.

14. WINK News, "Cape 'Tea Party' Cancelled; City Fears Too Many Attendees," Mar. 3, 2009.

15. Meghan Barr and Ryan J. Foley, "Occupy Protests Cost Nation's Cities at Least $13M," Associated Press, Nov. 13, 2011.

16. Perry Chiaramonte, "Tea Party Alleges Double Standard by Occupy-Friendly Mayor in Virginia," FoxNews.com, Nov. 28, 2011. Accessed Dec. 21, 2011. http://www.fox news.com/politics/2011/11/28/richmond-tea-party-claims-to-be-treated-unfairly-by -occupy-friendly-mayor/.

17. Patrik Jonsson, "Tea Party Activists Audited by City. Would That Happen to Occupy Protesters?" *Christian Science Monitor,* Nov. 29, 2011.

18. Annie Gowan, "As Occupy D.C. Movement Grows, So Does Tension," *Washington Post,* Dec. 17, 2010.

19. Darrell Issa, "Oversight Chairman Issa Asks Interior Secretary Salazar to Explain Illegal Camping in McPherson Square and Justify Destruction of Stimulus-Funded Upgrades" (U.S. House Committee on Oversight and Government Reform press release, Dec. 12, 2010).

20. Paul Courson, "Occupy DC Demonstrators Bolstered by Migrating NYC Occupiers," CNN.com, Jan. 2, 2012. http://articles.cnn.com/2012-01-02/us/us_occupy -migration_1_protest-camps-tent-city-demonstrators?_s=PM:US.

21. Steny Hoyer and Nancy Pelosi, "Un-American Attacks Can't Derail Health Care Debate," *USA Today,* Aug. 10, 2009.

22. Jacqueline Klingebiel, "Pelosi and the Tea Party 'Share Views'," ABC News, Feb. 28, 2010.

23. Bryan Fung, "Pelosi Gets Behind Occupy Wall Street," *TalkingPointsMemo.com*, Oct. 6, 2011. http://tpmdc.talkingpointsmemo.com/2011/10/pelosi-gets-behind -occupy-wall-street.php.

24. Kevin Bogardus, "Pelosi's Wealth Grows by 62 percent," *The Hill, On the Money blog*, June 15, 2011. http://thehill.com/blogs/on-the-money/801-economy/166599-pelosis -net-worth-rises-62-percent.

25. John Wildermuth, "Pelosi's Husband Prefers a Low Profile," *San Francisco Chronicle*, Jan. 1, 2007.

26. Carolyn C. Webber, "Development of Ideas About Balanced Budgets," Appendix D in Aaron Wildavsky, *How to Limit Government Spending* (Berkeley: University of California Press, 1980), p. 172.

27. "Time Series Chart of U.S. Government Spending." Accessed Dec. 20, 2011. http:// www.usgovernmentspending.com/spending_chart_1902_2015USp_F0xF0fF0sF0l.

28. *Ibid.*

29. Author's calculation, based on data from *usgovernmentspending.com.*

30. "Time Series Chart of Government Revenue," USgovernmentspending.com.

31. Admiral Mike Mullen, chairman of the Joint Chiefs of Staff, presentation at the Detroit Marriott at the Renaissance Center, Detroit, Mich., Aug. 26, 2010. Accessed Dec. 20, 2011. http://www.econclub.org/Multimedia/Transcripts/Admiral%20 Mullen%20Speech%20082610.pdf.

32. "Debt to the Penny and Who Holds It." Accessed Dec. 7, 2011. http://www.treasury direct.gov/NP/BPDLogin?application=np.

33. "US National Debt and Deficit History," chart 2, *usgovernmentspending.com.* Accessed Dec. 18, 2011. http://www.usgovernmentspending.com/spending_chart_1792 _2016USp_13s1li011mcn_H0f.

34. Ibid. For the amount of the Confederate portion of the Civil War debt, I have assumed it was comparable to or less than that of the USA, since the unrecognized Confederacy had trouble finding foreign buyers for its debt.

35. Author's calculations, based on data from "US National Debt and Deficit History," chart 2, cited above.

36. Joint Economic Committee, Republican staff, "What Is the Tipping Point?" Chart comparing debt at time of crisis or bailout, for Greece, Ireland, Portugal, and USA. Accessed Dec. 21, 2011. http://jec.senate.gov/republicans/public/?File_id=b35ec023 -c803-4bc0-8540-d2cbe0868794&a=Files.Serve&typ.%20.%20.

37. Alex Klein, "Fitch Threatens to Downgrade U.S. Credit Rating," *NYmag.com*. Accessed Dec. 21, 2011. http://nymag.com/daily/intel/2011/11/fitch-threatens-to-down grade-us-credit-rating.html; "Moody's warns the US it could be downgraded again before 2013," *Buenos Aires Herald,* Edition No. 3267, Aug. 8, 2011. Accessed Dec. 21, 2011. http://buenosairesherald.com/article/75365/moodys-warns-the-us-it-could-be -downgraded-again-before-2013.

38. Congressional Budget Office, "The Long-Term Budget Outlook," alternative fiscal scenario, table 1-2, p. 6. http://cbo.gov/ftpdocs/102xx/doc10297/06-25-LTBO.pdf.

39. Joint Economic Committee, Republican staff, "2015: Downgrade Day (Avoiding Europe's Fate)," May 28, 2010. Accessed Dec. 21, 2011. http://www.jec.senate.gov/repub licans/public/?a=Files.Serve&File_id=3472468a-4acc-4db0-9bc9-3bfbde139ea5.

40. "U.S. Federal Budget Analyst, Interest Analysis," *usgovernmentspending.com*. Accessed Dec. 21, 2011. http://www.usgovernmentdebt.us/federal_budget_interest.

41. Congressional Research Service, "The Congressional Budget Timetable," updated Mar. 20, 2008, Order Code 98-472 GOV. Accessed Dec. 18, 2011. http://www.senate .gov/reference/resources/pdf/98-472.pdf.

42. 2 U.S.C. 632, subsection (a), Annual Adoption of Concurrent Resolution on the Budget (emphasis added). Accessed Dec. 18, 2011. http://www.law.cornell.edu/uscode/ usc_sec_02_00000632--000-.html.

43. Author's calculation of ten-year deficit effect of Obama FY 2012 budget, based on CBO, An Analysis of the President's Budgetary Proposals for Fiscal Year 2012 (Apr. 2011), and CBO, Budget and Economic Outlook: An Update (Aug. 2011), summary tables 1, 2; tables 1.1, 1.2, 1.4, 1.5, 1.7, and 1.8.

44. Statement from Co-Chairs of the Joint Select Committee on Deficit Reduction, Nov. 21, 2011. Accessed Dec. 18, 2011, emphasis added. http://www.cspan.org/ uploadedFiles/Content/Special/Deficit_Committee/Reaction_to_SuperCommittee .pdf.

Chapter 2: What Czars Don't Know

1. Adam Smith, *An Inquiry into the Nature and Causes of the Wealth of Nations* 1776, IV.2.4-IV.2.9.

2. Don Lavoie, *Rivalry and Central Planning: The Socialist Calculation Debate Reconsidered* (Cambridge: Cambridge University Press, 1986), pp. 78–116.

3. Ludwig von Mises, *Socialism* (Indianapolis: Liberty Classics, 1981 (1922)), p. 101.

4. Ludwig von Mises, *Economic Calculation in the Socialist Commonwealth,* reprinted in F.A. Hayek (ed.), *Collectivist Economic Planning* (London: Routledge& Kegan Paul, 1935).

5. *Ibid.*

6. President Obama, speech at the headquarters of Solyndra Inc., Fremont, California,

May 26, 2010. Accessed Jan. 11, 2011. http://www.whitehouse.gov/the-press-office/remarks-president-economy-0.

7. Sean Higgins, "Van Jones, Other Liberals Defend Green Jobs Programs, Shift Focus From Jobs," Capital Hill Blog, *Investor's Business Daily*, Oct. 4, 2011, emphasis added. http://blogs.investors.com/capitalhill/index.php/home/35-politicsinvesting/3816-van-jones-liberals-green-jobs-solyndra-obama.

8. President Obama, remarks at Quincy, Ill., Apr. 28, 2010. http://www.gpoaccess.gov/presdocs/2010/DCPD-201000312.pdf.

9. Richard Reeves, "The Sayings of Chairman Barney," *Real Clear Politics*, Dec. 2, 2011. http://www.realclearpolitics.com/articles/2011/12/02/the_sayings_of_chairman_barney_112253.html.

10. "The Fannie Mae Dice Roll Continues," Review & Outlook, *Wall Street Journal*, Nov. 11, 2009.

11. Barney Frank, Fox News interview, July 14, 2008. http://www.foxnews.com/story/0,2933,432173,00.html.

12. President Bush, speech, Phoenix, Ariz., Mar. 26, 2004.

13. Joseph Rago and Paul A. Gigot, "On Taxes, 'Modeling,' and the Vision Thing," *Wall Street Journal*, Dec. 24, 2011.

14. *Ibid.*

15. *Ibid.*

16. William Schambra, "Obama and the Policy Approach," *National Affairs,* Fall 2009. http://www.nationalaffairs.com/publications/detail/obama-and-the-policy-approach.

17. *Ibid.*

18. Peter J. Boettke, "Economics for Yesterday, Today, and Tomorrow," *Journal of Private Enterprise,* Spring 2011.

19. Glenn Beck on his Fox News Channel program, June 8, 2010. http://www.foxnews.com/story/0,2933,594265,00.html#ixzz1ibeDeFyS.

20. "With Assist from Glenn Beck, University of Chicago Press Book Tops Amazon Rankings," *Publishers Weekly,* June 10, 2010.

21. Steven Rattner, "The 2012 Rivals Can Be Named: Hayek vs. Keynes," *Financial Times*, Sept. 12, 2011.

22. John Maynard Keynes, *The General Theory of Employment, Interest and Money,* Book 3, chapter 10, part 6, p. 116.

23. Exchange on "Global Public Square," CNN, Aug. 12, 2011. http://globalpublicsquare.blogs.cnn.com/2011/08/12/gps-this-sunday-krugman-calls-for-space-aliens-to-fix-u-s-economy/.

24. F. A. Hayek, Bruce Caldwell, ed., *The Collected Works of F. A. Hayek, Volume 9: Contra Keynes and Cambridge: Correspondence, Essays* (University of Chicago Press, 1995), 1996. p. 243.

25. P.J. O'Rourke, *Parliament of Whores,* 1991, p. xxiv.

26. F. A. Hayek, Bruce Caldwell, ed., *The Collected Works of F. A. Hayek, Volume 9: Contra Keynes and Cambridge: Correspondence, Essays* (Chicago: University of Chicago Press, 1995), p. 249.

27. F. A. Hayek, "The Use of Knowledge in Society," reprinted in *Individualism and Economic Order* (Chicago: University of Chicago Press, 1980), p. 77.

28. Frédéric Bastiat, "What Is Seen and What Is Not Seen," section 1.1. http://www.econlib.org/library/Bastiat/basEss1.html.

29. Mario Rizzo, "Yes, Paul: It is Hayek versus Keynes," *ThinkMarkets Blog,* Dec. 7, 2011 http://thinkmarkets.wordpress.com/2011/12/07/yes-paul-it-is-hayek-versus-keynes/.

30. Russ Feingold, "Feingold's Statement on Czars," *New York Times*, Oct. 6, 2009.
31. Jonah Goldberg, "Re: Czars," The Corner, *National Review Online*, Dec. 15, 2008. http://www.nationalreview.com/corner/174803/re-czars/jonah-goldberg.
32. Michael McAuliff, "Obama Tells Congress He's Keeping His Czars," *Huffington Post*, Apr. 15, 2011. http://www.huffingtonpost.com/2011/04/15/obama-czars-signing -statement_n_849963.html.
33. John Breshnahan, "Byrd: Obama in Power Grab," *Politico*, Feb. 25, 2009. http://www .politico.com/news/stories/0209/19303.html.
34. Arthur Ekirch Jr., *The Decline of American Liberalism* (New York: Longmans, Green, and Co., 1955), pp. 151–52.
35. Theodore Roosevelt, quoted at http://www.whitehouse.gov/about/presidents/theodore roosevelt.
36. H. L. Mencken, "Roosevelt: An Autopsy," in *Prejudices* (Baltimore: John Hopkins Paperbacks, 1996), pp. 61–62.
37. Charles A. Beard quoted in Arthur A. Ekirch Jr., *Ideologies and Utopias: The Impact of the New Deal on American Thought* (Chicago: Quadrangle Books, 1955), p. 132.
38. Gordon Tullock, "Welfare Costs of Monopolies, Tariffs, and Theft," *Western Economic Journal 5* (June 1967): pp. 224–32.
39. Charles B. Spahr, *An Essay on the Present Distribution of Wealth in the United States* (Boston: Thomas Y. Crowell, 1896), p. 27.

Chapter 3: The Truth Cartel

1. Walter Cronkite, "The First Priority of Humankind . . ." Presented to the United Nations, New York, Oct. 1999. http://web.archive.org/web/20071011173432/http:// www.ikosmos.com/wisdomeditions/essays/mw/cronkite01.htm.
2. Clark Peterson, "Frank Zappa: He's Only 38 and He Knows How to Nasty," *Relix Magazine*, Nov. 1979.
3. A. J. Liebling, "Do You Belong in Journalism?" *New Yorker*, May 14, 1960, pp. 104–12.
4. Thomas Jefferson, letter to Richard Price, Jan. 8, 1789. http://www.loc.gov/exhibits/ jefferson/60.html.
5. Thomas Hazlett, "The Wireless Craze, The Unlimited Bandwidth Myth, The Spectrum Auction Faux Pas, and the Punchline to Ronald Coase's 'Big Joke.'," AEI-Brookings Joint Center for Regulatory Studies, Jan. 2001. http://mason.gmu.edu/~thazlett/pubs/ The%20Wireless%20Craze.pdf.
6. Pingdom, "Internet 2010 in numbers," *Royal Pingdom*, Jan. 12, 2011. http://royal .pingdom.com/2011/01/12/Internet-2010-in-numbers.
7. Peter Voskamp, "GOP Attempt to Overturn FCC's Net Neutrality Rules Fails in Senate," *The Wrap*, Reuters, Nov. 10, 2011.
8. "Evening News Viewership, by Network 1980–2006," Pew Research Center's Project for Excellence in Journalism, Mar. 12, 2007. http://www.journalism.org/node/ 1346.
9. Brian Stetler, "CBS Evening News Ratings Tie 20-Year Low," *NY Times Media Decoder*, Aug. 24, 2010.
10. Chris Ariens, "Evening News Ratings: Week of Nov. 28," *TVNewser*, Dec. 6, 2011.
11. "U.S. Daily Newspaper Circulation Versus Number of Households," Pew Research Center's Project for Excellence in Journalism, Mar. 13, 2006.
12. "Number of U.S. Daily Newspapers, 5-Year Increments," Pew Research Center's Project for Excellence in Journalism, Mar. 12, 2007.

13. Joseph Plambeck, "Newspaper Circulation Falls Nearly 9%," *New York Times,* Apr. 26, 2010.

14. Michelle Malkin, "Fairness Doctrine Watch: Schumer Likens Conservative Opinion to Pornography," *MichelleMalkin.com*, Nov. 4, 2008. http://michellemalkin.com/2008/11/04/fairness-doctrine-watch-schumer-likes-conservative-opinion-to-pornography/.

15. Michael O'Brien, "Obama Open to Newspaper Bailout Bill," *The Hill,* Sept. 20, 2009. http://thehill.com/blogs/blog-briefing-room/news/59523-obama-open-to-newspaper-bailout-bill.

16. Office of Sen. Ben Cardin, "Senator Cardin Introduces Bill That Would Allow American Newspapers to Operate as Non-Profits," (press release) Mar. 24, 2009. http://cardin.senate.gov/newsroom/press/release/senator-cardin-introduces-bill-that-would-allow-american-newspapers-to-operate-as-non-profits.

17. Dave Murray, "Obama Concernced about Newspapers," post-gazette.com, Sept. 20, 2009. http://old.post-gazette.com/pg/09263/999253-482.stm.

18. Mark Joyella, "Traffic Data: Cable News, Led by CNN, Crushing Newspapers on the Web," *Mediaite.com*, May 10, 2011. http://www.mediaite.com/online/traffic-data-cable-news-led-by-cnn-crushing-newspapers-on-the-web/.

19. "Statistics," *Facebook.com*, retrieved Dec. 11, 2011. http://www.facebook.com/press/info.php?statistics.

20. Reported by Dylan Stableford, "Drudge Report Drives More Traffic Than Facebook and Twitter Combined, Study Says," *The Cutline, Yahoo! News*, Aug. 11, 2011. http://news.yahoo.com/blogs/cutline/drudge-report-drives-more-traffic-facebook-twitter-combined-193516280.html.

21. Kamelia Angelova, "Glenn Beck: Why This Is The Most Dangerous Era Of Our Lifetime," *Business Insider,* Dec. 27, 2011.

22. Ibid.

23. BITG research by Richard Greenfield.

24. Lauren A. E. Schuker, "Glenn Beck Faces Big New Test as New Show Bows," *Wall Street Journal,* Sept. 12, 2011.

25. Glenn Thrush, "Pelosi: 'I'm not afraid of August,'" *Politico,* July 23, 2009, http://www.politico.com/blogs/glennthrush/0709/Pelosi_Im_not_afraid_of_August.html.

26. Rich Noyes, "TV's Tea Party Travesty," Media Research Center, Mar. 2010. http://www.mrc.org/specialreports/2010/TeaParty/Scorning.aspx.

27. Annie Gowen, "City: Rat Population Has 'Exploded' Around Occupy D.C. Camps," *Washington Post, Breaking News Blog,* Jan. 9, 2012. http://www.washingtonpost.com/blogs/post_now/post/city-rat-population-has-exploded-around-occupy-dc-camps/2012/01/09/gIQA6AoylP_blog.html.

28. Tim Graham, "Omitting for Obama: How the Old Media Deliberately Censored New Media Scoops in 2009," Media Research Center, 2010. http://www.mrc.org/specialreports/2010/OmittingforObama/ExecutiveSummary.aspx.

29. Dan Gainor, "Fire and Ice," Business & Media Institute, Media Research Center, May 17, 2006. http://www.mrc.org/bmi/reports/2010/Fire_and_Ice.html.

30. W. Michael Cox and Richard Alm, "Creative Destruction," *Library of Economics and Liberty.* http://www.econlib.org/library/Enc/CreativeDestruction.html.

31. Tom Price, "Journalism Standards in the Internet Age," *CQ Researcher*, vol 20–35, Oct. 8, 2010.

32. David Brooks and Gail Collins, "Old Media vs. New Media," *NY Times Opinionator Blog,* June 30, 2010. http://opinionator.blogs.nytimes.com/2010/06/30/old-media-v-new-media/.

33. *Ibid.*
34. Brink Lindsey, Jonah Goldberg, and Matt Kibbe, "Where Do Libertarians Belong: A Reason Debate," *Reason.com*. Aug.–Sept. 2010. http://reason.com/archives/2010/07/12/where-do-libertarians-belong/singlepage.
35. Brian Stetler, "Debunkers of Fictions Sift the Net," *New York Times*, Apr. 4, 2010.
36. Rick Santelli, *Squawk Box, CNBC.* http://www.youtube.com/watch?v=or-EKjfVCoA.
37. Robert Seidman, "Cable News Ratings for Tuesday, Jan. 27, 2009," *TV by the Numbers*, Jan. 28, 2009. http://tvbythenumbers.zap2it.com/2009/01/28/cable-news-ratings-for-tuesday-january-27-2009/11700/.
38. Michael Polanyi, *Personal Knowledge: Towards a Post-Critical Philosophy* (Chicago: University of Chicago Press, 1958).

Chapter 4: Don't Hurt Others and Don't Take Their Stuff

1. Transcript, Van Jones Address to Netroots Nation 2011. Retrieved from Northwest Progressive Institute. http://www.nwprogressive.org/weblog/2011/07/transcript-van-jones-urges-netroots-to-lead-the-way-in-rebuilding-the-american-dream.html.
2. http://vanjones.net/.
3. Jeff Zeleny, "A Socialist? Obama Calls Back to Insist No," *New York Times,* Mar. 8, 2009.
4. "Remarks by the President on the Economy in Osawatomie, Kansas," *WhiteHouse.gov.* http://www.whitehouse.gov/the-press-office/2011/12/06/remarks-president-economy-osawatomie-kansas.
5. Saul Alinsky, *Rules for Radicals* (New York: Vintage Books, 1989), p. 130.
6. Frédéric Bastiat, "That Which is Seen, and That Which is Not Seen" (1850). http://bastiat.org/en/twisatwins.html.
7. Transcript, Van Jones Address to Netroots Nation 2011, *op. cit.*
8. Adam Smith, *The Theory of Moral Sentiments* (1789), Part 2, section II, reprinted by Library Classics, (1984) Indianapolis, Indiana pp. 83–84.
9. Peter Hamby, "Axelrod Suggests 'Tea Party' Movement Is 'Unhealthy,'" *CNN.com*, Apr. 19, 2009. http://politicalticker.blogs.cnn.com/2009/04/19/axelrod-suggests-tea-party-movement-is-unhealthy/.
10. Organizing for America memo, "2 Phone Calls on 9/11," Sept. 11, 2009. Retrieved from *Heritage Foundation.* http://blog.heritage.org/wp-content/uploads/2009/09/highlightedversion.jpg
11. Jonathan Allen and John Bresnahan, "Sources: Joe Biden Likened Tea Partiers to Terrorists," *Politico*, Aug. 1, 2011. http://www.politico.com/news/stories/0811/60421.html.
12. Alicia Ciccone, "Occupy Wall Street Causing Problems on Main Street," *Huffington Post*, Oct. 4, 2011. http://www.huffingtonpost.com/2011/10/04/occupy-wall-street-poses-challenge-to-main-street_n_993306.html.
13. Emma Brown and Del Quentin Wilber, "Air and Space Museum Closes after Guards Clash with Protesters," *Washington Post*, Oct. 8, 2011.
14. John Nolte, "Occupy Wall Street: The Rap Sheet So Far," *Big Government.com*, Dec. 9, 2011. http://biggovernment.com/jjmnolte/2011/10/28/occupywallstreet-the-rap-sheet-so-far/.
15. Meghan Barr and Ryan J. Foley, "Occupy Protests Cost Nation's Cities at Least $13M," Associated Press, Nov. 13, 2011.
16. Alessandra Rizzo and Meera Selva, "Police Fire Tear Gas as Protesters Riot in Rome," Associated Press, Oct. 15, 2011.

17. Matt Kibbe, "What Sets the Tea Party Apart," *Human Events*, Nov. 14, 2011. http://www.humanevents.com/article.php?id=47501.

18. Cady Lang, "Chained Up," *360 Magazine*, Dec. 13, 2011. http://360magazine.org/2011/12/chained-up/.

19. *Ibid.*

20. *Ibid.*

21. Craig Kanalley, "Occupy Wall Street: At Zuccotti Park, Conflict Arises Among Occupiers," *Huffington Post*, Oct. 22, 2011. http://www.huffingtonpost.com/craig-kanalley/occupy-wall-street-zuccotti-park_b_1026400.html.

22. *Ibid.*

23. Transcript, Van Jones Address to Netroots Nation 2011.

24. Hernando De Soto, "The Real Mohamed Bouaziz," *Foreign Policy*, Dec. 16, 2011. http://www.foreignpolicy.com/articles/2011/12/16/the_real_mohamed_bouazizi?page=full.

25. Amy Bingham, "Occupy D.C. Protesters Mar. Through Washington Demanding Jobs," ABC News, Oct. 6, 2011. http://abcnews.go.com/blogs/politics/2011/10/occupy-d-c-protesters-march-through-washington-demanding-jobs/.

26. Mary Bruce, "Obama Says Wall St. Protests Voice Widespread Frustrations," ABC News. Oct. 6, 2011. http://abcnews.go.com/blogs/politics/2011/10/obama-says-wall-st-protests-voice-widespread-frustrations/.

27. David Jackson, "Occupy Protesters Decry Obama's 'Silence' on Arrests," *USA Today*, Nov. 23, 2011.

28. *Ibid.*

29. Transcript, Van Jones Address to Netroots Nation 2011.

30. Rebuild the Dream website, *Contract for the Dream*, http://contract.rebuildthedream.com/.

31. Christopher F. Karpowitz, J. Quin Monson, Kelly D. Patterson, and Jeremy C. Pope, "Tea Time in America? The Impact of the Tea Party Movement on the 2010 Midterm Elections," *PS: Political Science & Politics*, 44, 2011, pp. 303–309.

32. Rebuild the Dream website, *op. cit.*

33. Jonah Goldberg, *Liberal Fascism: The Secret History of the American Left, from Mussolini to the Politics of Change* (New York: Random House, 2009), pp. 141–42.

34. *Ibid.*

35. Walter Isaacson, *Steve Jobs* (New York: Simon & Schuster, 2011), pp. 568–69.

Chapter 5: When America Beats Washington

1. George W. Bush, interview with Candy Crowley on CNN, Dec. 2008. Aired Nov. 14, 2010. http://transcripts.cnn.com/TRANSCRIPTS/1011/14/sotu.02.html.

2. "Transcript of Speaker Pelosi's Speech," *New York Times*, Sept. 29, 2008. http://www.nytimes.com/2008/09/30/washington/30pelositranscript.html?pagewanted=all.

3. USLegal, http://definitions.uslegal.com/c/collusion/.

4. Nick Gillespie and Matt Welch, "Death of the Duopoly," *Wall Street Journal*, June 18, 2011.

5. Tim Graham, "Jimmy Carter Lies on NPR: 'I Have Never Criticized the Tea Party Movement,'" *Newsbusters.org*, Dec. 2, 2010. http://newsbusters.org/blogs/tim-graham/2010/12/02/jimmy-carter-lies-npr-i-have-never-criticized-tea-party-movement#ixzz1hOZ59gfa.

6. Robert Higgs, *Crisis and Leviathan: Critical Episodes in the Growth of American Government* (New York: Oxford University Press, 1989).

7. Andreas Madestam et al., "Do Political Protests Matter? Evidence from the Tea Party Movement," Abstract from Harvard University seminar, Dec. 4, 2011. http://www.people.fas.harvard.edu/~veuger/papers/Political%20Protests%20—%20Evidence%20from%20the%20Tea%20Party.pdf.

8. David Freddoso, "Pelosi on Health Care: 'We Have to Pass the Bill So You Can Find Out What Is In It,'" *Washington Examiner*, Mar. 9, 2010.

9. David Espo, "Specter's Defection to Democrats Roils Republicans," *Associated Press*, Apr. 29, 2009. http://www.breitbart.com/article.php?id=D97S56DG0.

10. U.S. Senate, Roll Call Vote 396, Dec. 24, 2009, on final passage of H.R. 3590, Patient Protection and Affordable Care Act. The bill passed the Senate 60 to 39, with Senator Specter (D-PA) casting the 60th vote. Accessed Mar. 4, 2012. http://www.senate.gov/legislative/LIS/roll_call_lists/roll_call_vote_cfm.cfm?congress=111&session=1&vote=00396.

11. Josh Kraushaar, "After Specter Switch: Buyer's Remorse?" *Politico*, May 4, 2009. http://www.politico.com/news/stories/0509/22092_Page2.html.

12. Sam Stein, "NRSC's Cornyn: We Won't Call for Repealing All of Health Care," *Huffington Post,* May 23, 2010.

13. Jeremy P. Jacobs, "NRCC Stops Short Of Predicting Winning Majority," *Hotline ON CALL Blog, National Journal,* Oct. 5, 2010. http://hotlineoncall.nationaljournal.com/archives/2010/10/nrcc_stops_shor.php.

14. Michael Steele on Fox News Channel's *Hannity,* Jan. 4, 2010. http://www.youtube.com/watch?v=33gmv5WV09Y.

15. Mark Preston. "Cornyn Expresses Optimism, Caution on 2010." *CNN.com*, Sept. 8, 2009. http://politicalticker.blogs.cnn.com/2009/09/08/cornyn-expresses-optimism-caution-on-201/.

16. Scott Johnson, "The Tea Leaves in Last Week's Primaries," *PowerLineBlog*, June 28, 2010. http://www.powerlineblog.com/archives/2010/06/026628.php.

17. Amy Gardner, "Gauging the Scope of the Tea Party Movement in America," *Washington Post*, Oct. 24, 2010.

18. Profile of Mike Mulvaney, *Townhall.com*. http://townhall.com/election-2012/election-2010/state/sc/candidate/john-mick-michael-mulvaney/.

19. FEC Report filed by Mulvaney campaign. http://query.nictusa.com/pdf/724/10930239724/10930239724.pdf#navpanes=0.

20. Tim Padgett, "South Carolina's 5th Congressional District: John Spratt vs. Mick Mulvaney," *Time,* Oct. 6, 2010.

21. Jamie Self, "In Quick Visit, GOP's Mulvaney Enlists Tea Party Support at Home," *The Herald* (South Carolina), Oct. 31, 2010. http://www.heraldonline.com/2010/10/31/2573522/fight-for-us-house-district-5.html#storylink=misearch.

22. "Polls Close After Busy Day," *The Herald* (South Carolina), Nov. 2, 2010.

23. South Carolina State Election Commission, http://www.enr-scvotes.org/SC/19077/40477/en/summary.html#.

24. Tim Padgett, "South Carolina's 5th Congressional District: John Spratt vs. Mick Mulvaney."

Chapter 6: Smaller Government and More Individual Freedom

1. Congressman Tim Scott, speaking to John King, "Interview with Congressman-Elect Tim Scott," *John King, USA, Real Clear Politics,* Nov. 5, 2010. http://www.realclearpolitics.com/articles/2010/11/05/interview_with_congressman-elect_tim_scott_107879.html.

2. David Slade, "Foes Search for Differences," [Charleston] *Post and Courier*, June 19, 2010.
3. Ewen MacAskill, "Jimmy Carter: Animosity Towards Barack Obama Is Due to Racism," *Guardian*, Sept. 16, 2009.
4. Zev Chafets, "Tea for Tim," *The Daily Beast*, Nov. 7, 2010. http://www.thedailybeast.com/newsweek/2010/11/07/tim-scott-black-republican-tea-party-favorite.html.
5. Tim Scott, via TeamScott, "Tim Scott Statement on NAACP Resolution Condemning Tea Party as 'Racist,'" press release, *votetimscott.com*, July 13, 2010. http://www.votetimscott.com/2010/07/13/tim-scott-statement-on-naacp-resolution-condemning-tea-party-as-racist/.
6. "FEC FORM 3, Reports of Receipts and Disbursements," *Rand Paul for US Senate*, June 22, 2010. http://query.nictusa.com/pdf/220/10020414220/10020414220.pdf#navpanes=0.
7. Josh Kraushaar, "McConnell bats for Grayson," *Politico*, May 4, 2010.
8. Kentucky State Board of Elections, State Wide Primary Results. http://results.enr.clarityelections.com/KY/15261/30235/en/summary.html.
9. Jennifer Agiesta, "GOP turnout jumps in Kentucky," *Behind the Numbers Blog, Washington Post*, May 19, 2010.
10. Rand Paul, "Rand Paul, libertarian? Not quite," *USA Today*, Aug. 9, 2010. http://www.usatoday.com/news/opinion/forum/2010-08-10-column10_ST2_N.htm.
11. Kentucky State Board of Elections, 2010 State Wide Election Results. http://results.enr.clarityelections.com/KY/22208/45378/en/summary.html.
12. Kathy Kiely. "Conservative insurgents shake up Utah incumbent," *USA Today*, May 8, 2010.
13. Lisa Riley Roche, "Sen. Bob Bennett makes it official: He endorses Tim Bridgewater," *Deseret News*, June 11, 2010.
14. 2010 Utah General Election Results, *Deseret News*, Nov. 2, 2010.
15. Jamshid Ghazi Askar, "Constitutional divide: Sen. Mike Lee, others battle to define a living document," *Deseret News*, Feb. 18, 2011.
16. "Sen. Bob Bennett Ousted at Utah GOP Convention," *USA Today*, May 9, 2010.
17. Josh Kraushaar, "NRSC endorses Crist," *Politico*, May 12, 2009. http://www.politico.com/blogs/scorecard/0509/NRSC_to_endorse_Crist.html.
18. Dick Armey and Matt Kibbe, "Political Establishment, Like Failing CEOs, Tries to Repel Tea Party's Hostile Takeover," *Investor's Business Daily*, Sept. 24, 2010.
19. Meghashyam Mali, "GOP Senator Says Tea Party Challenges 'Killed Off' Efforts For Republican Majority," *Hill*, Dec. 25, 2011.
20. Aaron Blake and Reid Wilson, "Stopping Dem 60 'Real Hard,' Cornyn Fears," *Hill*, Apr. 21, 2009.
21. Juana Summers, "Lugar says GOP could lose his seat without him," *Politico*, Dec. 25, 2011. http://www.politico.com/blogs/politico-live/2011/12/lugar-says-gop-could-lose-indiana-senate-seat-without-108653.html.
22. "Congressman Boehner: Republicans Are Fighting For The Largest Possible Spending Cuts," press release, *boehner.house.gov*, Mar. 31, 2011. http://boehner.house.gov/News/DocumentSingle.aspx?DocumentID=233149.
23. Molly K. Hooper, "Tea Party-Backed Freshmen Win Plum Committee Assignments," *Hill*, Dec. 12, 2010.
24. James Rosen, "Tim Scott's star rockets to the top," *State*, Sep. 25, 2011.
25. Jesse Hyde and Kelly M. Henriod, "The Face of Change," *Deseret Morning News*, Oct. 18, 2010. http://www.deseretnews.com/article/700074427/The-face-of-change-Can-tea-partys-Mike-Lee-make-a-difference.html.

26. Shailagh Murray, "Republican Lawmakers Gird for Rowdy Tea Party," *Washington Post*, July 18, 2010.

27. Manu Raju and Scott Wong, "In Utah, Hatch and Lee Part Ways," *Politico*, Apr. 4, 2011. http://dyn.politico.com/printstory.cfm?uuid=1DE811B0-EA28-9131-043030F C36F021FB.

28. Judy Wiessler, "Sen. Paul Simon looks to 'buck the tide'/ Presidential hopeful makes his campaign intentions official," *Houston Chronicle*, May 19, 1987. http://www.chron .com/CDA/archives/archive.mpl/1987_463765/sen-paul-simon-looks-to-buck-the -tide-presidential.html.

29. *Ibid.*

30. Orrin Hatch, "A joint resolution proposing an amendment to the Constitution of the United States to require a balanced budget," Senate Joint Resolution 1, US Senate, 112th Congress, 2011. http://thomas.loc.gov/cgi-bin/bdquery/z?d105:S.J.Res1:

31. Orrin Hatch, "A joint resolution proposing an amendment to the Constitution of the United States relative to balancing the budget," Senate Joint Resolution 3, US Senate, 112th Congress, 2011. http://thomas.loc.gov/cgi-bin/bdquery/D?d112:3:./list/bss/ d112SJ.lst.

32. Mike Lee, "A joint resolution proposing an amendment to the Constitution of the United States requiring that the federal budget be balanced," Senate Joint Resolution 5, US Senate, 112th Congress, 2011. Http://thomas.loc.gov/cgi-bin/bdquery/z?d112:s.j .res.00005:.

33. Elspeth Reeve, "GOP Infighting Update: Cantor Could Lead Rebellion Against Boehner," *National Journal*, Apr. 4, 2011.

34. Manu Raju and Scott Wong, "In Utah, Hatch and Lee Part Ways," *op. cit.*

35. Jesse Hyde and Kelly M. Henriod, "The Face of Change," *op. cit.*

36. Orrin Hatch, "Joint resolution proposing a balanced budget amendment to the Constitution of the United States," Senate Joint Resolution 10, US Senate, 112th Congress, 2011.

37. Manu Raju and Scott Wong, "In Utah, Hatch and Lee Part Ways," *op. cit.*

38. *Ibid.*

39. Dick Armey and Matt Kibbe, "What Congress Should Cut," *Wall Street Journal*, Jan. 19, 2011.

40. Dean Clancy, "Report Card: Grading the Ten-Year Budget Plans," *FreedomWorks*. Accessed Jan. 9, 2011. http://www.freedomworks.org/blog/dean-clancy/report-card -grading-the-budget-plans.

41. The Tea Party Debt Commission. Accessed Jan. 9, 2011. http://www.freedomworks .org/tea-party-debt-commission.

42. The Tea Party Budget. Accessed Jan. 20, 2011. http://www.freedomworks.org/the-tea -party-budget.

Chapter 7: Looters and Moochers

1. Adam Smith, *The Wealth of Nations,* Book I, Chapter X, Part II, p. 152.

2. Jeffrey Immelt, "2008 Annual Report to Shareholders," Feb. 6, 2009. http://www.ge .com/ar2008/pdf/ge_ar_2008_letter.pdf.

3. Timothy P. Carney, "How GE's green lobbying is killing U.S. factory jobs," *Examiner*. http://washingtonexaminer.com/op-eds/2009/08/timothy-p-carney-how-ges-green -lobbying-killing-us-factory-jobs#ixzz1ksqW4kbp.

4. Matthew Mosk, "General Electric Wages Never-Say-Die Campaign for Jet Engine Contract," *The Blotter*, ABC News, Mar. 9, 2011. http://abcnews.go.com/Blotter/ge-top-corporate-spender-lobbying/story?id=13087750.

5. Public Campaign, "For Hire: Lobbyists or the 99%? How Corporations Pay More for Lobbyists Than in Taxes," Dec. 2011. http://publicampaign.org/sites/default/files/ReportTaxDodgerLob byingDec6.pdf.

6. Track the Money, *Recovery.gov*. http://www.recovery.gov/Transparency/Recipient ReportedData/Pages/RecipientSearch.aspx?recipname=General%20Electric.

7. Elizabeth Williamson and Paul Glader, "General Electric Pursues Pot of Government Stimulus Gold," *Wall Street Journal*, Nov. 17, 2009. http://online.wsj.com/article/SB125832961253649563.html.

8. Timothy P. Carney, "Obamanomics: General Electric Wins Big with the White House," in *Washington Examiner*, Dec. 9, 2009.

9. General Electric Summary, 2010 PAC Data, *OpenSecrets.org*. http://www.opensecrets.org/pacs/lookup2.php?strID=C00024869&cycle=2010.

10. Lobbying Database, *OpenSecrets.org*, Calculations by the Center for Responsive Politics based on data from the Senate Office of Public Records, Feb. 6, 2012. http://www.opensecrets.org/lobby/index.php.

11. Gerald P. O'Driscoll Jr., "An Economy of Liars," *Wall Street Journal*, Apr. 20, 2010.

12. "The visible hand," *Economist*, Jan. 21, 2012. http://www.economist.com/node/21542931.

13. Lorraine Woellert and John Gittelsohn, "Fannie-Freddie Fix at $160 Billion with $1 Trillion Worst Case," *Bloomberg*, June 13, 2010.

14. Robert Higgs, *Crisis and Leviathan: Critical Episodes in the Growth of American Government* (New York: Oxford University Press, 1989).

15. Harold Demsetz, "Information and Efficiency: Another Viewpoint," *Journal of Law and Economics* 12 (Apr. 1969): 1–22.

16. Jimmy Carter, "The President's Proposed Energy Policy," Apr. 18, 1977. Vital Speeches of the Day, vol. 43, no. 14, May 1, 1977, pp. 418–420. http://www.pbs.org/wgbh/americanexperience/features/primary-resources/carter-energy/.

17. "How dependent are we on foreign oil?," Energy in Brief, *EIA.gov*, June 24, 2011. http://www.eia.gov/energy_in_brief/foreign_oil_dependence.cfm.

18. Eric Lipton and Clifford Kraus, "A Gold Rush of Subsidies in Clean Energy Search," *New York Times*, Nov. 11, 2011.

19. *Ibid.*

20. *Ibid.*

21. Subcommittee on Oversight and Investigations Staff, internal memorandum to Members, Subcommittee on Oversight and Investigation, "Hearing on 'Solyndra and The DOE Loan Guarantee Program,'" Committee on Energy and Commerce, Sept. 12, 2011. http://republicans.energycommerce.house.gov/Media/file/Hearings/Oversight/091411/Memo.pdf.

22. Memorandum, "The Solyndra Story," Committee on Energy and Commerce, Sept. 14, 2011. http://republicans.energycommerce.house.gov/Media/file/Hearings/Oversight/091411/SolyndraStoryFinalMemo.pdf.

23. Mark Hemingway, "White House Video Touted Solyndra as a Stimulus Success Story," *Weekly Standard Blog*, Sept. 10, 2011. http://www.weeklystandard.com/blogs/white-house-video-touted-solyndra-stimulus-success-story_593071.html.

24. Loans Award Summary: Solyndra, Inc. Track the Money, *Recovery.gov*. http://www.recovery.gov/Transparency/RecipientReportedData/pages/RecipientProjectSummary508.aspx?AwardIdSur=19015.

25. Eric Lipton and John M. Broder, "In Rush to Assist a Solar Company, U.S. Missed Signs," *New York Times,* Sept. 22, 2011.

26. Matea Gold and Stuart Pfeifer, "Solar Firm's Obama Links Probed," *Los Angeles Times,* Sept. 17, 2011.

27. Jim Snyder, "Kaiser Spoke to White House About Solyndra," *Bloomberg,* Nov. 9, 2011. http://www.bloomberg.com/news/2011-11-09/kaiser-spoke-to-white-house-about-solyndra.html.

28. Amanda Carey, "Solyndra Officials Made Numerous Trips to White House, Logs Show," *Daily Caller,* Sept. 8, 2011. http://dailycaller.com/2011/09/08/solyndra-officials-made-numerous-trips-to-the-white-house-logs-show/.

29. "Solyndra Not Sole Firm to Hit Rock Bottom Despite Stimulus Funding," *FoxNews.com,* Sept. 15, 2011. http://www.foxnews.com/politics/2011/09/15/despite-stimulus-funding-solyndra-and-4-other-companies-have-hit-rock-bottom/.

30. Elisha Maldonado, "Solyndra Bankruptcy: Company Violated Loan Terms, But Got More Federal Money," *International Business Times,* Sept. 29, 2011. http://www.ibtimes.com/articles/222186/20110929/solyndra-bankruptcy-loan-violation-obama-feds.htm.

31. Joe Stephens and Carol D. Leonnig, "Solyndra loan deal: Warning about legality came from within Obama administration," *Washington Post,* Oct. 7, 2011.

32. Matthew Daly, "Solyndra Bankruptcy: Obama Administration Considered Bailout," *Huffington Post,* Nov. 2, 2011. http://www.huffingtonpost.com/2011/11/02/solyndra-bankruptcy-obama-administration-bailout_n_1072737.html.

33. "Solyndra Case Reveals Gateway Between Administration Loans, Obama Allies," *FoxNews.com,* Nov. 16, 2011. http://www.foxnews.com/politics/2011/11/16/solyndra-case-reveals-gateway-between-administration-loans-obama-allies/.

34. Matthew L. Wald, "Solar Firm Aided by Federal Loans Shuts Doors," *New York Times,* Aug. 31, 2011.

35. Jim McElhatton, "Congressman irked by Solyndra bonuses, equipment destruction," *Washington Times*, Jan. 20, 2012.

36. "Biden praised stimulus-backed Ener1 one year before company went bankrupt," *Daily Caller,* Jan. 26, 2012. http://dailycaller.com/2012/01/26/biden-praised-ener1-one-year-ago-in-speech-that-declared-administration-was-sparking-whole-new-industries/.

37. Brent Snavely, "Volt Production on Hold for 5 Weeks," *Detroit Free Press*, Mar. 2, 2012.

38. Tom Gantert, "Chevy Volt Costing Taxpayers up to $250K Per Vehicle," *Michigan Capitol Confidential*, Dec. 21, 2011. http://www.mackinac.org/16192.

39. Brent Snavely, "Volt Production on Hold for 5 Weeks," *op. cit.*

40. Jerry Hirsch, "General Electric Says it Will Buy 25,000 Electric Vehicles in 2015," *Los Angeles Times*, Nov. 12, 2010.

41. Joel Gehrke, "GM Laying Off 1300 Due to Low Volt Sales," *Beltway Confidential, Washington Examiner*, Mar. 2, 2012.

42. Aamer Madhani, "GOP's Hatch urged $20M in earmarks for bankrupt clean energy firm," *USA Today,* Oct. 29, 2011.

43. Aamer Madhani, "Failed Energy Projects Cross U.S. Party Lines," *USA Today*, Oct. 14, 2011.

44. *Ibid.*

45. U.S. Energy Information Administration, Independent Statistics & Analysis. http://www.eia.gov/oil_gas/natural_gas/data_publications/crude_oil_natural_gas_reserves/cr.html.

46. American Petroleum Institute, "The State of American Energy 2011." http://www.scribd.com/doc/46074917/The-State-of-American-Energy.

47. U.S. Energy Information Administration, Independent Statistics & Analysis. http://www.eia.gov/dnav/pet/pet_move_wkly_dc_NUS-Z00_mbblpd_4.htm.
48. U.S. Census Bureau, History, 2010 Fast Facts. http://www.census.gov/history/www/through_the_decades/fast_facts/2010_fast_facts.html.
49. Gross Domestic Product, Bureau of Economic Analysis, U.S. Department of Commerce. http://www.bea.gov/national/index.htm#gdp.
50. Jim Morrill, "Duke guaranteeing $10 million line of credit for DNC," *charlotte observer.com,* Mar. 12, 2011. http://www.charlotteobserver.com/2011/03/12/2133391/duke-guaranteeing-10m-line-of.html.
51. United States Climate Action Partnership. http://www.us-cap.org/.
52. Holman W. Jenkins Jr., "A Fine Clean Coal Mess: Duke Energy Loses its Bet on Cap and Trade," *Wall Street Journal,* Dec. 15, 2010.
53. "Duke Energy Reaches Agreement with DOE to Accept $204 million in Stimulus Funds to Support Grid Modernization," Duke Energy news release, May 13, 2010. http://www.duke-energy.com/news/releases/2010051301.asp.
54. Holman W. Jenkins Jr., "A Fine Clean Coal Mess," *op. cit.*
55. Clive Thompson, "A Green Coal Baron?" *New York Times Magazine,* June 22, 2008.
56. "Cap and Trade: We Need to Get It Right," Duke Energy. http://www.duke-energy.com/pdfs/CapNTrade_Fact_Sheet_FINAL.PDF.
57. Thompson, "A Green Coal Baron?" *op. cit.*
58. Bruce Henderson, "Lobbying pays off for Duke," *charlotteobserver.com,* Oct. 9, 2009. http://www.charlotteobserver.com/2009/10/09/992164/lobbying-pays-off-for-duke.html.
59. "Duke Energy CEO Jim Rogers Takes Heat at Company's Annual Meeting for Promoting President Obama's War on Fossil Fuels," press release, National Center for Public Policy Research, May 5, 2011. http://www.nationalcenter.org/PR-Duke_Energy_Results_050511.html.
60. "Duke Energy's Support of President Obama's Cap-and-Trade Policy to Be Challenged by Stockholders at Company Shareholder Meetings Thursday," press release, National Center for Public Policy Research, May 6, 2011 http://www.nationalcenter.org/PR-Duke_Energy_050610.html.
61. Henderson, "Lobbying pays off for Duke," *op. cit.*
62. Mark L. Vachon and Jeffrey R. Immelt, "To our investors, customers and other stakeholders," *Annual Report,* Ecomagination, General Electric, June 20, 2011. Accessed Jan. 3, 2012. http://www.ecomagination.com/progress/overview/letter/.
63. Scott Malone, "GE's Immelt wishes he had soft-pedaled green talk," Reuters, May 3, 2011. http://www.reuters.com/article/2011/05/03/us-ge-green-idUSTRE7427F920110503.
64. Eric Lipton and Clifford Kraus, "A Gold Rush of Subsidies in Clean Energy Search," *op. cit.*
65. Carol Browner, Ron Klain, and Larry Summers, Memorandum for the President, Oct. 25, 2010. http://s3.documentcloud.org/documents/265143/summers-renewable-energy-memo2010.pdf.
66. *Ibid.*
67. Warren Meyer, "The Looming Failure of Obamacare, Part 3: Rent-Seeking," *Forbes,* Feb. 24, 2011. http://www.forbes.com/sites/warrenmeyer/2011/02/24/the-looming-failure-of-obamacare-part-3-rent-seeking/.
68. Jim Drinkard, "Drugmakers go furthest to sway Congress," *USA Today,* Apr. 25, 2005.

69. Paul Blumenthal, "The Legacy of Billy Tauzin: The White House–PhRMA Deal," Sunlight Foundation, Feb. 12, 2010. http://sunlightfoundation.com/blog/2010/02/12/the-legacy-of-billy-tauzin-the-white-house-phrma-deal/.

70. *Ibid.*

71. Jeanne Cummings, "Wielding influence in health care fight," *Politico*, Dec. 25 2009. http://dyn.politico.com/printstory.cfm?uuid=BD18F267-18FE-70B2-A8F5960026D227DF.

72. David D. Kirkpatrick, "White House Affirms Deal on Drug Cost," *New York Times*, Aug. 5, 2009.

73. Cummings, "Wielding influence in health care fight," *op. cit.*

74. Alicia Mundy, "White House Assures Drug Makers on Reimportation," *Wall Street Journal*, July 7, 2009.

75. Tom Hamburger, "Activists say poor nations' access to affordable drugs stymied," *Los Angeles Times*, Aug. 20, 2009.

76. Ryan Grim, "Internal Memo Confirms Big Giveaways In White House Deal With Big Pharma," *Huffington Post*, Sept. 13, 2009, updated May 25, 2011. http://www.huffingtonpost.com/2009/08/13/internal-memo-confirms-bi_n_258285.html.

77. Kirkpatrick, "White House Affirms Deal on Drug Cost," *op. cit.*

78. Blumenthal, "The Legacy of Billy Tauzin," *op. cit.*

79. David D. Kirkpatrick, "Drug Industry to Run Ads Favoring White House Plan," *New York Times*, Aug. 8, 2009.

80. David Kirkpatrick and Duff Wilson, "Health Reform in Limbo, Top Drug Lobbyist Quits," *New York Times*, Feb. 11, 2010.

81. Wes Allison, "End no-bid contracts above $25,000: No sign of action," *Politifact.com*, Jan. 6, 2010. http://www.politifact.com/truth-o-meter/promises/obameter/promise/30/end-no-bid-contracts-above-25000/.

82. David Willman, "Cost, need questioned in $433-million smallpox drug deal," *Los Angeles Times*, Nov. 13, 2011.

83. Will Rahn, "McCaskill asks for investigation into Obama administration's sole-source vaccine contract," *Daily Caller*, Nov. 24, 2011. http://dailycaller.com/2011/11/24/mccaskill-asks-for-investigation-into-obama-administrations-sole-source-vaccine-contract/.

84. David Willman, *op. cit.*

85. *Ibid.*

86. Aaron Kiersh, "Pharmaceuticals / Health Products: Background," *OpenSecrets.org*, Mar. 2010. http://www.opensecrets.org/industries/background.php?cycle=2012&ind=H04.

87. *Ibid.*

88. Olga Pierce, "Medicare Drug Planners Now Lobbyists, With Billions at Stake," *ProPublica*, Oct. 20, 2009. http://www.propublica.org/article/medicare-drug-planners-now-lobbyists-with-billions-at-stake-1020.

89. General Electric, Ronald Reagan documentary. http://www.ge.com/reagan/video.html.

90. Michael Reagan, "Ronald Reagan's Son Remembers The Day When GE Fired His Dad," *Investor's Business Daily*, Feb. 4, 2011. http://news.investors.com/Article/562237/201102041911/Ronald-Reagans-Son-Remembers-The-Day-When-GE-Fired-His-Dad.htm?p=2.

91. Timothy P. Carney, "Obamanomics: General Electric Wins Big with the White House," *op. cit.*

Chapter 8: Scrap the Code

1. Steven Bertoni, "Warren Buffett Biggest Money Loser On Forbes 400," *Forbes*, Sept. 22, 2011.
2. Arthur B. Kennickell, "Tossed and Turned: Wealth Dynamics of U.S. Households, 2007–2009," U.S. Federal Reserve website. http://www.federalreserve.gov/pubs/feds/2011/201151/201151pap.pdf (accessed Dec.20, 2011).
3. Warren E. Buffett, "Stop Coddling the Super-Rich," *New York Times*, Aug. 15, 2011.
4. Jake Tapper, "President Obama to Propose Millionaire's Tax Called 'Buffett Rule,'" ABC News, Sept. 17, 2011. http://abcnews.go.com/blogs/politics/2011/09/president-obama-to-propose-millionaires-tax-called-buffett-rule/.
5. Brad Knickerbocker, "Obama pushes 'Buffett Rule' to tax the wealthy. GOP cries 'class warfare!,'" *Christian Science Monitor*, Sept. 18, 2011.
6. Berkshire Hathaway's 2010 Annual Report on page 56 notes: "At Dec. 31, 2010 . . . net unrecognized tax benefits were $1,005 million," or $1.005 billion. http://www.berkshirehathaway.com/2010ar/2010ar.pdf.
7. "WarrenBuffett, hypocrite," *New York Post*, Aug. 28, 2011.
8. Ross Boettcher, "Warren Watch: Tax Case," *Omaha World-Herald*, Sept. 4, 2011.
9. *Ibid.*
10. "The Most Serious Problems Encountered by Taxpayers," Internal Revenue Service. http://www.irs.gov/pub/irs-utl/2010arcmsp1_taxreform.pdf.
11. "Commissioner of Internal Revenue Douglas H. Shulman's Keynote Speech Before the AICPA Fall Tax Meeting," press release, Internal Revenue Service, Oct. 26, 2010. http://www.irs.gov/newsroom/article/0,,id=229675,00.html.
12. Berkshire Hathaway Lobbying Data 2010, *OpenSecrets.org.* http://www.opensecrets.org/lobby/clientsum.php?id=D000021757&year=2010.
13. David Keating, "A Taxing Trend: The Rise in Complexity, Forms, and Paperwork Burdens," *NTU Policy Paper 128,* National Taxpayers Union, Apr. 18, 2011. http://www.ntu.org/news-and-issues/taxes/tax-reform/complexity.html, p. 2.
14. "The Most Serious Problems Encountered by Taxpayers," Internal Revenue Service.
15. *Ibid.*
16. SOI Tax Stats—Individual Statistical Tables by Tax Rate and Income Percentile, Internal Revenue Service. http://www.irs.gov/taxstats/indtaxstats/article/0,,id=133521,00.html.
17. Contract from America. www.contractfromamerica.org.
18. Thomas Jefferson, letter to Samuel Kercheval, July 12, 1816, *The Writings of Thomas Jefferson: 1816–1826,* 1899, pp. 40–41.
19. James Madison, "Property," Mar. 29, 1792, in William T. Hutchinson et al., eds., *The Papers of James Madison,* Mar. 29, 1792, Doc. 23, vol. 1, ch. 16 (Chicago and London: University of Chicago Press, 1962–77, vols. 1–10).
20. Revenue Act of 1861, sec. 49, 12 Stat. 292, at 309, Aug. 5, 1861.
21. TaxAnalysts, "Tax History Museum: 1861–1865." http://www.taxhistory.org/www/website.nsf/Web/THM1861?OpenDocument.
22. David G. Davies, *United States Taxes and Tax Policy* (Cambridge: Cambridge University Press, 1986), p. 22.
23. *Pollack v. Farmer's Loan and Trust Co.,* 158 U.S. 601 (1895).
24. Quoted text is from the Revenue Act of 1861. The Civil War income tax was upheld unanimously by the Supreme Court in *Springer v. United States,* 102 U.S. 586 (1881).

The Court ruled that the tax, which had expired in 1872, was an excise (i.e., an indirect tax) and neither a head tax nor a real-estate or property tax (i.e., it was not a direct tax).

25. *Pollack v. Farmer's Loan and Trust Co.,* 158 U.S. 601 (1895), dissenting opinion of Justice Henry Billings Brown. In his dissent, Justice Brown railed: "The [Court's] decision involves nothing less than the surrender of the taxing power to the moneyed class. . . . Even the spectre of socialism is conjured up to frighten Congress from laying taxes upon the people in proportion to their ability to pay them." A year later, in 1896, Brown would assure a place for himself in history by authoring the opinion of the Court in *Plessy v. Ferguson*, which upheld racial discrimination in public transportation and popularized the term "separate but equal."

26. U.S. Constitution, Amendment XVI (1913).

27. Louis Alan Talley, "Federal Taxation: An Abbreviated History," *CRS Report on History of Federal Taxes*, Jan. 19, 2001. http://www.taxhistory.org/thp/readings.nsf/ArtWeb/2 D52A4CFD2844FAB85256E22007840E6?OpenDocument.

28. Tax Foundation, "U.S. Federal Individual Income Tax Rates History, 1913–2011 (Nominal and Inflation-Adjusted Brackets)." Accessed Mar. 5, 2012. http://www.tax foundation.org/taxdata/show/151.html.

29. Quoted in TaxAnalysts, "Tax History Museum, 1901–32: The Income Tax Arrives." http://www.taxhistory.org/www/website.nsf/Web/THM1901?OpenDocument.

30. U.S. Department of the Treasury, "History of the U.S. Tax System." http://www.policy almanac.org/economic/archive/tax_history.shtml.

31. *Ibid.*

32. G. Davies, *United States Taxes and Tax Policy,* p. 24, *op. cit.*

33. U.S. Department of the Treasury, "History of the U.S. Tax System."

34. Davies, *United States Taxes and Tax Policy, op. cit.*

35. Historical Top Tax Rate, *Tax Facts*, Tax Policy Center, Jan. 31, 2011 http://www.tax policycenter.org/taxfacts/displayafact.cfm?DocID=213&Topic2id=20&Topic3id=22.

36. Peter Sperry, "The Real Reagan Economic Record: Responsible and Successful Fiscal Policy." Heritage Foundation Backgrounder, Mar. 1, 2001. No. 1414.

37. J. D. Foster, "Tax Cuts, Not the Clinton Tax Hike, Produced the 1990s Boom," Heritage Foundation WebMemo No. 1835. Accessed Dec. 26, 2011. www.heritage.org/ research/taxes/wm1835.cfm.

38. "Federal Income Tax is Highly Progressive After Recent Cuts," Joint Economic Committee. Research Report 109–36, May 2006.

39. Duanjie Chen and Jack Mintz, "New Estimates of Effective Corporate Tax Rates on Business Investment," *Cato Institute Tax & Budget Bulletin*, No. 64 Feb. 2011.

40. Lauren Fox, "'Dubious Distinction' for U.S. Corporate Tax Rate," *US News*, Mar. 1, 2012. http://www.usnews.com/news/blogs/washington-whispers/2012/03/01/dubious -distinction-for-us-corporate-tax-rate.

41. Global 500, *CNN Money*. http://money.cnn.com/magazines/fortune/global500/2010/ full_list/index.html.

42. "Tax Compliance Challenges to Corporate Tax Enforcement and Options to Improve Securities Basis Reporting: Statement of David M. Walker Comptroller General of the United States," GAO 2006.

43. John McCormack, "GE Filed 57,000-Page Tax Return, Paid No Taxes on $14 billion in Profits," *The Weekly Standard Blog*, Nov. 17, 2011. http://www.weeklystandard .com/blogs/ge-filed-57000-page-tax-return-paid-no-taxes-14-billion-profits_609137 .html.

44. "Study of the Overall State of the Federal Tax System and Recommendations for Sim-

plification, Pursuant to Section 8022(3)(B) of the Internal Revenue Code of 1986," Joint Committee on Taxation, Apr. 2001. http://www.house.gov/jct/s-3-01vol1.pdf.

45. "About the IRS Form 1040," PRAComment.gov. http://www.pracomment.gov/About-the-PRA-Initiative/about1040.

46. Congressional Committees Database, *OpenSecrets.org.* http://www.opensecrets.org/cmteprofiles/index.php.

47. Robert E. Hall and Alvin Rabushka, *The Flat Tax* (Stanford, Calif.: Hoover Institution Press, 1995), p. 84. http://www.hoover.org/publications/books/8329.

48. Laurence Kotlikoff, "The Economic Argument for a Flat Tax," Testimony before The Joint Economic Committee, May 17, 1995.

49. Veronique de Rugy, "Tax Rates and Tax Revenue The Mellon Income Tax Cuts of the 1920s," *Tax and Budget Bulletin,* Cato Institute, Feb. 2003. http://www.cato.org/pubs/tbb/tbb-0302-13.pdf.

50. Daniel Mitchell, Ph.D., "The Historical Lessons of Lower Tax Rates," Heritage Foundation, Aug. 13 2003. http://www.heritage.org/research/reports/2003/08/the-historical-lessons-of-lower-tax-rates.

51. John McManus, "U2 criticism sits uncomfortably alongside low tax rate obsession," *Irish Times,* June 27, 2011. http://www.irishtimes.com/newspaper/finance/2011/0627/1224299635130.html.

52. Ralph Vartabedian, "Estimate of Heinz Fortune Doubled," *Los Angeles Times,* June 27, 2004.

53. Gayle Fee and Laura Raposa, "Sen. John Kerry skips town on sails tax," *Boston Herald,* July 23, 2010.

54. Donovan Slack, "Kerry will pay Mass. tax on R.I. yacht," *Boston Globe,* July 28, 2010. http://www.boston.com/news/local/massachusetts/articles/2010/07/28/kerry_will_pay_mass_tax_on_ri_yacht/.

55. Matt Negrin, "Bono advises Obama on poverty," *Politico,* Apr. 30, 2010. http://www.politico.com/politico44/perm/0410/stuck_in_a_meeting_ba03afe5-8545-45e1-9423-7af263885048.html.

56. *Ibid.*

57. Daniel Anderson, "ObamaCare: Burned by the Tanning Tax," *FreedomWorks blog*, Feb. 8, 2012. http://www.freedomworks.org/blog/daniel-anderson/obamacare-burned-by-the-%E2%80%9Ctanning-tax%E2%80%9D.

Chapter 9: A Standard of Value

1. Phil Mattingly and Robert Schmidt, "Monetary Policy: Fed Critic Ron Paul's Power Play," *Bloomberg Businessweek,* Dec. 2, 2010. http://www.businessweek.com/magazine/content/10_50/b4207035613107.htm.

2. *Ibid.*

3. Ludwig von Mises, The Theory of Money and Credit, Liberty Fund Inc., 1981.

4. Carl Menger, *Principles of Economics,* New York University Press, 1976: p. 257.

5. Ludwig von Mises, The Theory of Money and Credit, *op. cit.*

6. "Smoke 'Em if You Got 'Em: Cigarette Black Markets in U.S. Prisons and Jails." http://tpj.sagepub.com/content/81/2/142.abstract, p. 623.

7. For more on the subject, see Matt Kibbe, "Mind, Historical Time and the Value of Money: A Tale of Two Methods," *Market Process* 6, no. 1 (Spring 1988).

8. Richard Ebeling, "Free Market Money—Instead of Political Manipulation," The Future of Freedom Foundation. http://www.fff.org/freedom/0290b.asp.

9. Lawrence H. White, "Competing Money Supplies," Library of Economics and Liberty. http://www.econlib.org/library/Enc/CompetingMoneySupplies.html.

10. Ludwig von Mises, "Omnipotent Government: The Rise of the Total State and Total War." (orig. 1944). Reprinted by Liberty Fund Press, 2011.

11. Franklin D. Roosevelt: "Executive Order 6102—Requiring Gold Coin, Gold Bullion and Gold Certificates to Be Delivered to the Government," Apr. 5, 1933. Online by Gerhard Peters and John T. Woolley, *The American Presidency Project*. http://www.presidency.ucsb.edu/ws/?pid=14611.

12. Ralph Benko, "U.S. Elites Begin to Confront The Paper Dollar," *Forbes*, Aug. 29, 2011. http://www.forbes.com/sites/ralphbenko/2011/08/29/u-s-elites-begin-to-confront-the-paper-dollar/.

13. Detlev S. Schlichter, "Forty Years of Paper Money," *Wall Street Journal,* Aug. 15, 2011. http://online.wsj.com/article/SB10001424053111903918104576500811399421094.html?mod=googlenews_wsj.

14. Lewis E. Lehrman, "It's Not the Debt Ceiling—It's the Dollar," *American Spectator*, June 9, 2011. http://spectator.org/archives/2011/06/09/its-not-the-debt-ceiling-its-t/print.

15. Edmund Conway, "Abandoning the gold standard was a seminal moment, and one we're now all paying for," *Telegraph*, Aug. 13, 2011.

16. Jon Stewart, "QE2: We're Not Printing Money, We're 'Imagineering' Money," *Wall Street Journal*, Dec. 12, 2010.

17. Overview of the Federal Reserve System. http://www.federalreserve.gov/pf/pdf/pf_1.pdf#page=4.

18. John Maynard Keynes, The Economic Consequences of the Peace, Cosmo Classics, 1919.

19. Jonathan Sibun, "Inflation: History shows we've got it easy," *Telegraph*, Nov. 16, 2010. http://www.telegraph.co.uk/finance/economics/8135039/Inflation-History-shows-weve-got-it-easy.html

20. "R.I.P. Zimbabwe Dollar," Cato Institute. http://www.cato.org/zimbabwe.

21. "Zimbabwe inflation 'incalculable,'" BBC. http://news.bbc.co.uk/2/hi/africa/7115651.stm.

22. "A crisis it can't paper over," Los Angeles Times, July 14, 2008.

23. "Zimbabwe to print first $100 trillion note," CNN. http://articles.cnn.com/2009-01-16/world/zimbawe.currency_1_zimbabwe-dollar-south-african-rand-dollar-note?_s=PM:WORLD.

24. Sibun, "Inflation: History shows we've got it easy," *op. cit.*

25. "Zimbabwe's Novel Currency," *Freakonomics*. http://www.freakonomics.com/2009/04/24/zimbabwes-novel-currency/.

26. George J.W. Goodman, "The German Hyperinflation, 1923," *Commanding Heights*. http://www.pbs.org/wgbh/commandingheights/shared/minitext/ess_germanhyperinflation.html.

27. *Ibid.*

28. "Terms of the Treaty of Versailles," BBC. http://www.bbc.co.uk/schools/gcsebitesize/history/mwh/ir1/thetreatyrev1.shtml.

29. "Germany Set to Make Final World War I Reparation Payment," ABC News. http://abcnews.go.com/International/germany-makes-final-reparation-payments-world-war/story?id=11755920#.TvfZCTUeO8A.

30. "Better as Wallpaper: Weimar Republic Papiermark (1922-1923)," *Life*. http://www.life.com/gallery/60591/image/2643031/failed-currencies#index/6.

31. *Ibid.*

32. "Washington's Top 5 Missed Opportunities in 2011," *Fox News*. http://www.foxnews.com/opinion/2011/12/20/washingtons-top-5-missed-opportunities-in-2011/.

33. Interview, *Meet the Press*, Aug. 2011. http://www.youtube.com/watch?feature=player_embedded&v=-_N0Cwg5iN4.

34. Overview of Federal Reserve System. http://www.federalreserve.gov/pf/pdf/pf_1.pdf #page=4.

35. "Achieving a Stable Dollar," *Free Banking*. http://www.freebanking.org/2011/10/06/achieving-a-stable-dollar/.

36. Ludwig von Mises, *Human Action*, Chapter 20, Section 9, Contemporary Books, 3rd Revised Edition, 1966.

37. Peter Schiff "Mortgage Bankers Speech," Nov. 13, 2006. http://www.youtube.com/watch?v=jj8rMwdQf6k&feature=youtube.

38. Federal Reserve Board, Selected Interest Rates, Historical Data. http://www.federalreserve.gov/releases/h15/data.htm.

39. Bureau of Labor Statistics, "Employment, Hours, and Earnings from the Current Employment Statistics survey (National)." http://data.bls.gov/pdq/SurveyOutputServlet?request_action=wh&graph_name=CE_cesbref1.

40. "Global Economy 'as Strong as I've Seen,' Paulson Says," *Wall Street Journal*, Mar. 6, 2007. http://blogs.wsj.com/washwire/2007/03/06/global-economy-as-strong-as-ive-ever-seen-says-paulson/

41. "Dow, S&P break records," *CNN Money*. http://money.cnn.com/2007/10/09/markets/markets_0500/index.htm.

42. Rick Ferri, "Thank Goodness for Index Funds," *Forbes*, Dec. 19, 2011. http://www.forbes.com/sites/rickferri/2011/12/19/thank-goodness-for-index-funds/.

43. "After the Crash," *Economist*, Aug. 2011. http://www.economist.com/blogs/dailychart/2011/08/us-stockmarket-declines-and-gdp.

44. Henry Hazlitt, *What You Should Know About Inflation* (Princeton, NJ: D. Van Nostrand, 1965).

45. "Jobless Rate Falls to 9.7%, Giving Hope Worst Is Over," *New York Times*, Feb. 2, 2006.

46. Thomas Sowell, "Fed Up with the Fed." http://www.creators.com/opinion/thomas-sowell/fed-up-with-the-fed.html.

47. Cleveland Fed. http://www.clevelandfed.org/research/data/credit_easing/index.cfm.

48. Simon Johnson and James Qwak, *13 Bankers,* Pantheon, 2010.

49. *Ibid.*

50. John Mason, "Monetaray [*sic*] Policy in 2011: Looking Back," *Wall Street Pit*, Jan. 6, 2012. http://wallstreetpit.com/88418-monetaray-policy-in-2011-looking-back.

51. Robert E. Lucas Jr., "The U.S. Recession of 2007-201?" Millman Lecture, May 19, 2011. http://www.econ.washington.edu/news/millimansl.pdf.

52. Consumer Price Index—Jan. 2012, Bureau of Labor Statistics. http://www.bls.gov/news.release/cpi.nr0.htm.

53. "Inflation Nation," *New York Times*, May 3, 2009.

54. Gerald O'Driscoll, "The Federal Reserve's Covert Bailout of Europe," *Wall Street Journal*, Dec. 28, 2011.

55. "Fed's $16 trillion Dollar Secret Slush Fund Props Up Our Way Of Life," *Business Insider*. http://www.businessinsider.com/feds-16-trillion-dollar-secret-slush-fund-props-up-our-way-of-life-2011-7#ixzz1hgHQxuwi.

56. Ron Paul, "The Fed Undermines Foreign Policy." http://news.goldseek.com/RonPaul/1301932800.php.

57. "The Countdown Begins: Just One Hour Until The Fed Releases Bailout Documents," *Business Insider*. http://www.businessinsider.com/the-countdown-begins-just-one-hour-until-the-fed-releases-bailout-documents-2010-12

58. "Foreign Banks Tapped Fed's Secret Lifeline Most at Crisis Peak," *Bloomberg News.* http://www.bloomberg.com/news/2011-04-01/foreign-banks-tapped-fed-s-lifeline -most-as-bernanke-kept-borrowers-secret.html.

59. "Federal Reserve Document Dump Reveals Lending Secrets," Campaign for Liberty. http://www.campaignforliberty.com/blog.php?view=41475

60. "Secret Fed Loans Gave Banks $13 billion Undisclosed to Congress," *Bloomberg News.* http://www.bloomberg.com/news/2011-11-28/secret-fed-loans-undisclosed-to -congress-gave-banks-13-billion-in-income.html.

61. Ibid.

62. Erik Holm, "Buffett Buys Goldman Stake in 'Economic Pearl Harbor' (Update2)," *Bloomberg,* Sept. 24, 2008. http://www.bloomberg.com/apps/news?pid=newsarchive& sid=axN8Gl5_fsxA.

63. Charles Piller, "Buffett, champion of bailout, is also leading beneficiary," McClatchy Washington Bureau, Apr. 5, 2009. http://www.mcclatchydc.com/2009/04/05/v -print/65496/buffett-champion-of-bailout-is.html.

64. Julie Crawshaw, "WSJ: Buffett Foils IRS With Latest Tax Break," *Money News, Newsmax,* Aug. 31, 2011. http://www.moneynews.com/StreetTalk/Buffett-berkshire-IRS -Tax/2011/08/31/id/409259.

65. Shira Ovide, "Warren Buffett Made at Least $1.2 billion from GE," *Wall Street Journal,* Sept. 13, 2011.

66. Timothy P. Carney, "Is Barack buddy Buffett betting on bank bailout?," *Examiner.* http:// washingtonexaminer.com/politics/2011/08/barack-buddy-buffett-betting-bank-bailout.

67. Lizzie O'Leary and Andrew Frye, "Geithner AIG Recusal Was 'After the Fact,' Issa Says (Update2)," *Bloomberg,* Jan. 27 2010. http://www.bloomberg.com/apps/news?pid =newsarchive&sid=aDV3KdbP2Ap8&pos=6.

68. Ibid.

69. Silla Brush, "Paulson to testify that AIG bailout was correct," the Hill, Jan. 26, 2010. http://thehill.com/homenews/house/78191-paulson-to-stand-by-aig-bailout.

70. Lizzie O'Leary and Andrew Frye, "Geithner AIG Recusal Was 'After the Fact,' Issa Says (Update2)," op. cit.

71. "Tough Questions for Geithner on AIG Bailout," Associated Press Video. http://www .youtube.com/watch?v=VgtprlxOcks.

72. Louise Story and Gretchen Morgenson, "In U.S. Bailout of A.I.G., Forgiveness for Big Banks," *New York Times,* June 29, 2010.

73. "Testimony of Martin A. Weiss, Specialist in International Trade and Finance, Congressional Research Service, before the House Committee on Financial Services Hearing on 'The Role of the International Monetary Fund and Federal Reserve in Stabilizing Europe,'" Congressional Research Service. http://www.house.gov/apps/ list/hearing/financialsvcs_dem/crs_statement_for_the_record_5.20.10.pdf.

74. "Who's on the Hook for the IMF's Greek Bailout?," *Wall Street Journal.*

75. "Fed may give loans to IMF to help euro zone," Reuters. http://www.reuters.com/ article/2011/12/04/us-eurozone-imf-fed-idUSTRE7B30X320111204.

76. John H. Cochrane, "Restoring Robust Economic Growth in America" Conference, Hoover Institution, Stanford University, Dec. 2 2011. http://faculty.chicagobooth .edu/john.cochrane/research/papers/taylor_panel.pdf.

77. "U.S. Debt Not So Far from Greece's," American Enterprise Institute. http://blog .american.com/2010/05/us-debt-not-so-far-from-greeces/.

78. Hazlitt, *What You Should Know about Inflation* (1964).

79. Larry White, "Achieving a Stable Dollar," Free Banking, Oct. 6, 2011. http://www .freebanking.org/2011/10/06/achieving-a-stable-dollar/.

80. "Poll: Public wants to rein in the Fed," *Washington Examiner*. http://washington examiner.com/blogs/beltway-confidential/2009/07/poll-public-wants-rein-fed.
81. Overview of the Financial System. http://www.federalreserve.gov/pf/pdf/pf_1.pdf# page=4.
82. Larry White, "Achieving a Stable Dollar," *op. cit.*
83. Lewis E. Lehrman, "It's Not the Debt Ceiling—It's the Dollar," op. cit.
84. Hans Sennholz, Money and Freedom, Libertarian Press, 1985.

Chapter 10: A Teaching Moment

1. 20 USC § 1681–Sex. http://www.law.cornell.edu/uscode/20/1681.html.
2. *Grove City College v. Bell*, 465 U.S. 555, 579 (1984).
3. David M. Lascell, "Grove City College v. Bell: What the Case Means Today." http:// www2.gcc.edu/orgs/GCLawJournal/articles/spring%202010/Grove%20City%20 v%20Bell.pdf.
4. Milton Friedman, *Capitalism and Freedom* (Chicago: University of Chicago Press, 1962), p. 85.
5. Sam Dillon, "Top Test Scores from Shanghai Stuns Educators," *New York Times*, Dec. 7, 2010.
6. *Ibid.*
7. Paul E. Peterson, Ludger Woessmann, Eric A. Hanushek, and Carlos X. Lastra-Anadon, "Globally Challenged: Are U.S. Students Ready to Compete?" *Harvard Study*, http://www.hks.harvard.edu/pepg/PDF/Papers/PEPG11-03_GloballyChallenged .pdf.
8. Sam Dillon, "U.S. Students Remain Poor at History, Tests Show," *New York Times*, June 15, 2011. http://www.nytimes.com/2011/06/15/education/15history.html.
9. Susan Snyder and Kristen A. Graham, "Report Confirms Shortcomings in City Schools," *Philadelphia Inquirer*, Sept. 7, 2011. http://articles.philly.com/2011-09-07/ news/30123328_1_report-crime-school-violent-crimes.
10. Andrea Canning and Lezzel Tanglao, "Ohio Mom Kelley Williams-Bolar Jailed for Sending Kids to Better School District," ABC News, Jan. 26, 2011. http://abcnews .go.com/US/ohio-mom-jailed-sending-kids-school-district/story?id=12763654# .TuqW67JFuso.
11. Gregory Kane, "Schools Commit Fraud by Failing to Educate," *Washington Examiner*, Jan. 2011. http://washingtonexaminer.com/opinion/columnists/2011/01/schools -commit-fraud-failing-educate.
12. Tina Kaufmann, "Crying, Akron Mom Kelley Williams-Bolar Begs Ohio Parole Board to Pardon Her." *newsnet5.com*, July 20, 2011. http://www.newsnet5.com/dpp/news/ local_news/akron_canton_news/crying-akron-mom-kelley-williams-bolar-begs-ohio -parole-board-to-pardon-her#ixzz1gemkpcKW.
13. "Youth Violence." Centers for Disease Control and Prevention, National Center for Injury Prevention and Control. http://www.cdc.gov/ViolencePrevention/pdf/YV-Data Sheet-a.pdf.
14. *Ibid.*
15. "Facing the School Dropout Dilemma," American Psycological Association. http:// www.apa.org/pi/families/resources/school-dropout-prevention.aspx.
16. "1 in 10 U.S. High School Is Dropout Factory," Associated Press, Oct. 29, 2007. http:// www.msnbc.msn.com/id/21531704/ns/us_news-education/t/us-high-schools-dropout -factory/#.Tu5obzUeO8A.

17. Gary Fields, "The High School Dropout's Economic Ripple Effect," *Wall Street Journal*. Oct. 21, 2008. http://online.wsj.com/article/SB122455013168452477.html.

18. "1 in 10 U.S. High School Is Dropout Factory," Associated Press, *op. cit.*

19. Dropout Prevention and Recovery, National Conference of State Legislatures. http://www.ncsl.org/default.aspx?tabid=12884.

20. "The High School Dropout's Economic Ripple Effect," *Wall Street Journal, op. cit.*

21. Ezra Klein, "American Schools More Segregated Today Than When Martin Luther King Jr. Was Killed," *Washington Post,* Jan. 2011.

22. "Public School Per-Student Spending Increases as State Funding Decreases," Fox News, May 26, 2011. http://www.foxnews.com/politics/2011/05/26/public-school-student-spending-increases-state-funding-decreases/#ixzz1gw0vBaFV.

23. *Ibid.*

24. Senate Bill 1, Commonwealth Foundation. http://www.commonwealthfoundation.org/doclib/20110207_POLICYPOINTSSenateBill1.pdf.

25. Anthony Williams, "Pennsylvania Kids Deserve School Choice," *Wall Street Journal,* May 12, 2010.

26. David L. Kirp, "Bridging the Achievement Gap," *Los Angeles Times.* Sept. 22, 2010.

27. Adam B. Shaeffer, "They Spend WHAT? The Real Cost of Public Schools," Cato Institute. http://www.cato.org/pubs/pas/pa662.pdf.

28. "More Dramatic Education Reforms–Such as School-Choice Vouchers–Needed," Foundation for Education Reform & Accountability. http://www.nyfera.org/?page_id=3597.

29. Andrew J. Coulson, "President to Call for Big New Ed. Spending. Here's a Look at How that's Worked in the Past." Cato Institute, Jan. 27, 2010. http://www.cato-at-liberty.org/president-to-call-for-big-new-ed-spending-heres-a-look-at-how-thats-worked-in-the-past/.

30. *Ibid.*

31. Andrew J. Coulson, "DC Vouchers Solved? Generous Severance for Displaced Workers," Cato Institute. http://www.cato-at-liberty.org/dc-vouchers-solved-generous-severance-for-displaced-workers/.

32. Terry Jeffrey, "Send Your Children to D.C. Public Schools, Mr. President-Elect." *Town hall.com,* Nov. 12, 2008. http://townhall.com/columnists/terryjeffrey/2008/11/12/send_your_children_to_dc_public_schools,_mr_president-elect/p age/2.

33. Adam B. Schaeffer, "They Spend WHAT? The Real Cost of Public Schools," *op. cit.*

34. Coulson, "President to Call for Big New Ed. Spending," *op. cit.*

35. "Union Members–2010," Bureau of Labor Statistics. http://www.bls.gov/news.release/union2.nr0.htm

36. Matt Di Carlo and Esther Quintero, "Quote, Unquote," *theshankerblog,* Albert Shanker Institute. http://shankerblog.org/?p=2562.

37. Report: Right to Work States are Winning the Future, http://demint.senate.gov/public/index.cfm?p=JimsBlog&ContentRecord_id=c21045dc-6672-45ba-9475-92814eabd9fe.

38. Center for Responsive Politics, *OpenSecrets.org.*

39. "Teachers Unions Oppose Educational Reform," Teachers Unions Exposed. http://teachersunionexposed.com/blocking.cfm.

40. John Stossel, "Unions: Good for Bad Teachers, Bad for Kids," Fox Business. http://www.foxbusiness.com/on-air/stossel/blog/2011/11/06/unions-good-bad-teachers-bad-kids.

41. "Protecting Bad Teachers," Teachers Unions Exposed. http://teachersunionexposed.com/protecting.cfm.

42. *Ibid.*
43. *Ibid.*
44. John Stossel, "How to Fire an Incompetent Teacher," *Reason.* http://reason.com/archives/2006/10/01/how-to-fire-an-incompetent-tea.
45. "Protecting Bad Teachers," Teachers Unions Exposed.
46. *Ibid.*
47. *Ibid.*
48. John Stossel, "Unions: Good for Bad Teachers, Bad for Kids." *op. cit.* Fox Business.
49. Milton Friedman, *Capitalism and Freedom*, p. 95.
50. Mona Charen, "Wanting to Abolish the Department of Education Is Not Radical," *National Review.* http://www.nationalreview.com/articles/229936/wanting-abolish-department-education-not-radical/mona-charen.
51. Veronique de Rugy and Marie Gryphon, "Elimination Lost: What Happened to Abolishing the Department of Education?," Cato Institute. http://www.cato.org/research/articles/gryphon-040211.html.
52. Mona Charen, "Wanting to Abolish the Department of Education Is Not Radical," *op. cit.*
53. "Parent Satisfaction Higher in Private Schools," *Education Report.* http://www.educationreport.org/pubs/mer/article.aspx?id=9813.
54. Friedman, *Capitalism and Freedom,* p. 94.
55. Cecilia Elena Rouse, "Private School Vouchers and Student Achievement: An Evaluation of the Milwaukee Parental Choice Program." http://papers.nber.org/papers/w5964.
56. Joseph Lawler, "The 'Failure' of School Vouchers in Milwaukee," *American Spectator.* Apr. 15, 2010. http://spectator.org/blog/2010/04/15/the-failure-of-school-vouchers/print.
57. Farai Chideya, "'The Great Deluge': A Katrina Post-Mortem," NPR. http://www.npr.org/templates/story/story.php?storyId=5421017.
58. "The New Orleans School Voucher Program," Reason.tv. http://reason.com/blog/2010/08/18/reasontv-the-new-orleans-schoo.
59. "New Orleans Voucher Program First Day—Lines Around the Block." http://www.youtube.com/watch?v=4vGCJu9xMJY.
60. Alexandra Fenwick, "Charter Schools Rise in New Orleans After Hurricane Katrina," *US News.* http://www.usnews.com/news/articles/2009/12/23/charter-schools-rise-in-new-orleans-after-hurricane-katrina.
61. Andrew J. Coulson, "DC Vouchers Solved? Generous Severance for Displaced Workers," *op. cit.*
62. U.S. Constitution, Article 1, section 8, clause 17.
63. Jason Richwine, "D.C. Voucher Students: Higher Graduation Rates and Other Positive Outcomes." Heritage Foundation. http://www.heritage.org/research/reports/2010/07/dc-voucher-students-higher-graduation-rates-and-other-positive-outcomes.
64. *Ibid.*
65. *Ibid.*
66. "The President Says He Wants to Do 'What's Best For Kids.' So Why Won't He Save a Proven Program That Helps Low-Income Students?," Reason.tv. http://reason.tv/video/show/barack-obama-the-dc-school-vou.
67. *Ibid.*
68. Adam B. Shaeffer, "Tax Credits, Not Vouchers, Are Keeping School Choice a Viable Option," Cato Institute, June 25, 2009. http://www.cato.org/pub_display.php?pub_id=10315.

69. Greg Foster and Christian d'Andrea, "An Empirical Evaluation of the Florida Tax Credit Scholarship Program," Friedman Foundation for School Choice. http://www.edchoice.org/CMSModules/EdChoice/FileLibrary/383/FL%20Poll%200709.pdf.

70. Andrew Lefevre, "A Decade of Success: Pennsylvania's Educational Improvement Tax Credit," Commonwealth Foundation, Apr. 17, 2011. http://www.commonwealthfoundation.org/research/detail/a-decade-of-success-pennsylvanias-educational-improvement-tax-credit.

71. "What It Costs to Go to College," College Board. http://www.collegeboard.com/student/pay/add-it-up/4494.html.

72. *Ibid.*

73. Lindsey Burke, "Pell Grant Increase Would Not Solve the College Cost Problem," Heritage Foundation, Nov. 16, 2010. http://www.heritage.org/research/reports/2010/11/pell-grant-increase-would-not-solve-the-college-cost-problem.

74. "Trends in College Pricing. College Board." http://trends.collegeboard.org/downloads/College_Pricing_2011.pdf.

75. *Ibid.*

76. Dick Armey, "Texas Needs Higher Education Reform," *Houston Chronicle*, Apr. 18, 2011.

77. Christopher Shea, "The End of Tenure?," *New York Times*, Sept. 3, 2010.

78. Jay P. Greene, "Administrative Bloat at American Universities: The Real Reason for High Costs in Higher Education," Goldwater Institute, Aug. 17, 2010. http://goldwaterinstitute.org/article/administrative-bloat-american-universities-real-reason-high-costs-higher-education.

79. Tamar Lewin, "College Graduates' Debt Burden Grew, Yet Again, in 2010," *New York Times*, Nov. 2, 2011.

80. Catherine Lampell, "Many with New College Degree Find the Job Market Humbling," *New York Times*, May 18, 2011.

81. "Unfulfilled Expectations: Recent College Graduates Struggle in a Troubled Economy," Rutgers University. http://www.heldrich.rutgers.edu/sites/default/files/content/Work_Trends_May_2011.pdf.

82. Lindsey Burke, "Pell Grant Increase Would Not Solve the College Cost Problem," *op. cit.*

83. Gary Wolfram, "Making College More Expensive: The Unintended Consequences of Federal Tuition Aid," *Cato Institute Policy Analysis, no. 531*, Jan. 25, 2005. http://www.cato.org/pub_display.php?pub_id=3344.

84. Jonathan Moore, "No Strings Attached," Hoover Institution, May 1, 1998. http://www.hoover.org/publications/policy-review/article/6669.

85. "Grove City College Cost." http://www.gcc.edu/current_cost.php.

86. "Tuition Expected To Jump Next Semester," Hillsdale College, Mar. 10, 2011. http://www.hillsdalecollegian.com/tuition-expected-to-jump-next-semester-1.2102376#.TvCU3TUeO8A.

87. Tamar Lewin, "College Graduates' Debt Burden Grew, Yet Again, in 2010," *op. cit.*

88. Justin Pope, "Analysis: Is Student Loan, Education Bubble Next?," MSNBC, Nov. 6, 2011. http://www.msnbc.msn.com/id/45183544/ns/us_news-life/t/analysis-student-loan-education-bubble-next/#.TvCF5DUeO8A.

89. "Kelli Space, $200,000 in Debt, Starts Site to Solicit Donations," *Huffington Post*, Nov. 22, 2010. http://www.huffingtonpost.com/2010/11/22/kelli-space-two-hundred-thousand-in-debt_n_787074.html.

90. "Peter Schiff Exposes College Scam—Interviews Kelli Space" (1 of 2). http://www.youtube.com/watch?v=llrmq8q3E24&feature=player_embedded#!.

91. Richard Vedder, "Why Did 17 million Students Go to College?" *The Chronicle of Higher Education*, Oct. 20, 2010.

92. *Ibid.*

93. Linsey Davis, "Facebook and PayPal's Peter Thiel Pays College Students to Drop Out," ABC News, May 26, 2011. http://abcnews.go.com/Technology/facebook-paypals -peter-thiel-pays-college-students-drop/story?id=13693632#.TvC4jTUeO8A.

94. Cady Lang, "Chained Up," *360 Magazine,* Dec. 13, 2011. http://360magazine.org/ 2011/12/chained-up/.

95. Michael Barone, "Will College Bubble Burst from Public Subsidies?," *Washington Examiner.* http://washingtonexaminer.com/politics/2011/07/will-college-bubble-burst -public-subisidies.

96. Justin Pope, "Analysis: Is Student Loan, Education Bubble Next?," *op. cit.*

97. "One in Four State Lawmakers Lack Bachelor's Degree," FoxNews.com, June 16, 2011, http://www.foxnews.com/politics/2011/06/16/one-in-four-state-lawmakers-have-no -college-degree/.

Chapter 11: Losing Patients

1. Javier Panzar, "Transcript: Robert Reich's Speech at Occupy Cal," *Daily Californian*, Nov. 18, 2011. http://www.dailycal.org/2011/11/18/transcript-robert-reichs-speech-at/.

2. Barack Obama, "Remarks by the President in Health Insurance Reform Town Hall," White House Press Office, Aug. 11, 2009. http://www.whitehouse.gov/the_press_ office/Remarks-by-the-President-at-Town-Hall-on-Health-Insurance-Reform-in -Portsmouth-New-Hampshire\.

3. James Taranto, "We're Going to Let You Die," *Wall Street Journal*, Oct. 14, 2009.

4. United Kingdom Office for National Statistics. http://www.statistics.gov.uk/statbase.

5. Joint Economic Committee, Republican staff, "The UK De-Bureaucratizes Health Care: We Should Too," Sept. 22, 2010, p. 2. http://jec.senate.gov/republicans/public/ ?a=Files.Serve&File_id=9bf72ff0-f2ad-4486-9dd7-e8305d5d61a6.

6. Milton Friedman, "Gammon's Law Points to Health-Care Solution," *Wall Street Journal,* Nov. 12, 1991.

7. UK National Health Service, National Institute for Health and Clinical Excellence (NICE), "Measuring Effectiveness and Cost Effectiveness: the QALY." http://www .nice.org.uk/newsroom/features/measuringeffectivenessandcosteffectivenesstheqaly .jsp (accessed Aug. 5, 2010). See also Randeep Ramesh, "This UK Patient Avoided the NHS List and Flew to India for a Heart Bypass. Is Health Tourism the Future?" *Guardian,* Feb. 1, 2005. http://www.guardian.co.uk/uk/2005/feb/01/health.india.

8. Helen Briggs, "Critics Condemn Bowel Cancer Drug Rejection," *BBC News Health,* Aug. 24, 2010. http://www.bbc.co.uk/news/health-11060968.

9. Nadeem Esmail, "The Private Cost of Public Queues," Fraser Institute, Mar./Apr. 2011. Accessed Jan. 17, 2012. http://www.fraserinstitute.org/uploadedFiles/fraser-ca/ Content/research-news/research/articles/private-cost-of-public-queues-march2011 .pdf.

10. Tanya Talaga, "Woman Dies In ER As AG Finds Little Movement," thestar.com, Dec. 6, 2010. Accessed Jan. 19, 2012. http://www.thestar.com/news/canada/article/9025 81—woman-dies-waiting-in-er-as-ag-finds-little-movement.

11. "Palin Doubles Down On 'Death Panels'," *Politico,* Aug. 13, 2009, http://news.yahoo .com/s/politico/20090813/pl_politico/26078.

12. David Gratzer, "The Ugly Truth About Canadian Health Care," *City Journal*, Summer 2007.
13. §§ 6301 and 10602 of the Patient Protection and Affordable Care Act, P.L. 111-148, as amended by P.L. 111-152. http://www.ama-assn.org/ama1/pub/upload/mm/399/ppaca-consolidated.pdf.
14. §§ 3403 and 10320 of the Patient Protection and Affordable Care Act, P.L. 111-148, as amended by P.L. 111-152. http://www.ama-assn.org/ama1/pub/upload/mm/399/ppaca-consolidated.pdf.
15. Joint Economic Committee, Republican staff, "Rationer-in-Chief: The 'Berwick' Confirmation Hearing That Wasn't," July 19, 2010. http://jec.senate.gov/republicans/public/index.cfm?p=CommitteeNews&ContentRecord_id=16af1da1-20c7-46ed-8282-edd399a03f92.
16. "Rethinking Comparative Effectiveness Research," interview with Dr. Donald Berwick, Biotechnology Health Care, June 2009. http://www.ncbi.nlm.nih.gov/pmc/articles/PMC2799075/pdf/bth06_2p035.pdf. This and many other, similar, quotations are among the reasons why even the Democrat-controlled U.S. Senate refused to confirm Dr. Berwick as Medicare chief, allowing his recess appointment to expire at the end of 2011.
17. National Health Expenditure data, 2009. Accessed Jan. 18, 2012. https://www.cms.gov/NationalHealthExpendData/downloads/tables.pdf.
18. Nancy Pelosi, Mar. 10, 2009. Accessed Jan. 17, 2012. http://www.youtube.com/watch?v=hV-05TLiiLU.
19. Senate Republican Policy Committee, "159 Ways the Senate Bill Is a Government Takeover of Health Care," *gop.gov*, Feb. 25, 2010. Accessed Jan. 17, 2012. http://www.gop.gov/blog/10/02/25/159-ways-the-senate-bill.
20. *Ibid.*
21. Center for Health Transformation, Wall Chart: "1,968 New and Expanded Secretarial Powers Under the Health Reform Law." Accessed Jan. 16, 2012. http://www.healthtransformation.net/galleries/wallcharts/HHS_V7%20(Final).pdf.
22. House Ways & Means Committee Republicans, "The Wrong Prescription: Democrats' Health Overhaul Dangerously Expands IRS Authority," 2010-03-18. http://republicans.waysandmeans.house.gov/UploadedFiles/IRS_Power_Report.pdf.
23. Senate Finance Committee Republican tabulation of Joint Committee on Taxation estimates.
24. Curtis W. Copeland, "New Entities Created Pursuant to the Patient Protection and Affordable Care Act," Congressional Research Service, July 8, 2010. http://www.aamc.org/reform/summary/crsentities.pdf.
25. Estimate by Senate Budget Committee, Republican staff, 2010.
26. U.S. House Energy and Commerce Committee, Republicans, press release, "Final List of Health Care Law Waivers Now Available; Obama Administration Shields 4 million Americans From Its Own Law," Jan. 6, 2012. Accessed Jan. 19, 2012. http://energycommerce.house.gov/news/PRArticle.aspx?NewsID=9186. (The waivers expire in 2014, when Obamacare takes effect.)
27. Paul Connor, "Labor unions primary recipients of Obamacare waivers," Jan. 6, 2012. Accessed Jan. 19, 2012. http://dailycaller.com/2012/01/06/labor-unions-primary-recipients-of-obamacare-waivers/.
28. Kaiser Family Foundation, Kaiser Health Tracking Poll, Mar. 2011. Accessed Mar. 7, 2012. http://www.kff.org/kaiserpolls/upload/8166-f.pdf . See also Gallup, "Americans Divided on Repeal of 2010 Health Care Law," Feb. 27, 2012. Accessed Mar. 7, 2012.

http://www.gallup.com/poll/152969/Americans-Divided-Repeal-2010-Healthcare-Law.aspx.

29. The PJ Tatler, "Democrat Rep. Hochul: 'We're not looking to the Constitution' on the HHS Mandate," Feb. 27, 2012. http://pjmedia.com/tatler/2012/02/27/democrat-rep-hochul-were-not-looking-to-the-constitution-on-the-hhs-mandate/.

30. Shareef Mahdavi, "How to Compete Without Cutting Price [of LASIK] Eye Surgery," Mar. 2009. Accessed Mar. 7,2012. https://docs.google.com/viewer?url=http%3A%2F%2Fwww.sm2strategic.com%2Ffiles%2F2009%2520Mar%2520-%2520How%2520to%2520Compete%2520Without%2520Cutting%2520Price.RefractiveEyecare.pdf.

31. "Cost of LASIK Eye Surgery," *LasikSecrets.com*. Accessed Dec. 11, 2011. http://lasik-secrets.com/LASIK-cost.html (published Mar. 15, 2011).

32. John Mackey, "The Whole Foods Alternative to Obamacare: Eight Things We Can Do to Improve Health Care Without Adding to the Deficit," *Wall Street Journal*, Aug. 12, 2009.

33. John Mackey, "Defending the Morality of Capitalism," Whole Foods Market Blog, June 24, 2011. http://www2.wholefoodsmarket.com/blogs/jmackey/category/conscious-capitalism/.

34. John Mackey, "To Increase Jobs, Increase Economic Freedom," *Wall Street Journal*, Nov. 16, 2011. http://online.wsj.com/article/SB1000142405297020435800457703244215391170.html.

35. Nick Paumgarten, "Food Fighter: Does Whole Foods CEO know what's best for you?," *New Yorker*, Jan. 4, 2010. http://www.newyorker.com/reporting/2010/01/04/100104fa_fact_paumgarten.

36. John Mackey, "The Whole Foods Alternative to Obamacare," *op. cit.*

37. *Ibid.*

38. CNN presidential debate, Sept. 12, 2011. http://www.huffingtonpost.com/2011/09/12/tea-party-debate-health-care_n_959354.html.

39. Dick Armey, *The Freedom Revolution: The New Republican House Majority Leader Tells Why Big Government Failed, Why Freedom Works, and How We Will Rebuild America* (Washington, DC: Regnery Press, 1994), p. 213.

40. Centers for Medicare and Medicaid Services, U.S. National Health Expenditure data, 2009. https://docs.google.com/viewer?url=https%3A%2F%2Fwww.cms.gov%2FNationalHealthExpendData%2Fdownloads%2Fhighlights.pdf.

41. *Ibid.*

42. Health Care in the United States. Accessed Jan. 19, 2012. http://en.wikipedia.org/wiki/Health_care_in_the_United_States.

43. David Gratzer, "The Ugly Truth About Canadian Health Care," *City Journal*, Summer 2007. Accessed Jan. 19, 2012. http://www.city-journal.org/html/17_3_canadian_healthcare.html.

44. Deroy Murdock, "28 States Suing Over Obamacare," *Newsmax*, Feb. 18, 2011. http://www.newsmax.com/Murdock/healthcare-obamacare/2011/02/18/id/386576.

Chapter 12: A Time for Choosing

1. This summary reflects an analysis by the Republican staff of the Committee on the Budget, U.S. House of Representatives, based on figures from the Tax Foundation, the Congressional Budget Office, and the Census Bureau. Cited in Paul Ryan's "Roadmap for America's Future." http://www.roadmap.republicans.budget.house.gov/

2. A. Gary Shilling's *Insight* newsletter, Sept. 2009. http://www.agaryshilling.com/index
.html. Cited in Ryan's "Roadmap for America's Future."

3. Two other huge entitlements could be added to this list, to make it the "big five." One
is the federal tax code subsidy for employer-sponsored health benefits. The other is
Obamacare, which, if not repealed, will come on line in 2014. Thus, all but one of the
largest federal programs are health care entitlements.

4. The total U.S. population in 2010 was 309 million, according to the U.S. Census
Bureau, National Totals 2011; Table 1: Annual Estimates of the Population for the
United States, Regions, States, and Puerto Rico: Apr. 1, 2010 to July 1, 2011. Accessed
Dec. 23, 2011. http://www.census.gov/popest/data/national/totals/2011/index.html.
Total Social Security enrollment in 2010 was 54 million (or 17.5 percent of the popu-
lation), according to the 2011 Social Security trustees report, p. 2. Accessed Dec. 23,
2011. http://www.ssa.gov/oact/tr/2011/tr2011.pdf. Total Medicare enrollment in 2010
was 47.5 million (or about 15.4 percent of the population), according to the 2011
Medicare trustees report, Table II.B.1: Medicare Data for Calendar Year 2010, p. 9.
Accessed Dec. 23, 2011. http://www.cms.gov/ReportsTrustFunds/downloads/tr2011
.pdf. Total Medicaid enrollment at the end of 2010 was 51.5 million (or 16.6 percent of the population), according to the Kaiser Commission on Medicaid and the
Uninsured, "Medicaid Enrollment: Dec. 2010 Data Snapshot," Dec. 2011. Accessed
Dec. 23, 2011. http://www.kff.org/medicaid/upload/8050-04.pdf (Note: There is significant enrollment overlap between these three programs; figures should not be added
together.)

5. Social Security Administration, *Income of the Population 55 or Older*, 2008, Table
2.A1. Cited in "Policy Basics: Top Ten Facts about Social Security on the Program's
75th Anniversary," Center on Budget and Policy Priorities, Aug. 13, 2010. Accessed
Dec. 24, 2011. http://www.cbpp.org/cms/index.cfm?fa=view&id=3261#_ftnref15.

6. *The Path to Prosperity: Restoring America's Promise* (Fiscal Year 2012 Budget Resolution,
House Committee on the Budget, Paul Ryan of Wisconsin, Chairman), p. 13. Accessed
Dec. 23, 2011. http://budget.house.gov/UploadedFiles/PathToProsperityFY2012.pdf.

7. White House Office of Management and Budget, *President's Budget for Fiscal Year
2012,* Historical Tables, Table 3.2: Outlays by Function and Subfunction, 1962–2016,
and Table 8.5: Outlays for Mandatory and Related Programs, 1962–2016. Figure for
functions 571 (Medicare) and 651 (Social Security) are from table 3.2; figures for Medicaid are from table 8.5. All figures are based on 2011 (estimated) outlays. Accessed
Dec. 23, 2011). http://www.whitehouse.gov/omb/budget/Historicals.

8. Author's estimate, based on current program growth rates.

9. *The Path to Prosperity: Restoring America's Promise*, figure 3, p. 16.

10. Merriam-Webster Online. http://www.merriam-webster.com/dictionary/entitlement
(accessed Dec. 24, 2011). Emphasis added.

11. See *Helvering v. Davis* (1937), *Flemming v. Nestor* (1960).

12. U.S. Constitution, Amendment X.

13. *Ibid.,* Article I, section 8, clause 1.

14. *Ibid.,* Article I, section 8, clause 3.

15. The most notable case being *U.S. v. Butler* (1936), then making its way through the
courts. This case involved a federal tax on farmers established under the Agricultural
Adjustment Act. Was the tax but a means to an unconstitutional end (regulating farm
prices) that invaded the reserved powers of the states under the Tenth Amendment?
And in *Schechter Poultry Corp. v. U.S.*, 295 US 495 (1935), the Court would have to
decide whether the crown jewel of the New Deal, the National Recovery Administra-

tion, with its intrusive industrial codes, exceeded Congress's power to regulate interstate commerce.

16. US Congress, House Committee on Ways & Means, "Brief for Petitioners Helvering and Welch," in Analysis of the Social Security System: Hearings before a Subcommittee of the House Committee on Ways and Means, 83rd Congress, 1st Session, 1953, Appendix II, Miscellaneous Documents, pp. 1427–1440.

17. *Helvering v. Davis* (1937), 301 U.S. 619.

18. Peter Suderman, "The Individual Mandate's Tax Troubles," *Reason.com*, June 30, 2011. http://reason.com/blog/2011/06/30/the-individual-mandates-tax-tr.

19. Robert Pear, "Changing Stance, Administration Now Defends Insurance Mandate as a Tax," *New York Times,* July 17, 2010.

20. Dean Clancy, "Team Obama changes its story—again!—on whether health mandate is a tax," FreedomWorks blog, Feb. 15, 2012. http://www.freedomworks.org/blog/dean-clancy/is-the-health-care-mandate-a-tax-or-not (accessed Mar. 7, 2012).

21. *Flemming v. Nestor* (1960).

22. "The 1936 Government Pamphlet on Social Security," Social Security Administration. http://www.ssa.gov/history/ssn/ssb36.html (accessed Dec. 27, 2011).

23. "Why Social Security?," Social Security Administration, 1937. http://www.social security.gov/history/whybook.html (accessed Dec. 27, 2011).

24. Arthur M. Schlesinger Jr., *The Age of Roosevelt, Vol. 2, The Coming of the New Deal, 1933–1935*; (1958), pp. 308–309. Quoted in: Congressional Budget Office, "Social Security: A Primer," 14, n. 14 (Sept. 2001). Accessed Dec. 14, 2011. http://www.cbo.gov/ftpdocs/32xx/doc3213/EntireReport.pdf.

25. One politician who has touched them and lived is President Obama. In the name of "economic stimulus," he pushed through a temporary, one-year, 30 percent reduction in the employee half of the payroll tax in 2011, and repeated the feat in 2012, without incurring any visible harm. No one suggested that Social Security benefits would be endangered in any way, or that he was trying to "scrap" FDR's signature domestic achievement. It seems the tax really is "politics all the way through."

26. Paul Ryan, "Roadmap for America's Future." http://www.roadmap.republicans.budget.house.gov/.

27. And since higher wages are a result of higher productivity, we literally cannot "grow" our way out of the Social Security problem.

28. Michael Clingman, et al., "Internal Real Rates of Return Under the OASDI Program for Hypothetical Workers," Social Security Administration, Actuarial Note Number 2009.5, July 2010. http://www.ssa.gov/oact/NOTES/ran5/index.html. See also Michael Clingman, et al., "Moneys Worth Ratios Under the OASDI Program for Hypothetical Workers," Social Security Administration, Actuarial Note Number 2009.7, July 2010. http://www.ssa.gov/oact/NOTES/ran7/index.html.

29. Merrill Matthews, "Perry is Right: There Is a Texas Model for Fixing Social Security: Public employees in three Texas counties have benefited from an 'Alternate Plan' for 30 years," *Wall Street Journal*, Sept. 24, 2011, emphasis added.

30. The Tea Party Budget, Nov. 17, 2011. http://www.freedomworks.org/the-tea-party-budget.

31. "Speech by President *Lyndon B. Johnson*, July 30, 1965," *Public Papers of the Presidents of the United States*: Lyndon B. Johnson, 1965. Volume II, entry 394, pp. 811–815. Washington, D. C.: Government Printing Office, 1966.

32. Social Security Act, Section 1801 [42 U.S.C. 1395].

33. Ken Terry, "Medicaid Expansion May Fail Because of Doctors' Refusal to See Patients," *CBS Money Watch*, Nov. 29, 2009. Accessed Jan. 18, 2012. http://www.cbs

news.com/8301-505123_162-43840953/medicaid-expansion-may-fail-because-of
-doctors-refusal-to-see-patients/.

34. Avik S. A. Roy, "UVa Study: Surgical Patients Are 13% More Likely to Die Than
Those Without Insurance," July 17, 2010. Accessed Jan. 18, 2012. http://www.avikroy
.org/2010/07/uva-study-surgical-patients-on-medicaid.html.

35. Dean Clancy, "Rand Paul Unveils Bold, Simple Medicare Reform," *FreedomWorks
blog*, Mar. 15, 2012. http://www.freedomworks.org/blog/dean-clancy/rand-paul
-introduces-medicare-reform.

36. Rachel Slajda, "Obama Pokes fun at 'Don't Touch my Medicare People,'" Talking
Points Memo, July 28, 2009. http://tpmlivewire.talkingpointsmemo.com/2009/07/
obama-pokes-fun-at-dont-touch-my-medicare-people.php.

37. Ronald Reagan, "A Time for Choosing," Speech to the University of Texas, Oct. 27,
1964. http://www.reagan.utexas.edu/archives/reference/timechoosing.html#_top.

Chapter 13: Disintermediation Politics

1. Chris Anderson, "The Long Tail in a Nutshell," July 11, 2006. http://thelongtail.com/
about.html.

2. Michael Scherer, "Obama's Health Czar: Behind the Scenes but Leading the Charge,"
Time Politics, Mar. 3 2009. http://www.time.com/time/politics/article/0,8599,1882709
,00.html#ixzz1isjNYT1U.

3. Michelle Malkin, "Waivers for Favors: Big Labor's Obamacare Escape Hatch," Jan.
28, 2011. http://michellemalkin.com/2011/01/28/waivers-for-favors-big-labors-obama
care-escape-hatch/.

4. "Union Members Summary," Bureau of Labor Statistics, Jan. 27, 2012. http://www
.bls.gov/news.release/union2.nr0.htm.

5. Tom Fitton, "Why Did Unionized Companies Get So Many Obamacare Waivers?"
Big Government, Sep. 13, 2011. http://workplacechoice.org/2011/09/13/why-did-
unionized-companies-get-so-many-obamacare-waivers/.

6. Timeline Of A Right-Wing Media Smear: Hoffa's Call To Vote Became "A Call
For Violence," *MediaMatters*, Sep. 6, 2011. http://mediamatters.org/print/research/
201109060015.

7. Socrata, "Waivers–final table," *OpenData*. http://opendata.socrata.com/Government/
waivers-final-table/x63r-3x8s.

8. John Perry Barlow, "A Declaration of the Independence of Cyberspace," *Projects.eff.org*,
Feb. 6, 1996. https://projects.eff.org/~barlow/Declaration-Final.html..

9. Andy Greenberg, "As SOPA Looms, John Perry Barlow On 'The Right To Know,'"
Forbes, Dec. 16, 2011. http://www.forbes.com/sites/andygreenberg/2011/12/16/as
-sopa-looms-john-perry-barlow-on-the-right-to-know/

10. Thomas Jefferson, "Thomas Jefferson to Isaac McPherson," Aug. 13, 1813. http://
press-pubs.uchicago.edu/founders/documents/a1_8_8s12.html.

11. Julie Borowski, "SOPA and PIPA Would Destroy Internet Freedom," *FreedomWorks*,
Jan. 13, 2012. http://www.freedomworks.org/blog/jborowski/sopa-and-pipa-would
-destroy-internet-freedom.

12. Julian Sanchez, "SOPA: An Architecture for Censorship," *Cato Institute,* Dec. 20,
2011. http://www.cato-at-liberty.org/sopa-an-architecture-for-censorship/.

13. Micah Sifry, "PDM Editorial: Why We're Against PIPA/SOPA And For the Internet,"
TechPresident, Jan. 17, 2012. http://techpresident.com/news/21635/pdm-editorial
-why-were-against-pipasopa-and-Internet

14. Carl Franzen, "How The Web Killed SOPA and PIPA," *TPM*, Jan. 20, 2012. http://idealab.talkingpointsmemo.com/2012/01/how-the-web-killed-sopa-and-pipa.php.

15. Mike Lee, Twitter post, Twitter. https://twitter.com/#!/SenMikeLee.

16. Ed Henry, "Chris Dodd warns of Hollywood backlash against Obama over anti-piracy bill," *Fox News*, Jan. 19, 2012. http://www.foxnews.com/politics/2012/01/19/exclusive-hollywood-lobbyist-threatens-to-cut-off-obama-2012-money-over-anti/.

17. Lydia DePillis, "Disorganized: What happened to Obama's massive network of grassroots activists?," *New Republic*, Oct. 29, 2009. http://www.tnr.com/article/politics/disorganized?page=0,0.

18. Micah Sifry, "The Obama Disconnect: What Happens When Myth Meets Reality," *TechPresident*, Dec. 31, 2009. http://techpresident.com/blog-entry/the-obama-disconnect.

19. *Ibid.*

20. Kathleen Hall Jamieson, ed., "Electing the President 2008: The Insiders' View," quoted in Sifry, "The Obama Disconnect," pp. 37–38.

21. Michael O'Brien, "Dems say Tea Party rally shows dissipating opposition to health reform," *Hill*, Mar. 16, 2010.

22. Matt Bai, "Does Anyone Have a Grip on the G.O.P.?," *New York Times*, Oct. 12, 2011.

23. "Transcript: Van Jones urges netroots to lead the way in rebuilding the American dream," *NW Progressive*, July 1, 2011. http://www.nwprogressive.org/weblog/2011/07/transcript-van-jones-urges-netroots-to-lead-the-way-in-rebuilding-the-american-dream.html.

24. *Ibid.*

Chapter 14: The Revolution Will Be Chosen

1. Jordan Zakarin, "Stephen Colbert, The Next Ronald Reagan? Satirical Political Career Parallels Former President's," *Huffington Post*, Jan. 17, 2012. http://www.huffingtonpost.com/jordan-zakarin/colbert-super-pac-south-carolina_b_1210877.html.

2. Sam Stein, "Obama Compares himself to Reagan, JFK . . . But not Bill Clinton," *Huffington Post*, May. 25, 2011. http://www.huffingtonpost.com/2008/01/16/obama-compares-himself-to_n_81835.html..

3. *Ibid.*

4. Bernard Bailyn, *The Ideological Origins of the American Revolution* (Cambridge, MA: Harvard University Press, 1992), p. vi.

5. Paul Johnson, *George Washington: The Founding Father* (New York: HarperCollins, 2005).

6. George Washington, "Farewell Address on His Departure from the Presidency," Sep. 19, 1796. http://www.ourdocuments.gov/doc.php?flash=true&doc=15&page=transcript

7. Bernard Bailyn, *The Ideological Origins of the American Revolution*, p. 319.

8. *Ibid.*

INDEX